Vital Statistics on American Politics

Vital Statistics on American Politics

Harold W. Stanley
University of Rochester

Richard G. Niemi
University of Rochester

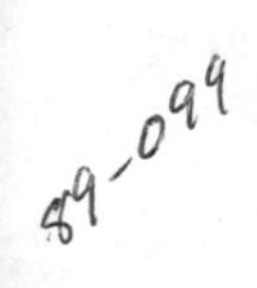

A Division of Congressional Quarterly Inc.
1414 22nd Street, N.W., Washington, D.C. 20037

Printed in the United States of America

Second printing

Library of Congress Cataloging-in-Publication Data

Stanley, Harold W. (Harold Watkins).
Vital statistics on American politics.

Bibliography: p.
Includes index.
1. United States—Politics and government—Statistics.
I. Niemi, Richard G. II. Title.
JK274.S74 1988 320.973'021 88-3594
ISBN 0-87187-472-5
ISBN 0-87187-471-7 (pbk.)

To

Margaret Louise Stanley,

Duncan Gelineau Stanley,

and

Andrew David (Niemi) Peckham

Contents

Tables and Figures

Acknowledgments

Completing this volume required the assistance of many people, at times giving the project the look and feel of a small industry. Our largest debt is to Carolyn Whitfield, who initially pulled together the tables and figures that form the backbone of the book; she then tracked down diverse bits of all-too-elusive information with her usual amazing efficiency. Without her assistance, the book would still be in its infant stage.

Shrikant Dash and Annette Steinacker combed sources for material to include in several chapters. Itai Sened updated selected tables, thereby increasing their value. Charles E. Smith tracked down references and addresses in the quest for permissions. Christine Montoney helped with the questions and answers.

This book tested the patience and good will of several typists, a test Mary Heinmiller, Tim Fox, and Dana Loud passed with high marks. Helaine McMenomy organized this critical activity.

G. Bingham Powell facilitated matters by providing assistance and support. Randy Calvert, Bruce Jacobs, John Mueller, William Riker, Alan Stockman, and David Weimer dealt graciously with repeated interruptions to explain how to find needed figures and what they might mean. As always, they were very willing to tell us where to go and what to do.

Herbert Alexander, Richard Baker, John Bolland, Kevin Coleman, George Edwards, Sheldon Goldman, Charles Hadley, David Huckabee, Malcolm Jewell, Gary Orfield, Tom Smith, and Stephen Wayne provided timely assistance with pieces of the work. We thank Edward Carmines and David Rohde for their thorough review of the final manuscript and Burdett Loomis, Paul Quirk, Elliot Slotnick, and David Vogler, who helped in the early stages of the project.

Joyce Donley, Michael Horn, Sue Robertson, and Robert Taylor gave needed advice and assistance on calculations, graphics, and word processing.

Reference librarians provided initial encouragement and sustaining support. Phyllis Andrews, Dave Reynolds, and Brad Smith at the University of Rochester, and Linda Watson at the University of Alabama dealt patiently and productively with requests.

Some could be mentioned for what they did to thwart completion of this project. After work began, one editor was named interim dean, the other a visiting research professor. Fortunately for us, Brian Thompson and Harvey Kline provided resources and work environments that made completion more likely rather than less.

Our families were understanding and supportive during the many evenings and weekends spent working on the book—even as we devoted bits of time on holidays to advance the project just a little more.

At CQ Press Joanne Daniels encouraged us from the start and persuaded us to push for an early completion date: a wise mix of anxiety, humor, and patience kept us on track. Nancy Lammers and Kerry Kern helped us negotiate the technical details of publication, Carolyn Goldinger and Tracy White gave us the benefit of their careful editing, and Kathryn Suárez and Ellen Kresky labored over promotion and advertising.

Introduction

This volume presents a convenient collection of more than two hundred figures and tables essential to understanding American politics. The range of topics covered, the treatment of topics over long time spans, the emphasis on up-to-date coverage, and the Guide to References for Political Statistics, page 369, mean this book can be an invaluable aid for the reader intent on understanding and keeping up with American politics.

The volume covers a wide range of topics. In addition to the standard subjects such as elections, Congress, the presidency, and the judiciary, the book provides information on the media, interest groups, foreign, social, and economic policy, and a variety of issues related to state and local government. Coverage is not limited to "hard" data such as votes cast and offices won; rankings of public officials' reputations, content analyses of media coverage, and public opinion data about policy issues are included. The information ranges from simple lists to compilations of outcomes based on implicit analytical concerns. A historical perspective is maintained throughout; depending on available data, the longest possible time periods are covered, even with public opinion data. The sources of material range from the findable to the fugitive: reference volumes, government publications, political science journals, and monographs, among others.

The chapter organization follows introductory American government textbooks. Readers will recognize, of course, that any such organization is somewhat arbitrary and that information relevant to a specific topic may be found in a variety of places. For example, public opinion data about specific policies are found in the policy chapters, while the public opinion chapter is reserved for more general topics such as party identification and liberal-conservative outlooks. The list of tables and figures, along with the index, should make use of the volume straightforward.

The guide provides help for those seeking data beyond that contained here. Literally thousands of tables and figures on the topics covered in this volume and on related topics can be found in the works cited.

The quantity and quality of statistical information have grown enormously in recent years, and this trend has yet to peak. But statistics have a bad image. Even the numerically innocent know that "there're lies, damn lies, and statistics" and that "figures don't lie but liars can figure." But anyone seeking to understand politics—past, present, or future—would be ill-advised to take refuge in such skepticism. Increasingly, both public debates and political analyses contain points couched in or accompanied by statistics. Democracy turns in part on the ability of an informed public to follow such debates and analyses. Now more than ever, understanding politics requires an ability to comprehend numerical data and the assumptions behind them.

Although data are more essential and more readily available, the interpretive skills are all too often lacking. Unless one knows how to read them, tables and figures can be less than useful; they can be intimidating, incomprehensible, and boring. Yet properly understood, tables and figures can be a resource of considerable value.

This volume will not teach statistical methodologies, but it will foster a greater familiarity with the appropriate cautions about reading too much or too little into tables and figures. This introduction, the chapter introductions, the chapter questions, and the guide are all intended to enhance the reader's understanding of how to make better use of tabular information. They are designed to help the reader to extract the maximum amount of information from tables, to understand the level of accuracy in tabular information as well as the various sources of and kinds of inaccuracies and to find additional information, including up-to-date information that must be found in serial publications rather than books.

Instructors who adopt the book may request a teacher's manual containing the answers to the questions and additional topics for discussion.

Some readers, particularly students who are accustomed to working with numbers as they appear in textbooks, are sometimes frustrated, perhaps even mystified, when confronted with whole tables of numbers. An important point of departure for these readers is to realize that this book is based principally on simple numerical data, not on the results of complicated statistical manipulations. The fanciest statistics presented are averages or medians. Regression coefficients, chi-squares, and the like can be revealing and useful, and increasingly political science has become methodologically sophisticated so that many journal articles are opaque to those without the ability to cope with advanced statistics. But this book fills a more fundamental need for a single volume encompassing a broad range of data about American politics and as such should be useful to the methodologically skilled and unskilled alike.

The figures and tables are easy to read. Many are merely lists, but very useful lists. They are often lengthy because they may cover as many as two hundred years. Long historical stretches mean change, and that creates some complexities, as, for example, when the names of the dominant parties change so that going back in time introduces unfamiliar labels. Footnotes to the tables and figures contain the necessary explanations as well as important qualifications and details; they must be read to understand the table or figure content. Following conventional practice, large numbers are expressed in units of thousands or millions to enhance readability. This, too, can lead to minor problems for readers unaccustomed to reading tabular material, but a bit of practice will overcome any such difficulties. In general, a little care and caution in reading and interpreting numbers is all that is required.

The Accuracy of Published Data

Errors in Data

The material selected for this volume is intended to be the most accurate, up-to-date information possible from the most reputable sources available. But anyone who has used statistical information realizes that it is almost never completely error free. This is inevitably true here as well. Consider, for example, Tables 12-4 and 12-5. Both are taken from a major publication of the U.S. Census Bureau, a publication devoted to presentation of statistical information about the United States. The figures reported in both tables typically match. For example, the figure $52,293 million of "total social welfare expenditures" for 1960 noted in Table 12-5 shows up, correctly rounded, as $52.3 billion in Table 12-4. Similarly, most federal versus state and local breakdowns in Table 12-5 match exactly the breakdowns in Table 12-4. Yet inexplicably, the figures for 1980 do not quite match; total expenditures were $492,797 million according to Table 12-5 but $492.5 billion according to Table 12-4; the federal expenditures were $302,616 million versus $302.8 billion, and so forth.

Why do such discrepancies and other kinds of errors (or what appear to be errors) occur? The answer varies.

Rounding. Sometimes what appears to be an error is simply a matter of when rounding is done. For example, 20.2 plus 20.4 equals 41 if one adds and then rounds, but equals 40 if one rounds and then adds. Almost certainly this explains why the 1960 federal and state and local expenditures in Table 12-5 (24,957 and 27,337) do not add up exactly to the total shown (summing to 52,294 rather than 52,293). A similar sort of "error" occurs when percentages sum to 99.8 or 100.2 rather than to 100 plus or minus 1 percent.

Exact Date of Data Collection. Accurate interpretation of data depends on knowing the precise date of collection and the period covered. Sometimes this is obvious. For example, the unemployment rate "at the end of the year" may differ if the phrase means the average of the November and December figures rather than the December figures alone. The time factor can be more subtle—for example, if a U.S. senator-elect dies and someone from the other party is appointed to fill the seat, the number of Democrats and Republicans elected will differ slightly from the number of Democrats and Republicans who actually take office a few months later. Even seemingly similar time spans sometimes conceal important differences. Dollar amounts for given years are likely to differ if one uses calendar years rather than fiscal years.

Handling of "Minor" Categories. "Minor" categories may be uncounted, ignored, or dropped for analytical reasons. Often, for example, votes are given only for the candidates of the two major parties. The small number of votes for the Socialist, Libertarian, and Prohibition candidates, not to mention the stray ballots cast for Mickey Mouse or "none of the above," are unreported or lumped together under "other." Thus a vote may be correctly reported as 42.7 percent (of the total vote) and just as correctly reported as 42.9 percent (of the two-party vote). Occasionally minor categories create more complicated problems. For example, in New York State, the same candidate may be nominated by two parties, such as the Democratic party and the Liberal party. The percentage of Democratic votes then differs from the percentage of votes received by the Democratic candidate.

Changes in Measurement Techniques. Changes in the way measurements are made can produce different figures and can lead to time series that are not fully comparable. A classic example is survey measurements, in which researchers "improve" the questions, only to find that they cannot measure change in public opinion because the new results are not comparable to those of earlier polls. Sometimes, however, changes are forced on reluctant researchers. For example, the "market basket" of items in the Consumer Price Index (Table 13-2) has changed over time. The cost of fountain pens or carbon paper might have been reasonable items in the 1950s but not in the 1980s; VCRs could hardly have been included until recently.

Ad Hoc Problems. All sorts of small discrepancies can occur, with ad hoc explanations for each one. An example that nearly everyone is familiar with involves the counting of presidents. Ronald Reagan is usually said to be the fortieth president. But he is only the thirty-ninth individual to hold the office; Grover Cleveland is counted twice because his two terms were separated by four years. So is the correct number thirty-nine or forty? It depends on precisely what one means. A less obvious problem occurs in counting Supreme Court nominations that failed. In 1987 Douglas Ginsburg was publicly announced as President Reagan's choice, but his name was withdrawn before it was formally submitted to the Senate. Technically, was he nominated? This kind of subtlety is exacerbated when we deal with events of the distant past. It would be easy, for example, to think that the two listings of the nomination of Edward King by President John Tyler are a typographical error. In fact, King was nominated twice, and the nomination was twice withdrawn in a fight between the president and Congress (Table 9-4).

Solutions to Errors in Data

Awareness that data may contain inaccuracies is no reason to ignore the data; nor is it an excuse to ignore the possible inaccuracies. A consideration of some "solutions" to data errors helps illustrate this point. The solutions, like the problems discussed above, are suggestive rather than exhaustive.

Sometimes errors are relatively obvious and can be easily corrected. Misprints occur, for example. One can encounter references to the 535 members of the House of Representatives when obviously the whole Congress is meant. Checking with alternative or more authoritative sources when mistakes are suspected can help remedy such problems.

Outlandish or illogical numbers should also be checked. A classic example of finding and explaining nonsensical results is the case of two researchers who were not willing to believe data from the 1950 Census showing "a surprising number of widowed fourteen-year-old boys and, equally surprising, a decrease in the number of widowed teenage males at older ages." [1] They wrote a "detective story" about how they traced the problem to systematic errors in the way certain data were entered into the census records.

Another method—one that should always be used—is to check footnotes and accompanying text for exceptions and special comments. Recognize that the problem may not really be error, but misreading. Consider the table on U.S. casualties in Vietnam (Table 11-7). For 1973-1984 the bottom row shows there were no U.S. military forces in Vietnam but 1,139 battle deaths—surely an anomaly. But the note reveals that there were troops in Vietnam for nearly a month during this time—the zero indicates the force count as of 31 December 1973, and U.S. forces were withdrawn on 27 January 1973. In addition, forces dying of wounds incurred earlier or those who were missing and later classified as deceased are also considered battle deaths.

Another solution is what is formally called sensitivity analysis. When values are inexact or differ across sources, one needs to ask how sensitive the conclusion is to the precise values used. If the true values differed by some specified amount from the reported values, would the conclusion change? If not, one can be more confident about the conclusion. Similarly, if sources differ, consider the actual values from several sources. If the conclusion to be drawn does not vary with the different values, the discrepancies are only a minor problem. In the welfare expenditures example, almost any conclusion about social welfare would be the same whether 1980 expenditures were $4.925 billion (Table 12-4) or $4.928 billion (Table 12-5), even though the difference represents three million dollars.

In examining data over time, one way to avoid possible errors is to be sure the data are truly comparable. Again, one must check that the data were collected uniformly or know what the differences are over time and their probable effects. Occasionally guesses about probable error can be confirmed by formal tests. An excellent example is a study in which both old and new survey questions were asked. Differences that had previously been attributed to changes in the electorate over time were shown to be methodological artifacts.[2]

One should also examine data, perhaps especially data over time, for "outliers." If a series of values, say the percentages of votes for the Republican candidate in a given district, are 52, 56, 49, 85, 50, one must check the accuracy of the 85 percent. Is the 85 a transposition of 58? If 85 is the correct number, what is the reason for it? Was the candidate essentially unopposed that year? What conclusion should be drawn if the 85 were omitted?

Finally, after taking all reasonable steps to be sure the data are as good as can be obtained, checking multiple sources, and so on, one should indicate known errors. It is better to point out that there is some question about certain figures than to pretend that they are perfect. If a loftier reason does not come to mind, being straightforward about inaccuracies at least prevents readers from lobbing them back as if the author were too ignorant to even notice the problems.

Obtaining Additional Material

This book provides essential figures and tables, but the coverage is far from exhaustive. Many readers may want data with a slightly different twist or of another sort altogether. The Guide to References for Political Statistics should help orient readers who seek information beyond that contained here. In addition, the sources given for the tables and figures in this book should also be considered in such searches.

Data on current events can be found in newspapers, weekly news magazines, the *Congressional Quarterly Weekly Report*, and the *National Journal*. Indexes for the *Weekly Report*, *National Journal*, and for major newspapers are a valuable guide. The *National Newspaper Index* and the *National Magazine Index* cover many sources.

Readers need to appreciate how useful reference librarians are to those seeking information. Librarians for government documents collections are also invaluable resources. Interlibrary loans can help secure less readily available volumes, although principal reference works and current material seldom circulate in this fashion.

For some material, one may need to contact organizations that compile or disseminate the data. Various directories are available—of party organizations, interest groups, associations, research institutions, and state agencies. At the federal level, Congressional Quarterly's *Washington Information Directory* is a valuable guide to potential sources. The Council of State Governments, with directories such as *State Administrative Officials Classified by Functions* and *State Elective Officials and the Legislatures* provide a similar service at the state level. (See also the references cited in the introduction to Chapter 10.)

For this volume, machine-readable data constituted a valuable source for several tables and figures. Descriptions of available machine-readable data would require another volume. The Inter-University Consortium for Political and Social Research (ICPSR) at the University of Michigan has the largest collection of such data and publishes an annual guide to resources. Most major research universities are members of the consortium. To learn how to obtain data, one should contact the official university representative of the ICPSR.

These hints are merely starting suggestions for those who wish to go beyond this volume to track down particular pieces of information. We hope the reader will find the extensive coverage in this obviously nonexhaustive volume to be convenient and invaluable.

Notes

1. Ansley J. Coale and Frederick F. Stephan, "The Case of the Indians and the Teen-Age Widows," *Journal of American Statistical Association* 57 (1962): 338.
2. John L. Sullivan, James E. Piereson, and George E. Marcus, "Ideological Constraint in the Mass Public: A Methodological Critique and Some New Findings," *American Journal of Political Science* 22 (1978): 233-249.

1

The Constitution

Constitutions are documents about rights and authority. At first blush, little about them suggests statistics. However, a great many numbers relate to the fundamental laws that govern the states and the nation. Such numbers, while significant, tend to be straightforward and simple: dates of constitutional revision and amendment, length of gubernatorial terms, requirements for voter registration, and so on. In addition, some important information is found in lists showing, for example, which state constitutions have a certain component, such as the line-item veto.

The image of the U.S. Constitution as a document written on parchment with quill pens is a powerful legacy from the past but a misleading image for understanding the Constitution in the present. The bicentennial year celebrations focused attention on the Constitutional Convention of 1787, but the U.S. Constitution has evolved dramatically over the past two hundred years (Table 1-3). The document, both in content and meaning, has changed as a result of civil war, formal amendments, and Supreme Court rulings. Amendments are not things of the past either; several have been proposed since the 1960s, and a few are still pending (Tables 1-5 and 1-6).

The federal political structure, delineated in the Constitution, has also undergone significant transformations. For instance, the first ten amendments, the Bill of Rights, originally limited only the federal government, but Supreme Court decisions have interpreted almost all of these rights to limit state governments as well (Table 1-4). Other data about federal and state constitutions and their changes (e.g., Tables 1-2, 1-7, and 1-8) also reveal the continuing evolution of the basic framework of the U.S. political system.

Because the federal constitution is a brief document that has been changed little during U.S. history, many may think that this is characteristic of all constitutions. State constitutions vary considerably in their length and in their age (Table 1-2). Some also have been amended frequently, and constitutional change has sometimes swept across the entire country, as when Progressives around the turn of the century mounted a major reform effort. Primaries flourish today as one legacy of the Progressive reform movement (Table 4-9). Progressive reformers also pushed the initiative, referenda, and recall; most states have constitutionally adopted at least one of these procedures (Table 1-7).

Constitutions attest to the fundamental values underlying the political order, supposedly capturing and constraining the prevailing political consensus. Although surveys have found public support for civil liberties such as free speech to be less than broadly based (Table 1-9), one of the major contributions of the U.S. Constitution is precisely the protection of minority rights against majority wishes.

Because individuals often fail to agree, even on so-called fundamental issues, and because any change in a constitution may have sweeping effects, constitutions attract controversy. And not surprisingly, data relevant to constitutional issues also reflect controversy. In a number of instances, public opinion reveals clear majority preferences—on school prayer (Table 1-6) and the balanced budget (Table 1-6), for example—and yet legislators have failed to enact these constitutional amendments. This may be understandable, as when the outnumbered opposition is intense or raises legal impediments. The discrepancy between majority opinion and political action serves as a helpful reminder about the distinction between opinion and behavior and raises questions about the meaning, interpretations, and implications of such survey data.

Constitutions reach beyond the words they contain. Vital pieces of the political fabric, such as political parties, are not mentioned in the U.S. Constitution. But much that was unmentioned has increasingly come under the Constitution and the jurisdiction of the federal courts. Voter registration requirements, for example, were originally left to the states, but federal court decisions and the 1965 Voting Rights Act have caused greater uniformity among the states since 1965 (Tables 1-15 and 1-17). Similarly, reapportionment of legislative seats, an area the federal courts initially refused to review because it raised "political questions," has changed dramatically since the early 1960s. With its "one person, one vote" ruling, the Supreme Court has imposed strict standards on legislative districts (Table 1-16).

Constitutions are words, not numbers. But it is surprising how many statistics are relevant to the understanding of constitutions.

Table 1-1 The States: Historical Data and Current Populations

State	*Population*[a]	*Date organized as territory*	*Date admitted to Union*	*Chronological order of admission to Union*
Alabama	3,893,888	March 3, 1817	December 14, 1819	22
Alaska	401,851	August 24, 1912	January 3, 1959	49
Arizona	2,718,215	February 24, 1863	February 14, 1912	48
Arkansas	2,286,435	March 2, 1819	June 15, 1836	25
California	23,667,902	[b]	September 9, 1850	31
Colorado	2,889,964	February 28, 1861	August 1, 1876	38
Connecticut	3,107,576	-	January 9, 1788[c]	5
Delaware	594,338	-	December 7, 1787[c]	1
Florida	9,746,324	March 30, 1822	March 3, 1845	27
Georgia	5,463,105	-	January 2, 1788[c]	4
Hawaii	964,691	June 14, 1900	August 21, 1959	50
Idaho	943,935	March 4, 1863	July 3, 1890	43
Illinois	11,426,518	February 3, 1809	December 3, 1818	21
Indiana	5,490,224	May 7, 1800	December 11, 1816	19
Iowa	2,913,808	June 12, 1838	December 28, 1846	29
Kansas	2,363,679	May 30, 1854	January 29, 1861	34
Kentucky	3,660,777	[b]	June 1, 1792	15
Louisiana	4,205,900	March 26, 1804	April 30, 1812	18
Maine	1,124,660	[b]	March 15, 1820	23
Maryland	4,216,975	-	April 28, 1788[c]	7
Massachusetts	5,737,037	-	February 6, 1788[c]	6
Michigan	9,262,078	January 11, 1805	January 26, 1837	26
Minnesota	4,075,970	March 3, 1849	May 11, 1858	32
Mississippi	2,520,638	April 7, 1798	December 10, 1817	20
Missouri	4,916,686	June 4, 1812	August 10, 1821	24
Montana	786,690	May 26, 1864	November 8, 1889	41
Nebraska	1,569,825	May 30, 1854	March 1, 1867	37
Nevada	800,493	March 2, 1861	October 31, 1864	36
New Hampshire	920,610	-	June 21, 1788[c]	9
New Jersey	7,364,823	-	December 18, 1787[c]	3
New Mexico	1,302,894	September 9, 1850	January 6, 1912	47
New York	17,558,072	-	July 26, 1788[c]	11
North Carolina	5,881,766	-	November 21, 1789[c]	12
North Dakota	652,717	March 2, 1861	November 2, 1889	39
Ohio	10,797,630	May 7, 1800	March 1, 1803	17
Oklahoma	3,025,290	May 2, 1890	November 16, 1907	46
Oregon	2,632,105	August 14, 1848	February 14, 1859	33
Pennsylvania	11,863,895	-	December 12, 1787[c]	2
Rhode Island	947,154	-	May 29, 1790[c]	13
South Carolina	3,121,820	-	May 23, 1788[c]	8
South Dakota	690,768	March 2, 1861	November 2, 1889	40

(Table continues)

Table 1-1 *(Continued)*

State	*Population*[a]	*Date organized as territory*	*Date admitted to Union*	*Chronological order of admission to Union*
Tennessee	4,591,120	June 8, 1790[d]	June 1, 1796	16
Texas	14,229,191	[b]	December 29, 1845	28
Utah	1,461,037	September 9, 1850	January 4, 1896	45
Vermont	511,456	[b]	March 4, 1791	14
Virginia	5,346,818	-	June 25, 1788[c]	10
Washington	4,132,156	March 2, 1853	November 11, 1889	42
West Virginia	1,949,644	[b]	June 20, 1863	35
Wisconsin	4,705,767	April 20, 1836	May 29, 1848	30
Wyoming	469,557	July 25, 1868	July 10, 1890	44

Note: "-" indicates one of the original thirteen states.

[a] As of 1980.

[b] No territorial status before admission to Union.

[c] Date of ratification of U.S. Constitution.

[d] Date Southwest Territory (identical boundaries as Tennessee's) was created.

Source: Council of State Governments, *Book of the States, 1986-1987* (Lexington, Ky.: Council of State Governments, 1986), 465-468.

Table 1-2 State Constitutions

State	*Number of constitutions*[a]	*Dates of adoption*	*Present Constitution*			
					Number of amendments	
			Effective date	Estimated length (number of words)	*Submitted to voters*	*Adopted*
Alabama	6	1819, 1861, 1865, 1868, 1875, 1901	November 28, 1901	174,000	656	452
Alaska	1	1956	January 3, 1959	13,000	28	20
Arizona	1	1911	February 14, 1912	28,876	187	104
Arkansas	5	1836, 1861, 1864, 1868, 1874	October 30, 1874	40,720	156	71
California	2	1847, 1879	July 4, 1879	33,350	756	449
Colorado	1	1876	August 1, 1876	45,679	227	108
Connecticut	4	1818, 1965	December 30, 1965	9,564	24	23
Delaware	4	1776, 1792, 1831, 1897	June 10, 1897	19,000		115
Florida	6	1839, 1861, 1865, 1868, 1886, 1968	January 7, 1969	25,100	63	41
Georgia	10	1777, 1789, 1798, 1861, 1865, 1868, 1877, 1945, 1976, 1982	July 1, 1983	25,000	11	10
Hawaii	1	1950	August 21, 1959	17,453	85	77
Idaho	1	1889	July 3, 1890	21,500	183	103
Illinois	4	1818, 1848, 1870, 1970	July 1, 1971	13,200	7	3
Indiana	2	1816, 1851	November 1, 1851	9,377	65	36
Iowa	2	1846, 1857	September 3, 1857	12,500	48	45
Kansas	1	1859	January 29, 1861	11,865	107	80
Kentucky	4	1792, 1799, 1850, 1891	September 28, 1891	23,500	54	26
Louisiana	11	1812, 1845, 1852, 1861, 1864, 1868, 1879, 1898, 1913, 1921, 1974	January 1, 1975	36,146	24	15
Maine	1	1819	March 15, 1820	13,500	181	153
Maryland	4	1776, 1851, 1864, 1867	October 5, 1867	41,134	227	195

(Table continues)

Table 1-2 *(Continued)*

			Present Constitution			
					Number of amendments	
State	*Number of constitutions*[a]	*Dates of adoption*	Effective date	Estimated length (number of words)	*Submitted to voters*	*Adopted*
Massachusetts	1	1780	October 25, 1780	36,690	141	116
Michigan	4	1835, 1850, 1908, 1963	January 1, 1964	20,000	41	15
Minnesota	1	1857	May 11, 1858	9,500	203	109
Mississippi	4	1817, 1832, 1869, 1890	November 1, 1890	23,500	124	54
Missouri	4	1820, 1865, 1875, 1945	March 30, 1945	42,000	100	62
Montana	2	1889, 1972	July 1, 1973	11,866	17	10
Nebraska	2	1866, 1875	October 12, 1875	20,048	276	183
Nevada	1	1864	October 31, 1864	20,770	165	100
New Hampshire	2	1776, 1784	June 2, 1784	9,200	271	141
New Jersey	3	1776, 1844, 1947	January 1, 1948	17,086	48	36
New Mexico	1	1911	January 6, 1912	27,200	213	104
New York	4	1777, 1822, 1846, 1894	January 1, 1895	80,000	270	203
North Carolina	3	1776, 1868, 1970	July 1, 1971	11,000	30	24
North Dakota	1	1889	November 2, 1889	31,000	208	119
Ohio	2	1802, 1851	September 1, 1851	36,900	241	142
Oklahoma	1	1907	November 16, 1907	68,800	254	114
Oregon	1	1857	February 14, 1859	25,965	347	174
Pennsylvania	5	1776, 1790, 1838, 1873, 1968	1968[b]	21,675	24	19
Rhode Island	2	1842	May 2, 1843	19,026	84	44
South Carolina	7	1776, 1778, 1790, 1861, 1865, 1868, 1895	January 1, 1896	22,500	638	454
South Dakota	1	1889	November 2, 1889	23,300	178	92
Tennessee	3	1796, 1835, 1870	February 23, 1870	15,300	55	32

Texas	5	1845, 1861, 1866, 1869, 1876	February 15, 1876	62,000	430	283
Utah	1	1895	January 4, 1896	17,500	121	73
Vermont	3	1777, 1786, 1793	July 9, 1793	6,600	206	49
Virginia	6	1776, 1830, 1851, 1869, 1902, 1970	July 1, 1971	18,500	19	16
Washington	1	1889	November 11, 1889	29,400	139	76
West Virginia	2	1863, 1872	April 9, 1872	25,600	96	59
Wisconsin	1	1848	May 29, 1848	13,500	161	118
Wyoming	1	1889	July 10, 1890	31,800	90	51

Note: Constitutions as of December 31, 1985. For more details on the constitutions, see source.

[a] The constitutions include those Civil War documents customarily listed by the individual states. In Connecticut and Rhode Island, colonial charters served as the first constitutions.

[b] Certain sections of the Constitution were revised in 1967-1968. Amendments proposed and adopted are since 1968.

Source: Book of the States, 1986–1987, 14-15.

Table 1-3 Length of Time between Congressional Approval and Actual Ratification of the Twenty-six Amendments to the U.S. Constitution

Amendment		*Time required for ratification*	*Year ratified*
I-X	Bill of Rights	2 years, 2½ months	1791
XI	Lawsuits against states	11 months	1795
XII	Presidential elections	6½ months	1804
XIII	Abolition of slavery	10 months	1865
XIV	Civil rights	2 years, 1 month	1868
XV	Suffrage for all races	11 months	1870
XVI	Income tax	3 years, 6½ months	1913
XVII	Senatorial elections	11 months	1913
XVIII	Prohibition	1 year, 1 month	1919
XIX	Women's suffrage	1 year, 2 months	1920
XX	Terms of office	11 months	1933
XXI	Repeal of prohibition	9½ months	1933
XXII	Limit on presidential terms	3 years, 11 months	1951
XXIII	Washington, D.C., vote	9 months	1961
XXIV	Abolition of poll taxes	1 year, 4 months	1964
XXV	Presidential succession	1 year, 10 months	1967
XXVI	Eighteen-year-old suffrage	3 months	1971

Source: Congressional Research Service, *The Constitution of the United States: Analysis and Interpretation* (Washington, D.C.: U.S. Government Printing Office, 1973), 23-44. 92d Cong., 2d sess., S. Doc. 92-82.

Table 1-4 Incorporation of the Bill of Rights to Apply to State Governments

Year	*Issue and amendment*	*Supreme Court case*	*Vote*
[1868 Fourteenth Amendment to Constitution passed][a]			
1897	Eminent domain (V)	*Chicago, Burlington & Quincy RR v. Chicago* 166 U.S. 266	9:0
1927	Freedom of speech (I)	*Fiske v. Kansas* 274 U.S. 380	9:0
1931	Freedom of press (I)	*Near v. Minnesota* 283 U.S. 697	5:4
1932	Counsel in capital criminal cases (VI)	*Powell v. Alabama* 287 U.S. 45	7:2
1934	Free exercise of religion (I)	*Hamilton v. Regents of the U. of California* 293 U.S. 245	9:0
1937	Freedom of assembly and petition (I)	*De Jonge v. Oregon* 299 U.S. 253	8:0
1947	Separation of church and state (I)	*Everson v. Board of Education of Ewing Township* 330 U.S. 1	5:4
1948	Public trial (VI)	*In re Oliver* 33 U.S. 257	7:2
1961	Unreasonable searches and seizures (IV)	*Mapp v. Ohio* 367 U.S. 643	6:3
1962	Cruel and unusual punishment (VIII)	*Robinson v. California* 370 U.S. 660	6:2
1963	Counsel in all criminal cases (VI)	*Gideon v. Wainwright* 372 U.S. 335	9:0
1964	Self-incrimination (V)	*Malloy v. Hogan* 378 U.S. 1	5:4
		Murphy v. Waterfront Commission 378 U.S. 52	9:0
1965	Right to confront adverse witnesses (VI)	*Pointer v. Texas* 380 U.S. 400	7:2
1967	Impartial jury (VI)	*Parker v. Gladden* 385 U.S. 363	8:1
1967	Obtaining and confronting favorable witnesses (VI)	*Washington v. Texas* 388 U.S. 14	9:0
1967	Speedy trial (VI)	*Klopfer v. North Carolina* 386 U.S. 213	9:0
1968	Jury trial in non-petty criminal cases (VI)	*Duncan v. Louisiana* 391 U.S. 145	7:2
1969	Double jeopardy (V)	*Benton v. Maryland* 395 U.S. 784	7:2

Note: Enumerated rights not incorporated: grand jury indictment, trial by jury in civil cases, excessive fines and bail, right to bear arms, and safeguards on quartering troops in private homes.

[a] The Fourteenth Amendment's due process clause is the basis for applying the Bill of Rights to the states.

Sources: Henry J. Abraham, *The Judiciary: The Supreme Court in the Governmental Process,* 6th ed. (Boston: Allyn and Bacon, 1983), 68-80; votes from *U.S. Supreme Court Reports.*

Table 1-5 State Action on Recently Proposed Constitutional Amendments

	Proposed amendment			
State	Reapportionment[a]	Equal rights[b]	Balanced budget[c]	Ban abortion[d]
Alabama	yes	n.a.	yes	yes
Alaska	n.a.	yes	yes	no or n.a.
Arizona	yes	n.a.	yes	no or n.a.
Arkansas	yes	n.a.	yes	yes
California	n.a.	yes	no or n.a.	no or n.a.
Colorado	yes	yes	yes	no or n.a.
Connecticut	n.a.	yes	no or n.a.	no or n.a.
Delaware	n.a.	yes	yes	yes
Florida	yes	n.a.	yes	no or n.a.
Georgia	yes	n.a.	yes	no or n.a.
Hawaii	n.a.	yes	no or n.a.	no or n.a.
Idaho	yes	r	yes	yes
Illinois	r[e]	n.a.	no or n.a.	no or n.a.
Indiana	yes	yes	yes	yes
Iowa	yes	yes	yes	no or n.a.
Kansas	r[e]	yes	yes	no or n.a.
Kentucky	yes	r	no or n.a.	yes
Louisiana	yes	n.a.	yes	yes
Maine	n.a.	yes	no or n.a.	no or n.a.
Maryland	r[e]	yes	yes	no or n.a.
Massachusetts	n.a.	yes	no or n.a.	yes
Michigan	n.a.	yes	no or n.a.	no or n.a.
Minnesota	yes	yes	no or n.a.	no or n.a.
Mississippi	yes	n.a.	yes	yes
Missouri	yes	n.a.	yes	yes
Montana	yes	yes	no or n.a.	no or n.a.
Nebraska	yes	r	yes	yes
Nevada	yes	n.a.	yes	yes
New Hampshire	yes	yes	yes	no or n.a.
New Jersey	n.a.	yes	no or n.a.	yes
New Mexico	yes	yes	yes	no or n.a.
New York	n.a.	yes	no or n.a.	no or n.a.
North Carolina	r[e]	n.a.	yes	no or n.a.
North Dakota	yes	yes	yes	no or n.a.
Ohio	n.a.	yes	no or n.a.	no or n.a.
Oklahoma	yes	n.a.	yes	yes
Oregon	n.a.	yes	yes	no or n.a.
Pennsylvania	n.a.	yes	yes	yes
Rhode Island	n.a.	yes	no or n.a.	yes
South Carolina	yes	n.a.	yes	no or n.a.
South Dakota	yes	r	yes	yes

(Table continues)

Table 1-5 *(Continued)*

State	Proposed amendment			
	Reapportionment[a]	Equal rights[b]	Balanced budget[c]	Ban abortion[d]
Tennessee	yes	r	yes	yes
Texas	r[e]	yes	yes	no or n.a.
Utah	yes	n.a.	yes	yes
Vermont	n.a.	yes	no or n.a.	no or n.a.
Virginia	yes	n.a.	yes	no or n.a.
Washington	r[e]	yes	no or n.a.	no or n.a.
West Virginia	n.a.	yes	no or n.a.	no or n.a.
Wisconsin	n.a.	yes	no or n.a.	no or n.a.
Wyoming	yes	yes	yes	no or n.a.

Note: "Yes" indicates state legislature approved the amendment or sent a petition to Congress for a constitutional convention; "no" indicates state legislature rejected the amendment or a proposal to petition for a convention; "n.a." indicates no action was taken; and "r" indicates previous appeal was rescinded. The equal rights amendment was initiated by Congress and submitted to the states for ratification. The other three proposed amendments were initiated by petition from state legislatures.

[a] Reapportionment: States acted to petition Congress for a constitutional convention on this issue following two Supreme Court "one person, one vote" decisions concerning how states were apportioned for their state legislatures. As a result, some states called for a convention to consider an amendment that would allow one house of a state legislature to be apportioned on a basis other than population.

[b] Equal Rights: This amendment, as proposed by Congress and voted on by the states, read: "Section 1. Equality of rights under the law shall not be denied or abridged by the United States or by any State on account of sex. Section 2. The Congress shall have the power to enforce, by appropriate legislation, the provisions of this article. Section 3. This amendment shall take effect two years after the date of ratification."

[c] Balanced Budget: This proposed amendment has various forms. In its simplest form, Congress would be required to approve a balanced federal budget each year. In other forms there is a provision that a three-fifths majority of Congress could vote not to balance the budget in any given year.

[d] Abortion: Some states have called for a constitutional convention to consider an amendment that would ban abortions. The most common approach among the various proposed amendments is to apply the constitutional protection of due process against the denial of life and property to unborn children.

[e] Passed by only one house of each of the state legislatures.

Sources: Reapportionment: *Congressional Quarterly Weekly Report* (1969), 1372-1373; equal rights: *Public Opinion* (August/September 1981), 39 (reprinted with permission of American Enterprise Institute for Public Policy Research); Congressional Research Service, *The Constitution of the United States,* 43; balanced budget: *Congressional Record* citations to state communications relating to constitutional conventions, *The Gallup Report* (September 1985), 11; abortion: *Congressional Record* citations to state communications relating to constitutional conventions.

Table 1-6 Public Opinion on Issues Relating to Proposed Constitutional Amendments (percent)

Proposed amendment/year	*Favor*	*Oppose*	*Don't know or no opinion*
Abortion			
1974	47	44	9
1981	45	46	9
1983	50	43	7
Reapportionment			
1964	47	30	23
1969	52	23	25
Supreme Court decision banning school prayer			
1963	24	70	6
1971	28	67	6
1974	31	66	3
1975	35	62	3
1977	33	64	2
1982	37	60	3
1983	40	57	4
1985	43	54	3
1986	37	61	2
Equal rights[a]			
1975	58	24	18
1976	57	24	19
1978	58	31	11
1980	58	31	11
1981	63	32	5
1982	56	34	10
1984	63	31	6
Balanced budget[a]			
1976	78	13	9
1981 (April)	70	22	8
1981 (September)	73	19	8
1982	74	17	9
1983	71	21	8
1985	49	27	24

Note: Questions: (Abortion) "The U.S. Supreme Court has ruled that a woman may go to a doctor to end her pregnancy at any time during the first three months of pregnancy. Do you favor or oppose this ruling?" (Reapportionment, 1964) "As you know, the U.S. Supreme Court has ruled that the number of representatives of both the lower house and the Senate in all state legislatures must be in proportion to population. In most states, this means reducing the number of legislators from the rural areas and increasing the number from urban areas. Do you approve or disapprove of this ruling?" (Reapportionment, 1969) "The U.S. Supreme Court has required states to change their legislative districts so that each member of the upper house represents the same number of people. Some people would like to return to the earlier method of electing members of the upper house

Table 1-6 *(Continued)*

---

according to counties or other units regardless of population. Would you favor continuing the present equal districting plan or returning to the earlier plan?" (School prayer) "The U.S. Supreme Court has ruled that no state or local government may require the reading of the Lord's Prayer or Bible verses in public schools. What are your views on this—do you approve or disapprove of the court ruling?" (Equal rights) "Have you heard or read about the Equal Rights Amendment to the U.S. Constitution which would prohibit discrimination on the basis of sex? Do you favor or oppose this amendment?" (Balanced budget) "Have you heard or read about the proposal for a constitutional amendment which would require the federal government to balance the national budget each year? A proposed amendment to the Constitution would require Congress to approve a balanced federal budget each year. Government spending would have to be limited to no more than expected revenues, unless a three-fifths majority of Congress voted to spend more than expected revenues. Would you favor or oppose this amendment to the Constitution?" (Slightly different wording in 1976.)

[a] Of those who were aware of the proposed amendment (except 1984 for equal rights and 1976 for balanced budget). Between 88 and 91 pecent of those asked were aware of the equal rights amendment. Between 53 and 66 percent of those asked were aware of the proposed balanced budget amendment.

Sources: Abortion: *The Gallup Poll* (Wilmington, Del.: Scholarly Resources Inc., 1983), 140; reapportionment: *The Gallup Poll* (New York: Random House, 1972), 1897, 2205-2206; school prayer (1963, 1971): *The Gallup Poll* (1972), 1837; school prayer (1974-1986): General Social Surveys, National Opinion Research Center, University of Chicago; equal rights: *The Gallup Poll* (1982), 140, (1984), 242; balanced budget: *The Gallup Poll* (1972), 679, *The Gallup Poll* (1982), 125, 231, (1983), 127, and *The Gallup Report* (September 1985), 10-11.

Table 1-7 State Provisions for Initiative, Referendum, and Recall

State	*Initiative*[a]	*Referendum*[b]	*Recall*[c]
Alabama			
Alaska	direct	petition	all but judiciary
Arizona	direct	legislation and petition	all elected officials
Arkansas	direct	petition	
California	direct	petition and constitutional requirement	all elected officials
Colorado	direct	legislature and petition	all elected officials
Connecticut		legislature	
Delaware			
Florida		constitutional requirement	
Georgia		constitutional requirement	all elected officials
Hawaii			
Idaho	direct	petition	all but judiciary
Illinois		legislature	
Indiana			
Iowa		constitutional requirement	
Kansas		constitutional requirement	all but judiciary
Kentucky		all three	
Louisiana			all but judiciary
Maine	indirect	all three	
Maryland		petition	
Massachusetts	indirect	petition	
Michigan	indirect	all three	all but certain judges
Minnesota			
Mississippi			
Missouri	direct	legislature and petition	
Montana	direct	legislature and petition	all elected or appointed officials
Nebraska	direct	petition	
Nevada	indirect	petition	all elected officials

State	Initiative[a]	Referendum[b]	Recall[c]
New Hampshire			
New Jersey		legislature and constitutional requirement	
New Mexico		constitutional requirement and petition	
New York		constitutional requirement	
North Carolina		constitutional requirement	
North Dakota	direct	petition	all elected officials
Ohio	both	petition and constitutional requirement	
Oklahoma	direct	all three	
Oregon	direct	petition	all elected officials
Pennsylvania		constitutional requirement	
Rhode Island		constitutional requirement	
South Carolina			
South Dakota	indirect	petition	
Tennessee			
Texas			
Utah	both	petition	
Vermont			
Virginia		legislature and constitutional requirement	
Washington	both	all three	all elected except certain types of judges
West Virginia			
Wisconsin		legislature and constitutional requirement	all elected officials
Wyoming	direct	petition	

[a] Initiative: Allows proposed state laws to be placed on a ballot by citizen petition and enacted or rejected by the electorate. "Direct" means measures may be placed on the ballot with a specific number of signatures and no legislative action; requirements for number of signatures vary. "Indirect" means a measure must be submitted to the legislature for consideration before it can be placed on the ballot.

[b] Referendum: State law passed by the legislature is referred to voters before it goes into effect. Referendum may be held by citizen petition, voluntary submission by the legislature, or, for certain types of decisions, such as tax increases, may be a constitutional requirement.

[c] Recall: Voters are allowd to remove state elective officials in a recall election. Number of signatures needed ranges from 10 to 40 percent; percentage is based on last vote for the office in question or general election. Sometimes percentage is modified by geographical or jurisdictional restrictions.

Source: Book of the States, 1986-1987, 214-217.

Table 1-8 Governors' Terms, Limits, Powers, and Other Statewide Elected Officials

State	*Length of term in 1900*	*Length of term in 1984*	*Year of change*	*Maximum number of consecutive terms*	*Item veto*[a]	*Other statewide elected officials*[b] Number of officials	Number of agencies
Alabama	2	4	1902	2	yes	17	8
Alaska		4		2	yes	1	0
Arizona	[c]	4	1970	No limit	yes	8	6
Arkansas	2	2		No limit	yes	6	6
California	4	4		No limit	yes	10	7
Colorado	2	4	1958	No limit	yes	18	6
Connecticut	2	4	1950	No limit	yes	5	5
Delaware	4	4		2[d]	yes	5	5
Florida	4	4		2	yes	7	7
Georgia	2	4	1942	2	yes	12	8
Hawaii		4		No limit	yes	14	2
Idaho	2	4	1946	No limit	yes	6	6
Illinois	4	4		No limit	yes	14	6[e]
Indiana	4	4		2	no	6	6
Iowa	2	4	1974	No limit	yes	6	6
Kansas	2	4	1974	2	yes	15	6
Kentucky	4	4		1	yes	10	8
Louisiana	4	4		2	yes	21	10
Maine	2	4	1958	2	no	0	0
Maryland	4	4		2	yes	3	3
Massachusetts	1	4	1920, 1966[f]	No limit	yes	13	6
Michigan	2	4	1966	No limit	yes	35	7
Minnesota	2	4	1962	No limit	yes	5	5
Mississippi	4	4		1	yes	13	9
Missouri	4	4		2[d]	yes	5	5
Montana	4	4		No limit	yes	10	6
Nebraska	2	4	1966	2	yes	26	8

Nevada	4	4		2	no	23	7
New Hampshire	2	2		No limit	no	5	1
New Jersey	3	4	1949	2	yes	0	0
New Mexico	[c]	4	1916, 1970	1	yes	19	8
New York	2	4	1938	No limit	yes	3	3
North Carolina	4	4		2[d]	[g]	9	9
North Dakota	2	4	1964	No limit	yes	13	11
Ohio	2	4	1958	2	yes	28	6
Oklahoma		4		2	yes	9	7
Oregon	4	4		2	yes	5	5
Pennsylvania	4	4		2	yes	4	4
Rhode Island	1	2	1912	No limit	no	4	4
South Carolina	2	4	1926	2	yes	8	8
South Dakota	2	4	1974	2	yes	9	7
Tennessee	1	4	1954	2	yes	3	1
Texas	2	4	1974	No limit	yes	33	8
Utah	4	4		No limit	yes	14	4
Vermont	2	2		No limit	no	5	5
Virginia	4	4		1	yes	2	2
Washington	4	4		2	yes	8	8
West Virginia	4	4		No limit	yes	5	5
Wisconsin	2	4	1970	No limit	yes	5	5
Wyoming	4	4		No limit	yes	4	4

[a] Provisions to override vary, requiring as many as two-thirds of the legislators elected. For details, see source.
[b] Popularly elected executive branch officials and the number of agencies involving these officials.
[c] Arizona admitted in 1912, started with 2 years; New Mexico admitted in 1912 with 4 years, went to 2 years in 1916, and back to 4 years in 1970.
[d] Two terms only, whether or not consecutive.
[e] Governor has administrative control over agencies.
[f] Massachusetts went from 1 year to 2 years in 1920, and from 2 years to 4 years in 1966.
[g] Implied, no formal provision.

Sources: Book of the States, 1986-1987, 37-38; length of term and year of change: Congressional Quarterly, *Congressional Quarterly's Guide to U.S. Elections*, 2d ed. (Washington, D.C.: Congressional Quarterly, 1985), 130-131.

Table 1-9 Public Opinion on Civil Liberties (percent)

Issue/year	*Allow*[a]	*Don't forbid*[b]
Public speeches against democracy		
1940	25	46
1974	56	72
1976a	55	80
1976b	52	79

Issue/year	*Allow to speak*	*Allow to teach college*	*Keep book in library*
Atheist[c]			
1954	37	12	35
1964[d]	—	—	61
1972	65	40	61
1973a	65	41	61
1973b	62	39	57
1974	62	42	60
1976	64	41	60
1977	62	39	59
1978	63	—	60
1980	66	45	62
1982	64	46	61
1984	68	46	64
1985	65	45	61
Admitted communist[c]			
1954	27	6	27
1972	52	32	53
1973a	60	39	58
1973b	53	30	54
1974	58	42	59
1976	55	41	56
1977	55	39	55
1978	60	—	61
1980	55	41	57
1982	56	43	57
1984	59	46	60
1985	57	44	57
Racist[c]			
1943[e]	17	—	—
1976	61	41	60
1977	59	41	61
1978	62	—	65
1980	62	43	64
1982	59	43	60
1984	57	41	63
1985	55	42	60

Table 1-9 *(Continued)*

Note: "—" indicates not available.
[a] Question: "Do you think the United States should allow public speeches against democracy?"
[b] Question: "Do you think the United States should forbid public speeches against democracy?"
[c] Question: "There are always some people whose ideas are considered bad or dangerous by other people. For instance, somebody who (is against all churches and religion/admits he is a communist/believes that blacks are genetically inferior). If such a person wanted to make a speech in your (city/town/community), should he be allowed to speak? Should such a person be allowed to teach in a college or university, or not? If some people in your community suggested that a book he wrote (against churches and religion/[promoting communism]/which said blacks are inferior) should be taken out of your public library, would you favor removing this book?"
[d] In 1964 the question was as follows: "Suppose a man admited in public that he did not believe in God. Do you think a book he wrote should be removed from a public library?"
[e] In 1943 the question was as follows: "In peacetime, do you think anyone in the United States should be allowed to make speeches against certain races in this country?"

Sources: Public speeches against democracy: Howard Schuman and Stanley Presser, *Questions and Answers in Attitude Surveys* (New York: Academic Press, 1981); 1943, 1964, and 1973b: National Opinion Research Center surveys; 1954: Samuel A. Stouffer, *Communism, Conformity, and Civil Liberties* (Garden City, N.Y.: Doubleday, 1955), 32-34, 40-43; 1973a: Clyde Z. Nunn et al., *Tolerance for Nonconformity* (San Francisco: Jossey-Bass, 1978), 40-43; data for all other years from General Social Surveys.

Table 1-10 States with the Death Penalty, Number of Executions (1940-1985), and Number on Death Row (1987)

State	Method	*Number executed*					*Number awaiting execution*[b]
		1940s	1950s	1960s	1970s	1980s[a]	
Alabama	electrocution	50	20	5	0	1	81
Alaska	none	0	0	0	0	0	0
Arizona	gas chamber	9	8	4	0	0	64
Arkansas	lethal injection	38	18	9	0	0	33
California	gas chamber	80	74	30	0	0	195
Colorado	gas chamber	13	3	6	0	0	2
Connecticut	none[c]	10	5	1	0	0	0
Delaware	hanging	4	0	0	0	0	6
Florida	electrocution	65	49	12	1	12	259
Georgia	electrocution	130	85	14	0	6	109
Hawaii	none	0	0	0	0	0	0
Idaho	lethal injection or firing squad	0	3	0	0	0	14
Illinois	lethal injection	18	9	2	0	0	103
Indiana	electrocution	7	2	1	0	2	40
Iowa	none	7	1	2	0	0	0
Kansas	none	5	5	5	0	0	0
Kentucky	electrocution	34	16	1	0	0	30
Louisiana	electrocution	47	27	1	0	7	49
Maine	none	0	0	0	0	0	0
Maryland	gas chamber	45	6	1	0	0	18
Massachusetts	none	9	0	0	0	0	0
Michigan	none	0	0	0	0	0	0
Minnesota	none	0	0	0	0	0	0
Mississippi	gas chamber or lethal injection	60	36	10	0	1	45
Missouri	gas chamber	15	7	4	0	0	47
Montana	lethal injection or hanging	1	0	0	0	0	5
Nebraska	electrocution	2	2	0	0	0	14
Nevada	lethal injection	10	9	2	1	1	39
New Hampshire	none[c]	0	0	0	0	0	0
New Jersey	lethal injection	14	17	3	0	0	25
New Mexico	lethal injection	2	3	1	0	0	0
New York	none	114	52	10	0	0	0
North Carolina	gas chamber or lethal injection	112	19	1	0	2	65
North Dakota	none	0	0	0	0	0	0
Ohio	electrocution	51	32	7	0	0	77
Oklahoma	lethal injection, hanging, or firing squad	13	7	6	0	0	68

Table 1-10 *(Continued)*

State	*Method*	*Number executed* 1940s	1950s	1960s	1970s	1980s[a]	*Number awaiting execution*[b]
Oregon	none	12	4	1	0	0	2
Pennsylvania	electrocution	36	31	3	0	0	87
Rhode Island	none	0	0	0	0	0	0
South Carolina	electrocution	61	26	8	0	1	46
South Dakota	none[c]	1	0	0	0	0	0
Tennessee	electrocution	37	8	1	0	0	56
Texas	lethal injection	74	74	29	0	10	242
Utah	firing squad or lethal injection	4	6	1	1	0	7
Vermont	none[c]	1	2	0	0	0	0
Virginia	electrocution	35	23	6	0	4	35
Washington	lethal injection or hanging	16	6	2	0	0	7
West Virginia	none	11	9	0	0	0	0
Wisconsin	none	0	0	0	0	0	0
Wyoming	lethal injection	2	0	1	0	0	3
Total[d]		1,284	717	191	3	47	1,874

[a] "1980s" includes through 1985.
[b] As of April 1987.
[c] Statute but no sentences.
[d] Included in total count are 23 federal executions not shown by state (1940s, 13; 1950s, 9; 1960s, 1).

Sources: Method: *Book of the States, 1986-1987*, 399; number awaiting execution: *New York Times*, April 23, 1987, B12 (copyright © 1987 by the New York Times Company, reprinted by permission); number executed: U.S. Bureau of the Census, *Statistical Abstract of the U.S., 1987* (Washington, D.C.: U.S. Government Printing Office, 1986), 176.

Table 1-11 Public Opinion on the Death Penalty, 1936-1986 (percent)

Date	*Favor*	*Oppose*	*Don't know*
April 1936	62	33	5
December 1936	59	38	3
November 1937	61	33	7
October 1953	68[a]	26	6
April 1956	53	34	13
September 1957	47	34	18
March 1960	53	36	11
February 1965	45	43	12
July 1966	42	47	11
June 1967	54	38	8
January 1969	51	40	9
October 1971	48	41	11
February 1972	51	41	8
March 1972	53	39	8
November 1972	60	30	10
March 1973	60	35	5
March 1974	63	32	5
March 1975	60	33	7
March 1976	66	30	5
April 1976	67	27	7
March 1977	67	26	6
March 1978	66	28	6
July 1979	65	27	8
March 1980	67	27	6
March 1981	66	25	9
March 1982	74	21	6
June 1982	71	20	9
March 1983	73	22	5
March 1984	70	24	6
January 1985	72	20	8
March 1985	76	19	5
November 1985	75	17	8
January 1986	70	22	8
March 1986	71	23	5

Note: Questions: (1936-1937) "Are you in favor of the death penalty for murder?" (1953-February 1972, November 1972, April 1976, January 1981, January, November 1985) "Are you in favor of the death penalty for persons convicted of murder?" (all others) "Do you favor or oppose the death penalty for murder?"
[a] Includes qualified yes or qualified no.

Sources: 1936 through February 1972, November 1972, April 1976, January 1981, January 1985, and November 1985: Gallup surveys; others from General Social Surveys.

Table 1-12 Frequency of Legal Abortions, 1973-1985

	Total		*White*		*Nonwhite*	
Year	Number of abortions (thousands)	Percentage of pregnancies terminated by abortion	Number of abortions (thousands)	Percentage of pregnancies terminated by abortion	Number of abortions (thousands)	Percentage of pregnancies terminated by abortion
1973	774.6	19.3	548.8	17.4	195.8	25.9
1974	898.6	22.0	629.3	19.6	269.3	31.6
1975	1,034.2	24.9	701.2	21.5	333.0	35.9
1976	1,179.3	26.5	784.9	23.0	394.4	38.9
1977	1,316.7	28.6	888.8	25.0	427.9	40.4
1978	1,409.6	29.2	969.4	26.1	440.2	39.6
1979	1,497.7	29.6	1,062.4	27.1	435.3	38.2
1980	1,553.9	30.0	1,093.6	27.4	460.3	39.2
1981	1,577.3	30.0	1,107.8	27.4	469.6	39.2
1982	1,573.9	30.0	1,095.3	27.1	478.7	39.2
1983	1,575.0	30.4	1,084.4	27.4	490.6	40.1
1984	1,577.2	29.7	—	—	—	—
1985	1,588.6	29.8	—	—	—	—

Note: "—" indicates not available.

Sources: 1973-1981: Stanley K. Henshaw and Ellen Blaine, *Abortion Services in the United States, Each State, and Metropolitan Area, 1981-1982* (New York: Alan Guttmacher Institute, 1985), 64; 1982-1983: Stanley K. Henshaw, "Characteristics of U.S. Women Having Abortions, 1982-1983," *Family Planning Perspectives,* 19(1) (1987): 6-7; 1984-1985: Stanley K. Henshaw, Jacqueline Darroch Forrest, and Jennifer Van Vort, "Abortion Services in the United States, 1984 and 1985," *Family Planning Perspectives,* 19(2) (1987): 64 (reprinted with permission).

Table 1-13 Public Opinion on Abortion, 1962-1987 (percent)

	Abortion should be legal under these circumstances						
Year	Mother's health	Rape	Birth defect	Low income	Single mother	As form of birth control	Any reason
1962	77	—	55	15	—	—	—
1965	70	56	55	21	17	15	—
1969	80	—	63	23	—	—	—
1972	83	75	75	46	41	38	—
1973	91	81	82	52	47	46	—
1974	90	83	83	52	48	45	—
1975	88	80	80	51	46	44	—
1976	89	81	82	51	48	45	—
1977	89	81	83	52	48	45	37
1978	88	81	80	46	40	39	32
1980	88	80	80	50	46	45	39
1982	90	83	81	50	47	46	39
1983	87	80	76	42	38	38	33
1984	88	77	78	45	43	41	37
1985	87	78	76	42	40	39	36
1987	86	78	77	44	40	40	38

Note: Question: "Please tell me whether or not you think it should be possible for a pregnant woman to obtain a legal abortion [in the order asked in the survey] if there is a strong chance of serious defect in the baby? If she is married and does not want any more children? If the woman's own health is seriously endangered by the pregnancy? If the family has a very low income and cannot afford any more children? If she became pregnant as a result of rape? If she is not married and does not want to marry the man? The woman wants it for any reason?" "—" indicates not available.

Sources: 1962 and 1969: Gallup surveys; 1965: National Opinion Research Center surveys; 1972-1986: General Social Surveys.

Table 1-14 Public Opinion on Gun Control, 1959-1987 (percent)

Date	*Favor*	*Oppose*	*Don't know*
July 1959	75	21	4
December 1963	79	17	4
January 1965	73	23	4
September 1965	70	25	5
August 1966	67	29	3
August 1967	73	24	4
October 1971	72	24	4
May 1972	72	24	4
March 1972	70	27	3
March 1973	74	25	2
March 1974	75	23	1
February 1975	71	28	1
March 1975	74	24	3
February 1976	73	24	4
March 1976	72	27	1
March 1977	72	27	2
March 1980	69	29	2
March 1982	72	26	2
March 1984	70	27	3
March 1985	72	27	1
March 1987	70	28	2

Note: Question: "Would you favor or oppose a law which would require a person to obtain a police permit before he or she could buy a gun?"

Sources: 1959-1971: Gallup surveys; February 1975, February 1976: Survey Research Center, University of Michigan; others: General Social Surveys.

Table 1-15 Voter Registration and Type of Political Primary

State	*Type of primary*[a]	*Mail registration allowed for all voters*	*Minimum state residence requirement (days)*	*Closing date for registration before general election (days)*	*Automatic cancellation of registration for failure to vote after ___ years*
Alabama	O/D	no	1	10	
Alaska	B	yes	30	30	2
Arizona	C	no	50	50	2
Arkansas	O/D	no	[b]	20	4
California	C	yes	29	29	4
Colorado	C/F	no	32	32	2
Connecticut	C	no	[b]	21[c]	
Delaware	C	yes	[b]	3d Saturday in October[c]	4
Florida	C	no	[b]	30	2
Georgia	O/D	no	[b]	30	3
Hawaii	O	no	[b]	30	2
Idaho	O	no	30	17/10[d]	4
Illinois	O/D	no	30	28	4
Indiana	O/D	no	30	29[e]	2
Iowa	C/C	yes	[b]	10	4
Kansas	C/F	yes	20	20	4
Kentucky	C	yes	30	30	4
Louisiana	B	no	[b]	24[c]	4
Maine	C/F	yes	[b]	Election Day	
Maryland	C	yes	29	29	5
Massachusetts	C/S	no	[b]	28	
Michigan	O	no	30	30	10
Minnesota	C/S	yes	20	Election Day	4
Mississippi	O/D	no	30	10	4
Missouri	O/D	yes	[b]	28	
Montana	O	yes	30	30	4
Nebraska	C	no	[b]	10	
Nevada	C	no	30	30	2
New Hampshire	C/S	no	10	10	
New Jersey	C/F	yes	30	29	4
New Mexico	C	no	[b]	42	2
New York	C	yes	30	30	4
North Carolina	C	no	30	21[f]	8
North Dakota	O	no	30	[g]	
Ohio	C/C	yes	30	30	4
Oklahoma	C	no	[b]	10	4
Oregon	C	yes	20	Election Day	2
Pennsylvania	C	yes	30	30	2
Rhode Island	C/F	no	30	30	5
South Carolina	O/D	no	[b]	30	4

Table 1-15 *(Continued)*

State	*Type of primary*[a]	*Mail registration allowed for all voters*	*Minimum state residence requirement (days)*	*Closing date for registration before general election (days)*	*Automatic cancellation of registration for failure to vote after ___ years*
South Dakota	C	no	[b]	15	4
Tennessee	O/D	yes	50	30	4
Texas	O/D	yes	[b]	30	
Utah	O	yes	30	5	4
Vermont	O	no	[b]	17	4
Virginia	O/D	no	[b]	31	4
Washington	B	no	30	30	2
West Virginia	C	yes	30	30	4
Wisconsin	O	yes	10	Election Day	2
Wyoming	C/C	no	[b]	30	2

Note: No entry under cancellation column indicates no automatic purging of registration lists.

[a] "C" indicates closed where party enrollment is required at the time of registration; "C/F" indicates closed/first vote where at least some voters enroll in a party when they first vote in a primary; "C/C" indicates closed/change where voters may change their party enrollment at the polls; "C/S" indicates semi-closed where registered independents may vote in either party's primary; "O" indicates open where voters receive ballots for both parties and choose one in the voting booth; "O/D" indicates open/declare where voters publicly declare which party's ballot they want; and "B" indicates blanket primaries where voters can choose among the candidates from all the parties.

[b] No residence requirement.

[c] Closing date differs for primary election. In Connecticut the closing date is 14 days before the primary; in Delaware, 21 days; and in Louisiana, 30 days.

[d] With precinct registrar, 17 days before the general election; with county clerk, 10 days.

[e] With deputy registrar, 45 days before the general election.

[f] Business days.

[g] No voter registration.

Sources: Book of the States, 1986-1987, 208. Type of primary compiled by Barbara Norrander, San Jose State University, 1987, personal communication.

Table 1-16 Legislative Reapportionment Deviations from Equality in Size of Congressional and State Legislative Districts, 1960s and 1980s (percent)

	Congressional districts			State legislative districts					
				Senate			House		
	1960s		1980s	*1960s*		*1980s*	*1960s*		*1980s*
State	Positive	Negative	total	*Positive*	*Negative*	*total*	*Positive*	*Negative*	*total*
Alabama	21.4	17.2	2.45	582	83.4	8.50	239	78.7	9.80
Alaska	AL	AL	AL	408	59.3	9.77	36	39.6	9.99
Arizona	52.9	54.3	0.08	613	91.7	8.40	87	64.4	8.40
Arkansas	28.8	25.4	0.73	59	29.4	9.15	78	72.9	9.15
California[a]	424.4	27.0	0.08	1,432	96.4	4.60	55	63.9	3.60
Colorado	49.1	55.4	0.002	51	66.6	3.98	37	70.6	4.94
Connecticut	63.2	24.5	0.46	138	62.6	3.92	840	97.8	8.35
Delaware	AL	AL	AL	167	84.0	9.78	357	87.3	25.10[b]
Florida	60.3	42.5	0.13	618	92.7	1.05	498	94.5	0.46
Georgia	108.9	31.0	—	664	82.1	9.99	864	90.9	9.94
Hawaii	AL	AL	<0.01	151	66.3	18.60	92	59.5	8.60
Idaho	22.9	22.9	0.04	517	94.0	5.35[c]	48	91.2	5.35[c]
Illinois	31.6	33.6	0.03	226	69.2	1.75	181	39.7	2.80
Indiana	64.6	31.4	2.96	76	54.9	4.04[c]	96	66.2	4.45[c]
Iowa	12.3	10.4	0.05	373	46.2	0.71	421	69.7	1.78
Kansas	23.9	14.3	0.34	529	70.5	6.50	293	88.8	9.90
Kentucky	40.8	19.2	1.39	165	43.6	7.52	123	62.9	13.47
Louisiana	31.6	35.2	0.42[c]	197	62.6	8.40	287	77.2	9.69
Maine	4.3	4.3	0.001	60	54.0	10.18	105	62.8	10.94
Maryland	86.3	37.3	0.35	360	83.5	9.80	181	77.0	15.70
Massachusetts	11.6	12.3	1.09	55	33.6	—	130	83.9	—
Michigan	85.3	71.4	<0.01	234	72.1	16.24	90	52.4	16.34
Minnesota	13.2	12.0	0.01	95	48.0	4.61	281	67.6	3.93
Mississippi	39.9	32.3	—	184	67.9	4.61[c]	282	77.8	4.90[c]
Missouri	17.3	12.4	0.18	22	24.1	6.10	99	85.8	9.30
Montana	18.7	18.7	AL	556	92.6	—	74	87.6	—

Nebraska	12.8	14.0	0.23	57	42.5	9.43	[d]	[d]	[d]
Nevada	AL	AL	0.60	658	96.6	8.20	639	91.9	9.70
New Hampshire	9.3	9.3	0.24	64	37.3	7.60	284	99.7	13.74
New Jersey	44.8	36.9	0.69[a]	222	83.2	7.70	42	51.2	7.70
New Mexico	AL	AL	0.87[c]	783	93.7	9.83[c]	103	86.7	9.87[c]
New York	15.1	14.4	1.64	48	33.6	5.29	34	86.6	8.17
North Carolina	18.7	36.9	1.76[c]	199	50.6	9.46	116	88.7	9.66
North Dakota	5.4	5.4	AL	225	63.6	9.93	52	51.7	9.93
Ohio	79.5	41.6	0.68	52	20.8	8.88	37	85.6	9.67
Oklahoma	42.5	41.3	0.58	554	75.2	5.60	216	77.9	10.98
Oregon	18.2	40.0	0.15	25	49.3	3.73	34	35.7	5.34
Pennsylvania	31.9	27.7	0.24	145	77.1	1.93[c]	158	91.8	2.82[c]
Rhode Island	7.0	7.0	0.02	151	97.9	—	121	94.4	10.47[b]
South Carolina	33.9	31.4	0.28[a]	317	83.6	—	53	55.1	9.88
South Dakota	46.3	46.3	AL	122	48.9	12.90	84	61.2	12.40
Tennessee	58.2	43.6	2.40	120	63.2	10.22	121	90.8	1.66
Texas	118.5	48.5	0.28	303	52.8	1.82[a]	65	46.9	9.95[a]
Utah	28.6	28.6	0.43	81	73.9	7.80	133	91.4	5.41
Vermont	AL	AL	AL	43	77.3	16.18	1,991	97.4	19.33[c]
Virginia	36.0	21.1	1.81	188	47.9	10.65	259	49.8	5.11[a]
Washington	25.2	16.0	0.06	152	65.5	5.40	102	56.4	5.70
West Virginia	13.4	18.6	0.50	336	36.4	8.96	112	76.9	9.94
Wisconsin	40.1	34.2	0.14	73	37.7	1.23	121	50.7	1.74
Wyoming	AL	AL	AL	147	74.4	63.70	70	50.6	89.40

Note: "AL" indicates at large district (only one congressional representative). 1960s figures represent the maximum percentage deviation (positive and negative) from the average district population. 1980s figures are total deviations from the average (the sum of the largest deviations above and below the average); positive and negative deviations were not available. 1960s data are from 1962; 1980s data are as of April 1983. "—" indicates not available.

[a] New plan needed.

[b] Plan contains inadvertant errors which increase total deviation, but which were not yet corrected by technical amendments.

[c] Subject to court review.

[d] Nebraska's state legislature is unicameral.

Sources: 1960s: Robert G. Dixon, Jr., *Democratic Representation: Reapportionment in Law and Politics* (New York: Oxford University Press, 1968) Appendices A-B (copyright © 1968, Oxford University Press, reprinted by permission); 1980s: Bernard F. Grofman, "Criteria for Districting," *UCLA Law Review* 33 (1985): 175-176 (copyright © 1985, Regents of the University of California, all rights reserved).

Table 1-17 Jurisdictions Subject to Federal Preclearance of Election Law Changes and to Minority Language Provisions of the Civil Rights Act

Coverage limited to preclearance provisions	*Coverage limited to minority language provisions*	*Combined coverage under preclearance and minority language provisions*
Alabama	California (35)	Alaska
Connecticut (3)	Colorado (33)	Arizona
Georgia	Connecticut (1)	California (4)
Idaho (1)	Florida (2)	Colorado (1)
Louisiana	Hawaii (3)	Florida (5)
Massachusetts (9) [a]	Idaho (2)	Hawaii (1)
Mississippi	Kansas (3)	Louisiana (1)
New Hampshire (10) [a]	Maine (1)	Michigan (2)
North Carolina (37)	Michigan (7)	Mississippi (1)
South Carolina	Minnesota (2)	New York (3)
Virginia	Montana (7)	North Carolina (3)
Wyoming (1)	Nebraska (2)	South Dakota (2)
	Nevada (4)	Texas
	New Mexico (32)	Virginia (1)
	North Carolina (1)	
	North Dakota (5)	
	Oklahoma (25)	
	Oregon (2)	
	South Dakota (6)	
	Utah (4)	
	Washington (5)	
	Wisconsin (4) [a]	
	Wyoming (5)	

Note: "Preclearance" means that changes in election laws must be approved by the U.S. Justice Department. Numbers in parentheses indicate the number of counties in the state affected by the provisions. If there are no parentheses, coverage is statewide.
[a] Number of towns or townships.

Source: United States Commission on Civil Rights, *The Voting Rights Act: Unfulfilled Goals* (Washington, D.C.: U.S. Government Printing Office, 1981), 97-100.

Questions

1. Aside from Hawaii and Alaska, what were the last five states to be admitted to the United States—in order beginning with the last one admitted (Table 1-1)?

2. The U.S. Constitution has fewer than five thousand words. What is the median length of U.S. state constitutions (Table 1-2)? The U.S. Constitution has been amended twenty-six times. Except for fairly recent constitutions (those less than twenty-five years old), what is the minimum number of amendments adopted by a state, and which state was that?

3. Of the sixteen amendments to the U.S. Constitution since passage of the Bill of Rights, ten have dealt with federal elections, terms of office of those elected, or succession if those elected are unable to serve. Which ten amendments are these (Table 1-3)? The main motivation of three of these ten was to ensure women and minorities the right to vote; Amendments Fifteen and Nineteen were obviously two of them. What was the other and why was it necessary?

4. More than half of the rights incorporated to the states (Table 1-4) were done so under one chief justice (Table 9-5). Who was that?

5. How many states must approve a proposed amendment before it is considered ratified? How many states must petition Congress in order for Congress to call a constitutional convention? The balanced budget and abortion amendments are still considered "live" possibilities. How close are these state-initiated petitions to requiring Congress to call for a convention (Table 1-5)?

6. For which of the five proposed amendments shown in Table 1-6 has public opinion been very closely divided, with a plurality sometimes on one side and sometimes on the other? For the remaining four issues, has a majority of those with opinions favored or opposed the sense of the proposed amendment? (A prayer amendment, which some have proposed, would permit some kinds of prayers in public schools.)

7. How many states have no provisions at all for initiatives, referenda, or recall (Table 1-7)? How many have no such provisions and

in addition have no limit on the number of consecutive terms a governor can serve (Tables 1-7 and 1-8)? Which states are they? How many, in addition to the above, have four-year rather than two-year terms for governor? Which are they?

8. Since 1960, how many states have changed from two-year to four-year terms for governor (Table 1-8)? How many presently have two-year terms?

9. What is shown by the "forbid-allow" comparison in the top panel of Table 1-9?

10. The climate for dissenting opinions has changed dramatically since the early 1950s (Table 1-9). In what way? Suppose another question were asked: "Should (an atheist, Communist, racist) be allowed to teach in high school?" What would be the result? (Exact percentages are not needed, but how would the results compare with the percentages in Table 1-9 and why?)

11. Including the states with a statute but no recent sentences, how many states have the death penalty (Table 1-10)? Which two states have more than two hundred inmates awaiting execution and have already executed ten or more people in the 1980s?

12. What has been the trend in public opinion about the death penalty since 1970 (Table 1-11)? Has the same trend characterized public opinion on gun control (Table 1-14)?

13. What proportion of pregnancies among whites ended in abortion in 1983 (Table 1-12)? Among nonwhites in the same year? What has happened to the rates since the late 1970s?

14. In what period did public opinion on abortion change dramatically (Table 1-13)? What has happened to public opinion since 1980?

15. Note the results for surveys taken one month apart—in February and March of 1975 and again in 1976 (Table 1-14). There are at least two possible explanations for differences in surveys conducted at different points in time. What are these explanations? Which do you think is the most likely to be correct and why?

16. Combining all types of open primaries and all types of closed primaries, are there more of the former or of the latter (Table 1-15)?

If one wished to promote party loyalty (voters generally voting in the same party's primary from one election to the next), which type of primary would one favor most? Why?

17. Registration is required fifty days ahead of the general elections in Arizona, and residence requirements are fifty days in Arizona and Tennessee (Table 1-15). At the other extreme, some states have election day registration (North Dakota has no registration at all) and have no residency requirement. What effect are these variations likely to have on voter turnout?

18. In the 1960s—prior to the Supreme Court's one person, one vote rulings, how many states had a total deviation (positive plus negative deviations) of greater than 50 percent for congressional districts (Table 1-16)? Of greater than 2 percent in the 1980s? Of greater than 100 percent in state senates in the 1960s? Of greater than 10 percent in the 1980s?

19. Based on the number of whole states that are under preclearance provisions, at which region was the Civil Rights Act originally aimed (Table 1-17)? Is there any region that is completely free of the preclearance requirement? Nearly free?

2

The Mass Media

The mass media thrive on numbers. Nearly every American adult has heard of audience ratings games—serious games with millions and millions of dollars and many individual careers at stake—played by television, newspapers, radio, and magazines. Will the top-ranked television show remain first in the ratings, and how much will it help the show that follows it? Can a "national newspaper," such as *USA Today*, be profitable? Will a radio station increase its audience ratings—and what kind of audience will it attract—by playing more hard rock? How many extra copies and how much more advertising will a weekly news magazine sell with excerpts of soon-to-be-published political memoirs—and how much can the publisher afford to pay for those excerpts? So much money is at stake that media organizations annually spend millions of dollars to find the answers to such questions.

Politics, as it relates to the media, also involves numbers. Some questions simply involve market share and audience, much like the questions noted above: How many and what kinds of individuals pay attention to political news stories, candidate advertisements, campaign debates, and so on? Of course, these matters, while very important, are relatively straightforward. More complicated and controversial are other matters that involve numbers. Some critics charge, for example, that television emphasizes only the "horse-race" aspect of political campaigns (who is ahead and by how much) to the exclusion of issues (Figure 2-4 and Table 2-5), that both print and electronic media give too much emphasis to the very early presidential primaries and caucuses (Table 2-6), and that the president receives too much coverage while Congress and the states receive too little (Figure 2-3).

Despite these concerns about numbers as they apply to politics and the media, data are not as publicly available as one might think or hope. General information on how many people watch, read, and listen to the media is readily obtainable (Tables 2-1 through 2-3), but specific information about political material is not. Some material is proprietary—for example, a candidate's private surveys—and therefore mostly unavailable to researchers or to students. But there are other reasons for the unavailability. One is that television is relatively new (serious coverage of presidential campaigns began only in 1952, and extended coverage only in the 1960s) and is still changing (televised House proceedings began in 1979 and Senate proceedings in 1986). This means that researchers have not yet settled on exactly what data are most relevant and therefore most in need of continued collection. This is especially true of data that go beyond sheer numbers of viewers. Note, for example, that some interesting information about television and newspaper coverage has been tabulated for only a single year (Figure 2-3 and Table 2-6), and that in another instance a useful series stops in 1980 (Table 2-5).

Fortunately, data collection and publication have expanded and improved, and researchers are beginning to see longer time series of significant information about politics and the media (e.g., Tables 2-4 and 2-7, Figure 2-2). Moreover, the media themselves are increasingly well preserved. Magazines are saved and are relatively well indexed. Major newspapers are widely available and well indexed, and small newspapers—though often kept only locally—combine to give widespread coverage of politics as practiced and perceived throughout the country. CBS News has published transcripts and indexes of its news programs since 1975 to facilitate research. Network television news programs since 1968 have been stored at Vanderbilt University; the archives are indexed and available to researchers. These efforts at preservation mean that studies can be made of the past as well as of contemporary events. Indeed, some of the most interesting studies of politics and the media are yet to come because they will be able to cover long expanses of time.

As in all areas of research, data about the media are rarely self-interpreting. One specific problem here is that the media both shape the news and reflect it. The shift in emphasis from parties to candidates (Figure 2-2) is a case in point. To some degree this shift simply reflects the weakening hold of political parties over American voters, a process that began as long ago as the turn of the century, that is, well before the advent of television. On the other hand, the power of television to bring individual candidates directly into one's living room has accelerated the declining influence of party organizations in particular and of party affiliation more generally.

Problems of interpretation—especially whether the media cause or simply reflect events—thus make inferences about media influence difficult. The usual response to such problems of inference is to bring additional data to bear on the subject. With more and more data now becoming available, researchers can safely anticipate better answers to questions about media audiences, coverage, emphasis, and influence as they relate to the political process.

Table 2-1 Growth and Reach of Selected Media, 1950-1986

	Percentage of households with						*Daily newspaper circulation*[g]	
Year	Telephone service[a]	Radios[b]	Television sets[c]	Cable TV[d]	VCRs[e]	*Average TV viewing per day (hours)*[f]	Number (millions)	Per capita (number)
1950	—	92.6	9	—	—	4.6	53.8	.354
1960	78.5	96.3	87	—	—	5.1	58.9	.327
1970	87.0	98.6	95	—	—	5.9	62.1	.305
1975	—	98.6	97	—	—	6.1	60.7	.282
1980	93.0	99.0	98	19.8	1.1	6.6	62.2	.275
1981	—	99.0	98	25.3	1.8	6.8	61.4	.267
1982	—	99.0	98	29.0	3.1	6.8	62.5	.269
1983	—	99.0	98	37.2	5.5	7.0	62.6	.267
1984	91.8	99.0	98	41.2	10.6	7.1	63.1	.267
1985	91.8	99.0	98	44.6	20.8	7.1	62.8	.263
1986	92.2	99.0	98	46.8	36.0	—	—	—

Note: "—" indicates not available.
[a] For occupied housing units. 1950 through 1980, as of April 1; thereafter, as of March.
[b] As of December 31.
[c] 1970-1975, as of September of prior year; all other years as of January of year shown.
[d] As of February.
[e] As of February. Excludes Alaska and Hawaii.
[f] Calendar year data.
[g] As of September 30, except 1950 and 1960 were as of October 1.

Sources: Telephone service: U.S. Bureau of the Census, *Statistical Abstract of the U.S., 1987* (Washington, D.C.: U.S. Government Printing Office, 1986), 531; radios: Radio Advertising Bureau, *Radio Facts* (New York: Radio Advertising Bureau, annual); television 1950-1960: National Broadcasting Company; television 1970-1986, cable, VCR: *Nielson Television Index* (Northbrook, Ill.: A. C. Nielsen); newspapers: *Editor & Publisher International Yearbook* (New York: Editor & Publisher).

Table 2-2 Use of Television, Radio, and Newspaper, Cross Section, 1986

	Total population (thousands)	*Television viewers*					*Radio listeners*		*Newspaper readers*	
		Prime time	Cable	Pay	Early news	Late news	Week-day	Week-end	Daily	Sun-day
Age										
18-24	27,990	75.3%	44.1%	33.1%	36.4%	30.9%	93.8%	81.6%	52.6%	58.7%
25-34	40,798	82.5	44.5	30.0	41.1	38.3	88.2	71.4	53.1	64.5
35-44	30,486	83.5	49.1	34.7	41.5	41.6	83.3	64.8	62.6	68.1
45-54	22,494	84.4	48.6	31.7	54.5	47.9	80.9	61.8	67.6	70.0
55-64	22,366	85.4	44.1	23.7	66.3	50.2	73.5	58.6	68.2	70.9
65 and older	26,465	83.3	36.8	9.9	74.5	45.1	62.5	52.9	65.4	63.3
Sex										
Male	81,025	81.4	45.3	28.2	48.5	40.9	83.8	67.5	61.8	65.7
Female	89,573	83.0	43.9	27.1	52.6	42.1	79.2	64.8	59.4	65.5
Race/ethnicity										
White	148,266	82.5	46.6	28.4	49.3	40.3	81.7	65.3	62.1	66.7
Black	18,639	80.7	30.8	22.6	63.3	52.1	80.1	72.6	51.9	59.2
Spanish speaking	6,639	80.5	45.0	27.8	41.0	40.0	82.3	67.5	52.0	59.5
Other	3,694	79.5	31.7	21.5	41.7	40.5	76.6	64.9	41.7	51.2
Education										
College graduate	28,587	80.7	50.7	31.2	45.5	43.5	86.4	66.5	70.2	78.9
Attended college	29,580	79.7	49.9	34.1	44.2	41.0	87.3	69.7	64.5	73.1
High school grad.	66,991	84.6	45.4	29.2	50.6	42.0	82.5	68.2	61.6	65.9
Not high school grad.	45,441	81.4	36.0	18.8	58.1	40.0	72.6	60.4	50.2	51.8
Employment										
Full-time	94,634	81.5	47.6	32.6	42.9	39.2	87.6	69.3	61.6	67.7
Part-time	10,214	82.3	44.4	29.1	43.7	40.2	87.5	72.8	63.2	69.1
Not employed	65,750	83.3	40.1	20.3	62.8	45.1	71.4	60.4	58.6	62.0

Household income										
Under $10,000	19,786	81.0	27.8	9.7	65.1	41.7	68.4	60.9	42.9	44.4
10,000-19,999	31,979	82.9	37.1	17.8	57.2	42.0	77.1	65.8	56.6	58.5
20,000-24,999	16,851	84.4	41.9	23.6	49.7	42.6	81.9	65.8	56.7	64.3
25,000-29,999	16,529	83.3	45.4	28.7	50.9	42.6	83.1	68.8	59.4	63.5
30,000-34,999	16,450	84.1	49.3	31.1	47.0	42.7	84.9	65.5	64.1	68.8
35,000-39,999	14,364	80.8	50.8	34.4	44.1	39.9	85.5	70.7	64.1	71.8
40,000-49,999	23,128	82.4	52.4	38.3	45.5	40.1	84.8	68.6	66.1	73.9
50,000 or more	31,512	80.3	52.5	37.6	43.8	41.2	86.4	64.9	70.6	77.2
Total	170,599	82.3	44.5	27.6	50.6	41.6	81.4	66.1	60.5	65.6

Note: For persons eighteen years old and over. Based on sample and subject to sampling error; see *Multimedia Audiences.*

Source: Statistical Abstract of the U.S., 1987, 531; *Multimedia Audiences* (New York: Mediamark Research, Spring 1986).

Table 2-3 Newspaper Circulation, 1850-1985

	Daily papers		
Year	Number	Circulation (thousands)	*Circulation as a percentage of population*
1850	254[a]	758[a]	3.3
1860	387[a]	1,478[a]	4.7
1870	574[a]	2,602[a]	6.5
1880	971[a]	3,566[a]	7.1
1890	1,610[a]	8,387[a]	13.3
1900	2,226[a]	15,102[a]	19.9
1904	2,452	19,633	23.9
1909	2,600	24,212	26.8
1914	2,580	28,777	29.0
1919	2,441	33,029	31.6
1921	2,334	33,742	31.1
1923	2,271	35,471	31.7
1925	2,116	37,407	32.2
1927	2,091	41,368	34.8
1929	2,086	42,015	34.5
1931	2,044	41,294	33.3
1933	1,903	37,630	30.0
1935	2,037	40,871	32.1
1937	2,065	43,345	33.6
1939	2,040	42,966	32.8
1947	1,854	53,287	36.7
1950	1,772	53,800	35.6
1954	1,820	56,410	34.6
1958	1,778	58,713	33.6
1960	1,763	58,900	32.8
1963	1,766	63,831	33.7
1965	1,751	60,400	31.1
1967	—	66,527	33.5
1970	1,748	62,100	30.5
1975	1,756	60,700	28.1
1978	1,756	62,000	27.9
1979	1,763	62,200	27.6
1980	1,745	62,200	27.5
1981	1,730	61,400	26.7
1982	1,711	62,500	26.9
1983	1,701	62,600	26.7
1984	1,688	63,100	26.6
1985	1,676	62,800	26.2

Note: "—" indicates not available.
[a] Includes a small number of periodicals.

Sources: Daily papers: *Statistical Abstract of the U.S., 1987,* 536, and U.S. Bureau of the Census, *Historical Statistics of the U.S.* (Washington, D.C.: U.S. Government Printing Office, 1975), 810; population: *Statistical Abstract of the U.S., 1977,* 5, *1987,* 8.

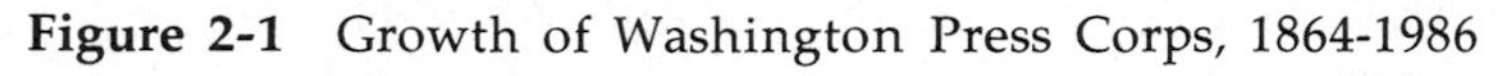

Figure 2-1 Growth of Washington Press Corps, 1864-1986

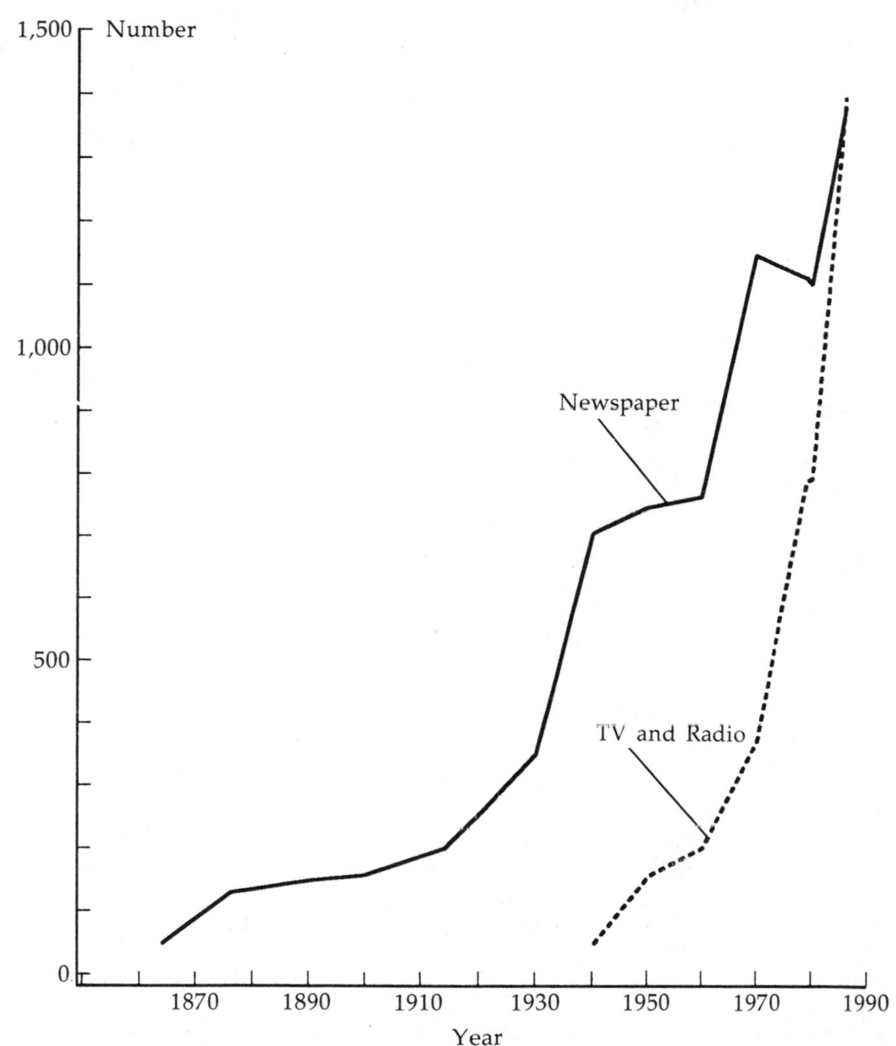

Sources: Samuel Kernell, *Going Public: New Strategies of Presidential Leadership* (Washington, D.C.: CQ Press, 1986), 57; updated by the editors from successive volumes of U.S. Congress, Joint Committee on Printing, *Official Congressional Directory* (Washington, D.C.: U.S. Government Printing Office).

Table 2-4 Presidential News Conferences with White House Correspondents, 1929-1987

President	*Average number of press conferences per month*	*Total press conferences*
Hoover (1929-1933)	5.6	268
Roosevelt (1933-1945)	6.9	998
Truman (1945-1953)	3.4	334
Eisenhower (1953-1961)	2.0	193
Kennedy (1961-1963)	1.9	64
Johnson (1963-1969)	2.2	135
Nixon (1969-1974)	0.5	37
Ford (1974-1977)	1.3	39
Carter (1977-1981)	1.2	59
Reagan (1981-1987)	0.5	42

Sources: Kernell, *Going Public,* 69; *National Journal* (May 2, 1987), 1068, updated by the editors.

Table 2-5 Subjects of Newspaper Stories on Presidential Campaigns, 1968-1980 (percent)

Year	*Campaign events*	*Domestic politics*	*Foreign affairs*	*Economic policy*	*Social problems*
1968	14	21	30	13	22
1972	42	24	18	10	7
1976	51	19	14	11	5
1980	52	29	5	7	6

Note: Calculations are based on the final month of the presidential campaigns.

Source: Doris Graber, "Hoopla and Horse-Race in 1980 Campaign Coverage: A Closer Look," in *Mass Media and Elections: International Research Perspectives,* ed. Winfried Schulz and Klaus Schönbach (Munich: Verlag Olschlager, 1983), 286.

Figure 2-2 Ratio of Mentions of Candidates to Parties by Selected Media, 1952-1980

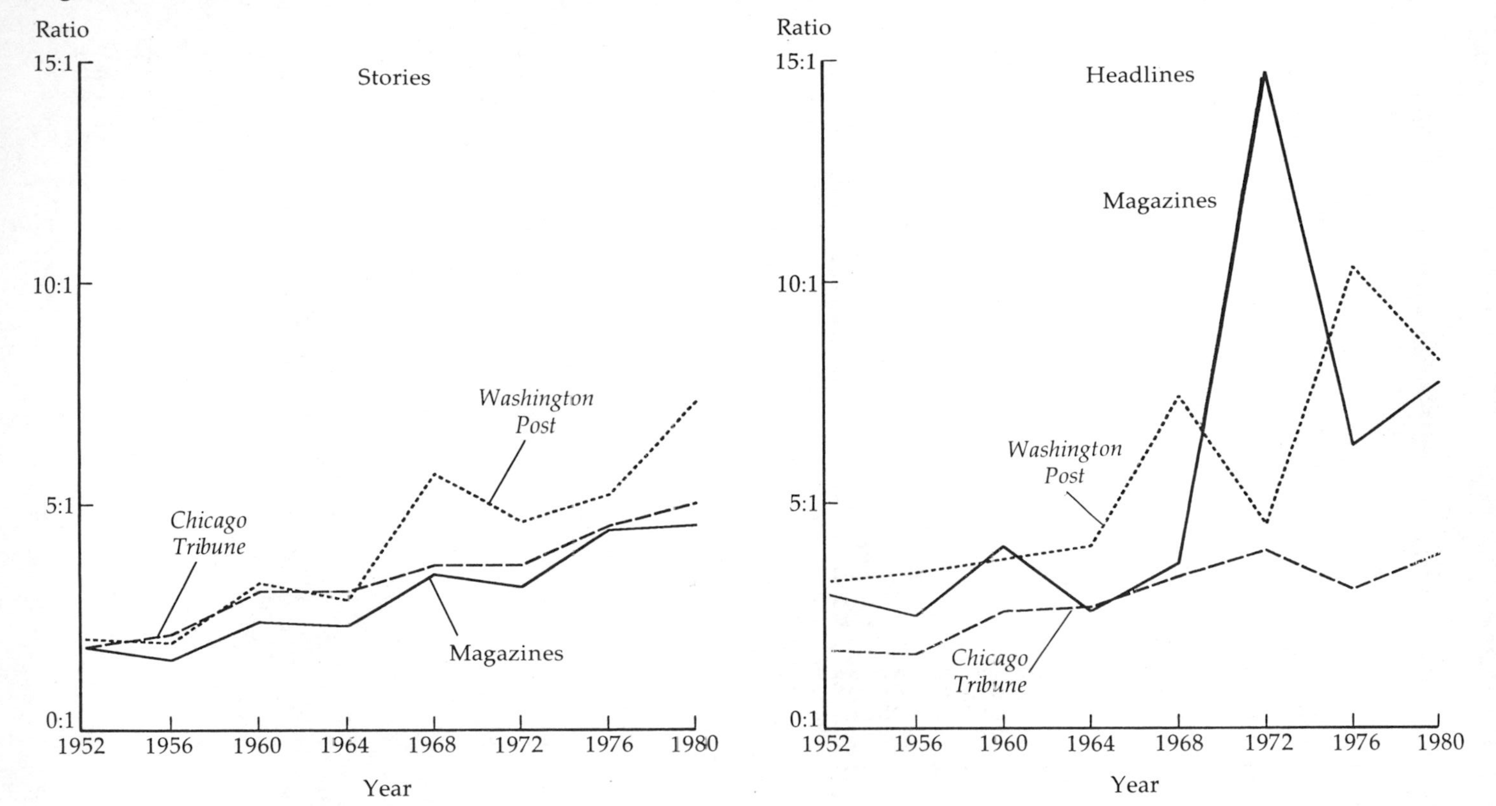

Note: Ratio of mentions of presidential candidates to mentions of political parties in election coverage during September and October of presidential election years. Selected media include *Chicago Tribune*, *Washington Post*, and three news magazines (*Newsweek*, *Time*, and *U.S. News & World Report*).

Source: Martin Wattenberg, *The Decline of American Political Parties, 1952-1984* (Cambridge, Mass.: Harvard University Press, 1986), 94-95.

Figure 2-3 CBS Coverage of 1980 Elections by Level of Office

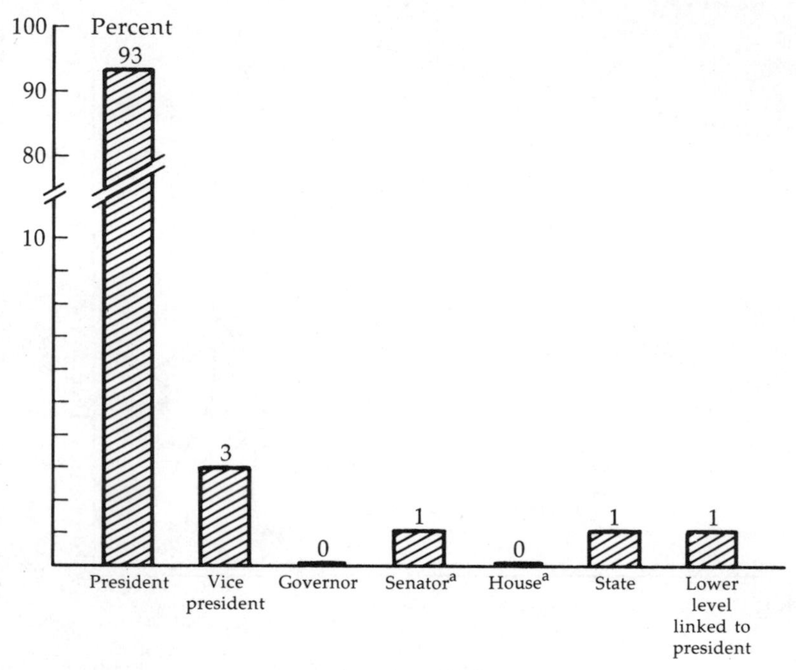

Note: Time was measured in seconds.
[a] Does not include stories that dealt with both the House and Senate—a total time of 245 seconds.

Source: Michael J. Robinson and Margaret A. Sheehan, *Over the Wire and on TV: CBS and UPI in Campaign 1980* (New York: Russell Sage Foundation, 1983), 169.

Table 2-6 Coverage of State Primaries and Caucuses, 1980

	CBS			*UPI*			*1980 Delegates*			
							Republican		Democrat	
State	News seconds	Percentage of total	Number of stories	Column inches	Percentage of total	Number of stories	*No.*	*%*	*No.*	*%*
New Hampshire	2,815	14	31	774	15	53	22	1	19	1
Iowa	2,940	14	19	679	13	45	37	2	50	2
Illinois	2,000	10	20	349	7	26	102	5	179	5
Pennsylvania	1,950	9	18	366	7	25	83	4	185	6
New York	1,515	7	19	307	6	21	123	6	282	8
Wisconsin	1,165	6	15	271	5	20	34	2	75	2
California	1,205	6	9	183	4	11	168	8	306	9
Massachusetts	1,450	7	15	160	3	12	42	2	111	3
Michigan	225	1	4	342	7	20	82	4	141	4
Maine	795	4	7	136	3	10	21	1	22	1
Ohio	915	4	8	105	2	8	77	4	161	5
Florida	700	3	7	105	2	7	51	3	100	3
South Carolina	470	2	6	172	3	11	25	1	37	1
Connecticut	395	2	5	123	2	7	35	2	54	2
Texas	345	2	5	119	2	7	80	4	152	5
District of Columbia	215	1	2	125	2	8	14	1	19	1
Puerto Rico	175	1	3	94	2	7	14	1	41	1
Maryland	50	-	1	108	2	7	30	2	59	2
Oregon	290	1	2	60	1	4	29	1	39	1
Indiana	125	1	3	54	1	4	54	3	80	2
Vermont	105	1	4	53	1	3	19	1	12	-
Kansas	15	-	1	67	1	4	32	2	37	1
Kentucky	85	-	1	51	1	4	27	1	50	2

(*Table continues*)

Table 2-6 *(Continued)*

	CBS			*UPI*			*1980 Delegates*			
							Republican		Democrat	
State	News seconds	Percentage of total	Number of stories	Column inches	Percentage of total	Number of stories	*No.*	*%*	*No.*	*%*
North Carolina	-	-	-	46	1	4	40	2	69	2
Oklahoma	-	-	-	43	1	3	34	2	42	1
Nebraska	95	-	1	30	1	2	25	1	24	1
Arizona	-	-	-	30	1	2	28	1	29	1
Nevada	-	-	-	29	1	2	17	1	12	-
Minnesota	160	1	2	19	-	1	34	2	75	2
New Jersey	145	1	4	17	-	1	66	3	113	3
Alabama	105	1	2	16	-	1	27	1	45	1
Arkansas	55	-	2	24	-	3	19	1	33	1
Delaware	-	-	-	16	-	1	12	1	14	-
Alaska	35	-	1	12	-	1	19	1	11	-
North Dakota	25	-	1	12	-	1	17	1	14	-
Tennessee	-	-	-	11	-	1	32	2	55	2
Louisiana	90	-	2	9	-	1	31	2	51	2
Virginia	-	-	-	5	-	1	51	3	64	2
Idaho	20	-	1	4	-	1	21	1	17	1
New Mexico	65	-	1	2	-	1	22	1	20	1
South Dakota	35	-	1	1	-	1	22	1	19	1
Montana	-	-	-	1	-	1	20	1	19	1
Mississippi	35	-	2	-	-	-	22	1	32	1
Colorado	20	-	1	-	-	-	31	2	40	1
Georgia	15	-	1	-	-	-	36	2	63	2
Hawaii	-	-	-	-	-	-	14	1	19	1
Missouri	-	-	-	-	-	-	37	2	77	2

Rhode Island	-	-	-	-	-	-	13	1	23	1
Utah	-	-	-	-	-	-	21	1	20	1
Washington	-	-	-	-	-	-	37	2	58	2
West Virginia	-	-	-	-	-	-	18	1	35	1
Wyoming	-	-	-	-	-	-	19	1	11	-
Total							1,994[a]		3,331[b]	

Note: "-" indicates zero or less than 0.5 percent.
[a] Includes Guam (4), and Virgin Islands (4).
[b] Includes Guam (4), Virgin Islands (4), Latin America (4), and Democrats Abroad (4).

Sources: Delegates: Congressional Quarterly, *Congressional Quarterly Almanac* (Washington, D.C.: Congressional Quarterly, 1980), 35-B, 90-B; CBS and UPI: Robinson and Sheehan, *Over the Wire and on TV*, 176, 177 (copyright © Russell Sage Foundation, used with permission).

Figure 2-4 Percentage of News Stories about Policy Issues

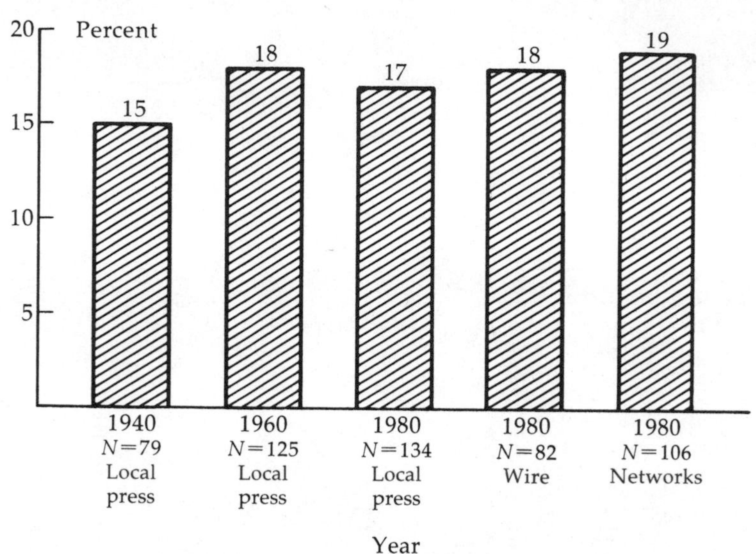

Note: "N" indicates number of news stories; "Local press" refers to *Boston Globe, Seattle Times,* and *Columbus Dispatch;* "Wire" refers to AP; and "Networks" refers to ABC, CBS, and NBC.

Source: Robinson and Sheehan, *Over the Wire and on TV,* 161.

Table 2-7 Public Use of Media to Follow Presidential Campaigns, 1952-1984 (percent)

Media	*1952*	*1956*	*1960*	*1964*	*1968*	*1972*	*1976*	*1980*	*1984*
Read newspaper articles about the election									
regularly			44	40	37	26	28	27[a]	24
often	39[b]	69[c]	12	14	12	14	17	29[d]	34
from time to time	40[e]		16	18	19	16	24	17[f]	19
once in a great while			7	6	7	4	10		
no	21	31	21	22	25	40	22	27[g]	23
Listened to speeches or discussions on radio									
good many	34[b]		15	12	12	8	12	14	10
several		45[c]	17	23	16	21	20	22	20
one or two	35[e]		10	12	12	13	16	15	16
no	30	55	58	52	59	59	52	50	55
Watched programs about the campaign on television									
good many	32[b]		47	41	42	33	37	28	25
several		74[c]	29	34	34	41	38	37	37
one or two	19[e]		11	13	13	16	15	22	24
no	49	26	13	11	11	9	10	13	14
Read about the campaign in magazines									
good many	15[b]		12	10	9	7	12	7	7
several		31[c]	15	16	12	15	24	19	16
one or two	26[e]		13	13	15	14	15	12	11
no	60	69	59	61	64	64	49	62	66

[a] Response offered was: "good many."
[b] Response offered was: "quite a lot" and "pretty much."
[c] Response offered was: "yes."
[d] Response offered was: "several."
[e] Response offered was: "not very much."
[f] Response offered was: "one or two."
[g] Response offered was: "none."

Source: National Election Studies codebooks, Center for Political Studies, Institute for Social Research, University of Michigan, Ann Arbor, Mich.

Table 2-8 Use and Trustworthiness of Media, 1959-1986 (percent)

	1959	*1961*	*1963*	*1964*	*1967*	*1968*	*1971*	*1972*	*1974*	*1976*	*1978*	*1980*	*1982*	*1984*	*1986*
Source of most news[a]															
Television	51	52	55	58	64	59	60	64	65	64	67	64	64	64	66
Newspapers	57	57	53	56	55	49	48	50	47	49	49	44	44	40	36
Radio	34	34	29	26	28	25	23	21	21	19	20	18	18	14	14
Magazines	8	9	6	8	7	7	5	6	4	7	5	5	6	4	4
People	4	5	4	5	4	5	4	4	4	5	5	4	4	4	4
Most believable[b]															
Television	29	39	36	41	41	44	49	48	51	51	47	51	53	53	55
Newspapers	32	24	24	23	24	21	20	21	20	22	23	22	22	24	21
Radio	12	12	12	8	7	8	10	8	8	7	9	8	6	8	6
Magazines	10	10	10	10	8	11	9	10	8	9	9	9	8	7	7
Don't know/no answer	17	17	18	18	20	16	12	13	13	11	12	10	11	9	12

[a] Question: "First, I'd like to ask you where you usually get most of your news about what's going on in the world today—from the newspapers or radio or television or magazines or talking to people or where?" (more than one answer permitted).
[b] Question: "If you got conflicting or different reports of the same news story from radio, television, the magazines, and the newspapers, which of the four versions would you be most inclined to believe—the one on the radio or television or magazines or newspapers?" (only one answer permitted).

Sources: 1959-1984: Television Information Office, "Public Attitudes Toward Television and Other Media in a Time of Change" (New York: Television Information Office, 1985), 3, 5; 1986: Television Information Office, "America's Watching: Public Attitudes Toward Television" (New York: Television Information Office, 1987), 18.

Table 2-9 Newspaper Endorsements of Presidential Candidates, 1972-1984

Year/candidate	*Papers*		*Circulation*	
	Number	Percentage	Number	Percentage
1972				
Nixon (R)	753	71	30,560,535	77
McGovern (D)	56	5	3,049,534	8
Uncommitted	245	23	5,864,548	15
1976				
Ford (R)	411	62	20,951,798	62
Carter (D)	80	12	7,607,739	23
Uncommitted	168	26	5,074,069	15
1980				
Reagan (R)	443	42	17,561,333	49
Carter (D)	126	12	7,782,078	22
Anderson[a]	40	4	1,614,740	4
Uncommitted	439	42	9,131,940	25
1984				
Reagan (R)	381	58	18,357,512	52
Mondale (D)	62	9	7,568,639	21
Uncommitted	216	33	9,611,058	27

[a] In 1980 John Anderson ran as an independent candidate.

Source: Editor & Publisher (November 7, 1972), 9; (October 30, 1976), 5; (November 1, 1980), 10; (November 3, 1984), 9.

Questions

1. What are the two biggest changes in media coverage in the 1980s (Table 2-1)? What implications do these developments have for political and news broadcasting?

2. If your target audience were young people, which media would you use most (Table 2-2)? If your target were the middle-aged or elderly, what would your media strategy be? What if your purpose were to reach relatively well-educated and well-to-do people?

3. What explains the decline in newspaper circulation as a percentage of the population, which began in the late 1940s (Table 2-3)? (Hint: see Table 2-1.) In the twentieth century, circulation as a percentage of population rose considerably over what it had been in the nineteenth century. An obvious inference is that this made the electorate more informed about political matters. Yet some historians have argued that this was not the case. How might one support such an argument in the face of the figures in Table 2-3? (Hint: one clue—but only a very partial answer—is suggested in Figure 3-1.)

4. Why has the average number of press conferences declined since Franklin Roosevelt's time (Table 2-4)? (Hint: Figure 2-1 suggests one reason.) Why did Richard Nixon have especially few press conferences?

5. If there were one hundred stories that mentioned parties in the *Chicago Tribune* in September and October of 1952, how many stories mentioned candidates (Figure 2-2)? What about 1980? Figure 2-2 is related to important changes in the way candidates campaign and voters choose now compared to as little as thirty years ago. Describe the connection between Figure 2-2 and Table 4-7.

6. It is frequently charged that the media today pay too much attention to the "horserace" aspects of political campaigns (who is ahead and who is behind) and too little attention to the issues. On the basis of Table 2-5, do you think this is true? Would you answer differently on the basis of Figure 2-4? Be careful. There are at least two points to make about Figure 2-4.

7. One reason for the differences between Table 2-5 and Figure 2-4 is the years included (Figure 2-4 does not include 1968, in which greater attention was paid to policies and problems). Why is it

likely that newspapers paid more attention to foreign affairs and to social problems in 1968 than in later years?

8. Although the differences in coverage in Figure 2-3 are striking, there are obvious explanations for disproportionate coverage of races for the presidency, state governorships, and Congress. What are these reasons?

9. Why is there so much media coverage of the New Hampshire primary and the Iowa caucuses (Table 2-6)? In 1980 both parties in fifteen states used caucuses (Alabama, Arizona, Colorado, Delaware, Hawaii, Iowa, Maine, Minnesota, Missouri, North Dakota, Oklahoma, Utah, Virginia, Washington, and Wyoming). In thirty states both parties used primaries. In the remaining five states (Arkansas, Mississippi, Montana, South Carolina, and Texas), one party used caucuses, the other a primary. Using news seconds of CBS coverage, was there more coverage of primary states or caucus states in 1980? Answer both in terms of overall coverage in the primary versus the caucus states and in terms of coverage per state. There are at least two reasons for the difference. What are they?

10. In Tables 2-7 and 2-8 there are two almost contradictory trends with regard to the amount of television viewing. What are they?

11. It is sometimes alleged that newspapers are more Republican than the general population. Based on newspaper endorsements (Table 2-9), presidential election outcomes (Table 3-8), and the population's party identification (Table 5-1), do you think that this allegation is true? Explain your reasoning with numbers drawn from the three tables mentioned.

3

Elections and Campaigns

Campaigns and elections provide an abundance of numbers. Indeed, if asked for examples of political statistics, most people would think first of election results. But votes are only part of the numbers election campaigns generate: opinion surveys and exit polls, for example, offer a wealth of information about who the voters are and why they chose as they did; summary statistics show which party and which types of candidates won and lost; financial disclosure requirements furnish detailed information about campaign costs and contributions.

Not only are there a great many electoral statistics, but they extend back to the early years of the country. Consider the much-researched topic of partisan realignment. Long time series on voter turnout and the partisan breakdown of the vote have allowed researchers to comb the nation's past for realignments—fundamental shifts in support for parties and the coalitions supporting them. Election returns from localities dominated by different ethnic or economic groups also have been used to reveal the links between those groups and the parties. Thus, periods of realignment and the length of time between them—scholarly consensus holds that realignments occurred in the 1850s, 1890s, and between 1928 and 1932—are important for understanding our political history and the role of electoral statistics in uncovering that history. Realignment years are useful groupings for presenting data on partisan changes (Tables 3-9 and 3-10).

Available data also document more recent trends in campaigns and elections: the decline in presidential voter turnout after 1960 (Figure 3-1), the electoral advantages of incumbency (Table 3-12), the increasingly long quests for the presidential nominations (Figure 3-3), the growing contributions from political action committees (Table 3-16), and the expense of political campaigns (Tables 3-13 and 3-14).

Added to the arsenal of statistics about elections in the past fifty years have been surveys of representative national, state, and local populations. These data have enlivened research on the identification and timing of electoral realignments. The partisan changes that have occurred since the mid-1960s are of particular interest. Most scholars see the period since the mid-1960s as one of "dealignment" rather than realignment—with voters more willing to vote for some nominees of both parties (Table 4-7) and with more frequent outcomes in which different parties carry the presidential and congressional vote in a district (Table 4-8). Public opinion surveys also allow researchers to move beyond reliance on the simple shape of overall election results. Extensive data on individual behavior and attitudes reveal patterns of voting turnout and support (Tables 3-1 and 3-7) and voters' opinions about the candidates, parties, and issues (e.g., Tables 3-6 and 5-1) that are much more detailed than previously available.

Despite this volume of data there are some gaps: survey data is nonexistent before the mid-1930s, and reliable, consistent surveys date principally from the 1950s; until 1980, presidential primary surveys were limited; even official election returns below the state level are only now being made readily available (by the Inter-University Consortium for Political and Social Research); surveys emphasizing nonpresidential voting are very limited prior to the mid-1970s; and campaign finance data are unavailable or uninformative in some states and systematically available for the federal level for just a little more than a decade.

These are serious gaps, and they impose limits on what we know about campaigns, elections, and parties. The lack of survey data on earlier realignments, for example, is troublesome because it robs researchers of helpful historical comparisons. Nonetheless, in the area of campaigns and elections, more than anywhere, there is almost an embarrassment of riches.

Figure 3-1 Voter Turnout, Presidential and Midterm Elections, 1824-1986

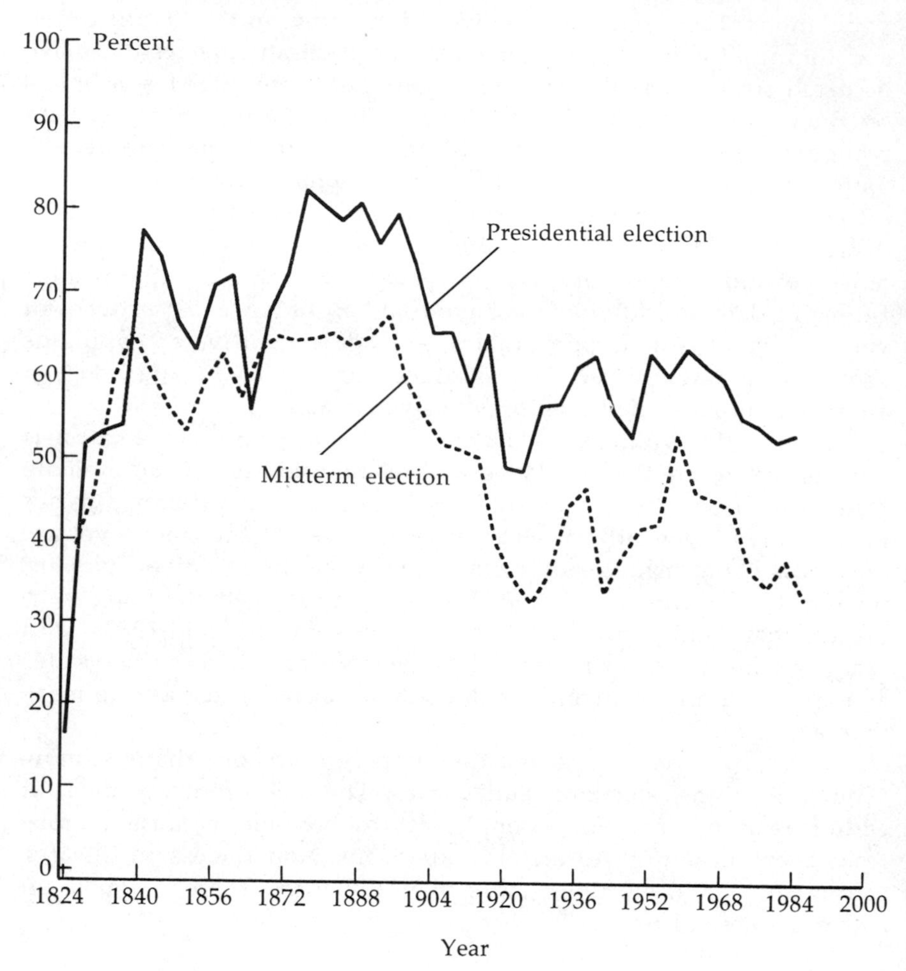

Sources: 1824-1984: Erik W. Austin and Jerome M. Clubb, *Political Facts of the United States Since 1789* (New York: Columbia University Press, 1986), 378-379; 1986: *Congressional Quarterly Weekly Report* (1987), 485.

Figure 3-2 Voter Turnout, Presidential Elections, 1868-1984, South and Nonsouth

Source: Walter Dean Burnham, "The Turnout Problem," in *Elections American Style*, ed. A. James Reichley (Washington, D.C.: Brookings, 1987), 113-114.

Table 3-1 Citizens Registered and Voting, 1972-1986 (percent)

	Percentage reporting they registered								*Percentage reporting they voted*							
	Presidential election years				Congressional election years				Presidential election years				Congressional election years			
	1972	*1974*	*1980*	*1984*	*1974*	*1978*	*1982*	*1986*	*1972*	*1976*	*1980*	*1984*	*1974*	*1978*	*1982*	*1986*
Race/ethnicity																
White	73	68	68	69	63	63	65	65	64	60	60	61	46	47	49	47
Black	65	58	60	66	54	57	59	64	52	48	50	55	33	37	43	43
Hispanic origin[a]	44	37	36	40	34	32	35	36	37	31	29	32	22	23	25	24
Sex																
Male	73	67	66	67	62	62	63	63	64	59	59	59	46	46	48	46
Female	71	66	67	69	61	62	64	65	62	58	59	60	43	45	48	46
Region[b]																
Northeast	—	65	64	66	62	62	62	62	—	59	58	59	48	48	49	44
Midwest	—	72	73	74	66	68	71	71	—	65	65	65	49	50	54	50
South	68	64	64	66	59	60	61	63	55	54	55	56	36	39	41	43
West	—	63	63	64	59	59	60	61	—	57	57	58	48	47	50	48
Age																
18-20	58	47	44	47	36	34	35	35	48	38	35	36	20	20	19	19
21-24	59	54	52	54	45	45	47	47	50	45	43	43	26	26	28	24
25-34	68	62	62	63	54	55	57	56	59	55	54	54	37	38	40	35
35-44	74	69	70	70	66	66	67	68	66	63	64	63	49	50	52	49
45-64	79	75	75	76	73	74	75	75	70	68	69	69	56	58	62	59
65 and older	75	71	74	76	70	72	75	77	63	62	65	67	51	55	59	61

Employment																
Employed	74	68	68	69	63	63	65	64	66	62	61	61	46	46	50	46
Unemployed	58	52	50	54	44	44	49	51	49	43	41	44	28	27	34	31
Not in labor force	70	65	65	68	61	63	64	66	59	56	57	58	43	46	48	48
Education																
8 years or less	61	54	53	53	54	53	52	51	47	44	42	42	34	34	35	33
1-3 years high school	63	55	54	54	54	52	53	52	52	47	45	44	35	35	37	34
4 years high school	74	66	66	67	61	62	62	63	65	59	58	58	44	45	47	44
1-3 years college	81	75	74	75	66	68	70	70	74	68	67	67	49	51	53	50
4 or more years college	87	83	84	83	76	76	79	76	83	79	79	79	61	63	66	59
Total	72	66	66	68	62	62	64	64	63	59	59	59	44	45	48	46

Note: "—" indicates not available.

[a] Persons of Hispanic origin may be of any race.

[b] For composition of regions, see Appendix, Table A-1.

Sources: U.S. Bureau of the Census, *Statistical Abstract of the U. S., 1987* (Washington, D.C.: U.S. Government Printing Office, 1986), 224, and U.S. Bureau of the Census, Current Population Reports, Series P-20, No. 414, *Voting and Registration in the Election of November 1986* (Washington, D.C.: U.S. Government Printing Office, 1987), and unpublished data.

Table 3-2 Presidential General Election Returns by State, 1984

	Electoral vote		*Popular vote*				*Popular vote (percentage)*	
State	Republican	Democrat	Republican	Democrat	Other	Total	Republican	Democrat
Alabama	9		872,849	551,899	16,965	1,441,713	60.5	38.3
Alaska	3		138,377	62,007	7,221	290,605	66.7	29.9
Arizona	7		681,416	333,854	10,627	1,025,897	66.4	32.5
Arkansas	6		534,774	338,646	10,986	884,406	60.5	38.3
California	47		5,467,009	3,922,519	115,895	9,505,423	57.5	41.3
Colorado	8		821,817	454,975	18,588	1,295,380	63.4	35.1
Connecticut	8		890,877	569,597	6,426	1,466,900	60.7	38.8
Delaware	3		152,190	101,656	726	254,572	59.8	39.9
District of Columbia		3	29,009	180,408	1,871	211,288	13.7	85.4
Florida	21		2,730,350	1,448,816	885	4,180,051	65.3	34.7
Georgia	12		1,068,722	706,628	770	1,776,120	60.2	39.8
Hawaii	4		185,050	147,154	3,642	335,846	55.1	43.8
Idaho	4		297,523	108,510	5,111	411,144	72.4	26.4
Illinois	24		2,707,103	2,086,499	25,486	4,819,088	56.2	43.3
Indiana	12		1,377,230	841,481	14,358	2,233,069	61.7	37.7
Iowa	8		703,088	605,620	11,097	1,319,805	53.3	45.9
Kansas	7		677,296	333,149	11,546	1,021,991	66.3	32.6
Kentucky	9		821,702	539,539	8,104	1,369,345	60.0	39.4
Louisiana	10		1,037,299	651,586	17,937	1,706,822	60.8	38.2
Maine	4		336,500	214,515	2,129	553,144	60.8	38.8
Maryland	10		879,918	787,935	8,020	1,675,873	52.5	47.0
Massachusetts	13		1,310,936	1,239,606	8,911	2,559,453	51.2	48.4
Michigan	20		2,251,571	1,529,638	20,449	3,801,658	59.2	40.2
Minnesota		10	1,032,603	1,036,364	15,482	2,084,449	49.5	49.7
Mississippi	7		582,377	352,192	6,535	941,104	61.9	37.4
Missouri	11		1,274,188	848,583	12	2,122,783	60.0	40.0

Montana	4		232,450	146,742	5,185	384,377	60.5	38.2
Nebraska	5		460,054	187,866	4,170	652,090	70.6	28.8
Nevada	4		188,770	91,655	6,242	286,667	65.8	32.0
New Hampshire	4		267,051	120,395	1,620	389,066	68.6	30.9
New Jersey	16		1,933,630	1,261,323	22,909	3,217,862	60.1	39.2
New Mexico	5		307,101	201,769	5,500	514,370	59.7	39.2
New York	36		3,664,763	3,119,609	22,438	6,806,810	53.8	45.8
North Carolina	13		1,346,481	824,287	4,593	2,175,361	61.9	37.9
North Dakota	3		200,336	104,429	4,206	308,971	64.8	33.8
Ohio	23		2,678,560	1,825,440	43,619	4,547,619	58.9	40.1
Oklahoma	8		861,530	385,080	9,066	1,255,676	68.6	30.7
Oregon	7		685,700	536,479	4,348	1,226,527	55.9	43.7
Pennsylvania	25		2,584,323	2,228,131	32,449	4,844,903	53.3	46.0
Rhode Island	4		212,080	197,106	1,306	410,492	51.7	48.0
South Carolina	8		615,539	344,459	8,531	968,529	63.6	35.6
South Dakota	3		200,267	116,113	1,487	317,867	63.0	36.5
Tennessee	11		990,212	711,714	10,068	1,711,994	57.8	41.6
Texas	29		3,433,428	1,949,276	14,867	5,397,571	63.6	36.1
Utah	5		469,105	155,369	5,182	629,656	74.5	24.7
Vermont	3		135,865	95,730	2,966	234,561	57.9	40.8
Virginia	12		1,337,078	796,250	13,307	2,146,635	62.3	37.1
Washington	10		1,051,670	807,352	24,888	1,883,910	55.8	42.9
West Virginia	6		405,483	328,125	2,134	735,742	55.1	44.6
Wisconsin	11		1,198,584	995,740	17,365	2,211,689	54.2	45.0
Wyoming	3		133,241	53,370	2,357	188,968	70.5	28.2
Total	525	13	54,455,075	37,577,185	620,582	92,652,842	58.8	40.6

Source: Richard M. Scammon and Alice V. McGillivray, comps. and eds., *America Votes 16: A Handbook of Contemporary American Election Statistics* (Washington, D.C.: Elections Research Center, Congressional Quarterly, 1985), 41.

Table 3-3 Presidential Primary Returns, 1984

State (date)	Democrats						Republicans		
	Glenn	Hart	Jackson	Mondale	Other	Total vote	Reagan	Other	Total vote
New Hampshire (2-28)	12.0%	37.3%	5.3%	27.9%	17.7%	101,131	86.1%	13.9%	75,570
Vermont (3-6)		70.0	7.8	20.0	21.1	74,059	98.7	1.3	33,643
Alabama (3-13)	20.8	20.7	19.6	34.6	4.3	428,283			
Florida (3-13)	10.8	39.2	12.2	33.4	4.4	1,182,190	100.0		344,150
Georgia (3-13)	17.9	27.3	21.0	30.5	3.3	684,541	100.0		50,793
Massachusetts (3-13)	7.2	39.0	5.0	25.5	23.3	630,962	89.5	10.5	65,937
Rhode Island (3-13)	5.1	45.0	8.7	34.5	6.8	44,511	90.7	9.3	2,235
Illinois (3-20)	1.2	35.2	21.0	40.4	2.1	1,659,425	99.9	0.1	595,078
Connecticut (3-27)	0.4	52.7	12.0	29.1	5.9	220,842			
New York (4-3)	1.1	27.4	25.6	44.8	1.0	1,387,950			
Wisconsin (4-3)	1.0	44.4	9.8	41.1	3.6	635,768	95.2	4.8	294,813
Pennsylvania (4-10)	1.4	33.3	16.0	45.1	4.3	1,656,294	99.3	0.7	621,206
District of Columbia (5-1)		7.1	67.3	25.6		102,731	100.0		5,692
Tennessee (5-1)	1.3	29.1	25.3	41.0	3.3	322,063	90.9	9.1	82,921
Louisiana (5-5)		25.0	42.9	22.3	9.8	318,810	89.7	10.3	16,687
Texas (5-5)							96.5	3.5	319,839
Indiana (5-8)	2.2	41.8	13.7	40.9	1.4	716,955	100.0		428,559
Maryland (5-8)	1.2	24.3	25.5	42.5	6.4	506,886	100.0		73,663
North Carolina (5-8)	1.8	30.2	25.4	35.6	7.0	960,857			
Ohio (5-8)		42.0	16.4	40.3	1.2	1,447,236	100.0		658,169
Nebraska (5-15)		58.2	9.1	26.6	6.1	148,855	99.0	1.0	146,648
Oregon (5-15)	2.7	58.5	9.3	27.6	1.9	399,679	98.0	2.0	243,346
Idaho (5-22)		58.0	5.7	30.1	6.3	54,722	92.2	7.8	105,687
California (6-5)	3.3	38.9	18.4	35.3	4.1	2,970,903	100.0	0.0	1,874,975

Montana (6-5)		9.0	1.1	5.9	83.9	34,214	92.4	7.6	71,887
New Jersey (6-5)		29.7	23.6	45.2	1.5	676,561	100.0		240,054
New Mexico (6-5)		46.7	11.8	36.1	5.3	187,403	94.9	5.1	42,994
South Dakota (6-5)		50.7	5.2	39.0	5.1	52,561			
West Virginia (6-5)		37.3	6.7	53.8	2.1	369,245	91.8	8.2	136,996
North Dakota (6-12)		85.2		2.8	12.0	33,555	100.0		44,109
Totals[a]	3.4	36.1	18.2	37.8	4.4	18,009,192	98.6	1.4	6,575,651

[a] Other Democratic votes include: 334,801 for McGovern; 123,649 for LaRouche; 77,697 "No preference"; 59,254 "Uncommitted"; 52,759 for Askew; 51,437 for Cranston; 33,684 for Hollings; 9,261 "None of the names shown"; 51,615 scattered. Other Republican votes include: 22,791 "Uncommitted"; 14,047 "Ronald Reagan no"; 12,749 for Stassen; 10,383 "No preference"; 8,237 "None of the names shown"; 22,457 scattered.

Source: America Votes 16, 67.

Table 3-4 Democratic Presidential Caucus Results, 1984

State (date)	Estimated turnout	Hart	Jackson	Mondale	Others	Uncommitted
Iowa (2-20)	85,000	16.5%	1.5%	48.9%	23.7%	9.4%
Maine (3-4)	16,830	50.2	0.4	45.4	0.8	3.2
Wyoming (3-10)	3,526	60.4	0.4	35.9	0.3	3.0
Hawaii (3-13)	2,830		4.2	32.3		63.5
Nevada (3-13)	5,000	52.3	0.6	37.7	2.2	7.2
Oklahoma (3-13)	42,800	43.3	3.7	38.9	4.0	10.1
Washington (3-13)	75,000	52.6	3.0	33.2	1.6	9.6
Delaware (3-14)	2,856	29.8	9.6	60.1		0.5
Alaska (3-15)	2,200	43.6	10.6	27.7		18.1
Arkansas (3-17)	22,202	30.3	19.9	44.0		5.8
Michigan (3-17)	132,002	32.2	16.7	50.4	0.2	0.5
Mississippi (3-17)	—	11.0	26.9	30.3		31.8
South Carolina (3-17)	40,000	12.7	25.0	9.1		53.2
Minnesota (3-20)[a]	66,000	7.0	2.0	62.0		29.0
Kansas (3-24)	11,553	41.8	3.3	48.7		6.2
Virginia (3-24-26)	25,505	14.7	26.7	30.4		28.2
Montana (3-25)	13,895	49.1	5.2	35.5	0.3	9.9
North Dakota (3-18-28)	5,000	35.8	2.8	29.9		31.5
Kentucky (3-31)	—	15.2	18.5	30.4		35.9
Wisconsin (4-7)	33,719	30.4	10.2	57.7		1.7
Arizona (4-14)	34,173	44.4	15.7	38.5		1.4
Missouri (4-18)	40,000	19.8	18.5	58.0		3.7
Vermont (4-24)	2,000	48.2	14.0	33.2		4.6
Utah (4-25)	9,506	50.5	3.1	19.5	0.6	26.3
Texas (5-5)[b]	—	27.1	16.4	50.0		6.5
Colorado (5-7)[b]	50,000	81.6	4.2	9.8		4.4
Idaho (5-24)	—	57.5	2.4	33.6		6.5

Note: "—" indicates not available.

[a] Minnesota results are based on 150 precincts, tabulated to form a weighted sampling of the state.

[b] Texas results are with about 60 percent of the precincts reporting; Colorado results are with 80 percent of the precincts reporting.

Source: Congressional Quarterly Weekly Report (1984), 1317.

Figure 3-3 Presidential Nominations, Campaign Length, 1968-1988

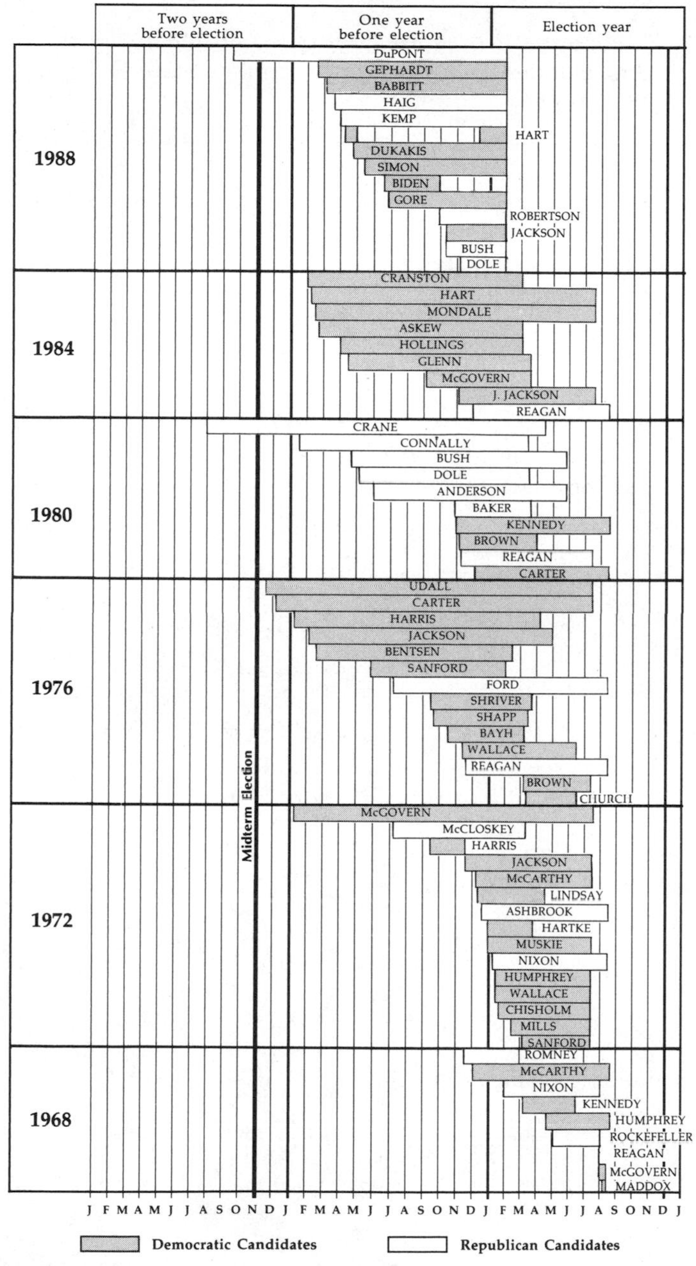

Note: Beginning of campaigns is determined by date of the formal announcement. Status of 1988 campaigns as of January 31, 1988.

Sources: 1968-1984: Congressional Quarterly, *Elections '80* (Washington, D.C.: Congressional Quarterly, 1980), and Congressional Quarterly, *Congressional Quarterly's Guide to U.S. Elections,* 2d ed. (Washington, D.C.: Congressional Quarterly, 1985), 387; 1988: *Congressional Quarterly Weekly Report* (1987), 2732.

Table 3-5 Convention Votes Presidential Candidates Received from Caucus State Delegates and Primary State Delegates, 1964-1984

Year/candidate	*Caucus states*	*Primary states*	*Number of convention votes*	*Percentage of convention*
1964 Republican convention				
Goldwater	74.5%	60.5%	883	67.5
Scranton	10.7	22.1	214	16.4
Rockefeller	0.6	16.8	114	8.7
Others	14.2	0.6	97	7.4
Total	*N*=655	*N*=653	1,308	100.0
1968 Democratic convention				
Humphrey	80.2	53.4	1,760.25	67.1
McCarthy	12.1	34.4	601	22.9
McGovern	3.8	7.5	146.5	5.6
Others	4.0	4.7	114.25	4.4
Total	*N*=1,346	*N*=1,276	2,622	100.0
1968 Republican convention				
Nixon	59.6	43.2	692	51.9
Rockefeller	14.4	27.9	277	20.8
Reagan	11.2	16.4	182	13.7
Others	14.7	12.4	182	13.7
Total	*N*=706	*N*=627	1,333	100.0
1972 Democratic convention				
McGovern	41.0	64.9	1,715.4	56.9
Jackson	30.0	11.5	534	17.7
Wallace	7.3	15.5	385.7	12.8
Others	21.7	8.1	380.9	12.6
Total	*N*=1,009	*N*=2,007	3,016	100.0
1976 Republican convention				
Ford	44.9	55.9	1,187	52.5
Reagan	55.1	43.9	1,070	47.4
Others	0.0	0.1	2	0.1
Total	*N*=693	*N*=1,566	2,259	100.0
1980 Democratic convention				
Carter	71.0	60.8	2,123	63.7
Kennedy	24.3	38.6	1,150.5	34.5
Others	4.7	0.5	57.5	1.7
Total	*N*=953	*N*=2,378	3,331	100.0

Table 3-5 *(Continued)*

Year/candidate	*Caucus states*	*Primary states*	*Number of convention votes*	*Percentage of convention*
1984 Democratic convention				
Mondale	56.3%	55.6%	2,191	55.9
Hart	29.6	31.2	1,200.5	30.6
Jackson	11.9	11.9	465.5	11.9
Others	2.3	1.3	66	1.7
Total	N=1,460	N=2,463	3,923	100.0

Note: Shown are major presidential candidates with substantial opposition. The table is based on first ballot votes before switches.

Sources: 1964-1980: Congressional Quarterly, *Elections '84* (Washington, D.C.: Congressional Quarterly, 1984), 50; 1984: compiled by the editors from Congressional Quarterly, *Congressional Quarterly Almanac, 1984* (Washington, D.C.: Congressional Quarterly, 1985), B68.

Table 3-6 Election Year Candidate Preferences, Gallup Poll, 1948-1984 (percent)

Year/candidate	*First poll of year*	*First poll after conventions*	*Early October*	*Final survey*	*Election results*
1948					
Truman (D)[a]	46 (+ 5)	37	40	45	50 (+ 5)
Dewey (R)	41	48 (+11)	46 (+ 6)	50 (+ 5)	45
1952					
Eisenhower (R)	59 (+28)	50 (+ 7)	53 (+12)	51 (+ 2)	55 (+11)
Stevenson (D)	31	43	41	49	44
1956					
Eisenhower (R)[a]	61 (+26)	52 (+11)	51 (+10)	60 (+19)	57 (+15)
Stevenson (D)	35	41	41	41	42
1960					
Kennedy (D)	43	44	49 (+ 3)	51 (+ 2)	50 (+0.2)
Nixon (R)	48 (+ 5)	50 (+ 6)	46	49	50
1964					
Johnson (D)[a]	75 (+57)	65 (+36)	64 (+35)	64 (+28)	61 (+23)
Goldwater (R)	18	29	29	36	38
1968					
Nixon (R)	43 (+ 9)	43 (+12)	43 (+12)	43 (+ 1)	43 (+0.7)
Humphrey (D)	34	31	31	42	43
Wallace (AIP)[b]	9	19	20	15	14
1972					
Nixon (R)[a]	53 (+19)	64 (+34)	60 (+26)	62 (+24)	61 (+23)
McGovern (D)	34	30	34	38	38
1976					
Carter (D)	47 (+ 5)	51 (+15)	47 (+ 2)	48	50 (+ 2)
Ford (R)[a]	42	36	45	49 (+ 1)	48
1980					
Reagan (R)	33	38	40	47 (+ 3)	51 (+10)
Carter (D)[a]	62 (+29)	39 (+ 1)	44 (+ 4)	44	41
Anderson (I)		13	9	8	7
1984					
Reagan (R)[a]	48 (+ 1)	55 (+15)	56 (+17)	59 (+18)	59 (+18)
Mondale (D)	47	40	39	41	41

[a] Incumbent
[b] American Independent Party

Sources: Congressional Quarterly Weekly Report (1984), 2648; 1984 final survey: *The Gallup Report* (November 1984), 31.

Table 3-7 Vote by Groups in General Elections, 1952-1984 (percent)

	1952		1956		1960		1964		1968			1972		1976			1980			1984	
	D	R	D	R	D	R	D	R	D	R	I[a]	D	R	D	R	I[a]	D	R	I[a]	D	R
Sex																					
Male	47	53	45	55	52	48	60	40	41	43	16	37	63	53	45	1	38	53	7	36	64
Female	42	58	39	61	49	51	62	38	45	43	12	38	62	48	51	-	44	49	6	45	55
Race/ethnicity																					
White	43	57	41	59	49	51	59	41	38	47	15	32	68	46	52	1	36	56	7	34	66
Nonwhite	79	21	61	39	68	32	94	6	85	12	3	87	13	85	15	-	86	10	2	87	13
Education																					
Grade school	52	48	50	50	55	45	66	34	52	33	15	49	51	58	41	1	54	42	3	51	49
High school	45	55	42	58	52	48	62	38	42	43	15	34	66	54	46	-	43	51	5	43	57
College	34	66	31	69	39	61	52	48	37	54	9	37	63	42	55	2	35	53	10	39	61
Employment																					
Manual	55	45	50	50	60	40	71	29	50	35	15	43	57	58	41	1	48	48	5	46	54
White collar	40	60	37	63	48	52	57	43	41	47	12	36	64	50	48	2	40	51	9	47	53
Professional and business	36	64	32	68	42	58	54	46	34	56	10	31	69	42	56	1	33	55	10	34	66
Age																					
Under 30	51	49	43	57	54	45	64	36	47	38	15	48	52	53	45	1	47	41	11	40	60
30-49	47	53	45	55	54	46	63	37	44	41	15	33	67	48	49	2	38	52	8	40	60
50 and older	39	61	39	61	46	54	59	41	41	47	12	36	64	52	48	-	41	54	4	41	59
Religion																					
Protestant	37	63	37	63	38	62	55	45	35	49	16	30	70	46	53	-	39	54	6	39	61
Catholic	56	44	51	49	78	22	76	24	59	33	8	48	52	57	41	1	46	47	6	39	61

(Table continues)

Table 3-7 *(Continued)*

	1952		*1956*		*1960*		*1964*		*1968*			*1972*		*1976*			*1980*			*1984*	
	D	R	D	R	D	R	D	R	D	R	I[a]	D	R	D	R	I[a]	D	R	I[a]	D	R
Political affiliation																					
Democrat	77	23	85	15	84	16	87	13	74	12	14	67	33	82	18	-	69	26	4	79	21
Independent	35	65	30	70	43	57	56	44	31	44	25	31	69	38	57	4	29	55	14	33	67
Republican	8	92	4	96	5	95	20	80	9	86	5	5	95	9	91	-	8	86	5	4	96
Region																					
East	45	55	40	60	53	47	68	32	50	43	7	42	58	51	47	1	43	47	9	46	54
Midwest	42	58	41	59	48	52	61	39	44	47	9	40	60	48	50	1	41	51	7	42	58
South	51	49	49	51	51	49	52	48	31	36	33	29	71	54	45	-	44	52	3	37	63
West	42	58	43	57	49	51	60	40	44	49	7	41	59	46	51	1	35	54	9	40	60
Union family	61	39	57	43	65	35	73	27	56	29	15	46	54	63	36	1	50	43	5	52	48
Total	45	55	42	58	50	50	61	39	43	43	14	38	62	50	48	1	41	51	7	41	59

Note: "-" indicates less than 0.5 percent.
[a] "I" indicates the vote for George Wallace in 1968, for Eugene McCarthy in 1976, and for John Anderson in 1980.

Source: The Gallup Report (November 1984), 32.

Table 3-8 Popular and Electoral Votes, 1789-1984

Year	*Number of states*	*Candidates*		*Electoral vote (number and percent)*		*Popular vote (number and percent)*
			(Federalist)		*(Federalist)*	
1789[a]	10		Washington		69	
					100%	
1792[a]	15		Washington		132	
					98%	
		(Democrat-Republican)	*(Federalist)*	*(Democrat-(Republican)*	*(Federalist)*	
1796[a]	16	Jefferson	Adams	68	71	
				49%	51%	
1800[a]	16	Jefferson	Adams	73	65	
				53%	47%	
1804	17	Jefferson	Pinckney	162	14	
		Clinton	King	92%	8%	
1808	17	Madison	Pinckney	122	47	
		Clinton	King	69%	27%	
1812	18	Madison	Clinton (Fusionist)	128	89	
		Genny	Ingersoll	59%	41%	
1816	19	Monroe (R)	King	183	34	
		Tompkins	Howard	83%	15%	
		(Democrat-Republican)		*(Democrat-Republican)*		
1820	24	Monroe	Adams (I-R)	231	1	
		Tompkins	Stockton	98%	0%	

(Table continues)

Table 3-8 *(Continued)*

Year	Number of states	Candidates		Electoral vote (number and percent)		Popular vote (number and percent)	
1824[b]	24	Jackson	Adams	99	84		
		Calhoun	Sanford	38%	32%		
		(Democrat-Republican)	*(National Republican)*	*(Democrat-Republican)*	*(National Republican)*	*(Democrat-Republican)*	*(National Republican)*
1828	24	Jackson	Adams	178	83	642,553	500,897
		Calhoun	Rush	68%	32%	56.1%	43.6%
1832	24	Jackson	Clay	219	49	701,780	484,205
		Van Buren	Sergeant	76%	17%	54.2%	37.4%
		(Democrat)	*(Whig)*	*(Democrat)*	*(Whig)*	*(Democrat)*	*(Whig)*
1836	26	Van Buren	Harrison	170	73[c]	764,176	550,816
		Johnson	Granger	58%	25%	50.8%	36.6%
1840	26	Van Buren	Harrison	60	234	1,128,854	1,275,390
		Johnson	Tyler	20%	80%	46.8%	52.9%
1844	26	Polk	Clay	170	105	1,339,494	1,300,004
		Dallas	Frelinghuysen	62%	38%	49.5%	48.1%
1848	30	Cass	Taylor	127	163	1,223,460	1,361,393
		Butler	Fillmore	44%	56%	42.5%	47.3%
1852	31	Pierce	Scott	254	42	1,607,510	1,386,942
		King	Graham	86%	14%	50.8%	43.9%
		(Democrat)	*(Republican)*	*(Democrat)*	*(Republican)*	*(Democrat)*	*(Republican)*
1856	31	Buchanan	Fremont	174	114	1,836,072	1,342,345
		Breckinridge	Dayton	59%	39%	45.3%	33.1%
1860	33	Douglas	Lincoln	12	180	1,380,202	1,865,908
		Johnson	Hamlin	4%	59%	29.5%	39.8%

1864	36	McClellan	Lincoln	21	212	1,812,807	2,218,388
		Pendleton	Johnson	9%	91%	45.0%	55.0%
1868	37	Seymour	Grant	80	214	2,708,744	3,013,650
		Blair	Colfax	27%	73%	47.3%	52.7%
1872	37	Greeley	Grant	d	286	2,834,761	3,598,235
		Brown	Wilson	d	78%	43.8%	55.6%
1876	38	Tilden	Hayes	184	185	4,288,546	4,034,311
		Hendricks	Wheeler	50%	50%	51.0%	47.9%
1880	38	Hancock	Garfield	155	214	4,444,260	4,446,158
		English	Arthur	42%	58%	48.2%	48.3%
1884	38	Cleveland	Blaine	219	182	4,874,621	4,848,936
		Hendricks	Logan	55%	45%	48.5%	48.2%
1888	38	Cleveland	Harrison	168	233	5,534,488	5,443,892
		Thurman	Morton	42%	58%	48.6%	47.8%
1892	44	Cleveland	Harrison	277	145	5,551,883	5,179,244
		Stevenson	Reid	62%	33%	46.1%	43.0%
1896	45	Bryan	KcKinley	176	271	6,511,495	7,108,480
		Sewall	Hobart	39%	61%	46.7%	51.0%
1900	45	Bryan	McKinley	155	292	6,358,345	7,218,039
		Stevenson	Roosevelt	35%	65%	45.5%	51.7%
1904	45	Parker	Roosevelt	140	336	5,028,898	7,626,593
		Davis	Fairbanks	29%	71%	37.6%	56.4%
1908	46	Bryan	Taft	162	321	6,406,801	7,676,258
		Kern	Sherman	34%	66%	43.0%	51.6%
1912	48	Wilson	Taft	435	8	6,293,152	3,486,333
		Marshall	Sherman	82%	2%	41.8%	23.2%
1916	48	Wilson	Hughes	277	254	9,126,300	8,546,789
		Marshall	Fairbanks	52%	48%	49.2%	46.1%
1920	48	Cox	Harding	127	404	9,140,884	16,133,314
		Roosevelt	Coolidge	24%	76%	34.2%	60.3%

(Table continues)

Table 3-8 *(Continued)*

Year	Number of states	Candidates		Electoral vote (number and percent)		Popular vote (number and percent)	
		(Democrat)	*(Republican)*	*(Democrat)*	*(Republican)*	*(Democrat)*	*(Republican)*
1924	48	Davis	Coolidge	136	382	8,386,169	15,717,553
		Bryant	Dawes	26%	72%	28.8%	54.1%
1928	48	Smith	Hoover	87	444	15,000,185	21,411,991
		Robinson	Curtis	16%	84%	40.8%	58.2%
1932	48	Roosevelt	Hoover	472	59	22,825,016	15,758,397
		Garner	Curtis	89%	11%	57.4%	39.6%
1936	48	Roosevelt	London	523	8	27,747,636	16,679,543
		Garner	Knox	90%	2%	60.8%	36.5%
1940	48	Roosevelt	Willkie	449	82	27,263,448	22,336,260
		Wallace	McNary	85%	15%	54.7%	44.8%
1944	48	Roosevelt	Dewey	432	99	25,611,936	22,013,372
		Truman	Bricker	81%	19%	53.4%	45.9%
1948	48	Truman	Dewey	303	189	24,105,587	21,970,017
		Barkley	Warren	57%	36%	49.5%	45.1%
1952	48	Stevenson	Eisenhower	89	442	27,314,649	33,936,137
		Sparkman	Nixon	17%	83%	44.4%	55.1%
1956	48	Stevenson	Eisenhower	73	457	26,030,172	35,585,245
		Kefauver	Nixon	14%	86%	42.0%	57.4%
1960	50	Kennedy	Nixon	303	219	34,221,344	34,106,671
		Johnson	Lodge	56%	41%	49.7%	49.5%
1964	50	Johnson	Goldwater	486	52	43,126,584	27,177,838
		Humphrey	Miller	90%	10%	61.1%	38.5%

1968	50	Humphrey	Nixon	191	301	31,274,503	31,785,148
		Muskie	Agnew	36%	56%	42.7%	43.4%
1972	50	McGovern	Nixon	17	520	29,171,791	47,170,179
		Shriver	Agnew	3%	97%	37.5%	60.7%
1976	50	Carter	Ford	297	240	40,830,763	39,147,793
		Mondale	Dole	55%	45%	50.1%	48.0%
1980	50	Carter	Reagan	49	489	35,483,883	43,904,153
		Mondale	Bush	9%	91%	41.0%	50.7%
1984	50	Mondale	Reagan	13	525	37,577,137	54,455,074
		Ferraro	Bush	2%	98%	40.6%	58.8%

Note: For details of the electoral system as well as popular and electoral votes polled by minor candidates, see source. Popular vote returns are shown since 1824 because of availability and because by that time most electors were chosen by popular vote.

[a] The elections of 1789-1800 were held under different rules, which did not include separate voting for president and vice president. Scattered electoral votes are not shown.

[b] All candidates in 1824 represented factions of the Democratic-Republican party. Figures are for the two candidates with the highest electoral votes. The two other candidates were Crawford and Clay with 41 and 37 electoral votes, respectively.

[c] Three Whig candidates ran in 1836. Their electoral votes totalled 113.

[d] The Democratic presidential nominee, Horace Greeley, died between the popular vote and the meeting of presidential electors. Democratic electors split 63 votes among several candidates, Congress refused to count the three Georgians who insisted on casting their votes for Greeley, and an additional 14 electoral votes were not cast.

Source: Congressional Quarterly's Guide to U.S. Elections, 269*ff,* 329*ff,* 1220*ff.*

Table 3-9 Party Winning Presidential Election by State, 1789-1984

	1789-1824			*1828-1856*			*1860-1892*			*1896-1928*			*1932-1964*			*1968-1984*		
State	D	F	O	D	R	O	D	R	O	D	R	O	D	R	O	D	R	O
Alabama	2	0	0	8	0	0	6	2	0	9	0	0	7	1	1	1	3	1
Alaska	-	-	-	-	-	-	-	-	-	-	-	-	1	1	0	0	5	0
Arizona	-	-	-	-	-	-	-	-	-	2	3	0	5	4	0	0	5	0
Arkansas	-	-	-	6	0	0	6	1	0	9	0	0	9	0	0	1	3	1
California	-	-	-	2	0	0	2	7	0	1	7	1	6	3	0	0	5	0
Colorado	-	-	-	-	-	-	0	4	1	5	4	0	4	5	0	0	5	0
Connecticut	2	8	0	2	6	0	4	5	0	1	8	0	5	4	0	1	4	0
Delaware	2	8	0	2	6	0	7	1	1	1	8	0	5	4	0	1	4	0
District of Columbia[a]	-	-	-	-	-	-	-	-	-	-	-	-	1	0	0	5	0	0
Florida	-	-	-	2	1	0	4	3	1	8	1	0	6	3	0	1	4	0
Georgia	8	2	0	5	3	0	7	0	1	9	0	0	8	1	0	2	2	1
Hawaii	-	-	-	-	-	-	-	-	-	-	-	-	2	0	0	3	2	0
Idaho	-	-	-	-	-	-	-	-	1	4	5	0	6	3	0	0	5	0
Illinois	2	0	0	8	0	0	1	8	0	1	8	0	7	2	0	0	5	0
Indiana	3	0	0	6	2	0	3	6	0	1	8	0	3	6	0	0	5	0
Iowa	-	-	-	2	1	0	0	9	0	1	8	0	4	5	0	0	5	0
Kansas	-	-	-	-	-	-	0	7	1	3	6	0	3	6	0	0	5	0
Kentucky	8	1	0	2	6	0	8	0	1	6	3	0	7	2	0	1	4	0
Louisiana	4	0	0	6	2	0	5	1	1	9	0	0	6	2	1	1	3	1
Maine	2	0	0	5	3	0	0	9	0	1	8	0	1	8	0	1	4	0
Maryland	4	6	0	1	6	1	7	1	1	4	5	0	6	3	0	3	2	0
Massachusetts	3	7	0	0	8	0	0	9	0	2	7	0	7	2	0	3	2	0
Michigan	-	-	-	4	2	0	0	9	0	0	8	1	5	4	0	4	1	0
Minnesota	-	-	-	-	-	-	0	9	0	0	8	1	7	2	0	4	1	0
Mississippi	2	0	0	7	1	0	5	1	1	9	0	0	6	1	2	1	3	1
Missouri	-	-	-	8	0	0	7	2	0	4	5	0	8	1	0	1	4	0
Montana	-	-	-	-	-	-	0	1	0	4	5	0	6	3	0	0	5	0
Nebraska	-	-	-	-	-	-	0	7	0	4	5	0	3	6	0	0	5	0

Nevada	-	-	-	-	-	-	1	6	1	5	4	0	7	2	0	0	5	0
New Hampshire	4	6	0	6	2	0	0	9	0	2	7	0	4	5	0	0	5	0
New Jersey	5	5	0	3	5	0	7	2	0	1	8	0	6	3	0	0	5	0
New Mexico	-	-	-	-	-	-	-	-	-	2	3	0	7	2	0	0	5	0
New York	6	3	0	5	3	0	4	5	0	1	8	0	6	3	0	2	3	0
North Carolina	8	1	0	5	3	0	5	2	1	8	1	0	9	0	0	1	4	0
North Dakota	-	-	-	-	-	-	-	-	-	2	7	0	3	6	0	0	5	0
Ohio	6	0	0	4	4	0	0	9	0	2	7	0	5	4	0	1	4	0
Oklahoma	-	-	-	-	-	-	-	-	-	4	2	0	6	3	0	0	5	0
Oregon	-	-	-	-	-	-	1	8	0	1	8	0	5	4	0	0	5	0
Pennsylvania	8	2	0	6	2	0	0	9	0	0	8	1	5	4	0	2	3	0
Rhode Island	4	5	0	2	6	0	0	9	0	2	7	0	7	2	0	3	2	0
South Carolina	8	2	0	6	0	2	4	3	1	9	0	0	7	1	1	1	4	0
South Dakota	-	-	-	-	-	-	0	1	0	1	7	1	3	6	0	0	5	0
Tennessee	8	0	0	3	5	0	6	1	1	7	2	0	6	3	0	1	4	0
Texas	-	-	-	3	0	0	7	0	0	8	1	0	7	2	0	2	3	0
Utah	-	-	-	-	-	-	-	-	-	2	7	0	6	3	0	0	5	0
Vermont	6	3	0	7	1	0	0	9	0	0	9	0	1	8	0	0	5	0
Virginia	8	2	0	8	0	0	5	1	1	8	1	0	6	3	0	0	5	0
Washington	-	-	-	-	-	-	0	1	0	2	6	1	6	3	0	1	4	0
West Virginia	-	-	-	-	-	-	5	3	0	1	8	0	8	1	0	3	2	0
Wisconsin	-	-	-	2	1	0	1	8	0	1	7	1	5	4	0	1	4	0
Wyoming	-	-	-	-	-	-	0	1	0	3	6	0	5	4	0	0	5	0
Total[b]	113	61	0	136	79	3	118	189	15	170	244	7	274	158	5	52	198	5

Note: "D" is the Democratic-Republican party from 1796 to 1820 and in 1828, the Jackson faction in 1824, and the Democratic party in 1832 and later; "F" is the Federalists from 1792 to 1816, Independent Democrat-Republicans in 1820, and the Adams faction in 1824; "R" is the National Republicans in 1828 and 1832, Whigs from 1836 to 1852, and the Republican party in 1856 and later. The "O" column refers to other (third-party) parties. Southern Democrats in 1860 are counted as Democratic. "-" indicates that the state was not yet admitted to the Union.

[a] Residents of the District of Columbia received the presidential vote in 1961.

[b] Fewer total votes for a given state within a party system indicate admission of the state during the party system or nonvoting in certain southern states in 1864, 1868, and 1872.

Source: Compiled by the editors from *Congressional Quarterly's Guide to U.S. Elections*, 269ff, 327.

Table 3-10 Party Victories in U.S. House Elections by State, 1860-1984

State	*1860-1895*			*1896-1931*			*1932-1965*			*1966-1984*		
	Dem.	Rep.	Other	Dem.	Rep.	Other	Dem.	Rep.	Other	Dem.	Rep.-	Other
Alabama	94	20	19	171	0	7	146	5	0	42	27	1
Alaska	-	-	-	-	-	-	4	0	0	3	9	0
Arizona	-	-	-	11	0	0	25	7	0	14	24	1
Arkansas	56	3	12	124	0	0	107	0	1	20	11	0
California[a]	27	45	11	10	86	80	178	146	121	232	170	4
Colorado	0	10	3	24	31	6	43	26	0	26	21	0
Connecticut	33	37	4	11	78	0	52	50	0	39	19	0
Delaware	15	2	2	5	14	0	9	8	0	2	8	0
Florida	18	9	1	61	0	0	111	8	0	86	39	0
Georgia	110	10	13	207	0	1	171	1	0	84	9	0
Hawaii	-	-	-	-	-	-	6	0	0	18	0	0
Idaho	0	4	0	0	25	3	20	14	0	0	18	0
Illinois	116	191	22	136	329	8	220	222	0	113	125	2
Indiana	107	99	19	96	139	1	84	109	0	54	49	0
Iowa	14	131	13	10	193	0	35	104	0	27	32	0
Kansas	0	64	12	23	114	8	16	91	0	11	38	1
Kentucky	143	19	31	149	54	0	122	25	0	42	23	1
Louisiana	69	25	2	136	0	2	140	0	0	57	10	3
Maine	1	76	9	4	71	0	8	41	0	7	12	0
Maryland	74	15	18	63	49	0	87	25	0	53	26	0
Massachusetts	22	166	21	60	208	5	102	134	3	83	29	2
Michigan	29	119	16	10	214	4	111	187	0	98	86	0
Minnesota	10	51	5	8	146	12	4	92	56	1	30	47
Mississippi	74	18	3	141	0	0	110	1	0	36	13	2
Missouri	142	42	40	202	89	0	159	48	0	77	19	0
Montana	1	3	0	13	13	2	24	11	0	11	8	0

Nebraska	3	30	6	17	55	37	21	50	0	2	26	0
Nevada	4	9	4	3	9	6	14	3	0	9	2	1
New Hampshire	11	33	3	3	33	0	3	31	0	5	13	0
New Jersey	53	58	5	64	135	2	84	158	0	92	54	0
New Mexico	-	-	-	7	5	0	29	0	0	9	12	0
New York[b]	238	306	73	284	327	120	368	371	26	229	141	12
North Carolina	79	31	37	157	11	9	193	9	0	76	29	0
North Dakota	0	4	0	0	43	1	2	32	0	4	9	0
Ohio	145	185	40	127	265	0	163	238	2	81	145	2
Oklahoma	-	-	-	70	27	0	115	15	0	42	13	0
Oregon	7	13	2	2	38	6	22	42	0	28	13	0
Pennsylvania	157	296	41	71	524	31	253	292	0	106	90	2
Rhode Island	7	34	2	13	34	0	32	2	0	16	2	0
South Carolina	64	28	6	127	0	0	104	0	0	40	17	1
South Dakota	0	9	0	3	44	0	7	27	0	7	11	0
Tennessee	92	49	23	140	39	4	120	37	1	48	33	0
Texas	110	6	16	298	7	0	364	6	3	200	34	0
Utah	-	-	-	6	23	2	23	11	0	9	13	1
Vermont	1	42	4	0	36	0	1	16	0	0	9	1
Virginia	82	21	41	166	16	1	151	15	0	38	59	1
West Virginia	40	15	6	23	75	0	84	16	0	37	5	0
Washington	0	6	0	6	61	4	55	55	0	53	16	0
Wisconsin	45	93	5	17	176	5	47	105	21	50	39	1
Wyoming	1	2	0	1	17	0	4	13	0	4	6	0

Note: "-" indicates that the state was not yet admitted to the Union.
[a] The relatively high number of "other" victories between 1896 and 1965 stems from a law that allowed cross-filings such that many candidates ran as both Republican and Democrat or another combination of parties.
[b] In New York the large number of "other" victories represent candidates endorsed by both major and minor parties.

Source: Inter-University Consortium for Political and Social Research, "Candidate and Constituency Statistics of Elections in the United States, 1788-1984," machine-readable data file (Ann Arbor, Mich.: Inter-University Consortium for Political and Social Research, 1986).

Table 3-11 House and Senate Election Results by Congress, 1854-1986

		House					Senate					
					Gains/losses					Gains/losses		
Year	*Congress*	Dem.	Rep.	Other	*Dem.*	*Rep.*	Dem.	Rep.	Other	*Dem.*	*Rep.*	*President*
1854	34th	83	108	43			42	15	5			
1856	35th	131	92	14	+48	−16	39	20	5	−3	+5	Buchanan (D)
1858	36th	101	113	23	−30	+21	38	26	2	−1	+6	
1860	37th	42	106	28	−59	−7	11	31	7	−27	+5	Lincoln (R)
1862	38th	80	103		+38	−3	12	39		+1	+8	
1864	39th	46	145		−34	+42	10	42		−2	+3	Lincoln (R)
1866	40th	49	143		+3	−2	11	42		+1	0	A. Johnson (R)
1868	41st	73	170		+24	+27	11	61		0	+19	Grant (R)
1870	42d	104	139		+31	−31	17	57		+6	−4	
1872	43d	88	203		−16	+64	19	54		+2	−3	Grant (R)
1874	44th	181	107	3	+93	−96	29	46		+10	−8	
1876	45th	156	137		−25	+30	36	39	1	+7	−7	Hayes (R)
1878	46th	150	128	14	−6	−9	43	33		+7	−6	
1880	47th	130	152	11	−20	+24	37	37	2	−6	+4	Garfield (R)
1882	48th	200	119	6	+70	−33	36	40		−1	+3	Arthur (R)
1884	49th	182	140	2	−18	+21	34	41		−2	+2	Cleveland (D)
1886	50th	170	151	4	−12	+11	37	39		+3	−2	
1888	51st	156	173	1	−14	+22	37	47		0	+8	Harrison (R)
1890	52d	231	88	14	+75	−85	39	47	2	+2	0	
1892	53rd	220	126	8	−11	+38	44	38	3	+5	−9	Cleveland (D)
1894	54th	104	246	7	−116	+120	39	44	5	−5	+6	
1896	55th	134	206	16	+30	−40	34	46	10	−5	+2	McKinley (R)
1898	56th	163	185	9	+29	−21	26	53	11	−8	+7	
1900	57th	153	198	5	−10	+13	29	56	3	+3	+3	McKinley (R)
1902	58th	178	207		+25	+9	32	58		+3	+2	Roosevelt (R)

1904	59th	136	250		−42	+43	32	58		0	0	Roosevelt (R)
1906	60th	164	222		+28	−28	29	61		−3	−3	
1908	61st	172	219		+8	−3	32	59		+3	−2	Taft (R)
1910	62d	228	162	1	+56	−57	42	49		+10	−10	
1912	63d	290	127	18	+62	−35	51	44	1	+9	−5	Wilson (D)
1914	64th	231	193	8	−59	+66	56	39	1	+5	−5	
1916	65th	210	216	9	−21	+23	53	42	1	−3	+3	Wilson (D)
1918	66th	191	237	7	−19	+21	47	48	1	−6	+6	
1920	67th	132	300	1	−59	+63	37	59		−10	+11	Harding (R)
1922	68th	207	225	3	+75	−75	43	51	2	+6	−8	Coolidge (R)
1924	69th	183	247	5	−24	+22	40	54	1	−3	+3	Coolidge (R)
1926	70th	195	237	3	+12	−10	47	48	1	+7	−6	
1928	71st	163	267	1	−32	+30	39	56	1	−8	+8	Hoover (R)
1930	72d	216	218	1	+53	−49	47	48	1	+8	−8	
1932	73d	313	117	5	+97	−101	59	36	1	+12	−12	Roosevelt (D)
1934	74th	322	103	10	+9	−14	69	25	2	+10	−11	
1936	75th	333	89	13	+11	−14	75	17	4	+6	−8	Roosevelt (D)
1938	76th	262	169	4	−71	+80	69	23	4	−6	+6	
1940	77th	267	162	6	+5	−7	66	28	2	−3	+5	Roosevelt (D)
1942	78th	222	209	4	−45	+47	57	38	1	−9	+10	
1944	79th	243	190	2	+21	−19	57	38	1	0	0	Roosevelt (D)
1946	80th	188	246	1	−55	+56	45	51		−12	+13	Truman (D)
1948	81st	263	171	1	+75	−75	54	42		+9	−9	Truman (D)
1950	82d	234	199	2	−29	+28	48	47	1	−6	+5	
1952	83d	213	221	1	−21	+22	47	48	1	−1	+1	Eisenhower (R)
1954	84th	232	203		+19	−18	48	47	1	+1	−1	
1956	85th	234	201		+2	−2	49	47		+1	0	Eisenhower (R)
1958	86th	283	154		+49	−47	64	34		+17	−13	
1960	87th	263	174		−20	+20	64	36		−2	+2	Kennedy (D)
1962	88th	258	176	1	−4	+2	67	33		+4	−4	
1964	89th	295	140		+38	−38	68	32		+2	−2	L. Johnson (D)

(Table continues)

Table 3-11 *(Continued)*

		House					*Senate*					
					Gains/losses					Gains/losses		
Year	*Congress*	Dem.	Rep.	Other	*Dem.*	*Rep.*	Dem.	Rep.	Other	*Dem.*	*Rep.*	*President*
1966	90th	248	187		−47	+47	64	36		−3	+3	
1968	91st	243	192		−4	+4	58	42		−5	+5	Nixon (R)
1970	92d	255	180		+12	−12	55	45		−4	+2	
1972	93d	243	192		−12	+12	57	43		+2	−2	Nixon (R)
1974	94th	291	144		+43	−43	61	38		+3	−3	
1976	95th	292	143		+1	−1	62	38		0	0	Carter (D)
1978	96th	277	158		−11	+11	59	41		−3	+3	
1980	97th	243	192		−33	+33	47	53		−12	+12	Reagan (R)
1982	98th	269	166		+26	−26	46	54		0	0	
1984	99th	253	182		−14	+14	47	53		+2	−2	Reagan (R)
1986	100th	258	177		+5	−5	55	45		+8	−8	

Note: Because of changes in the overall number of seats in the Senate and House, in the number of seats won by third parties, and in the number of vacancies, a Republican loss is not always matched precisely by a Democratic gain, or vice versa.

Sources: 1854: Congressional Quarterly, *Elections '84*, 106; 1856-1984: *Congressional Quarterly's Guide to U.S. Elections*, 1124; 1986: *Congressional Quarterly Weekly Report* (1986), 2811, 2843.

Table 3-12 Advantages of Incumbency in Reelection: Representatives, Senators, and Governors, 1960-1986

Year/office	*Number of incumbents* Ran	Won	Lost	*Winning election*	*Gaining over 60 percent of the vote*
1960					
House	400	374	26	93.5%	58.9%
Senate	29	28	1	96.6	41.3
Governor	13	7	6	53.8	15.4
1962					
House	396	381	15	94.3	63.6
Senate	34	29	5	85.3	26.4
Governor	24	15	9	62.5	12.5
1964					
House	389	344	45	88.4	58.5
Senate	32	28	4	87.5	46.8
Governor	14	12	2	85.7	42.9
1966					
House	402	362	40	90.1	67.7
Senate	29	28	1	96.6	41.3
Governor	21	14	7	66.7	23.8
1968					
House	401	396	5	98.8	72.2
Senate	24	20	4	83.3	37.5
Governor	13	9	4	69.2	15.4
1970					
House	391	379	12	96.9	77.3
Senate	29	23	6	79.3	31.0
Governor	24	17	7	70.8	4.2
1972					
House	380	367	13	95.6	77.8
Senate	25	20	5	80.0	52.0
Governor	9	7	2	77.8	44.5
1974					
House	383	343	40	89.6	66.4
Senate	25	23	2	92.0	40.0
Governor	22	17	5	77.3	36.4
1976					
House	381	368	13	96.6	69.2
Senate	25	16	9	64.0	40.0
Governor	7	5	2	71.4	28.6
1978					
House	378	359	19	95.0	76.6
Senate	22	15	7	68.1	31.8
Governor	21	16	5	76.2	28.6
1980					
House	392	361	31	90.7	72.9
Senate	25	16	9	55.2	40.0
Governor	10	7	3	70.0	30.0

(Table continues)

Table 3-12 *(Continued)*

Year/office	*Number of incumbents* Ran	Won	Lost	*Winning election*	*Gaining over 60 percent of the vote*
1982					
House	381	352	29	92.4%	68.9%
Senate	30	28	2	93.3	56.7
Governor	24	19	5	79.2	41.7
1984					
House	407	391	16	96.1	78.9
Senate	29	26	3	89.7	65.5
Governor	6	4	2	66.7	50.0
1986					
House	391	385	6	98.5	84.5
Senate	28	21	7	75.0	50.0
Governor	17	15	2	88.2	52.9

Note: Includes general elections only. Percentage gaining over 60 percent of the vote is calculated on the basis of the vote for the two major parties. "Off-off" year gubernatorial elections, held in Kentucky, Louisiana, Mississippi, New Jersey, and Virginia, are not included in the above totals. For these gubernatorial election outcomes, see *Congressional Quarterly's Guide to U.S. Elections.*

Sources: House and Senate, 1960-1978: Congressional Quarterly, *Elections '80,* 14; House and Senate, 1980-1982, and governor, 1964-1966: *America Votes;* 1984: *Congressional Quarterly Almanac* (1984), B7, B13, B19; and House and Senate, 1986, and governor, 1968-1986: *Congressional Quarterly Weekly Report.*

Table 3-13 Presidential Prenomination Campaign Finance, 1984

Candidate	*Net receipts*	*Federal matching funds*	*Individual contributors*	*Expenditures*	*Debts owed*
Democrats					
Askew	$ 3,327,176	$ 951,478	$ 1,683,918	$ 3,321,872	$ 25,000
Cranston	8,036,384	2,004,405	3,310,003	7,953,360	790,522
Glenn	14,096,528	3,150,850	6,539,944	14,051,781	2,851,922
Hart	23,244,098	4,775,150	8,481,519	23,039,575	4,374,168
Hollings	2,787,901	821,600	1,346,855	2,771,967	9,544
Jackson	9,751,326	2,857,053	5,037,122	9,654,265	345,875
Larouche	4,656,806	494,146	1,793,361	4,609,905	2,051,405
McGovern	1,803,688	612,735	805,208	1,790,363	146,899
Mondale	37,138,675	8,942,178	17,192,930	36,462,220	430,322
Total	105,200,513	24,609,594	46,385,803	104,034,457	11,198,271
Republican					
Reagan	28,649,441	10,100,000	16,358,445	27,658,297	150,000
Grand total[a]	$134,897,284	$34,895,967	$63,577,868	$132,718,316	$11,387,458

Note: Figures reflect activity from the start of the campaigns through December 31, 1984.
[a] Includes finances for four minor candidates, not shown separately.

Source: Federal Election Commission, "Final 1984 Presidential Statistical Report Released," press release, June 4, 1986, 3.

Table 3-14 Congressional Campaign Costs by Party and Incumbency Status, 1984 and 1986

Year/party/ status	*House*			*Senate*		
	Number of candidates	Receipts	Expenditures	Number of candidates	Receipts	Expenditures
1984						
Democrats	434	$105,421,690	$ 95,295,074	33	$ 69,194,647	$ 67,146,187
Incumbents	258	80,870,876	71,130,208	12	22,245,704	21,060,054
Challengers	152	15,801,634	15,538,963	17	23,568,852	22,897,607
Open seats	24	8,749,180	8,626,533	4	23,380,091	23,188,526
Republicans	382	90,455,879	82,115,412	35	78,137,391	76,314,077
Incumbents	154	50,597,557	42,932,329	17	52,570,233	50,996,668
Challengers	204	30,009,737	29,555,957	13	8,180,152	8,315,158
Open seats	24	9,848,585	9,627,126	5	17,387,006	17,002,251
Others	192	193,759	191,627	33	200,441	203,318
Total	1,008	$196,071,328	$177,602,742	101	$147,532,479	$143,663,582
1986						
Democrats	841	$139,500,941	$128,378,639	127	$ 91,775,796	$ 88,884,265
Incumbents	235	83,732,001	73,380,722	9	26,290,465	24,414,413
Challengers	430	25,533,843	25,308,685	75	40,419,960	39,779,421
Open seats	176	30,235,097	29,689,232	43	25,065,371	24,690,431
Republicans	596	117,635,274	110,312,250	92	122,194,367	122,148,362
Incumbents	161	65,901,124	59,054,984	18	64,012,012	64,781,363
Challengers	319	23,608,139	23,441,825	46	26,516,26	26,204,188
Open seats	116	28,126,011	27,815,441	28	31,666,094	31,162,811
Others	169	291,412	276,267	43	51,170	49,394
Total	1,606	$257,427,627	$238,967,156	262	$214,021,333	$211,082,021

Note: Figures are for general election candidates (primary and general election activity included) from January 1, 1983, to December 31, 1984, and January 1, 1985, to December 31, 1986.

Sources: Federal Election Commission, "FEC Releases Final Report on 1984 Congressional Races," press release, December 8, 1985, 6, and "1986 Congressional Spending Tops $450 Million," press release, May 10, 1987, 6-7.

Table 3-15 Campaign Contribution Sources for Congressional Candidates, 1983-1986 (percent)

	1983-1984		*1985-1986*	
Source	House	Senate	House	Senate
Individuals	48	63	49	65
Candidate contributions	2	2	2	1
Candidate loans	8	12	8	6
Party contributions	3	1	1	1
Nonparty (PAC) contributions	34	17	34	21
Other loans	1	0	1	1
Other	5	5	4	6

Note: Figures are for activity from January 1, 1983, to December 31, 1984, and January 1, 1985, to December 31, 1986.

Sources: Federal Election Commission, "FEC Releases Final Report on 1984 Congressional Races," 8, and Federal Election Commission, "1986 Congressional Spending Tops $450 Million," 5.

Table 3-16 Political Action Committee (PAC) Congressional Campaign Contributions by Type of PAC and Incumbency Status of Candidate, 1977-1986 (millions)

	House						*Senate*					
Year/PAC type	Dem.	Rep.	Incumbent	Challenger	Open seat[a]	Total	Dem.	Rep.	Incumbent	Challenger	Open seat[a]	Total
1977-1978												
Corporate	$ 2.6	$ 3.4	$ 3.8	$ 1.1	$ 1.1	$ 6.0	$ 0.9	$ 2.6	$ 1.8	$ 0.9	$ 0.8	$ 3.5
Trade association	3.9	4.7	5.2	1.5	1.9	8.6	0.9	1.7	1.3	0.7	0.6	2.6
Labor	7.0	0.2	4.6	1.2	1.4	7.2	2.4	0.3	1.2	0.9	0.6	2.7
Nonconnected	0.4	1.4	0.5	0.8	0.5	1.8	0.2	0.5	0.2	0.3	0.2	0.7
Total	14.4	10.0	14.7	4.6	5.1	24.4	4.5	5.2	4.5	3.0	2.2	9.7
1979-1980												
Corporate	4.8	7.5	8.1	2.6	1.5	12.2	2.1	4.8	2.7	3.3	0.9	6.9
Trade association	5.1	6.6	8.0	2.2	1.5	11.7	1.9	2.2	2.2	1.4	0.5	4.1
Labor	8.9	0.4	6.6	1.6	1.2	9.4	3.4	0.4	2.7	0.7	0.4	3.8
Nonconnected	0.9	2.1	1.0	1.4	0.7	3.1	0.5	1.4	0.5	1.1	0.3	1.9
Total	20.5	17.2	24.9	7.9	5.1	37.9	8.4	9.0	8.6	6.6	2.1	17.3
1981-1982												
Corporate	7.0	12.0	14.4	2.0	2.6	18.9	2.4	6.2	5.5	1.7	1.4	8.6
Trade association	7.2	9.7	12.4	2.1	2.3	16.8	2.2	2.8	3.7	0.8	0.5	5.0
Labor	14.7	0.7	8.5	4.3	2.6	15.4	4.5	0.4	3.0	1.3	0.5	4.9
Nonconnected	3.9	3.5	3.4	2.4	1.6	7.4	1.6	1.7	1.5	1.3	0.5	3.3
Total	34.2	26.8	40.8	10.9	9.4	61.1	11.2	11.4	14.3	5.2	3.0	22.6

1983-1984												
Corporate	10.6	13.4	19.2	2.7	2.1	24.0	3.8	10.2	10.9	1.1	2.0	14.1
Trade association	10.7	10.0	16.8	2.2	1.8	20.8	3.0	4.2	5.4	0.9	0.9	7.2
Labor	19.3	1.1	14.7	3.6	2.0	20.4	5.1	0.4	2.1	2.3	1.2	5.6
Nonconnected	4.8	4.5	5.0	3.0	1.3	9.3	3.1	2.7	2.8	2.0	1.0	5.8
Total	47.3	30.0	58.4	11.6	7.3	77.4	15.6	18.1	22.1	6.3	5.2	33.7
1985-1986												
Corporate	13.3	14.4	23.6	1.1	2.9	27.7	5.9	15.8	14.1	2.7	4.8	21.6
Trade association	12.6	11.4	19.8	1.3	2.8	24.0	4.2	6.2	6.7	1.6	2.1	10.5
Labor	21.5	1.6	15.1	4.4	3.6	23.1	7.2	0.7	2.8	3.2	1.9	7.9
Nonconnected	6.8	4.5	6.3	2.4	2.6	11.3	4.5	3.6	3.5	2.4	2.1	8.1
Total	$56.1	$33.4	$67.8	$9.4	$12.3	$89.5	$22.6	$27.4	$28.4	$10.3	$11.3	$49.9

Note: Figures are for amounts given to candiates in primary, general, run-off, and special elections during the two-year calendar period indicated.
[a] Open seat refers to candidates in elections in which an incumbent did not seek reelection.

Source: 1979-1984: *Statistical Abstract of the U.S., 1987,* 246; 1985-1986: Federal Election Commission, *Federal Election Commission Interim Report,* May 21, 1987, 67.

Questions

1. Nationally, turnout fell sharply with the 1920 election (Figure 3-1). What could account for this decline?

2. Around the turn of the century, southern turnout dropped sharply and has approached the levels attained in the 1890s only since the 1960s (Figure 3-2). What accounts for the drop and recovery?

3. Which four groups generally register and vote at the lowest rates (Table 3-1)? What might account for the gap in participation between these groups and others? What political implications might flow from these low participation rates?

4. Which states gave more than 65 percent of their popular vote in 1984 to Ronald Reagan (Table 3-2)? Which gave 45 percent or more to Walter Mondale? Which region is most supportive of Reagan? (Use the four regions as defined by the Census Bureau—see the Appendix.) Walter Mondale is from Minnesota. Did this have an effect on the vote in his home state and the surrounding area?

5. In the primaries in which John Glenn and Jesse Jackson both competed through March 13, each outdrew the other three times (Table 3-3), yet Glenn dropped out and Jackson stayed in the race. Give at least two possible reasons for this different reaction to their situations.

6. The Iowa caucus results differ in an obvious way from all the others (Table 3-4). What is this difference? How might you explain it? Is this explanation substantiated by the 1984 primary election results (Table 3-3)?

7. In some years the Democrats have had considerably more candidates than the Republicans, while in other years the Republicans have had more (Figure 3-3). What explains these differences? In 1972, 1980, and 1984, the incumbent president announced his candidacy relatively late. Were the incumbents uncertain about whether they would run?

8. Did Jimmy Carter in 1980 and Walter Mondale in 1984 receive more of their convention votes from caucus states or primary states (Table 3-5)?

9. What is the average difference between the Republican "vote" in the final Gallup survey and the Republican vote in the election (Table 3-6)? The Gallup organization has tried to improve its procedures since the disastrous (for its image) incorrect "call" in 1948. Does the evidence suggest an improvement?

10. Support for third-party candidates George Wallace in 1968 and John Anderson in 1980 came from very different parts of the electorate (Table 3-7). Describe their differing bases of support. In almost every election year, the lower the education level, the greater the support for the Democrats. What could explain this result?

11. How many times has the winning presidential candidate received a minority of the *two-party* popular vote (Table 3-8)? Which winning candidate received the smallest percentage of the *total* popular vote?

12. Using the U.S. Census Bureau definition of regions from the Appendix and Table 3-9, determine which region was the most Republican in presidential voting from 1896 to 1931 and from 1932 to 1964. Compared with its presidential level of support, was this region more or less Republican in its House voting (Table 3-10)?

13. Political scientists and historians speak of "realigning elections," elections in which there is a sharp shift in the partisanship or long-term voting habits of the electorate. What do the results of House elections in the last decade of the nineteenth century suggest about the timing of the realignment in that period (Table 3-11)?

14. Except for 1986, there is a perfect pattern in Table 3-12: House incumbents most often get more than 60 percent of the vote, incumbent governors least often. What might explain this pattern?

15. Which Democratic presidential candidate in 1984 raised the highest proportion of his funds from individual contributors (Table 3-13)? What was that proportion?

16. Did the average challenger or incumbent spend more in 1984 or 1986 (Table 3-14)? How much did the average House candidate spend in 1986? The average Senate candidate?

17. Did PACs give more money to incumbents or to challengers (Table 3-16)? Why? (Hint: see Table 3-12.)

18. PAC contributions to Senate campaigns increased by nearly 50 percent between 1983-1984 and 1985-1986 (Table 3-16). How much larger a proportion of campaign contributions did PACs give in 1985-1986 compared to 1983-1984 (Table 3-15)?

4

Political Parties

Political parties live and die by the numbers—numbers of supporters, candidates, contributors, and especially voters. Therefore, it is not surprising that a book of statistics on American politics contains a great deal of data about parties or that these data appear throughout the volume.

Parties can be profitably viewed from three different perspectives: parties in the electorate, parties in government, and parties as organizations. As Chapter 3 is devoted entirely to elections, and Chapter 5 includes considerable data about elements of voting (partisanship and party evaluations), in this chapter only a portion of the material is devoted to parties in the electorate, despite the overwhelming importance to parties of gathering votes. Although no sharp distinction is possible or intended, the emphasis here is on aspects of voting that relate more closely to parties as organizations. Thus, for example, a number of tables concern the topics of party-line versus split-ticket voting and partisan versus split outcomes (Tables 4-4 through 4-8). Such topics are useful for assessing the strength of parties and of partisanship.

The party-line voting tables draw on two kinds of data— aggregate data (about collectivities such as states and congressional districts) and individual data (about individual voters, chiefly drawn from sample surveys). Although the two are likely to indicate the same sort of conclusions, they are independent of one another and each tells something distinct. It is possible, for example, for there to be a large amount of split-ticket voting by individuals and yet a small number of split district outcomes. For example, a very large majority may support the Democratic candidate for governor and a much narrower majority support the Democratic candidate for president. Likewise, it is possible for many individuals to split their tickets and still have winning candidates from the same party; if those who split their tickets do so in opposite ways, they will offset each others' votes.

Many of the tables in Chapters 7 and 8 concern parties in government. Voting in Congress frequently takes on partisan tones, as does support for or opposition to the president. Party unity and presidential support scores therefore offer important perspectives on the continuing or changing significance of political parties. Like voting by the electorate, congressional voting is viewed from both individual and aggregate perspectives. How individual representatives and senators vote is important to their constituents and to organized interests, so publications and tabulations showing individual voting behavior have become widespread (see Tables 7-13 and 7-14). How unified party members are in their voting, the degree to which the parties oppose each other, and the extent to which there are other cohesive groups—such as the so-called Conservative Coalition of Republicans and southern Democrats—are all important analytically for understanding congressional behavior and practically for those who wish to influence congressional action (Tables 7-7 through 7-9 and Figure 7-2).

In this chapter the emphasis is on parties as organizations, beginning simply with their organizational identities (Table 4-1). The growth of presidential primaries is also documented (Table 4-9). Two additional topics are covered principally since the 1970s when data collection began in earnest. First, as is discussed further in Chapter 6, the establishment of the Federal Election Commission in 1973 has led to more extensive and more revealing data about expenditures (Tables 4-12 and 4-13). Second, just as surveys have expanded the kind of material available about voters, they have been used to provide insight into party elites, especially national convention delegates. The data that have been systematically collected are largely limited to demographic information (Table 4-10). And the information itself, plus the fact that it has been collected by multiple organizations, has led to less consistency than is desirable. Nevertheless, data about national convention delegates is likely to be collected again in 1988, with improvements in collection procedures.

It is fortunate, in any event, that some information is available about party elites. In part because of the decentralized nature of American parties, scholars only recently have begun systematically to study parties as organizations, especially at the national level. Consequently data are scarce; what is available are from limited time periods and a restricted range of localities. This systematic study has occurred just as Republican and Democratic national party organizations have responded to the declining importance of parties in the electorate by stepping up the services they provide to local and state party organizations in areas such as candidate recruitment, media consulting, polling information, and fund raising.

How parties fare in the altered context of American politics depends partially upon how parties as organizations respond to changes such as the growth of political action committees, increased campaign costs, and the pervasive reach and use of media, particularly television. In doing so, the parties may add to scholarly efforts to increase available information about their activities and organizational efforts. Ironically, the much-heralded decline of parties in the electorate may make parties as organizations a growth area of data collection over the next decade.

Figure 4-1 American Political Parties Since 1789

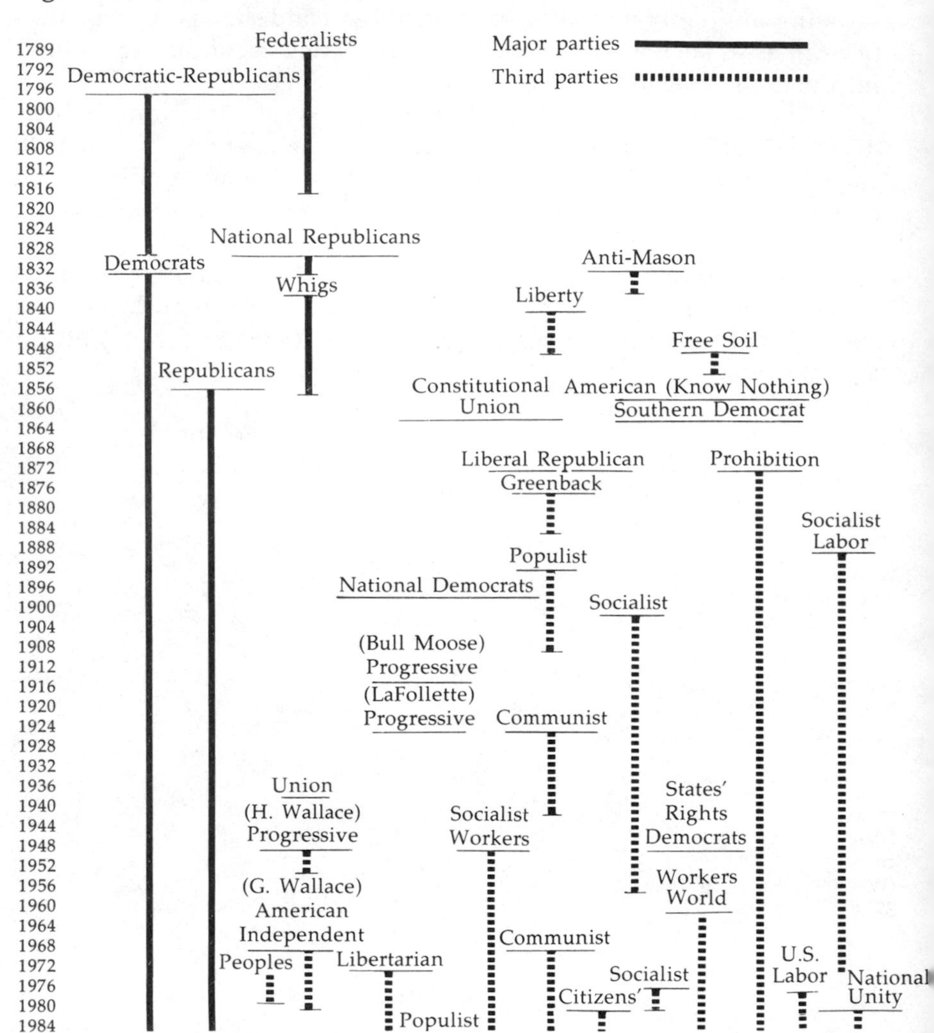

Note: The chart indicates the years parties either ran presidential candidates or held national conventions. The lifespan for many political parties can only be approximated because parties existed at the state or local level before they ran candidates in presidential elections, and parties continued to exist at local levels long after they ceased running presidential candidates.

Source: Congressional Quarterly, *Congressional Quarterly's Guide to U.S. Elections,* 2d ed. (Washington, D.C.: Congressional Quarterly, 1985), 224.

Table 4-1 Party Competition: The Presidency, 1968-1984

Number of times Republican presidential candidate carried the state (based on electoral votes)					
0	1	2	3	4	5
District of Columbia	Minnesota	Georgia	Alabama	Connecticut	Alaska
		Hawaii	Arkansas	Delaware	Arizona
		Maryland	Louisiana	Florida	California
		Massachusetts	Mississippi	Kentucky	Colorado
		Rhode Island	New York	Maine	Idaho
		West Virginia	Pennsylvania	Michigan	Illinois
			Texas	Missouri	Indiana
				North Carolina	Iowa
				Ohio	Kansas
				South Carolina	Montana
				Tennessee	Nebraska
				Washington	Nevada
				Wisconsin	New Hampshire
					New Jersey
					New Mexico
					North Dakota
					Oklahoma
					Oregon
					South Dakota
					Utah
					Vermont
					Virginia
					Wyoming

Source: Compiled by the editors from Richard M. Scammon and Alice V. McGillivray, comps. and eds., *America Votes 16: A Handbook of Contemporary American Election Statistics* (Washington, D.C.: Elections Research Center, Congressional Quarterly, 1985), 31, 33, 35, 37, 41.

Table 4-2 Party Competition in the States, 1968-1986

Percentage of Republican wins[a]				
0-20	21-40	41-60	61-80	81-100
Alabama	Alaska	Delaware	Colorado	Arizona
Arkansas	Montana	Illinois	Idaho	Indiana
California	Nebraska[b]	Maine	Iowa	New Hampshire
Connecticut	New Jersey	New York	Kansas	
Florida	Ohio		North Dakota	
Georgia	Oregon		South Dakota	
Hawaii	Pennsylvania		Utah	
Kentucky	Washington		Vermont	
Louisiana	Wisconsin		Wyoming	
Maryland				
Massachusetts				
Michigan				
Minnesota				
Mississippi				
Missouri				
Nevada				
New Mexico				
North Carolina				
Oklahoma				
Rhode Island				
South Carolina				
Tennessee				
Texas				
Virgina				
West Virginia				

[a] The governorship, control of the lower chamber, and control of the upper chamber are figured separately. That is, if in a given year the Republicans won the governorship and control of one chamber, they had 66.7 percent of the wins.
[b] Results are for the governorship only because the legislature is nonpartisan.

Source: Calculated by the authors. 1968-1984: Republican National Committee, *The 1985 Republican Almanac: State Political Profiles* (Washington, D.C.: Republican National Committee, 1985); 1985-1986: *National Journal* (December 7, 1985), 2810, 2818, (November 8, 1986), 2714, 2717.

Table 4-3 Party Competition by Region, 1896-1984 (percent)

	Party system			
Region/office	1860-1895	1896-1931	1932-1965	1966-1984
New England				
President	85.2	85.5	53.7	66.7
Governor	72.9	85.9	60.8	37.5
U.S. representative	76.7	82.7	57.7	34.9
U.S. senator	[a]	85.7	59.7	44.7
Middle Atlantic				
President	38.9	88.9	47.2	61.1
Governor	31.9	66.0	56.8	57.9
U.S. representative	53.1	63.4	52.8	39.8
U.S. senator	[a]	76.7	64.7	50.0
Midwest				
President	77.8	84.4	44.4	78.3
Governor	73.2	78.9	45.6	72.0
U.S. representative	55.8	73.5	57.1	52.3
U.S. senator	[a]	81.6	51.6	38.2
Plains				
President	88.9	77.8	57.4	78.6
Governor	86.7	73.6	64.1	42.9
U.S. representative	82.1	83.3	73.7	59.3
U.S. senator	[a]	76.2	73.1	50.0
South				
President	18.4	6.1	15.8	53.2
Governor	17.1	2.9	0.0	25.8
U.S. representative	17.7	4.0	4.5	27.6
U.S. senator	[a]	0.0	0.7	32.9
Border South				
President	8.6	56.8	22.2	56.0
Governor	14.0	38.6	16.7	34.8
U.S. representative	15.6	36.7	18.5	25.4
U.S. senator	[a]	41.2	24.6	38.2
Rocky Mountain				
President	73.3	57.8	35.2	91.7
Governor	63.0	44.7	40.0	30.0
U.S. representative	68.3	59.4	31.8	55.0
U.S. senator	[a]	44.3	30.5	56.9
Pacific Coast				
President	75.0	75.0	37.5	82.6
Governor	42.9	55.6	54.8	53.8
U.S. representative	57.1	63.1	38.6	38.1
U.S. senator	[a]	66.7	37.5	47.1

Note: Table entries are the percentages of all elections won by Republicans. For composition of regions, see Appendix Table A-3.

[a] Direct election of U.S. senators began after passage of the Seventeenth Amendment in 1913.

Source: Inter-University Consortium for Political and Social Research, "Candidate and Constituency Statistics of Elections in the United States, 1788-1984," machine-readable data file. (Ann Arbor, Mich.: Inter-University Consortium for Political and Social Research, 1986).

Table 4-4 Strength of Party Identification and the Presidential Vote, 1952-1984 (percent)

Year/candidate	*Strong Democrat*	*Weak Democrat*	*Independent Democrat*	*Independent*	*Independent Republican*	*Weak Republican*	*Strong Republican*	*Total*
1952								
Stevenson	84	62	61	20	7	7	2	42
Eisenhower	16	38	39	80	93	93	98	58
1956								
Stevenson	85	63	67	17	7	7	1	40
Eisenhower	15	37	33	83	93	93	99	60
1960								
Kennedy	91	72	90	46	12	13	2	49
Nixon	9	28	10	54	88	87	98	51
1964								
Johnson	95	82	90	77	25	43	10	68
Goldwater	5	18	10	23	75	57	90	32
1968								
Humphrey	92	68	64	30	5	11	3	46
Nixon	8	32	36	70	95	89	97	54
1972								
McGovern	73	49	61	30	13	9	3	36
Nixon	27	51	39	70	87	91	97	64
1976								
Carter	92	75	76	43	14	22	3	51
Ford	8	25	24	57	86	78	97	49
1980								
Carter	89	65	60	26	13	5	5	44
Reagan	11	35	40	74	87	95	95	56
1984								
Mondale	89	68	79	28	7	6	3	42
Reagan	11	32	21	72	93	94	97	58

Note: Results are from surveys in which voters are asked which party they identify with and who they voted for. The exact question is as follows: "Generally speaking, do you conider yourself a Republican, a Democrat, an Independent, or what?" If Republican or Democrat: "Would you consider yourself a strong (R/D) or a not very strong (R/D)?" If Idependent or other: "Do you think of yourself as closer to the Republican or Democratic party?"

Sources: 1952-1976: Warren E. Miller, Arthur H. Miller, and Edward J. Schneider, *American National Election Studies Data Sourcebook, 1952-1978* (Cambridge, Mass.: Harvard University Press, 1980), 334; updated by the editors from National Election Studies data.

Table 4-5 Party-line Voting in Presidential and Congressional Elections, 1956-1986 (percent)

	Presidential elections			*U.S. Senate elections*			*U.S. House elections*		
Year	Party-line voters[a]	Defectors[b]	Independents	Party-line voters[a]	Defectors[b]	Independents	Party-line voters[a]	Defectors[b]	Independents
1952	77	18	5	79	16	5	80	15	5
1956	76	15	9	79	12	9	82	9	9
1958				85	9	5	84	11	5
1960	79	13	8	77	15	8	80	12	8
1962				—	—	—	83	12	6
1964	79	15	5	78	16	6	79	15	5
1966				—	—	—	76	16	8
1968	69	23	9	74	19	7	74	19	7
1970				78	12	10	76	16	8
1972	67	25	8	69	22	9	75	17	8
1974				73	19	8	74	18	8
1976	74	15	11	70	19	11	72	19	9
1978				71	20	9	69	22	9
1980	70	22	8	71	21	8	69	23	8
1982				77	17	6	76	17	6
1984	81	11	8	72	20	9	70	23	7
1986				76	20	4	72	22	6

Note: "—" indicates not available. The base for percentages is all voters.

[a] Party identifiers who vote for the candidate of their party. Party identification is based on surveys in which voters are asked which party they identify with (see Table 4-4 for exact question). "Independent partisans," or so-called "leaners," are included here as party-line voters or defectors.

[b] Party identifiers who vote for the candidate of the other party.

Sources: Norman J. Ornstein et al., eds., *Vital Statistics on Congress, 1987-1988* (Washington, D.C.: Congressional Quarterly, 1987), 65; 1952 calculated by the editors from the National Election Studies data set.

Table 4-6 Partisan Division of Governors and State Legislatures

	Governor			Legislature				
				Upper house		Lower house		
State	Name	Party	Next up for reelection	*Democrats*	*Republicans*	*Democrats*	*Republicans*	Next up for reelection
Alabama	Guy Hunt	R[a]	1990	30	5	89	16	1990
Alaska	Steve Cowper	D	1990	8	11	24	16	1988[b]
Arizona	Evan Mecham	R[a]	1990	11	19	24	36	1988
Arkansas	Bill Clinton	D	1990	31	4	91	9	1988[b]
California	George Deukmejian	R	1990	24	15	44	36	1988[b]
Colorado	Roy Romer	D	1990	10	25	24	41	1988[b]
Connecticut	William A. O'Neill	D	1990	25	11	93	57	1988
Delaware	Michael N. Castle	R	1988	13	8	19	22	1988[b]
Florida	Bob Martinez	R[a]	1990	25	15	75	45	1988[b]
Georgia	Joe Frank Harris	D	1990	47	10	153	27	1988
Hawaii	John Waihee	D	1990	20	5	40	11	1988[b]
Idaho	Cecil D. Andrus	D	1990	14	26	20	64	1988
Illinois	James R. Thompson	R	1990	31	28	67	51	1988[b]
Indiana	Robert D. Orr	R	1988	20	30	48	52	1988[b]
Iowa	Terry Branstead	R	1990	30	20	58	42	1988[b]
Kansas	Mike Hayden	R[a]	1990	16	24	51	74	1988
Kentucky	Wallace Wilkinson	D	1991	29	9	72	28	1988[b]
Louisiana	Buddy Roemer	D	1991	87	18	34	5	1991
Maine	John McKernan	R[a]	1990	20	15	86	65	1988
Maryland	William Schaefer	D	1990	40	7	124	17	1990
Massachusetts	Michael Dukakis	D	1990	32	8	127	33	1988
Michigan	James Blanchard	D	1990	18	20	64	46	1988[c]
Minnesota	Rudy Perpich	D	1990	46	20	81	51	1988[c]
Mississippi	Ray Mabus	D	1991	45	7	113	9	1991
Missouri	John Ashcroft	R	1988	21	13	111	52	1988[b]

Montana	Ted Schwinden	D	1988	25	25	49	51	1988[b]
Nebraska	Kay Orr	R[a]	1990	[d]	[d]	[d]	[d]	1988[b]
Nevada	Richard Bryan	D	1990	9	12	29	13	1988[b]
New Hampshire	John Sununu	R	1988	5	14	133	263	1988
New Jersey	Thomas Kean	R	1989	24	16	38	42	1990
New Mexico	Garrey Carruthers	R[a]	1990	21	21	47	23	1988
New York	Mario Cuomo	D	1990	26	35	93	57	1988
North Carolina	James Martin	R	1988	40	10	84	36	1988
North Dakota	George Sinner	D	1988	27	26	45	61	1988[b]
Ohio	Richard Celeste	D	1990	15	18	60	39	1988[b]
Oklahoma	Henry Bellmon	R[a]	1990	31	15	70	31	1988[b]
Oregon	Neil Goldschmidt	D[a]	1990	17	13	31	29	1988[b]
Pennsylvania	Robert P. Casey	D[a]	1990	23	27	103	100	1988[b]
Rhode Island	Edward DiPrete	R	1988	38	12	80	20	1988
South Carolina	Carroll Campbell, Jr.	R[a]	1990	34	12	89	33	1988
South Dakota	George Mickelson	R	1990	10	25	22	48	1988
Tennessee	Ned McWherter	D[a]	1990	23	10	61	38	1988[b]
Texas	William P. Clements	R[a]	1990	25	6	94	56	1988[b]
Utah	Norman Bangerter	R	1988	8	21	27	48	1988[b]
Vermont	Madeleine Kunin	D	1988	19	11	76	74	1988
Virginia	Gerald Baliles	D	1989	31	9	65	33	1990
Washington	Booth Gardner	D	1988	24	25	61	37	1988[b]
West Virginia	Arch Moore, Jr.	R	1988	27	7	78	22	1988[b]
Wisconsin	Tommy Thompson	R[a]	1990	19	14	55	43	1988[b]
Wyoming	Mike Sullivan	D	1990	11	19	20	44	1988[b]

Note: As of January 1988, except in Louisiana, where Roemer was scheduled to be sworn in March 14 to succeed Edwin W. Edwards. Legislative divisions reflect seated members. Some vacancies exist.

[a] Change in party control from last election.

[b] Upper house elections are staggered so only some legislators are up for election in the year indicated.

[c] Lower house only, upper house in 1990.

[d] Nebraska's state legislature is nonpartisan and unicameral.

Sources: *Congressional Quarterly Weekly Report* (1986), 2260, 2894, 2895, (1988), 4; Council of State Governments, *The Book of the States, 1986-87* (Lexington, Ky.: Council of State Governments, 1986), 179-180; state legislative divisions: *National Journal* (November 14, 1987), 2920.

Table 4-7 Split-Ticket Voting, 1952-1984 (percent)

Year	*President-House*	*Senate-House*	*State-local*
1952	12	9	27
1956	16	10	30
1960	14	9	27
1964	15	18	41
1968	26	22	48
1972	30	23	56
1976	25	23	—
1980	34	31	59
1984	25	20	52

Note: "—" indicates not available. Entries are the percentages of voters who "split" their ticket by supporting candidates of different parties for the offices indicated. The state-local figure is based on a general question: "Did you vote for other state and local offices? Did you vote a straight ticket, or did you vote for candidates from different parties?"

Source: Martin Wattenberg, "The Hollow Realignment," *Public Opinion Quarterly* 51 (1987): 66.

Table 4-8 Split District Outcomes: Presidential and House Voting, 1900-1984

Year	*Total number of districts*[a]	*Number of districts with split results*[b]	*Percentage of total*
1900	295	10	3.4
1904	310	5	1.6
1908	314	21	6.7
1912	333	84	25.2
1916	333	35	10.5
1920	344	11	3.2
1924	356	42	11.8
1928	359	68	18.9
1932	355	50	14.1
1936	361	51	14.1
1940	362	53	14.6
1944	367	41	11.2
1948	422	90	21.3
1952	435	84	19.3
1956	435	130	29.9
1960	437	114	26.1
1964	435	145	33.3
1968	435	139	32.0
1972	435	192	44.1
1976	435	124	28.5
1980	435	143	32.8
1984	435	196	45.0

[a] Before 1952 complete data are not available on every congressional district.
[b] Congressional districts carried by a presidential candidate of one party and a House candidate of another party.

Sources: Ornstein, *Vital Statistics on Congress, 1987-1988,* 62.

Table 4-9 Presidential Primaries, 1912-1984

	Democratic party			*Republican party*		
Year	Number of primaries	Votes cast	Percentage of delegates selected through primaries	Number of primaries	Votes cast	Percentage of delegates selected through primaries
1912	12	974,775	32.9	13	2,261,240	41.7
1916	20	1,187,691	53.5	20	1,923,374	58.9
1920	16	571,671	44.6	20	3,186,248	57.8
1924	14	763,858	35.5	17	3,525,185	45.3
1928	17	1,264,220	42.2	16	4,110,288	44.9
1932	16	2,952,933	40.0	14	2,346,996	37.7
1936	14	5,181,808	36.5	12	3,319,810	37.5
1940	13	4,468,631	35.8	13	3,227,875	38.8
1944	14	1,867,609	36.7	13	2,271,605	38.7
1948	14	2,151,865	36.3	12	2,635,255	36.0
1952	15	4,928,006	38.7	13	7,801,413	39.0
1956	19	5,832,592	42.7	19	5,828,272	44.8
1960	16	5,686,664	38.3	15	5,537,967	38.6
1964	16	6,247,435	45.7	17	5,935,339	45.6
1968	15	7,535,069	40.2	15	4,473,551	38.1
1972	23	15,993,965	65.3	22	6,188,281	56.8
1976	30	16,052,652	76.0	29	10,374,125	71.0
1980	35	18,747,825	71.8	36	12,690,451	76.0
1984	30	18,009,217	62.1	25	6,575,651	71.0

Sources: Votes cast and number of primaries: Congressional Quarterly, *Congressional Quarterly's Guide to U.S. Elections*, 387-441; delegates selected 1912-1976: Christopher F. Arterton, "Campaign Organizations Confront the Media-Political Environment," in *Race for the Presidency: The Media and the Nomination Process*, ed. James David Barber (Englewood Cliffs, N.J.: Prentice-Hall, 1978), 7 (copyright © The American Assembly); 1980: *Congressional Quarterly Weekly Report* (1980), 1873; 1984: Congressional Quarterly, *Elections '84* (Washington, D.C.: Congressional Quarterly, 1984), 68-70.

Table 4-10 Profile of National Convention Delegates, 1944-1984 (percent)

	1944		*1968*		*1972*		*1976*		*1980*		*1984*	
	D	R	D	R	D	R	D	R	D	R	D	R
Women	11	9	13	27	40	29	33	31	49	29	51	46
Education												
High school or less	24	23	—	—	9	7	9	7	12	9	11	12
Some college	18	18	—	—	26	27	18	27	23	26	18	25
College graduate	12	16	19	—	22	19	13	19	26	22	20	28
More than college	46	41	44	34	41	45	56	40	40	41	51	35
Age (average)	52	54	49	49	42[a]	—	43	48	44[a]	49[a]	44	51
Black	—	—	5	2	15	4	11	3	15	3	18	4
Profession												
Lawyer	38	37	28	22	12	—	16	15	13	15	17	14
Union leader	2	—	4	—	5	—	6	—	5	—	6	—
Union member	—	—	—	—	16	—	21	—	27	—	27	5
Attending first convention	63	63	67	66	83	78	80	78	87	84	71	66
Religion												
Protestant	—	—	—	—	42	75	47	73	47	72	53	74
Catholic	—	—	—	—	26	—	34	18	37	22	32	22
Jewish	—	—	—	—	9	—	9	3	8	3	9	3
Ideology												
Liberal	—	—	—	—	54	12	40	3	46	2	50	2
Moderate	—	—	—	—	39	35	47	45	42	36	42	22
Conservative	—	—	—	—	7	53	8	48	6	58	5	76
Party office holder	—	—	—	—	72	92	63	85	60	60	42	62
Governor[b]	—	—	23	24	17	16	16	9	23	13	—	—
U.S. senator[b]	—	—	39	21	15	22	11	22	8	26	28	27
U.S. representative[b]	—	—	78	58	31	33	41	52	37	64	179	73

Note: "—" indicates not available.

[a] Median age.

[b] Absolute numbers, not percentages.

Sources: 1944, 1968: Barbara Farah, "Delegate Polls: 1944-1984," *Public Opinion* 7 (4) (1984): 43-45; 1972, 1980: Warren J. Mitofsky and Martin Plissner, "The Making of the Delegates, 1968-1980," *Public Opinion,* 3 (5) (1980): 37-43 (reprinted with permission of American Enterprise Institute for Public Policy Research); 1976: Farah, "Delegate Polls," and Mitofsky and Plissner, "The Making of the Delegates"; 1984: Mitofsky and Plissner, "The Making of the Delegates," and *New York Times,* July 15, 1984, 26 (copyright © 1984 by the New York Times Company, reprinted by permission); additional data for all years from *Congressional Quarterly Weekly Report* (1984), 1745, 2074; *Washington Post,* August 18, 1972, A1, August 15, 1976, A6, July 15, 1984, A16; William Crotty and John S. Jackson III, *Presidential Primaries and Nominations* (Washington, D.C.: CQ Press, 1985), 114; and Warren E. Miller and M. Kent Jennings, *Parties in Transition: A Longitudinal Study of Party Elites and Party Supporters* (New York: Russell Sage, 1986), 262-264 (copyright © 1986 by the Russell Sage Foundation, reprinted by permission). These sources overlap in their coverage and their results sometimes differ.

Table 4-11 Size of National Party Conventions, 1932-1988

	Delegates	
Year	Democrats	Republicans
1932	1,154	1,154
1936	1,100	1,003
1940	1,100	1,000
1944	1,176	1,056
1948	1,234	1,094
1952	1,230	1,206
1956	1,372	1,323
1960	1,521	1,331
1964	2,295	1,308
1968	2,522	1,333
1972	3,016	1,348
1976	3,008	2,259
1980	3,331	1,994
1984	3,933	2,235
1988	4,161	2,277

Sources: Democrats, 1932-1972: Richard C. Bain and Judith H. Parris, *Convention Decisions and Voting Records,* 2d ed. (Washington, D.C.: Brookings, 1973), Appendix C; 1976-1984: *Congressional Quarterly Weekly Report* (1976), 1873, (1980), 1879, (1984), 1629; 1988: Democratic National Committee; Republicans (all years): Republican National Committee.

Table 4-12 Financial Activity of the National Political Parties, 1977-1986 (millions)

Party	*1977-1978*	*1979-1980*	*1981-1982*	*1983-1984*	*1985-1986*
Democrat					
Raised	$26.4	$37.2	$39.3	$98.5	$61.8
Spent	26.9	35.0	40.1	97.4	62.7
Contributions	1.8	1.7	1.7	2.6	1.6
Coordinated expenditures[a]	0.4	4.9	3.3	9.0	6.4
Republican					
Raised	84.5	169.5	215.0	297.9	252.4
Spent	85.9	161.8	214.0	300.8	254.2
Contributions	4.5	4.5	5.6	4.9	3.5
Coordinated expenditures[a]	4.3	12.4	14.3	20.1	14.3

Note: Building funds and state and local election spending are not reported to the Federal Election Commission.

[a] Coordinated expenditures are governed under U.S. Code, Title 2, sec. 441a(d). Under this provision, House candidates may receive up to $5,000 from a national party committee and another $5,000 from a state or local party committee in direct contributions for each election the candidate contests. In a normal cycle, including one primary and one general election, the limit is $10,000. Senate candidates may receive up to $17,500 for a full election cycle in direct contributions from their party committees.

Party committees are also allowed to spend money on behalf of federal candidates, in addition to the money they may contribute directly. This spending may be coordinated with a candidate.

The limits on 441a(d) expenditures are as follows: (a) for Senate candidates and for House candidates from states with only one House district, two 1975 cents times the voting age population, or $20,000 in 1975 dollars adjusted for inflation, whichever is greater; (b) for all other House candidates, $10,000 in 1975 dollars adjusted for inflation. State parties are allowed to spend equal amounts on behalf of congressional candidates, and court decisions permit state and local parties to designate a national party committee as its agent for these expenditures.

Combining state and national party contribution and 441a(d) expenditure limits, the maximum amount a House candidate could receive from party committees in 1982 was $66,880. Senate limits ranged from a low of $101,260 to a high of $1,399,248, in California.

Source: Federal Election Commission, "Political Party Figures for '86 Election," press release, May 31, 1987, 1.

Table 4-13 Party Contributions and Coordinated Expenditures by Office and Party, 1976-1986

	Senate		*House*	
Year/party	Contributions	Expenditures	Contributions	Expenditures
1976				
Democrats	$468,795	$4,359	$1,465,629	$500
Republicans	930,034	113,976	3,658,310	329,583
1978				
Democrats	466,683	229,218	1,262,298	72,892
Republicans	703,204	2,723,880	3,621,104	1,297,079
1980				
Democrats	480,464	1,132,912	1,025,989	256,346
Republicans	677,004	5,434,758	3,498,323	2,203,748
1982				
Democrats	579,337	2,265,197	1,052,286	694,321
Republicans	600,221	8,715,761	4,720,959	5,293,260
1984				
Democrats	441,467	3,947,731	1,280,672	1,774,452
Republicans	590,922	6,518,415	4,060,120	6,190,309
1986				
Democrats	561,519	4,117,734	1,020,539	1,864,967
Republicans	757,165	10,077,756	2,611,103	4,204,736

Note: Includes direct contributions made by party committees to congressional candidates and coordinated expenditures made on their behalf.

Source: Ornstein, *Vital Statistics on Congress, 1987-1988,* 102.

Questions

1. Which third party survived the longest (Figure 4-1)?

2. Using the Guide to References for Political Statistics, find a source of third party votes for president. Which third party received the greatest percentage of the popular vote in an election? Why?

3. Which party has dominated presidential elections since 1968 (Table 4-1)? Which party has dominated state elections since 1968 (Table 4-2)? What does this imply about voting behavior during this period?

4. Lyndon Johnson in 1964 was the first southerner to be elected president since before the Civil War. Why? Table 4-3 should help.

5. What does Table 4-4 suggest about the significance of party as a voting cue?

6. Compare the voting of weak and independent Democrats and of weak and independent Republicans (Table 4-4). What does this suggest about the strength of party identification among weak versus independent partisans?

7. Is the proportion of defectors consistently greater in House voting than in presidential voting (Table 4-5)? In the presidential election of 1972, are the defectors most likely to have been Republican identifiers voting for McGovern or Democratic identifiers voting for Nixon? What about 1984—Republicans for Mondale or Democrats for Reagan? What about 1960—Republicans for Kennedy or Democrats for Nixon?

8. In which states are the legislative parties fairly evenly matched in at least one house in 1987, in other words, states in which neither party has more than 55 percent of the legislators (Table 4-6)? In which state legislatures is one party completely dominant, in other words, states in which one party has more than two-thirds of the legislators in both houses? How does this "snapshot" of one aspect of partisan competition compare with the picture presented in Table 4-2?

9. What percentage of U.S. voters supported candidates of different parties for president and U.S. House of Representatives before the

mid-1960s (Table 4-7)? Since the mid-1960s? What does this difference suggest about the significance of party as a voting cue?

10. How can it be that only 15 percent of the voters split their ticket in presidential and House voting but in one-third of the districts candidates of different parties led the congressional and presidential voting, as happened in 1964 (Tables 4-7 and 4-8)? Explain your answer with a hypothetical example.

11. Presidential primaries are a more important part of the nomination process now than years ago. When do you think they became more important (Table 4-9)? Note that between 1968 and 1972 the number of Democratic primaries rose by less than 50 percent but that the number of votes cast more than doubled. Give two hypotheses that might explain this combination of results. Note that turnout in the Republican primaries was greater in 1976 than in 1984. Why? (Hint: see Figure 3-3.)

12. Contrast the ideology of Democratic and Republican national convention delegates (Table 4-10). Compare the delegates' ideology with that of the nation's population (Table 5-3).

13. Speculate on why the political parties have increased the size of national party conventions in the past two decades (Table 4-11) and why the Democrats have tended to have larger conventions than Republicans.

14. Which party raised the most money for its candidates between 1977 and 1986 (Table 4-12)? Has the ratio of the dollars raised by Republicans to dollars raised by Democrats increased steadily over the period shown?

15. In 1986 the Republican party gave about $2.5 million to its House candidates, far less than in previous years (Table 4-13). At the same time, the party increased its contributions to Senate candidates. Why? (Hint: Table 3-11 may help.)

5

Public Opinion

Public opinion data are everywhere. They are perhaps most prominent in preelection polls showing who is ahead and who is behind, but they are more important and more often used as guides by candidates and officeholders about what the public thinks and how it would react to changes in public policies. Surveys are also used, in a more partisan way, by politicians, journalists, and interest groups to support their positions. And, in a slightly different form, they are even more widely used by advertisers and manufacturers to gauge consumer reactions to new products and services. Reflecting this frequent and varied use, this book is interspersed with public opinion data. The present chapter includes what might be called general perspectives on public opinion.

Figures 5-1, 5-2, and Tables 5-1 through 5-4 cover two of the most frequently cited components of public opinion—partisanship and political ideology. These characteristics merit emphasis due to their practical political significance. They are of interest not only to those who wish to understand scientifically why people behave as they do. They also attract the attention of those who analyze long-term political and social trends, and are of intense interest to those who track day-to-day politics.

From another perspective, these results are important because they illustrate the reliability and validity of public opinion polling as well as the hazards of gauging personal opinions. Figures 5-1 and 5-2, showing self-proclaimed party identification, are reasonably similar for the period they jointly cover. If public opinion data were totally unreliable, as some contend, such similarity would be unlikely. Moreover, these figures illustrate two aspects of reliability and validity. First, polling as few as fifteen hundred people tells something very real about the entire population; two separate organizations, as represented in Figures 5-1 and 5-2, would not obtain such similarity over several decades of interviewing if the results represented only those actually interviewed. (Of course, one must choose the fifteen hundred respondents according to scientific sampling procedures, as do all the major polling organizations.) Second, poll results are not completely dependent on exact question wording. The Gallup question focuses on the immediate situation ("In politics, as of today ..."), while the National Election Studies question is broader ("Generally speaking ..."), suggesting that the Gallup question might pick up more short-term fluctuations in partisanship. Yet the results are somewhat similar.

At the same time, differences between the two series indicate that we cannot consider one a mere clone of the other. The National Election Studies surveys probe those who claim to be independents to determine whether they lean toward one party or the other. The responses to this probe as well as other evidence (Table 4-4) raise the question of whether independents are really closet partisans. How we answer that question, as the contrast between the two plots in Figure 5-1 shows, has major implications for conclusions about the relative strengths of the parties. As has been emphasized in earlier introductions, even simple data descriptions involve interpretation.

Because surveys are not exact counts of the whole population, "sampling error" is often reported to convey the range within which the true population result lies. For example, results are said to be accurate to within plus or minus 3 percent. Yet even with greater precision (achieved by increasing the size of the sample), survey results still require interpretation. Suppose one could ask every American adult simultaneously whether he or she was a Democrat, an independent, or a Republican. There would then be no sampling error; because everyone was asked, the information would describe the entire U.S. population at that particular time. But that returns us to an equally vexing question: What does it mean to be an independent?

The "don't know" and "no opinion" responses to the liberal/conservative questions (Tables 5-3 and 5-4)—and in the other public opinion tables—illustrate a similar point. Whether pollsters ask about a general position or a specific issue, some proportion of the sample—often as many as 15 percent and sometimes many more—respond "don't know." It is not immediately apparent how to interpret such responses; some people have information about the subject matter but no opinion, some have no information and no opinion, and a few have no information but have an opinion anyway—and the pollster's decision about how to treat such responses can make a large difference. For example, in a preelection poll, should a pollster assume that those who have not yet chosen whom to support will eventually (1) split their votes between candidates in similar proportions as those who have already decided, (2) not vote, (3) divide evenly between the candidates, or (4) overwhelmingly support a particular candidate?

For public officials seeking guidance on public sentiment, no simple reading suffices because they must assess intensity as well as direction. Those seeking a theoretical understanding of politics face the same problem. For example, although more than public opinion accounted for the outcome, consider the Senate rejection of Judge Robert Bork's nomination to the Supreme Court (Table 9-4). Polls showed the public almost evenly divided on the matter, with a slight edge to those opposing the nomination. Such a close balance was misleading. Deeper political meaning turned on the intensity of those views. One senator said, "If you vote against Bork, those in favor of him will be mad at you for a week. But if you vote for him, those who don't like him will be mad at you for the rest of their lives." Understanding the importance of public opinion in politics requires more than a simple nose count. The salience of an opinion to the person holding it also counts.

In addition, a particular survey result usually tells little in isolation. The soundest interpretations depend upon several surveys stretching over time, often over a period of years. Consider the decline and budding recovery in public confidence in government (Figure 5-8). The confidence level at a particular time is a mere point, difficult or impossible to interpret. That point, when viewed with comparable points from similar surveys over the years, indicates a trend—decline, upsurge, constancy, whatever. Consequently, reports of public opinion increasingly emphasize long time series, as we do here and in other chapters (Figures 5-3 through 5-7). Such time series data can be usefully supplemented by cross-sections (Tables 5-2 and 5-4); such within-survey contrasts convey whether and how groups differ in attitudes.

A final note. Even a firm understanding of public opinion can be contradicted by events, as one cannot blindly equate opinion with behavior. The growth of racial tolerance in the South, such as it is, is a telling counterpoint to a political atmosphere formerly committed to white supremacy. As one respondent, a segregationist, told a pollster in the mid-1960s: "You asked me what I favored, not what I will accept graciously, not what I thought was right." [1]

Note

1. Donald R. Matthews and James W. Prothro, *Negroes and the New Southern Politics* (New York: Harcourt, Brace & World, 1966), 363.

Table 5-1 Partisan Identification, National Election Studies, 1952-1986 (percent)

	1952	*1954*	*1956*	*1958*	*1960*	*1962*	*1964*	*1966*	*1968*	*1970*	*1972*	*1974*	*1976*	*1978*	*1980*	*1982*	*1984*	*1986*
Strong Democrat	22	22	21	27	20	23	27	18	20	20	15	18	15	15	18	20	17	18
Weak Democrat	25	26	23	22	25	23	25	28	25	24	26	21	25	24	23	24	20	22
Independent Democrat	10	9	6	7	6	7	9	9	10	10	11	13	12	14	11	11	11	10
Independent	6	7	9	7	10	8	8	12	11	13	13	15	15	14	13	11	11	12
Independent Republican	7	6	8	5	7	6	6	7	9	8	11	9	10	10	10	8	12	11
Weak Republican	14	14	14	17	14	16	14	15	15	15	13	14	14	13	14	14	15	15
Strong Republican	14	13	15	11	16	12	11	10	10	9	10	8	9	8	9	10	12	10
Apolitical	3	4	4	4	3	4	1	1	1	1	1	3	1	3	2	2	2	2
Total	100	100	100	100	100	100	100	100	100	100	100	100	100	100	100	100	100	100
Number of interviews	1,784	1,130	1,757	1,808	1,911	1,287	1,550	1,278	1,553	1,501	2,694	2,505	2,850	2,283	1,613	1,418	2,236	2,166

Note: Question: "Generally speaking, do you consider yourself a Republican, a Democrat, an Independent, or what?" If Republican or Democrat: "Would you call yourself a strong (R/D) or a not very strong (R/D)?" If Independent or other: "Do you think of yourself as closer to the Republican or Democratic party?"

Sources: Warren E. Miller, Arthur H. Miller, and Edward J. Schneider, *American National Election Studies Data Sourcebook, 1952-1978* (Cambridge, Mass.: Harvard University Press, 1980), 81, and codebooks for such studies since 1978.

Figure 5-1 Partisan Identification, National Election Studies, 1952-1986

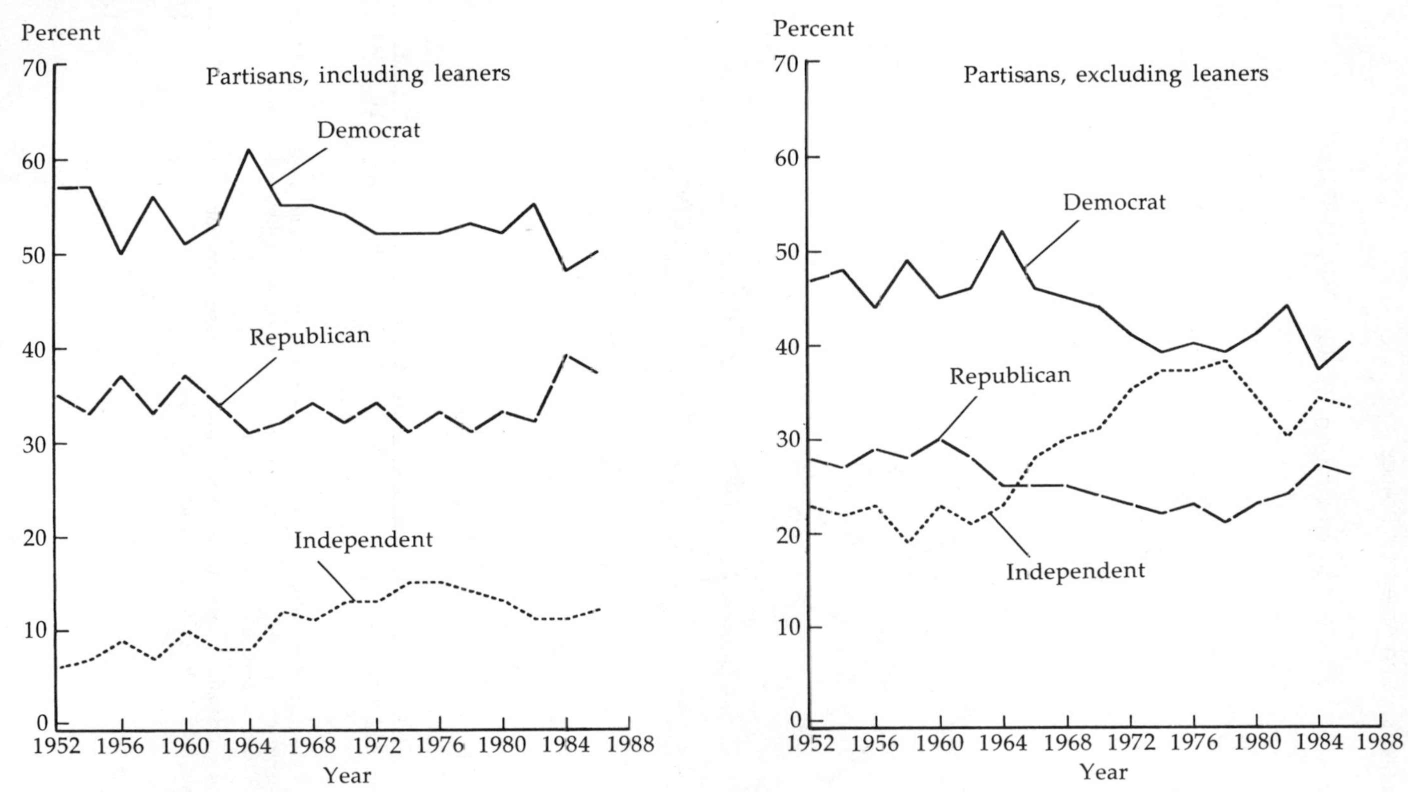

Note: See Table 5-1 for question. "Leaners" are independents who consider themselves closer to one party.

Source: Successive volumes of National Election Studies codebooks.

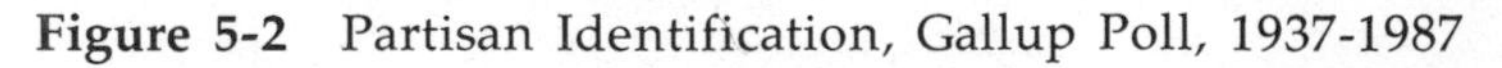

Figure 5-2 Partisan Identification, Gallup Poll, 1937-1987

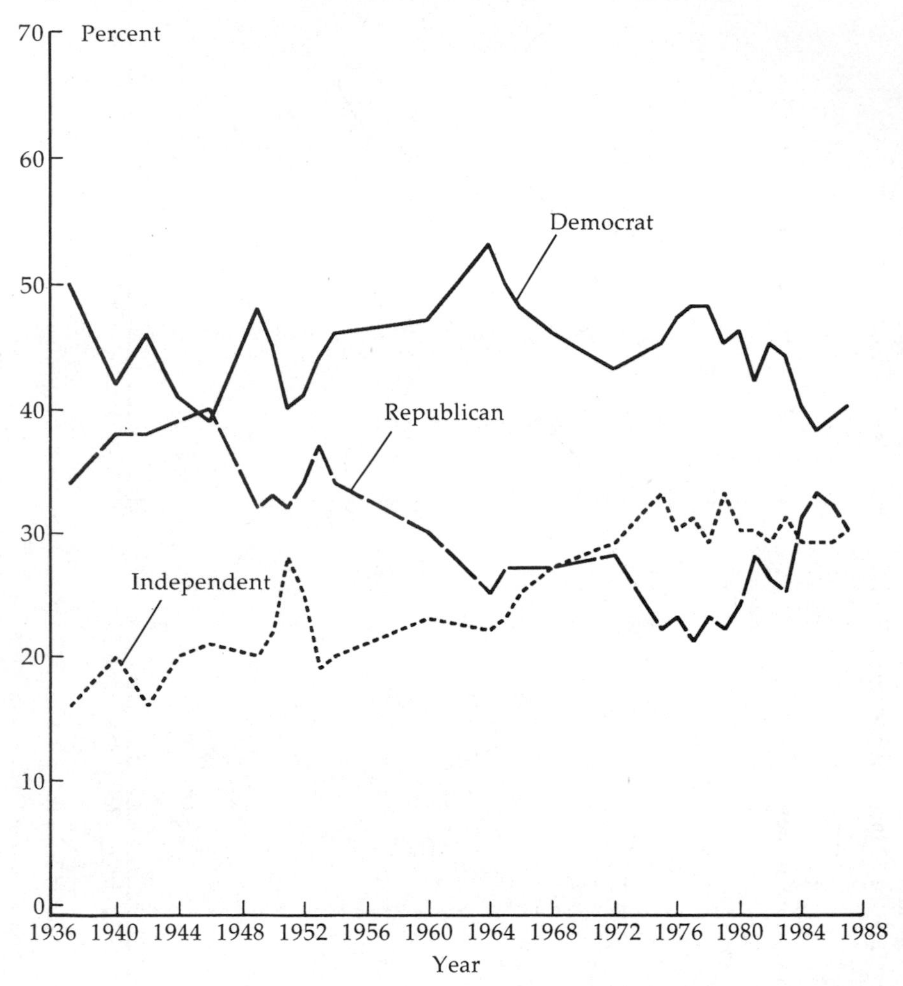

Note: Question: "In politics, as of today, do you consider yourself a Republican, a Democrat, or an Independent?" Respondents who gave replies other than Democrat, Republican, or Independent are excluded.

Sources: The Gallup Report (May 1987), 16-17, (January/February 1985), 21; *The Gallup Opinion Index* (July 1979), 34, (October 1967), 61.

Table 5-2 Partisan Identification, Cross Section, 1986

	Republican	*Democrat*	*Independent*	*Number of interviews*
Sex				
Men	33%	36%	31%	2,980
Women	31	42	27	2,949
Age				
Total under 30	35	33	32	1,241
18-24	34	33	33	593
25-29	36	34	30	648
30-49	30	38	32	2,258
Total 50 and over	32	45	23	2,405
50-64	31	44	25	1,223
65 and over	35	45	20	1,182
Region[a]				
East	32	39	29	1,486
Midwest	31	35	34	1,529
South	31	43	26	1,748
West	37	38	25	1,166
Race/ethnicity				
White	35	35	30	5,327
Black	9	73	18	525
Hispanic	24	49	27	330
Education				
Not high school graduate	23	53	24	1,262
High school graduate	30	39	31	1,975
College incomplete	40	31	29	1,449
College graduate	39	31	30	1,223
Occupation of chief wage earner				
Unskilled worker	26	45	29	1,121
Skilled worker	29	38	33	1,039
Manual worker	27	42	31	2,160
Clerical and sales	35	36	29	407
Professional and business	39	31	30	1,745

(Table continues)

Table 5-2 *(Continued)*

	Republican	*Democrat*	*Independent*	*Number of interviews*
Household income				
Under $25,000	28	44	28	3,077
Under $10,000	28	47	25	954
$10,000-$14,999	26	47	27	847
$15,000-$24,999	30	40	30	1,276
$25,000 and over	37	33	30	2,537
$25,000-$34,999	34	35	31	1,039
$35,000-$49,999	39	32	29	863
$50,000 and over	38	32	30	635
Religion				
Protestant	36	38	26	3,499
Catholic	27	43	30	1,636
Labor union				
Labor union family	26	44	30	1,150
Nonunion family	34	38	28	4,779
National	32	39	29	5,929

Note: Question: "In politics, as of today, do you consider yourself a Republican, a Democrat, or an Independent?" Data are from pooled surveys conducted between January and June 1986.

[a] For composition of regions, see the Appendix, Table A-2.

Source: The Gallup Report (July 1986), 21.

Table 5-3 Liberal or Conservative Self-Identification, 1973-1987

Date	*Extremely liberal*	*Liberal*	*Slightly liberal*	*Moderate*	*Slightly conservative*	*Conservative*	*Extremely conservative*	*Don't know*	*Number of interviews*
March 1973	4%	14%	13%	36%	13%	13%	3%	6%	1,484
March 1974	1	14	14	38	15	11	2	5	1,480
March 1975	3	12	13	38	16	10	2	5	1,478
March 1976	2	13	12	37	15	13	2	6	1,494
March 1977	2	11	14	37	16	12	3	5	1,524
March 1978	1	9	16	36	17	12	2	5	1,505
March 1980	2	8	14	40	18	12	3	2	1,451
March 1982	2	9	15	39	14	13	4	4	1,495
March 1983	2	8	12	40	18	13	2	4	801
March 1984	2	9	12	39	19	13	3	4	1,462
March 1985	2	11	11	37	18	14	3	4	1,525
March 1986	2	9	12	39	16	14	3	5	1,468
March 1987	2	12	13	37	16	12	2	4	1,437

Note: Question: "We hear a lot of talk these days about liberals and conservatives. I'm going to show you a seven-point scale on which the political views that people might hold are arranged from extremely liberal—point 1—to extremely conservative—point 7. Where would you place yourself on this scale?"

Source: General Social Surveys, National Opinion Research Center, University of Chicago.

Table 5-4 Liberal or Conservative Self-Identification, Cross Section, 1986

	Liberal			*Moderate*			*Conservative*				
	Far left	Substantially left	Moderately left	Slightly left	Middle of road	Slightly right	Moderately right	Substantially right	Far right	*No opinion*	*Number of interviews*
Sex											
Men	3%	4%	12%	15%	9%	22%	20%	7%	2%	6%	786
Women	3	4	14	12	12	21	18	6	3	7	766
Age											
Total under 30	4	7	15	14	9	21	15	6	2	7	318
18-24	6	6	12	14	10	23	14	4	2	9	138
25-29	2	7	18	15	8	18	14	10	2	6	180
30-49	2	3	15	15	9	23	19	5	3	6	596
Total 50 and over	3	2	9	12	13	20	23	7	4	7	630
50-64	2	3	7	14	12	21	23	8	3	7	311
65 and over	3	2	12	10	14	19	23	6	4	7	319
Region[a]											
East	3	3	13	12	15	22	19	3	1	9	378
Midwest	2	6	12	17	7	21	22	5	4	4	426
South	4	2	11	13	14	21	14	9	3	9	447
West	2	5	19	11	6	22	22	6	3	4	301
Race/ethnicity											
White	3	4	12	13	11	21	20	7	3	6	1,399
Black	3	5	18	19	11	20	9	3	2	10	136
Hispanic	1	9	13	19	4	14	25	6	1	8	104
Education											
Not high school graduate	4	3	10	12	10	17	19	7	4	14	338

High school graduate	3	4	13	12	13	22	17	6	4	6	531
College incomplete	2	4	13	14	11	26	18	4	2	6	360
College graduate	2	3	18	16	6	20	25	7	1	2	320
Political affiliation											
Democrat	3	5	19	17	11	20	13	4	2	6	615
Independent	4	4	13	15	16	19	16	4	2	7	375
Republican	2	2	7	18	7	27	29	10	4	4	514
Occupation of chief wage earner											
Unskilled worker	3	4	13	12	11	19	18	5	3	12	303
Skilled worker	2	5	17	10	8	20	19	8	4	7	265
Manual worker	3	5	14	11	10	20	18	6	3	10	568
Clerical and sales	3	5	13	17	12	27	13	6	0	4	108
Professional and business	3	4	14	16	8	23	21	7	2	2	451
Household income											
Under $25,000	4	4	11	10	12	22	17	6	3	11	824
Under $10,000	5	4	12	8	16	21	13	4	2	15	240
$10,000-$14,999	4	5	8	14	10	21	20	8	1	9	248
$15,000-$24,999	2	3	13	10	11	25	18	6	4	8	336
$25,000 and over	2	4	16	18	8	20	21	6	3	2	656
$25,000-$34,999	2	4	17	20	10	20	17	5	3	2	257
$35,000-$49,999	1	3	16	15	8	22	21	9	3	2	233
$50,000 and over	4	4	15	19	5	17	28	3	2	3	166
Religion											
Protestant	3	3	12	14	10	22	19	8	3	6	939
Catholic	1	5	15	12	12	23	20	3	3	6	418

(Table continues)

Table 5-4 *(Continued)*

	Liberal			*Moderate*			*Conservative*				
	Far left	Substantially left	Moderately left	Slightly left	Middle of road	Slightly right	Moderately right	Substantially right	Far right	*No opinion*	*Number of interviews*
Labor union											
Labor union family	2%	3%	17%	15%	11%	20%	19%	5%	3%	5%	299
Nonunion family	3	4	12	13	10	22	19	7	3	7	1,253
National	3	4	13	13	11	21	19	6	3	7	1,552

Note: Question: "People who are conservative in their political views are referred to as being right of the center and people who are liberal in their political views are referred to as being left of the center." (Respondent is handed a card with the categories above.) "Which one of these categories best describes your own political position?"

[a] For composition of regions, see Appendix, Table A-2.

Source: The Gallup Report (June 1986), 20-21.

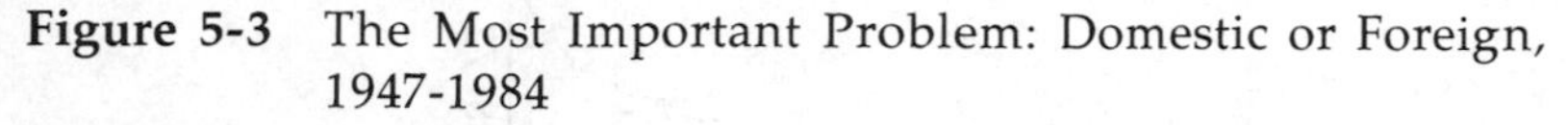

Figure 5-3 The Most Important Problem: Domestic or Foreign, 1947-1984

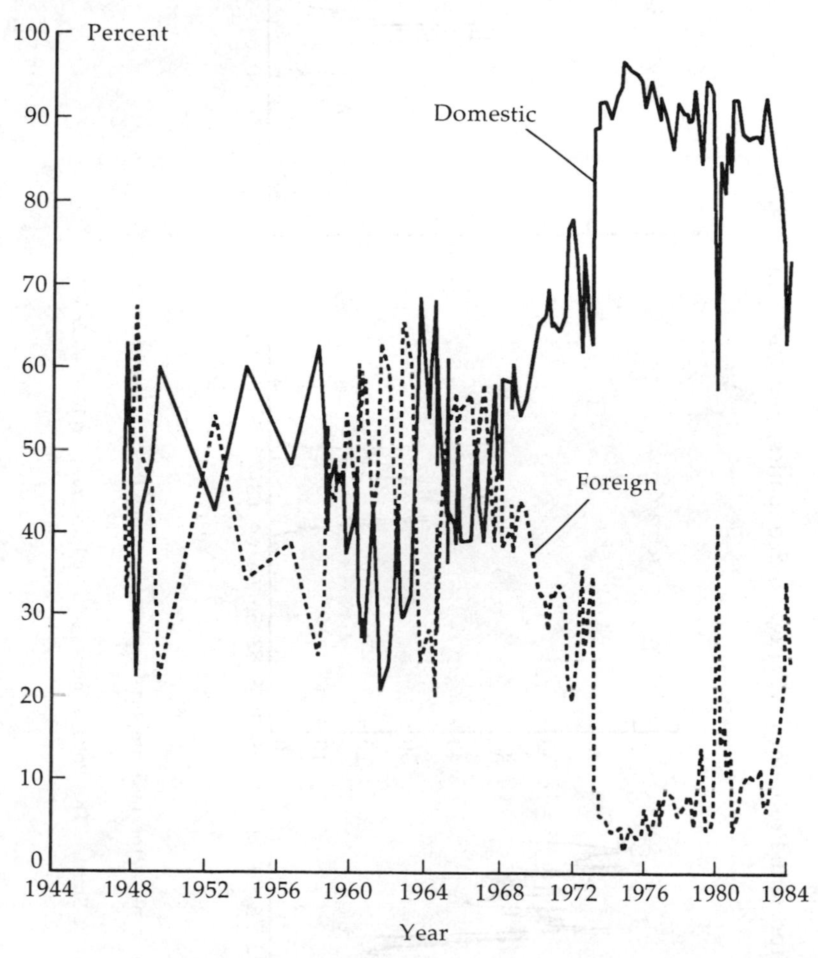

Note: Question: "What do you think is the most important problem facing this (the) country today?"

Source: Gallup polls as reported in Tom W. Smith, "The Polls: America's Most Important Problems," *Public Opinion Quarterly* 49 (1985): 268-274.

Figure 5-4 The Most Important Problem: Civil Rights, Economics, and Vietnam, 1947-1984

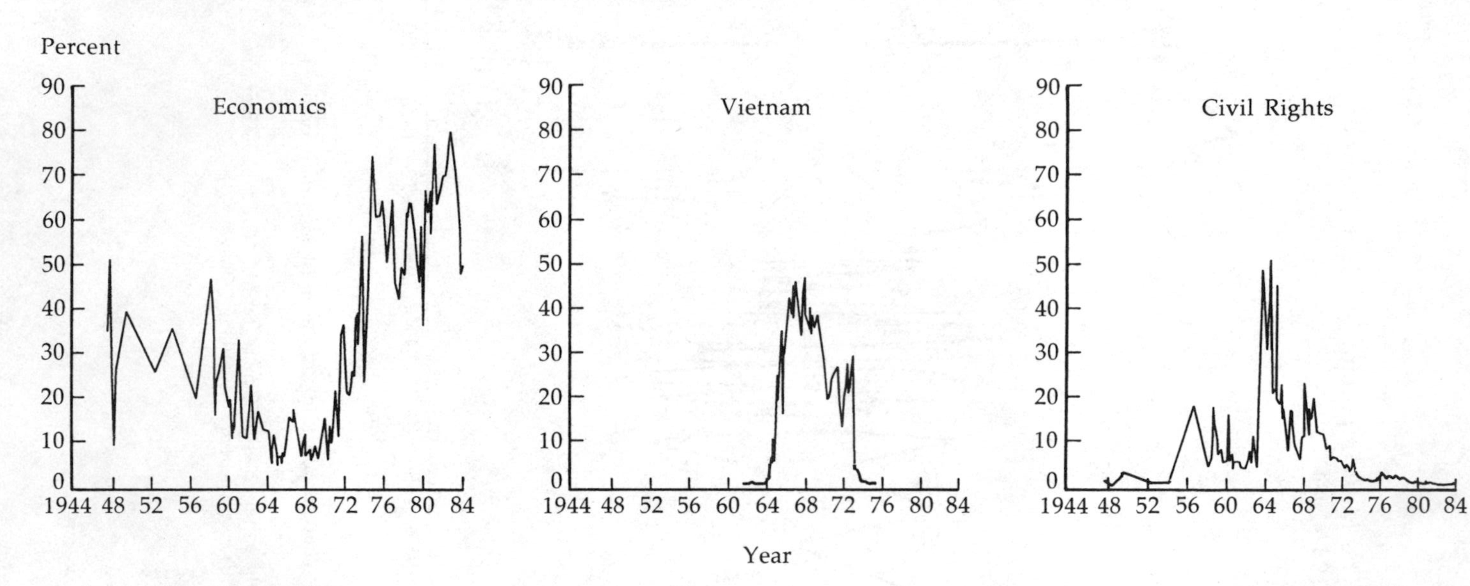

Note: Question: "What do you think is the most important problem facing this (the) country today?"

Source: Gallup polls as reported in Smith, "The Polls: America's Most Important Problems," 268-274.

Figure 5-5 The Party Better Able to Handle the Most Important Problem, 1945-1987

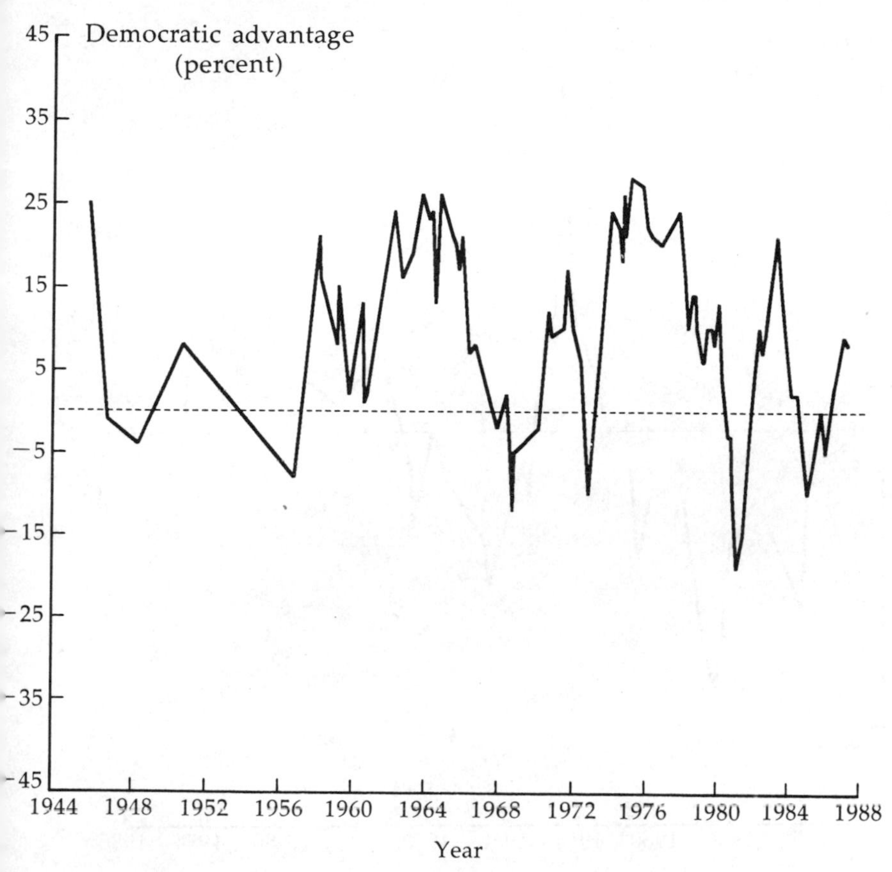

Note: Question: "Which political party do you think can do a better job of handling the problems you have just mentioned—the Republican party or the Democratic party?" "Democratic advantage" is the percentage responding Democratic minus the percentage responding Republican.

Source: The Gallup Report (May 1987), 9.

Figure 5-6 The Party More Likely to Keep the United States Out of War, 1951-1986

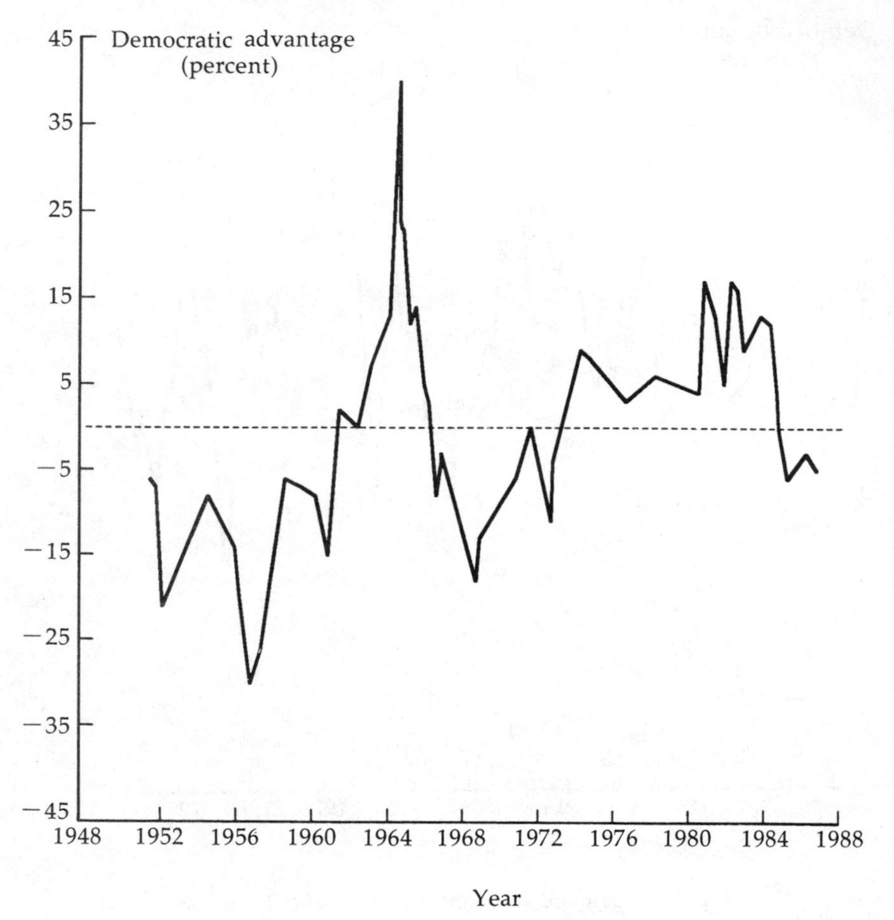

Note: Question: "Looking ahead for the next few years, which political party would be more likely to keep the United States out of World War III—the Republican or the Democratic party?" "Democratic advantage" is the percentage responding Democratic minus the percentage responding Republican.

Source: The Gallup Report (October 1986), 23.

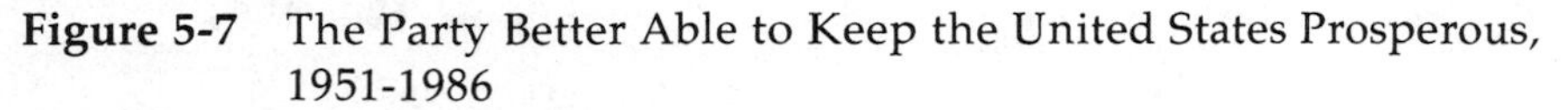

Figure 5-7 The Party Better Able to Keep the United States Prosperous, 1951-1986

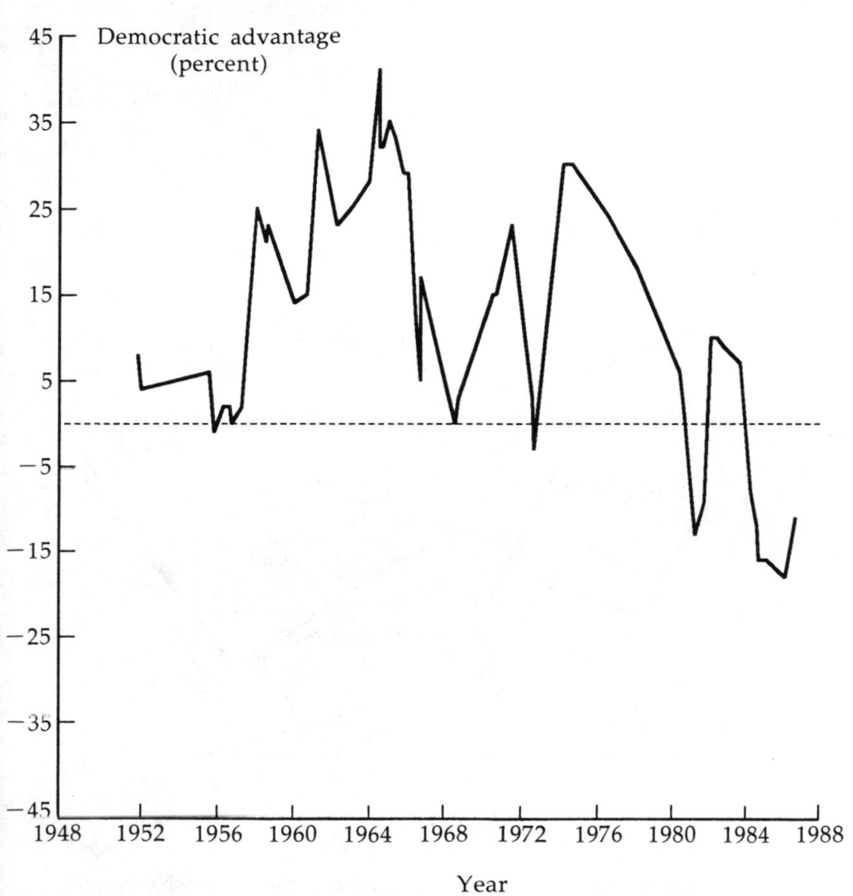

Note: Question: "Which political party—the Republican or the Democratic party—would do a better job of keeping the country prosperous?" "Democratic advantage" is the percentage responding Democratic minus the percentage responding Republican.

Source: The Gallup Report (October 1986), 23.

Figure 5-8 Individual Confidence in Government, 1964-1984

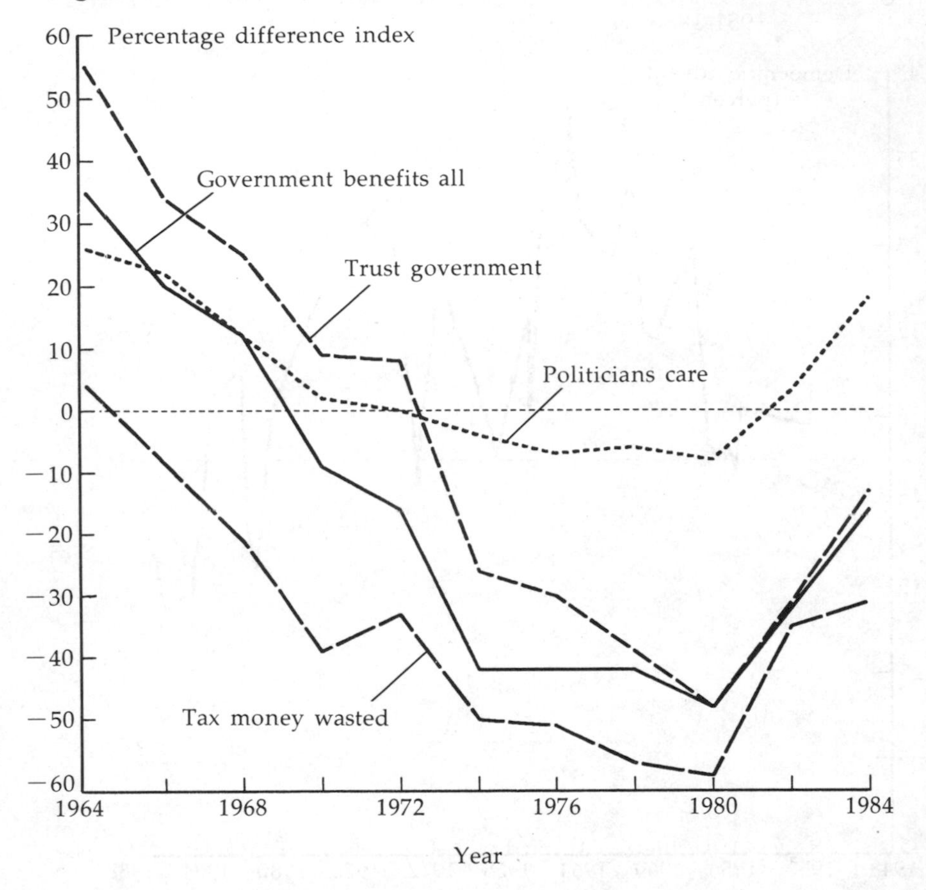

Note: Question: (Politicians care) "I don't think public officials care much what people like me think." (Trust government) "How much of the time do you think you can trust the government in Washington to do what is right—just about always, most of the time, or only some of the time?" (Government benefits all) "Would you say the government is pretty much run by a few big interests looking out for themselves or that it is run for the benefit of all people?" (Tax money wasted) "Do you think that people in the government waste a lot of money we pay in taxes, waste some of it, or don't waste very much of it?" The percentage difference index is calculated by subtracting the percentage giving a trusting response from the percentage giving a cynical response.

Sources: 1964-1982: Arthur H. Miller, "Is Confidence Rebounding?" *Public Opinion* 6 (3) (1983): 17 (reprinted with permission of American Enterprise Institute for Public Policy Research); 1984: National Elections Studies Codebook.

Questions

1. Compare the trends in party identification (for 1952-1984) in Figures 5-1 and 5-2. In what respects are the trends similar? How does it change the answer if you count "leaners" (those self-identified in Table 5-1 as "Independent Democrats" and "Independent Republicans") as partisans rather than independents?

2. What are the five most pro-Democratic groups in Table 5-2? The five most pro-Republican? People with low incomes tend to favor the Democrats. What other general characteristics (shown in Table 5-2) of low-income people are strongly associated with favoring the Democrats?

3. Do the overall trends on liberal and conservative shares of the population reflect political events of the 1970s and 1980s (Table 5-3)?

4. Here are three stereotypes to consider. Easterners are all a bunch of liberals. Young people are radicals; older people are reactionaries. The wealthier you are, the more conservative you are. To what degree, if at all, are these stereotypes correct (Table 5-4)? In answering this question, you might want to group the three categories under the liberal line as liberal and the three under the conservative line as conservative.

5. Account for the gross contours of change in the most important problem series (Figure 5-3). (Hint: see Figure 5-4.)

6. Discuss briefly the major events that might have caused the public to upgrade or downgrade the importance of the economy, Vietnam, and civil rights as issues between 1946 and 1984 (Figure 5-4).

7. More often than not, the Democrats had the advantage in judgments about the party better able to handle the most important problem (Figure 5-5). What is it about the figure that nonetheless helps explain why the Republicans have won more than half of the post-World War II presidential elections?

8. Specific campaign statements or themes account for some of the features of Figures 5-6 and 5-7, especially the huge spike in 1964 in Figure 5-6 and the Republican advantages in 1980 and 1984 in

Figure 5-7. What were these statements and themes? Based on these effects, how would you interpret the "party better able" responses? Are these responses long-term evaluations of parties?

9. What political events might explain the changes over time in individual confidence in government (Figure 5-8)? If adversaries wished to argue opposite sides of the case that the American public had lost confidence in its government, which facts and questions would each highlight?

6

Interest Groups

When people think about interest groups, they think about dollars. Not surprisingly, then, most of the information in this chapter and in related tables in other chapters is about money—who gives it, who spends it, who regulates it, and what effect it has. Even more surprising is the huge quantity of information available, which results chiefly from the large number of elections in the United States and the collection and publication of data about them. For example, the most recent campaign expenditures are shown for all 435 representatives and 100 senators (Tables 7-13 and 7-14), as well as the amounts of money spent by individual presidential candidates (Table 3-13), and more aggregated information about expenditures by congressional candidates (Table 3-14). The present chapter concentrates on the sources of these funds, especially on funds derived from organized groups.

One could, in fact, easily be inundated by numbers relating to organized interests. The publications of the Federal Election Commission (FEC) alone run to multiple volumes every two years, with detailed accountings of receipts and expenditures of candidates in federal elections. More volumes are produced, though inconsistently and much less systematically, by various state agencies. Because such information is so voluminous, it is often summarized as it is here: how much money was contributed to incumbents versus challengers in congressional campaigns (Table 3-14), how much was spent by various types of political action committees (PACs) (Table 6-4), interest organizations (Table 6-9), and so on.

However, this wealth of information has not been collected for many U.S. elections. The FEC only began operations in the mid-1970s. Although there were studies of campaign costs before then, present time series are often limited to a span of no more than fifteen years. In addition, laws regulating campaign contributions, expenditures, and interest groups' activities change so frequently that long time series are often unobtainable and would be misleading if they could be compiled. For example, the growth of PACs dates from 1974 because changes in the laws at that time allowed their establishment (Table 6-1).

Concern about money is not limited to the sums spent by candidates. Indeed, there is probably more concern over interest group spending and about where candidates' funds come from and what, if anything, that money buys. Fortunately, data are increasingly available on interest group finances and on candidates' fund raising as well as expenditures. Much of the data concern PACs, the dominant organizations through which interest groups raise and spend money. The primary information is about general categories of PACs (Tables 6-1, 6-4, and 6-5); the lists of PACs illustrate the variety of organizations that fall into these categories (Tables 6-2 and 6-6).

Because money is at the heart of interest group activities, matters of campaign finance law are directly relevant in this chapter. At the federal level these consist mainly of fairly straightforward contribution limits (Table 6-7). At the state level, there is a myriad of contribution and expenditure limits (Table 6-8).

Not all questions about interest groups involve money. Some other aspects of interest group activity that can be quantified are reflected in this volume. For example, several interest groups rate members of Congress on how favorable their votes were to the groups' interests. A number of recent ratings of each representative and senator are provided in Tables 7-13 and 7-14. Similarly, interest groups directly endorse candidates for election, with varying degrees of success (Table 6-10).

Another perennial question about interest groups is whether such groups in the aggregate reflect the interests of the general population. This is a difficult question on which to collect data, but one perspective is given in Table 6-9. The listings of PAC types and of specific PACs also provide some understanding of the variety of organized interests.

For obvious reasons no one is able to collect systematically what would surely be the most captivating data on the activities of organized interests, that is, bribes, threats, blackmail, and so forth. But political analysts now have a larger body of material on interest groups than ever before. Although much of this information is buried in hard-to-digest volumes on campaign contributions and spending or in seemingly bland lists showing what interests are represented, the data provide more knowledge and more research capabilities than ever before about the scope and potential influence of organized interests.

Table 6-1 Number of Political Action Committees (PACs), 1974-1987

	Connected[a]						
Date	Corporate	Labor	Trade/ membership/ health	Cooperative	Corporation without stock	*Nonconnected*[b]	*Total*
December 31, 1974	89	201	318[c]	—	—	—	608
November 24, 1975	139	226	357[c]	—	—	—	722
May 10, 1976	294	246	452[c]	—	—	—	992
December 31, 1976	433	224	489[c]	—	—	—	1146
December 31, 1977	550	234	438	8	20	110	1,360
December 31, 1978	785	217	453	12	24	162	1,653
August, 1979	885	226	483	13	27	206	1,840
December 31, 1979	950	240	514	17	32	247	2,000
July 1, 1980	1,107	255	544	23	41	309	2,279
December 31, 1980	1,206	297	576	42	56	374	2,551
July 1, 1981	1,253	303	579	38	64	441	2,678
December 31, 1981	1,329	318	614	41	68	531	2,901
July 1, 1982	1,417	350	627	45	82	628	3,149
December 31, 1982	1,469	380	649	47	103	723	3,371
July 1, 1983	1,514	379	664	50	114	740	3,461
December 31, 1983	1,538	378	643	51	122	793	3,525
July 1, 1984	1,642	381	662	53	125	940	3,803
December 31, 1984	1,682	394	698	52	130	1,053	4,009
July 1, 1985	1,687	393	694	54	133	1,039	4,000
December 31, 1985	1,710	388	695	54	142	1,003	3,992
July 1, 1986	1,734	386	707	56	146	1,063	4,092
December 31, 1986	1,744	384	745	56	151	1,077	4,157
July 1, 1987	1,762	377	795	56	152	967	4,409
December 31, 1987	1,775	364	865	59	145	957	4,165

Note: "—" indicates not available.

[a] Connected PACs are associated with a sponsoring organization that may pay operating and fund-raising expenses. They are typically subdivided by the type of sponsor: corporate (with stockholders), labor (unions), membership/trade/health (professional groups and associations of corporations), cooperatives (primarily agricultural), and corporations without stock.

[b] Nonconnected PACs do not have a sponsoring organization.

[c] For the years 1974-1976, trade/membership/health category includes all PACs except corporate and labor; no further breakdown available.

Source: Federal Election Commission, "FEC Releases New PAC Count," press release, January 12, 1987, 1; FEC update.

Table 6-2 The Largest Washington-Based PACs

Type of PAC/name
Corporate PACs
None
Labor PACs
Active Ballot Club
PAC of the United Food and Commercial Workers International Union
AFL-CIO Committee on Political Education (COPE)
AFSCME Public Employees Organized to Promote Legislative Equality
Air Line Pilots Association Political Action Committee
American Federation of Teachers Committee on Political Education
Carpenters' Legislative Improvement Committee
Committee on Letter Carriers Political Education
Communications Workers of America-COPE Political Contributions Committee
Democratic Republican Independent Voter Education Committee
PAC of the International Brotherhood of Teamsters, Chauffeurs, Warehousemen, and Helpers of America
Engineers Political Education Committee
PAC of the International Union of Operating Engineers
International Brotherhood of Electrical Workers Committee on Political Education
Ironworkers Political Action League
Machinists Non-Partisan Political League
Marine Engineers Beneficial Association Political Action Fund
National Education Association Political Action Committee
National Rural Letter Carriers Association Political Action Committee
Political Fund Committee of the American Postal Workers Union
Responsible Citizens' Political League—A Project of the Brotherhood of Railway and Airline Clerks
Seafarers Political Activity Donation
Sheet Metal Workers' International Association Political Action League
Trade/membership/health PACs
Action Committee for Rural Electrification
American Bankers Association (BANKPAC)
American Dental Political Action Committee
American Medical Association Political Action Committee
Association of Trial Lawyers of America Political Action Committee
Associated General Contractors Political Action Committee
Build-Political Action Committee (BUILDPAC)
PAC of the National Association of Home Builders
Dealers Election Action Committee
PAC of the National Automobile Dealers Association
Independent Insurance Agents of America Political Action Committee
League of Conservation Voters
National Association of Life Underwriters Political Action Committee
National Association of Retired Federal Employees Political Action Committee
National Rifle Association Political Victory Fund
U.S. League-Savings Association Political Elections Committee
Veterans of Foreign Wars Political Action Committee
Women's Campaign Fund

Table 6-2 *(Continued)*

Type of PAC/name
Nonconnected PACs
Campaign America
Supports Republican candidates
Campaign for Prosperity
Supports conservative candidates, especially those favoring free enterprise, traditional values, and a strong national defense
Committee for America
Supports Republican candidates
Council for a Livable World
Supports senatorial candidates who favor arms control
Democrats for the 80s
Freeze Voter
Supports a nuclear weapons freeze
Fund for a Conservative Majority
Fund for a Democratic Majority
Funds progressive candidates
Fund for America's Future
Supports Republican candidates
Human Rights Campaign Fund
Concerned with lesbian and gay civil rights issues and federal funding for AIDS treatment and research
Independent Action
Supports progressive candidates
National Abortion Rights Action League Political Action Committee
National Committee for an Effective Congress
Supports liberal or progressive candidates in marginal races
National Conservative Political Action Committee
National Political Action Committee
Supports candidates who advocate close Israeli-American relations
National Right to Life Political Action Committee
Republican Majority Fund
Ruff Political Action Committee
Supports candidates who support a free market economic system and a strong national defense
Voters for Choice
Assists congressional candidates who support legal abortion
Cooperative PACs
None
Corporation without stock PACs
Council for National Defense
Supports candidates who favor a strong national defense

Note: Listed are Washington-based political action committees with receipts or expenditures of $600,000 or more during 1985 and 1986.

Source: Congressional Quarterly, *Washington Information Directory, 1987-1988* (Washington, D.C.: Congressional Quarterly, 1987), 640-643.

Table 6-3 PACs: Receipts, Expenditures, Contributions, 1975-1986

Election cycle[a]	*Adjusted receipts*[b] *(millions)*	*Adjusted expenditures*[b] *(millions)*	*Contributions to congressional candidates (millions)*	*Percentage contributed to congressional candidates*
1975-1976	$ 54.0	$ 52.9	$ 22.6	42
1977-1978	80.0	77.4	34.1	43
1979-1980	137.7	131.2	55.2	40
1981-1982	199.5	190.2	83.6	42
1983-1984	288.7	266.8	105.3	36
1985-1986	352.9	338.3	132.2	37

[a] Data cover January 1 of the odd-numbered year to December 31 of the even-numbered year.
[b] Adjusted receipts and expenditures exclude funds transferred between affiliated committees.

Sources: 1975-1976: Joseph E. Cantor, "Political Action Committees: Their Evolution and Growth and Their Implications for the Political System" (Washington, D.C.: Congressional Research Service, 1982), Report no. 83, 87-88; others: Federal Election Commission, "FEC Releases First PAC Figures for 1985-86," press release, May 21, 1987, 1.

Table 6-4 Spending by Type of PAC, 1978-1986 (millions)

Year	*Corporate*	*Labor*	*Trade/ membership/ health*	*Other connected*[a]	*Non-connected*	*Total*
1978	$15.2	$18.6	$23.8	$ 17.4	$ 2.4	$ 77.4
1980	31.4	25.1	32.0	38.6	4.0	131.2
1982	43.3	34.8	41.9	64.3	5.8	190.2
1984	59.2	47.5	54.0	97.4	8.7	266.8
1986	79.6	58.3	73.5	115.6	11.3	338.3

Note: Adjusted expenditures exclude transfers of funds between affiliated committees. Detail may not add to totals because of rounding.
[a] This category combines the FEC categories of cooperatives and corporations without stock.

Source: Norman J. Ornstein et al., eds., *Vital Statistics on Congress, 1987-1988* (Washington, D.C.: Congressional Quarterly, 1987), 105.

Table 6-5 Contributions and Independent Expenditures by Type of PAC, 1983-1984

Type of PAC	*Number*[a]	*Receipts*[b]	*Contributed to candidates*[c] Amount	Percentage	*Independent expenditures*[d] Amount	Percentage
Corporate	1,682	$66,331,047	$39,008,465	59	$32,559	<.01
Labor	394	51,116,628	26,164,349	51	305,672	1
Trade/membership/health[e]	693	59,346,516	28,346,541	48	1,936,589	3
Realtors PAC		4,291,572	2,429,052	57	355,346	8
American Medical Association		4,032,365	1,839,464	46	450,020	11
NRA Political Victory Fund		3,331,630	700,324	21	785,516	24
Cooperative	52	4,485,621	2,621,713	58	13,750	0.3
Corporations without stock[e]	130	4,461,336	1,506,352	34	777,133	17
Council for National Defense		1,449,671	42,258	3	739,552	51
Nonconnected[e]	1,053	102,789,387	15,322,624	15	19,085,105	19
National Conservative PAC		19,514,822	128,241	1	10,243,753	52
National Congressional Club		5,703,035	104,533	2	948,032	17
Fund for Conservative Majority		5,500,208	221,648	4	2,177,628	40
Ruff PAC		3,707,512	220,848	6	2,020,225	54
Total	4,009	$288,690,535	$112,970,044	39	$22,150,808	8

[a] As of December 31, 1984.
[b] Adjusted for money transferred between affiliated committees.
[c] Figures include contributions to all federal candidates, including those who did not run for office during 1983-1984.
[d] Independent expenditures include money spent on behalf of candidates and against candidates. Some independent expenditures made in 1983-1984 pertained to 1982 candidates.
[e] Includes others not listed separately. The PACs listed are among those that spend the most independently.

Sources: Federal Election Commission, "FEC Releases New PAC Count," 1; receipts, contributions, independent expenditures: Federal Election Commission, "FEC Final Report for '84 Elections Confirms Majority of PAC Money Went to Incumbents," press release, December 1, 1985; independent expenditures for individual PACs: Federal Election Commission, "FEC Reports 1983-84 Independent Spending Activity," press release, October 4, 1985, 3.

Table 6-6 Top Twenty PACs in Overall Spending and in Contributions to Federal Candidates, 1985-1986

PAC	*Overall spending*
1. National Congressional Club (NC)[a]	$15,841,407
2. National Conservative Political Action Committee (NCPAC) (NC)	9,349,810
3. Fund for America's Future, Inc. (NC)	9,202,479
4. National Committee to Preserve Social Security PAC (NC)	6,190,561
5. Realtors Political Action Committee (TMH)	6,010,744
6. American Medical Association PAC (AMPAC) (TMH)	5,406,582
7. NRA Political Victory Fund (TMH)	4,763,529
8. League of Conservation Voters (TMH)	3,781,361
9. Campaign America (NC)	3,249,361
10. Campaign for Prosperity (NC)	3,247,810
11. Fund for a Democratic Majority (NC)	3,118,840
12. Democratic Republican Independent Voter Education Committee (DRIVE) (Teamsters) (L)	3,055,468
13. Auto Dealers for Free Trade PAC (NC)	2,986,398
14. Voter Guide (NC)	2,910,933
15. Association of Trial Lawyers of America PAC (ATLA) (TMH)	2,772,698
16. Fund for a Conservative Majority (NC)	2,728,143
17. National Education Association PAC (NEA) (L)	2,532,193
18. National Committee for an Effective Congress (NCEC) (NC)	2,497,965
19. UAW-V-CAP (United Auto Workers) (L)	2,397,490
20. Citizens for the Republic (NC)	2,355,862

PAC	*Contributions to federal candidates*
1. Realtors Political Action Committee (TMH)	$2,782,338
2. American Medical Association PAC (AMPAC) (TMH)	2,107,492
3. National Education Association PAC (NEA) (L)	2,055,133
4. UAW-V-CAP (United Auto Workers) (L)	1,621,055
5. National Association of Retired Federal Employees PAC (NARFE-PAC) (TMH)	1,491,895
6. Committee on Letter Carriers Political Education (L)	1,490,875
7. Democratic Republican Independent Voter Education Committee (D.R.I.V.E.) (Teamsters) (L)	1,457,196
8. Build PAC of the National Association of Home Builders (TMH)	1,424,240
9. Association of Trial Lawyers PAC (ATLA) (TMH)	1,404,000
10. Machinists Non-Partisan Political League (L)	1,364,550
11. Seafarers Political Activity Donation (SPAD) (L)	1,187,106
12. American Federation of State, County, and Municipal Employees (AFSCME) Public Employees Organized to Promote Legislative Equality (PEOPLE) (L)	1,112,075

Table 6-6 *(Continued)*

PAC	*Contributions to federal candidates*
13. Active Ballot Club, A Department of United Food and Commercial Workers International Union (L)	1,116,879
14. National Association of Life Underwriters PAC (TMH)	1,087,859
15. Dealers Election Action Committee of the National Automobile Dealers Association (NADA) (TMH)	1,059,650
16. Auto Dealers for Free Trade PAC (NC)	1,016,699
17. International Brotherhood of Electrical Workers COPE (L)	969,840
18. National PAC (NC)	952,000
19. Carpenters' Legislative Improvement Committee (L)	947,836
20. American Bankers Association BANKPAC (TMH)	934,440

Note: "L" indicates labor; "TMH" indicates trade/membership/health; "NC" indicates nonconnected.

[a] Figures for the National Congressional Club include approximately $7 million spent by JMI, required to be reported pursuant to a Consent Decree issued by the U.S. District Court for the Eastern District of North Carolina in May 1986, as well as joint fundraising activity on behalf of Senator Jesse Helms.

Source: Federal Election Commission, "First Complete PAC Figures for 1985-86," 10-11.

Table 6-7 Contribution Limits Under Federal Election Commission Act

	Recipient			
Source	Candidate or his/her authorized committee	National party committee[a]	Any other committee	Total contributions
Individual	$1,000 per election[b]	$20,000	$5,000	$25,000
Multicandidate committee[c]	5,000 per election	15,000	5,000	NL
Party committee	1,000-5,000 per election[d]	NL	5,000	NL
Republican or Democratic Senatorial Campaign Committee,[e] or the National Party Committee or a combination of both	17,500 to Senate candidate per calendar year in which candidate seeks election	NA	NA	NA
Any other committee or group[f]	1,000 per election	20,000	5,000	NL

Note: "NL" indicates no limit; "NA" indicates not applicable. Limits for national party committee, other committee, and total contributions are per calendar year.

[a] The following are considered national party committees: a party's national committee, the Senate campaign committees and the national congressional committees, provided they are not authorized by any candidate. Individual contributions made or earmarked to influence a specific election of a clearly identified candidate are counted as if made during the year in which the election is held.

[b] The following are considered separate elections: primary election, general election, runoff election, special election, and party caucus or convention which has authority to select the nominee.

[c] A multicandidate committee is any committee with more than fifty contributors which has been registered for at least six months and, with the exception of state party committees, has made contributions to five or more federal candidates.

[d] Limit depends on whether party committee is a multicandidate committee.

[e] Republican and Democratic Senatorial Campaign committees are subject to all other limits applicable to a multicandidate committee.

[f] Group includes an organization, partnership, or group of persons.

Source: U.S. Advisory Commission on Intergovernmental Relations, *The Transformation in American Politics: Implications for Federalism* (Washington, D.C.: U.S. Advisory Commission on Intergovernmental Relations, 1986), 266.

Table 6-8 State Campaign Finance: Tax Provisions, Contribution and Expenditure Limits, and Public Funding by State

State	*Tax provisions*	*Contribution limit*	*Expenditure limit*[a]
Alabama	Add-on: $1	none	none
Alaska	Credit: $100	$1,000 per year to single candidates	Governor: $0.40 times total population; House and Senate: $1 times district population divided by number of seats in district
Arizona	Deduction: $100	none	none
Arkansas	Deduction: $25	$1,500 per candidate per election	none
California	Deduction: $100 Add-on: $1, $5, $10, $25	none	none
Colorado	none	none	none
Connecticut	none	Governor: $2,000; amount differs for other offices; aggregate limit of $15,000 per primary or general election	none
Delaware	none	$1,000 per candidate for statewide elections; $500 in other elections	none
Florida	Legislative appropriations to state campaign fund	$3,000 per candidate per election for statewide candidates; $1,000 for legislative candidates and political committees	Governor: $0.75 times total votes cast for governor in last general election; cabinet: $0.25 times total votes cast for governor in last general election
Georgia	none	none	none

(Table continues)

Table 6-8 *(Continued)*

State	*Tax provisions*	*Contribution limit*	*Expenditure limit*[a]
Hawaii	Deduction: $500 aggregate to candidates abiding by spending limits; $100 per candidate or $100 to party committee Checkoff: $2	$2,000 per candidate per election	Governor: $1.25 times total number of registered voters in preceding general election; amount differs for other offices
Idaho	Credit: 50% of political contributions to $5 Checkoff: $1	none	none
Illinois	none	none	none
Indiana	none[b]	none	none
Iowa	Deduction: $100 Checkoff: $1 Add-on: $2	none	none
Kansas	none	$3,000 per election to candidate for statewide office; $750 for state legislative office	none
Kentucky	Deduction: $100 Checkoff: $2	$3,000 per candidate per election	none
Louisiana	none	none	none
Maine	Deduction: $100 Add-on: $1	$1,000 per candidate per election; aggregate ceiling of $25,000 per calendar year	none
Maryland[c]	Deduction: $100 Add-on: $2	$1,000 per candidate per election; $2,500 aggregate limit	Governor and lieutenant governor: approximately $911,000 for the 1990 primary and general elections; amount differs for other offices

Massachusetts	Add-on: $1	$1,000 per candidate per year; also to political parties and committees; minors limited to $25 per year	none
Michigan	Deduction: $50 Checkoff: $2	$1,700 per statewide candidate per election; $450 per state senate candidate; $250 per state representative candidate	Governor: $1 million for primary and $1 million for general election
Minnesota	Credit: 50% of political donations up to $50 if candidate abides by spending limits. Deduction: $100 Checkoff: $2	Candidates for governor: $60,000 in an election year and $12,000 in a nonelection year; amount differs for other offices	Governor: $600,000; amount differes for other offices
Mississippi	none	none, except $250 aggregate limit for certain judicial primaries	none
Missouri	none	none	none
Montana	Deduction: $100 Add-on: $1	Governor and lieutenant governor: $1,500; other statewide offices: $750; amount varies for other offices	none
Nebraska	none	none	none
Nevada	none	none	none
New Hampshire	none	$5,000	none
New Jersey	Deduction: $25 Checkoff: $1	Governor: $800 per candidate per primary or general election	General election: $0.70 per voter in last presidential election; primary: $0.35 per voter in last presidential election
New Mexico	none	none	none

(Table continues)

Table 6-8 *(Continued)*

State	*Tax provisions*	*Contribution limit*	*Expenditure limit*[a]
New York	none	Aggregate of $150,000 per year; statewide elections limited to total number of registered voters times $0.025; primary and other offices vary in amount.	none
North Carolina	Deduction: $25 Checkoff: $1	$4,000 per candidate per election	Media limit of $0.10 times voting age population
North Dakota	none	none	none
Ohio	none	none	none
Oklahoma[d]	Deduction: $100 Checkoff: $1	$5,000 per statewide candidate, organization, or political party; $1,000 to candidate for local office	none
Oregon	Credit: 50% of political contributions up to $25	none	none
Pennsylvania	none	none	none
Rhode Island	Checkoff: $1	none	none
South Carolina	none	none	none
South Dakota	none	$1,000 per year to any statewide candidate; $250 per year to any county and legislative office; $3,000 per year to any political party	none
Tennessee	none	none	none
Texas	none	none	none

Utah	Deduction: $50 Checkoff: $1	none	Media limit for governor of $100,000; amount differs for other offices
Vermont	none	$1,000 for statewide offices and legislature	none
Virginia	none	none	none
Washington	none	none	
West Virginia	none	$1,000 per election	none
Wisconsin	Checkoff: $1	Aggregate limit of $10,000 per year to candidates for state and local office and committees; amount varies	Governor: $302,025 for primary and $704,725 for general election; amounts vary for other offices
Wyoming	none	$1,000 per candidate for two-year campaign period; $25,000 aggregate ceiling	none

[a] Although other states may still have expenditure limits on the books, only those states that provide for public funding of candidates or political parties are permitted expenditure limits. See *Buckley v. Valeo,* 424 U.S. 1 (1976).

[b] Indiana funds the party in power through county license branch profits ($320,000 was reported in 1984 to have gone to the Republican party) and offers both parties a split of revenues derived from vanity license plate sales.

[c] A $2 tax add-on was enacted in 1974 and in operation in Maryland from 1975 to 1982 but actual disbursement of the funds was postponed. Legislation was enacted in April 1986 to spend the funds for the 1990 gubernatorial election, then dismantle the funding system.

[d] For all practical purposes, Oklahoma's law is defunct. In *Democratic Party of Oklahoma v. Estop, Oklahoma,* 625 P. 2d 271, the Oklahoma Supreme Court said that the legislature would have to correct the deficiencies. It has not. Thus, while the statute remains on the books, it cannot be implemented.

Sources: Herbert E. Alexander and Mike Eberts, *Public Financing of State Elections: A Data Book on Tax-Assisted Funding of Political Parties and Candidates in Twenty States* (Los Angeles: Citizens' Research Foundation, 1986), 15-24, 227; U.S. Advisory Commission on Intergovernmental Relations, *The Transformation in American Politics.* 300-301, 310-315, based on Herbert Alexander and Jennifer W. Frutig, *Public Financing of State Elections: A Data Book and Election Guide to Public Funding of Political Parties and Candidates in Seventeen States* (Los Angeles: Citizens' Research Foundation, 1982) and Council on Governmental Ethics, Council of State Governments, *Campaign Finance, Ethics, and Lobby Law: Blue-Book, 1984-85* (Lexington, Ky.: Council on State Governments, 1984).

Table 6-9 Organizational Focus of Groups in Comparison with Occupations of U.S. Adults

Organizational focus	*Percentage of organizations*	*Percentage of U.S. adults*	*Occupation*
Professional	17.0	9	Professional/technical
Business	71.0	7	Managerial/administrative
Unions	4.0	41	All other nonfarm workers
Agriculture	1.5	2	Farm
Unemployed	0.1	4	Unemployed
Education	4.0	4	In school
Handicapped	0.6	2	Unable to work
Senior citizens	0.8	12	Retired
		19	At home
Women	1.8		

Note: Percentages reflect characteristics as found in the 1980 census and in organizational directories published in 1981.

Source: Kay Lehman Schlozman and John T. Tierney, *Organized Interests and American Democracy* (New York: Harper and Row, 1986), 70 (copyright © 1986 by Kay Lehman Schlozman and John T. Tierney, reprinted by permission of Harper and Row Publishers, Inc.).

Table 6-10 Interest Group Endorsements and Election Outcomes for Congress, 1982 and 1984

	Senate		*House*	
Year/group	Number endorsed	Wins	Number endorsed	Wins
1982				
Liberal groups				
ADA	18	44%	138	73%
COPE	31	65	374	64
NCEC	15	60	103	71
Conservative groups				
ACA	15	47	144	78
BIPAC	17	47	103	37
NCPAC	3	0	86	81
1984				
Liberal groups				
ADA	9	44	73	59
COPE	28	54	368	64
NCEC	18	56	85	54
Conservative groups				
ACA	22	55	195	82
BIPAC	14	50	80	64
NCPAC	18	67	196	78

Note: "ADA" is Americans for Democratic Action; "COPE" is American Federation of Labor-Congress of Industrial Organizations, Commitee on Political Education; "NCEC" is National Committee for an Effective Congress; "ACA" is Americans for Constitutional Action; "BIPAC" is Business-Industry Political Action Committee; "NCPAC" is National Conservative Political Action Committee.

Source: Congressional Quarterly Weekly Report (1982), 2811-2816, (1984), 2971-2976.

Questions

1. Was average PAC spending more in 1986 than in 1976? (Use the number of PACs from December 31, 1976, and December 31, 1986, from Table 6-1 and PAC spending [adjusted expenditures] for 1975-1976 and 1985-1986 from Table 6-3.) One measure of inflation, the Consumer Price Index (Table 13-2), rose 92.6 percent between 1976 and 1986 ((328.4-170.5)/170.5). Did the increase in PAC spending over the same period surpass the increase in the rate of inflation as measured by the Consumer Price Index?

2. Are there PACs whose goals you are likely to agree with (Table 6-2)? Any you would strongly oppose? Which ones are they? (There is no right and wrong answer.) Which category do these PACs fall under? Why would you agree or disagree with these particular PACs?

3. Which type of PAC spends the most money (Table 6-4)? Which type currently spends the most per PAC (Tables 6-4 and 6-1). Corporate PACs spend relatively little per PAC (none is in the top twenty in spending or contributions—Table 6-6) and they are typically not based in Washington. How can it be, then, that corporations are thought to have considerable influence?

4. Do the different types of PACs follow roughly similar patterns in dividing their receipts between contributing to candidates and engaging in independent expenditures (Table 6-5)?

5. How much can a PAC contribute to a single candidate in a single year (Table 6-7)? To multiple candidates?

6. How many states have some sort of public funding (tax provisions) for political candidates (Table 6-8)? Why are tax deductions and credits considered public funding? In which state does buying a vanity license plate (those clever plates that spell things like ICOOK4U on a chef's license, 2THDR on a dentist's license, etc.) help support political candidates?

7. Which two states impose limits on media expenditures (Table 6-8)? In what circumstances can a state impose expenditure requirements? Why do you think there is this sort of restriction about imposing expenditure limits?

8. Do you think the political power of senior citizens (more or less equivalent to the retired population) is more reflective of their 0.8 percent of the nation's organizations or their 12 percent of the population (Table 6-9)? What about those in business (generally equivalent to those in managerial/administrative occupations)?

9. Do major liberal or conservative interest groups have a consistent edge in the number of endorsements they give and in the percentage of times their endorsed candidates win (Table 6-10)?

10. Look at the success rates for candidates endorsed by conservative groups in the Senate in 1982 (Table 6-10). If you add these three percentages (47 + 47 + 0) and divide by three, you find an average of 31.33. But that calculation obviously ignores the fact that NCPAC endorsed only three candidates, considerably fewer than the other conservative groups. What is the "weighted" average of success, the average that takes into account the number of candidates endorsed?

7

Congress

Statistics about Congress abound. Capsule descriptions of senators and representatives and their districts can easily run to over a thousand pages for each Congress (*Politics in America* and the *Almanac of American Politics*). Elections are held every two years, generating mounds of electoral and financial data. Recorded votes annually number more than four hundred in the House and more than three hundred in the Senate. It is thus hardly surprising that votes for Congress, votes in Congress, those who work for Congress, and those who benefit from (or are hurt by) congressional activities have been subject to extensive statistical scrutiny.

Congressional elections and roll call votes in Congress constitute the largest areas of research. Elections are covered in several other chapters, and the nature of electoral data is discussed in the introductions to Chapters 3 and 4. What is added here are a few tables that pertain to specific hypotheses about congressional elections. Losses by the president's party in midterm elections (Table 7-4) have long been of interest because of a strong regularity and because the pattern has a variety of implications for the way voters evaluate their representatives. The same is true of incumbency; the results are interesting in and of themselves (Table 7-5) and because of what they suggest about how voters make choices.

Congress generates other kinds of statistics. Simply apportioning members among the states (Table 7-1 and Figure 7-1) has led to a surprising amount of controversy and statistical calculation, which resulted in a fascinating, book-length treatment.[1] As the composition of Congress changes to include more women and minorities, these and other characteristics have also been tabulated and analyzed (Tables 7-2 and 7-3).

Cohesion within and contrasts between the political parties were the topics of some of the first statistical treatments of political subjects.[2] Increased numbers of roll calls and other recorded votes (Table 7-11) have done nothing to dampen this tradition. Party unity and presidential support by individual representatives and senators (Tables 7-13 and 7-14) and for groups (Tables 7-7 through 7-9, Figure 7-2) have become a standard part of congressional analyses.

As Congress becomes a larger and more complex operation, more interest has been expressed in its workload and structure. These aspects of Congress are represented here with information about staff size (Figure 7-3), numbers of measures considered and passed (Table 7-10 and Figure 7-4), numbers of votes (Table 7-11), and numbers of and leadership of committees (Table 7-12). Although these, too, at first might be considered insignificant or analytically useless tabulations, analyses of the relationships among committee staffs, congressional voting, voter behavior, and legislative output suggest otherwise.

For the statistically minded, the study of Congress has long been an inviting prospect. The traditional topics are still interesting because the turnover of personnel, the constant change in congressional leadership and of the president, changes in regional strength, and so on, make Congress anything but static. In addition, reforms of congressional procedures and of campaign finance since Watergate, changing technologies that result in electronic voting and the televising of proceedings in both chambers, and changes in the size and scope of the government bureaucracy Congress must deal with, are adequate reasons to scrutinize anew the data underlying one's understanding of Congress.

Notes

1. Michel Balinski and H.P. Young, *Fair Representation* (New Haven, Conn.: Yale University Press, 1982).
2. Stuart Rice, *Quantitative Methods in Politics* (New York: Knopf, 1928).

Table 7-1 Apportionment of Membership in the House of Representatives, 1789-1980

State	*1789*[a]	*1790*	*1800*	*1810*	*1820*	*1830*	*1840*	*1850*	*1860*	*1870*	*1880*	*1890*	*1900*	*1910*	*1930*[b]	*1940*	*1950*	*1960*	*1970*	*1980*
Alabama	-	-	-	1[c]	3	5	7	7	6	8	8	9	9	10	9	9	9	8	7	7
Alaska	-	-	-	-	-	-	-	-	-	-	-	-	-	-	-	-	1[c]	1	1	1
Arizona	-	-	-	-	-	-	-	-	-	-	-	-	-	1[c]	1	2	2	3	4	5
Arkansas	-	-	-	-	-	1[c]	1	2	3	4	5	6	7	7	7	7	6	4	4	4
California	-	-	-	-	-	-	2[c]	2	3	4	6	7	8	11	20	23	30	38	43	45
Colorado	-	-	-	-	-	-	-	-	-	1[c]	1	2	3	4	4	4	4	4	5	6
Connecticut	5	7	7	7	6	6	4	4	4	4	4	4	5	5	6	6	6	6	6	6
Delaware	1	1	1	2	1	1	1	1	1	1	1	1	1	1	1	1	1	1	1	1
Florida	-	-	-	-	-	-	1[c]	1	1	2	2	2	3	4	5	6	8	12	15	19
Georgia	3	2	4	6	7	9	8	8	7	9	10	11	11	12	10	10	10	10	10	10
Hawaii	-	-	-	-	-	-	-	-	-	-	-	-	-	-	-	-	1[c]	2	2	2
Idaho	-	-	-	-	-	-	-	-	-	-	1[c]	1	1	2	2	2	2	2	2	2
Illinois	-	-	-	1[c]	1	3	7	9	14	19	20	22	25	27	27	26	25	24	24	22
Indiana	-	-	-	1[c]	3	7	10	11	11	13	13	13	13	13	12	11	11	11	11	10
Iowa	-	-	-	-	-	-	2[c]	2	6	9	11	11	11	11	9	8	8	7	6	6
Kansas	-	-	-	-	-	-	-	-	1	3	7	8	8	8	7	6	6	5	5	5
Kentucky	-	2	6	10	12	13	10	10	9	10	11	11	11	11	9	9	8	7	7	7
Louisiana	-	-	-	1[c]	3	3	4	4	5	6	6	6	7	8	8	8	8	8	8	8
Maine	-	-	-	7[c]	7	8	7	6	5	5	4	4	4	4	3	3	3	2	2	2
Maryland	6	8	9	9	9	8	6	6	5	6	6	6	6	6	6	6	7	8	8	8
Massachusetts	8	14	17	13[d]	13	12	10	11	10	11	12	13	14	16	15	14	14	12	12	11
Michigan	-	-	-	-	-	1[c]	3	4	6	9	11	12	12	13	17	17	18	19	19	18
Minnesota	-	-	-	-	-	-	-	2[c]	2	3	5	7	9	10	9	9	9	8	8	8
Mississippi	-	-	-	1[c]	1	2	4	5	5	6	7	7	8	8	7	7	6	5	5	5
Missouri	-	-	-	-	1	2	5	7	9	13	14	15	16	16	13	13	11	10	10	9
Montana	-	-	-	-	-	-	-	-	-	-	1[c]	1	1	2	2	2	2	2	2	2
Nebraska	-	-	-	-	-	-	-	-	1[c]	1	3	6	6	6	5	4	4	3	3	3
Nevada	-	-	-	-	-	-	-	-	1[c]	1	1	1	1	1	1	1	1	1	1	2
New Hampshire	3	4	5	6	6	5	4	3	3	3	2	2	2	2	2	2	2	2	2	2
New Jersey	4	5	6	6	6	6	5	5	5	7	7	8	10	12	14	14	14	15	15	14

New Mexico	-	-	-	-	-	-	-	-	-	-	-	-	-	1[c]	1	2	2	2	2	3
New York	6	10	17	27	34	40	34	33	31	33	34	34	37	43	45	45	43	41	39	34
North Carolina	5	10	12	13	13	13	9	8	7	8	9	9	10	10	11	12	12	11	11	11
North Dakota	-	-	-	-	-	-	-	-	-	-	1[c]	1	2	3	2	2	2	2	1	1
Ohio	-	-	1[c]	6	14	19	21	21	19	20	21	21	21	22	24	23	23	24	23	21
Oklahoma	-	-	-	-	-	-	-	-	-	-	-	-	5[c]	8	9	8	6	6	6	6
Oregon	-	-	-	-	-	-	-	1[c]	1	1	1	2	2	3	3	4	4	4	4	5
Pennsylvania	8	13	18	23	26	28	24	25	24	27	28	30	32	36	34	33	30	27	25	23
Rhode Island	1	2	2	2	2	2	2	2	2	2	2	2	2	3	2	2	2	2	2	2
South Carolina	5	6	8	9	9	9	7	6	4	5	7	7	7	7	6	6	6	6	6	6
South Dakota	-	-	-	-	-	-	-	-	-	-	2[c]	2	2	3	2	2	2	2	2	1
Tennessee	-	1	3	6	9	13	11	10	8	10	10	10	10	10	9	10	9	9	8	9
Texas	-	-	-	-	-	-	2[c]	2	4	6	11	13	16	18	21	21	22	23	24	27
Utah	-	-	-	-	-	-	-	-	-	-	-	1[c]	1	2	2	2	2	2	2	3
Vermont	-	2	4	6	5	5	4	3	3	3	2	2	2	2	1	1	1	1	1	1
Virginia	10	19	22	23	22	21	15	13	11	9	10	10	10	10	9	9	10	10	10	10
Washington	-	-	-	-	-	-	-	-	-	-	1[c]	2	3	5	6	6	7	7	7	8
West Virginia	-	-	-	-	-	-	-	-	-	3	4	4	5	6	6	6	6	5	4	4
Wisconsin	-	-	-	-	-	-	2[c]	3	6	8	9	10	11	11	10	10	10	10	9	9
Wyoming	-	-	-	-	-	-	-	-	-	-	1[c]	1	1	1	1	1	1	1	1	1
Total	65	106	142	186	213	242	232	237	243	293	332	357	391	435	435	435	437[e]	435	435	435
Apportionment ratio[f]	30	33	33	35	40	48	71	93	127	131	152	174	194	211	281	301	345	410	469	521

Note: "-" indicates state not yet admitted to Union. Apportionment effective with congressional election two years after census.

[a] Original apportionment made in Constitution, pending first census.

[b] No apportionment was made in 1920.

[c] Representation accorded newly admitted states by the Congress, pending the next census.

[d] Twenty members were assigned to Massachusetts, but seven of these were credited to Maine when that area became a state.

[e] Normally 435, but temporarily increased two seats by Congress when Alaska and Hawaii became states.

[f] In thousands.

Sources: Congressional Quarterly, *Congressional Quarterly's Guide to Congress,* 3d ed. (Washington, D.C.: Congressional Quarterly, 1982), 699; U.S. Bureau of the Census, *Historical Statistics of the U.S.* (Washington, D.C.: U.S. Government Printing Office, 1975), 1085.

Figure 7-1 Apportionment of Membership in the House of Representatives by Region, 1910 and 1980

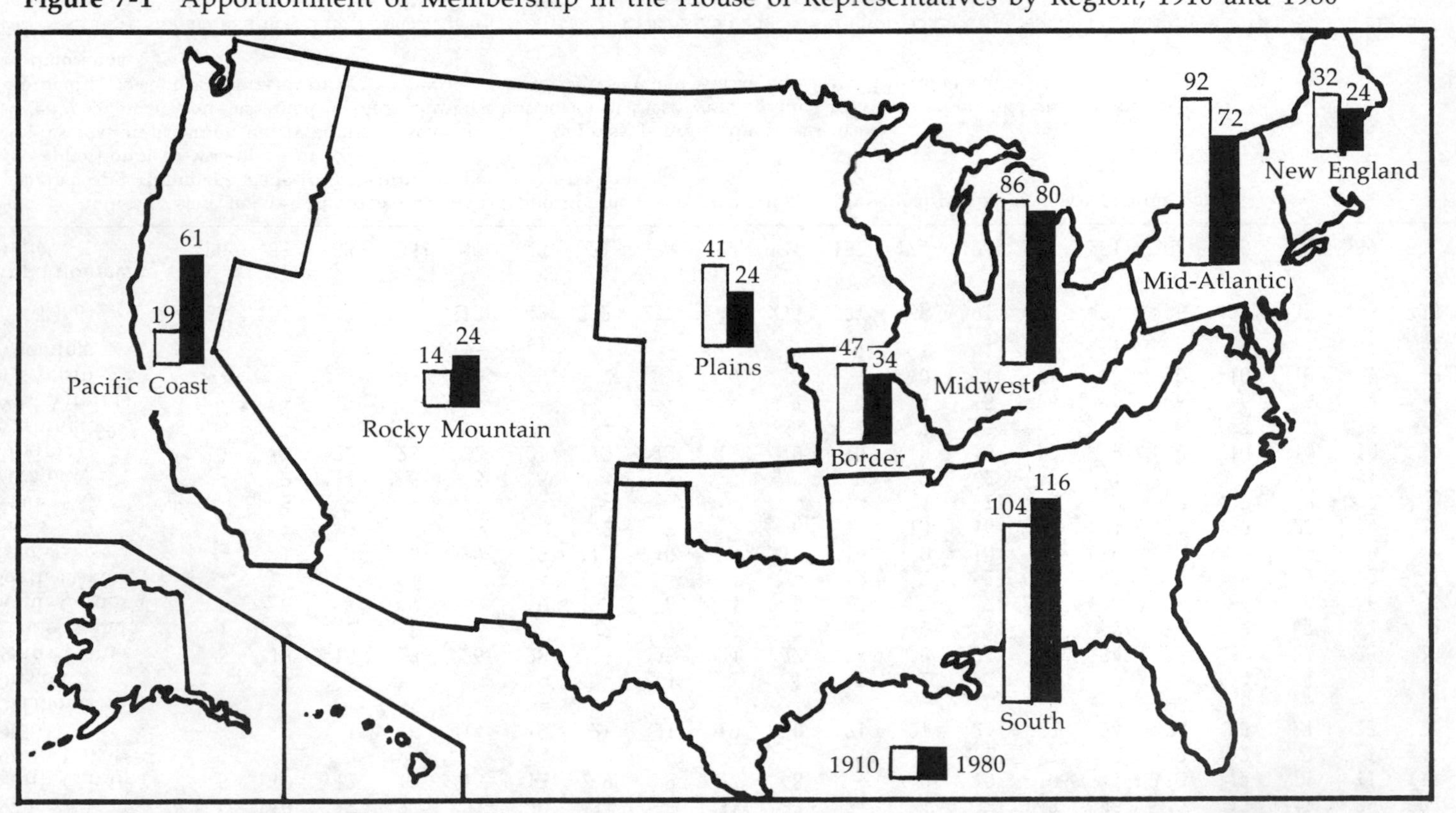

Source: Congressional Quarterly, *Congressional Quarterly's Guide to U.S. Elections,* 2d ed. (Washington, D.C.: Congressional Quarterly, 1985), 688.

Table 7-2 Members of Congress: Gender, Race, Marital Status, and Age, 1971-1987

				Age					
Congress	*Female*	*Black*	*Not married*[a]	Under 40	40-49	50-59	60-69	70-79	80 and over
Representatives									
92d (1971)	12	12	26	40	133	152	86	19	3
93d (1973)	14	15	34	45	132	154	80	20	2
94th (1975)	19	15	54	69	138	137	75	14	2
95th (1977)	18	16	56	81	121	147	71	15	0
96th (1979)	16	16	69	86	125	145	63	14	0
97th (1981)	19	17	86	94	142	132	54	12	1
98th (1983)	21	21	68	86	145	132	57	13	1
99th (1985)	20	20	69	71	155	131	59	17	2
100th (1987)	23	23	72	62	156	134	59	22	2
Senators									
92d (1971)	1	1	3	4	24	32	23	16	1
93d (1973)	0	1	4	3	25	37	23	11	1
94th (1975)[b]	0	1	6	5	21	35	24	15	0
95th (1977)	0	1	9	6	26	35	21	10	2
96th (1979)	1	0	5	10	31	33	17	8	1
97th (1981)	2	0	7	9	35	36	14	6	0
98th (1983)	2	0	10	7	28	39	20	3	3
99th (1985)	2	0	8	4	27	38	25	4	2
100th (1987)	2	0	11	5	30	36	22	5	2

Note: As of beginning of first session of each Congress. Figures for representatives exclude vacancies.

[a] Single, widowed, divorced, or separated.

[b] Includes Sen. John Durkin (D-N.H.), seated September 1975.

Sources: U.S. Bureau of the Census, *Statistical Abstract of the U.S., 1986* (Washington, D.C.: U.S. Government Printing Office, 1985), 249; 1987: Congressional Quarterly, *Politics in America, The 100th Congress* (Washington, D.C.: Congressional Quarterly, 1987), passim, and *Congressional Quarterly Weekly Report* (1986), 2863, 3175-3184, updated to include the eventual seating of Rep. Frank McClosky (D-Ind.), whose election had been contested.

Table 7-3 Members of Congress: Seniority and Occupation, 1981-1987

	Representatives								*Senators*							
			99th (1985)			100th (1987)					99th (1985)			100th (1987)		
Seniority and occupation	97th (1981)	98th (1983)[a]	*Total*	*Dem.*	*Rep.*	*Total*	*Dem.*	*Rep.*	97th (1981)	98th (1983)	*Total*	*Dem.*	*Rep.*	*Total*	*Dem.*	*Rep.*
Seniority[b]																
Under 2 years	77	83	48	16	32	50	27	23	19	5	8	5	3	13	11	2
2-9 years	231	224	239	136	102	220	118	102	51	61	55	21	34	42	17	25
10-19 years	96	88	104	66	38	116	78	38	17	21	28	13	15	35	19	16
20-29 years	23	28	33	23	10	36	24	12	11	10	7	6	1	7	6	1
30 years or more	8	11	11	11	0	12	10	2	2	3	2	2	0	3	2	1
Occupation[c]																
Agriculture	28	29	24	11	13	20	10	10	9	9	7	2	5	5	2	3
Business or banking	134	139	144	68	76	142	66	76	28	35	30	12	18	28	13	15
Education	59	43	37	24	13	38	24	14	10	12	10	3	7	12	6	6
Journalism	21	21	21	12	10	20	11	9	7	7	8	6	2	8	6	2
Law	194	201	190	122	69	184	122	62	59	61	61	32	29	62	35	27
Public service/ politics	52	49	65	42	23	94	59	35	13	2	11	4	7	20	13	7
Total	435	435[d]	435	253	182	435	258	177	100	100	100	47	53	100	55	45

Note: Members of Congress may state more than one occupation; therefore, sum may be greater than total.

[a] Data have been adjusted for the subsequent switching of parties by one representative and the representative elected to fill the vacancy created by the death of Rep. Benjamin Rosenthal (D-N.Y.).

[b] Represents consecutive years of service.

[c] Not all occupations reported are listed.

[d] Includes one vacancy.

Sources: Statistical Abstract of the U.S., 1986, 249, and *Congressional Quarterly Weekly Report* (1986), 2862, 3184, updated as in Table 7-2.

Table 7-4 Losses by President's Party in Midterm Elections, 1862-1986

Year	*Party holding presidency*	*President's party: gain/loss of seats in House*	*President's party: gain/loss of seats in Senate*
1862	R	−3	8
1866	R	−2	0
1870	R	−31	−4
1874	R	−96	−8
1878	R	−9	−6
1882	R	−33	3
1886	D	−12	3
1890	R	−85	0
1894	D	−116	−5
1998	R	−21	7
1902	R	9[a]	2
1906	R	−28	3
1910	R	−57	−10
1914	D	−59	5
1918	D	−19	−6
1922	R	−75	−8
1926	R	−10	−6
1930	R	−49	−8
1934	D	9	10
1938	D	−71	−6
1942	D	−55	−9
1946	D	−55	−12
1950	D	−29	−6
1954	R	−18	−1
1958	R	−48	−13
1962	D	−4	3
1966	D	−47	−4
1970	R	−12	2
1974	R	−48	−5
1978	D	−15	−3
1982	R	−26	1
1986	R	−5	−8

Note: Each entry is the difference between the number of seats won by the president's party in that midterm election and the number of seats won by that party in the preceding general election. Because of changes in the overall number of seats in the Senate and House, in the number of seats won by third parties, and in the number of vacancies, a Republican loss is not always matched precisely by a Democratic gain, or vice versa.

[a] Although the Republicans gained nine seats in the 1902 elections, they actually lost ground to the Democrats, who gained twenty-five seats after the increase in the overall number of representatives after the 1900 census.

Source: Norman J. Ornstein et al., eds., *Vital Statistics on Congress, 1987-1988* (Washington, D.C.: Congressional Quarterly, 1987), 51.

Table 7-5 House and Senate Incumbents Reelected, Defeated, or Retired, 1946-1986

			Defeated		*Reelected*	
Year	*Retired*[a]	*Number seeking reelection*	Primaries	General election	Total	Percentage of those seeking reelection
House						
1946	32	398	18	52	328	82.4
1948	29	400	15	68	317	79.3
1950	29	400	6	32	362	90.5
1952	42	389	9	26	354	91.0
1954	24	407	6	22	379	93.1
1956	21	411	6	16	389	94.6
1958	33	396	3	37	356	89.9
1960	26	405	5	25	375	92.6
1962	24	402	12	22	368	91.5
1964	33	397	8	45	344	86.6
1966	22	411	8	41	362	88.1
1968	23	409	4	9	396	96.8
1970	29	401	10	12	379	94.5
1972	40	390	12	13	365	93.6
1974	43	391	8	40	343	87.7
1976	47	384	3	13	368	95.8
1978	49	382	5	19	358	93.7
1980	34	398	6	31	361	90.7
1982	40	393	10	29	354	90.1
1984	22	409	3	16	390	95.4
1986	38	393	2	6	385	98.0
Senate						
1946	9	30	6	7	17	56.7
1948	8	25	2	8	15	60.0
1950	4	32	5	5	22	68.8
1952	4	31	2	9	20	64.5
1954	6	32	2	6	24	75.0
1956	6	29	0	4	25	86.2
1958	6	28	0	10	18	64.3
1960	5	29	0	1	28	96.6
1962	4	35	1	5	29	82.9
1964	2	33	1	4	28	84.8
1966	3	32	3	1	28	87.5
1968	6	28	4	4	20	71.4
1970	4	31	1	6	24	77.4
1972	6	27	2	5	20	74.1
1974	7	27	2	2	23	85.2
1976	8	25	0	9	16	64.0
1978	10	25	3	7	15	60.0
1980	5	29	4	9	16	55.2
1982	3	30	0	2	28	93.3
1984	4	29	0	3	26	89.6
1986	6	28	0	7	21	75.0

[a] Does not include persons who died or resigned from office before the election.

Source: Ornstein, *Vital Statistics on Congress, 1987-1988,* 56, 57.

Table 7-6 House and Senate Seats that Changed Party, 1954-1986

		Incumbent defeated		*Open seat*	
Year	*Total changes*	Democrat to Republican	Republican to Democrat	Democrat to Republican	Republican to Democrat
House					
1954	26	3	18	2	3
1956	20	7	7	2	4
1958	50	1	35	0	14
1960	37	23	2	6	6
1962	19	9	5	2	3
1964	57	5	39	5	8
1966	47	39	1	4	3
1968	11	5	0	2	4
1970	25	2	9	6	8
1972	23	6	3	9	5
1974	55	4	36	2	13
1976	22	7	5	3	7
1978	33	14	5	8	6
1980	41	27	3	10	1
1982	31	1	22	3	5
1984	22	13	3	5	1
1986	20	1	5	7	8
Senate					
1954	8	2	4	1	1
1956	8	1	3	3	1
1958	13	0	11	0	2
1960	2	1	0	1	0
1962	8	2	3	0	3
1964	4	1	3	0	0
1966	3	1	0	2	0
1968	9	4	0	3	2
1970	6	3	2	1	0
1972	10	1	4	3	2
1974	6	0	2	1	3
1976	14	5	4	2	3
1978	13	5	2	3	3
1980	12	9	0	3	0
1982	4	1	1	1	1
1984	4	1	2	0	1
1986	10	0	7	1	2

Note: This table reflects shifts in party control from immediately before to immediately after the November elections. It does not include party gains resulting from the creation of new districts and does not account for situations in which two districts were reduced to one, thus forcing incumbents to run against each other.

Source: Ornstein, *Vital Statistics on Congress, 1987-1988,* 52, 54.

Table 7-7 Party Unity and Polarization in Congressional Voting, 1953-1987 (percent)

Year	*House*	*Senate*
1953	52	—
1954	38	47
1955	41	30
1956	44	53
1957	59	36
1958	40	44
1959	55	48
1960	53	37
1961	50	62
1962	46	41
1963	49	47
1964	55	36
1965	52	42
1966	41	50
1967	36	35
1968	35	32
1969	31	36
1970	27	35
1971	38	42
1972	27	36
1973	42	40
1974	29	44
1975	48	48
1976	36	37
1977	42	42
1978	33	45
1979	47	47
1980	38	46
1981	37	48
1982	36	43
1983	56	44
1984	47	40
1985	61	50
1986	57	52
1987	64	41

Note: "—" indicates not available. Data indicate the percentage of all recorded votes on which a majority of voting Democrats opposed a majority of voting Republicans.

Sources: 1953-1986: Ornstein, *Vital Statistics on Congress, 1987-1988*, 208; 1987: *Congressional Quarterly Weekly Report* (1988), 101, 102.

Table 7-8 Party Support and Unity in Congressional Voting, 1954-1987 (percent)

	House			*Senate*		
Year	All Democrats	Southern Democrats	Republicans	All Democrats	Southern Democrats	Republicans
1954	80	—	84	77	—	89
1955	84	68	78	82	78	82
1956	80	79	78	80	75	80
1957	79	71	75	79	81	81
1958	77	67	73	82	76	74
1959	85	77	85	76	63	80
1960	75	62	77	73	60	74
1961	—	—	—	—	—	—
1962	81	—	80	80	—	81
1963	85	—	84	79	—	79
1964	82	—	81	73	—	75
1965	80	55	81	75	55	78
1966	78	55	82	73	52	78
1967	77	53	82	75	59	73
1968	73	48	76	71	57	74
1969	71	47	71	74	53	72
1970	71	52	72	71	49	71
1971	72	48	76	74	56	75
1972	70	44	76	72	43	73
1973	75	55	74	79	52	74
1974	72	51	71	72	41	68
1975	75	53	78	76	48	71
1976	75	52	75	74	46	72
1977	74	55	77	72	48	75
1978	71	53	77	75	54	66
1979	75	60	79	76	62	73
1980	78	64	79	76	64	74
1981	75	57	80	77	64	85
1982	77	62	76	76	62	80
1983	82	67	80	76	70	79
1984	81	68	77	75	61	83
1985	86	76	80	79	68	81
1986	86	76	76	74	59	80
1987	88	79	79	85	80	78

Note: "—" indicates not available. Data show percentage of members voting with a majority of their party on party unity votes. Party unity votes are those roll calls on which a majority of Democrats vote against a majority of Republicans. Percentages are calculated to eliminate the impact of absences.

Sources: 1954-1986: Ornstein, *Vital Statistics on Congress, 1987-1988,* 209; 1987: *Congressional Quarterly Weekly Report* (1988), 105.

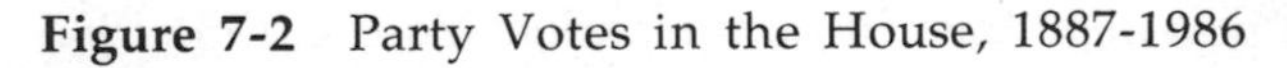

Figure 7-2 Party Votes in the House, 1887-1986

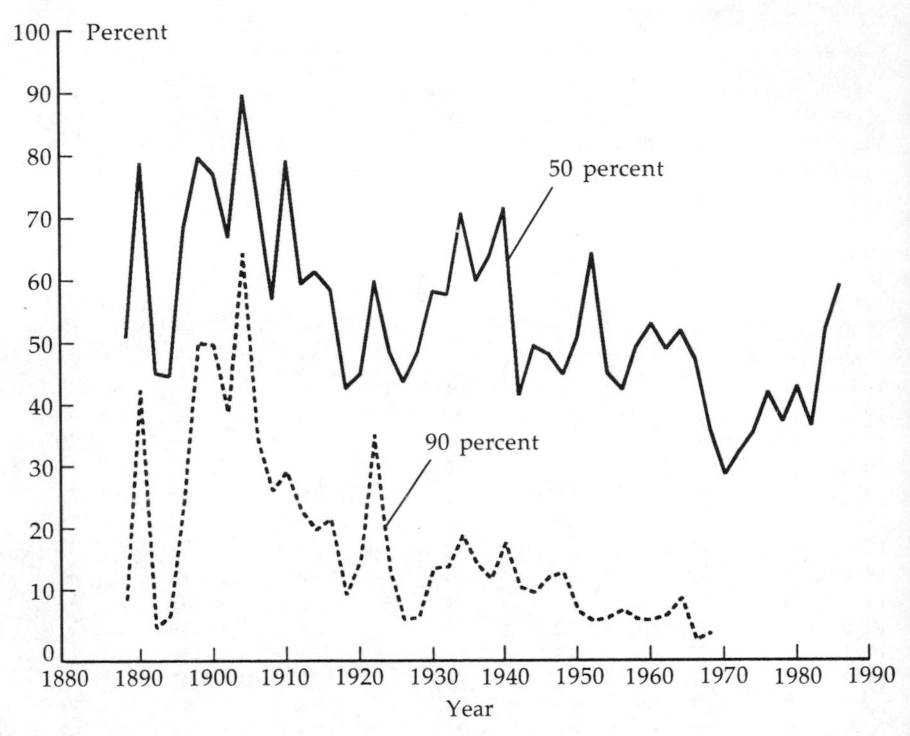

Note: A party vote occurs when the specified percentage (or more) of one party votes against the specified percentage (or more) of the other party. After 1969, figures for 90 percent party votes are unavailable.

Sources: 1887-1969: Joseph Cooper et al., "The Electoral Basis of Party Voting: Patterns and Trends in the U.S. House of Representatives, 1887-1969," in *The Impact of the Electoral Process,* ed. Louis Maisel and Joseph Cooper (Beverly Hills, Calif.: Sage, 1977), 139; 1970-1986: successive volumes of Congressional Quarterly, *Congressional Quarterly Almanac* (Washington, D.C.: Congressional Quarterly).

Table 7-9 Conservative Coalition Votes and Victories, 1957-1987 (percent)

	House		*Senate*	
Year	Votes	Victories	Votes	Victories
1957	16	81	11	100
1958	15	64	19	86
1959	13	91	19	65
1960	20	35	22	67
1961	30	74	32	48
1962	13	44	15	71
1963	13	67	19	44
1964	11	67	17	47
1965	25	25	24	39
1966	19	32	30	51
1967	22	73	18	54
1968	22	63	25	80
1969	25	71	28	67
1970	17	70	26	64
1971	31	79	28	86
1972	25	79	29	63
1973	25	67	21	54
1974	22	67	30	54
1975	28	52	28	48
1976	17	59	26	58
1977	22	60	29	74
1978	20	57	23	46
1979	21	73	18	65
1980	16	67	20	75
1981	21	88	21	95
1982	16	78	20	90
1983	18	71	12	89
1984	14	75	17	94
1985	13	84	16	93
1986	11	78	21	93
1987	9	88	8	100

Note: "Votes" is the percentage of all roll call votes on which a majority of voting southern Democrats and a majority of voting Republicans—the Conservative Coalition—opposed the stand taken by a majority of voting northern Democrats. "Victories" is the percentage of Conservative Coalition votes won.

Sources: 1957-1986: Ornstein, *Vital Statistics on Congress, 1987-1988,* 210; 1987: *Congressional Quarterly Weekly Report* (1988), 110-113.

Figure 7-3 Congressional Staff, 1955-1985

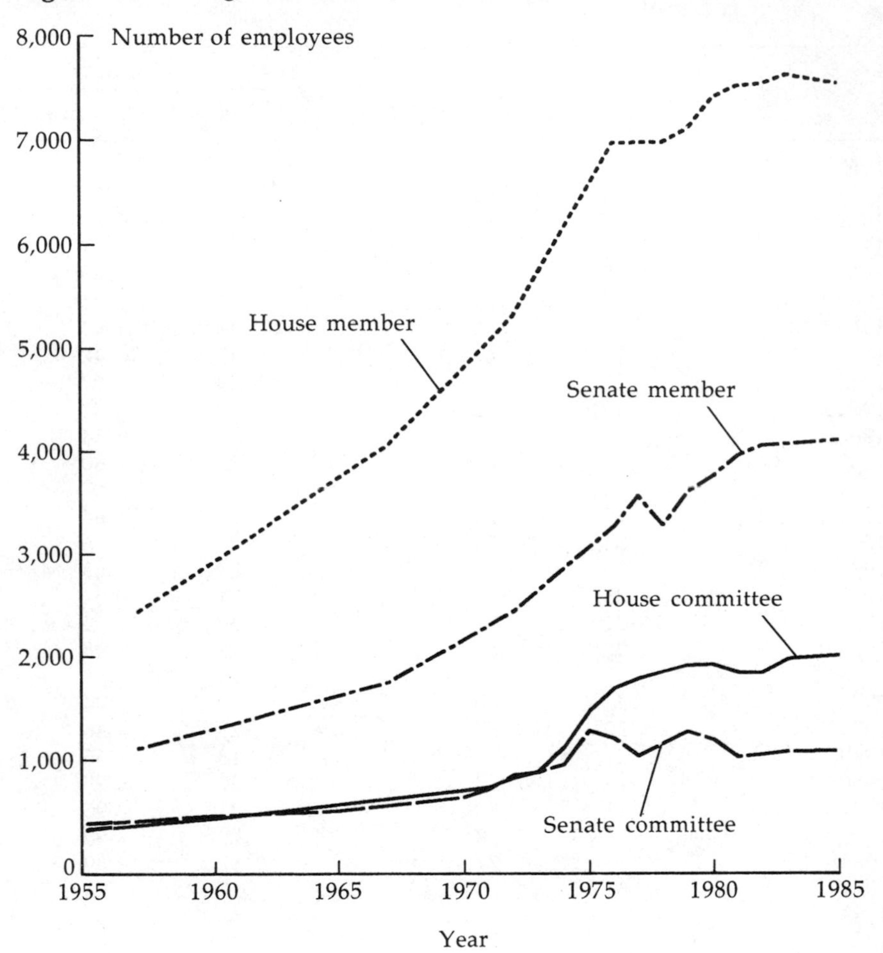

Source: Ornstein, *Vital Statistics on Congress, 1987-1988.*

Table 7-10 Bills, Acts, and Resolutions, 1947-1986

Congress	*Measures introduced*			*Measures enacted*		
	Total	Bills	Joint resolutions	Total	Public	Private
80th (1947-1948)	10,797	10,108	689	1,363	906	457
81st (1949-1950)	14,988	14,219	769	2,024	921	1,103
82d (1951-1952)	12,730	12,062	668	1,617	594	1,023
83d (1953-1954)	14,952	14,181	771	1,783	781	1,002
84th (1955-1956)	17,687	16,782	905	1,921	1,028	893
85th (1957-1958)	19,112	18,205	907	1,720	936	784
86th (1959-1960)	18,261	17,230	1,031	1,292	800	492
87th (1961-1962)	18,376	17,230	1,146	1,569	885	684
88th (1963-1964)	17,480	16,079	1,401	1,026	666	360
89th (1965-1966)	24,003	22,483	1,520	1,283	810	473
90th (1967-1968)	26,460	24,786	1,674	1,002	640	362
91st (1969-1970)	26,303	24,631	1,672	941	695	246
92d (1971-1972)	22,969	21,363	1,606	768	607	161
93d (1973-1974)	23,396	21,950	1,446	774	651	123
94th (1975-1976)	21,096	19,762	1,334	729	588	141
95th (1977-1978)	19,387	18,045	1,342	803	633	170
96th (1979-1980)	12,583	11,722	861	736	613	123
97th (1981-1982)	11,490	10,582	908	529	473	56
98th (1983-1984)	11,156	10,134	1,022	677	623	54
99th (1985-1986)	9,885	8,697	1,188	688	664	24

Note: Excludes simple and concurrent resolutions.

Source: United States Congress, *Calendars of the U.S. House of Representatives and History of Legislation,* 99th Cong., Final ed., 19-57 through 19-68.

Figure 7-4 Proportion of Measures Passed to Measures Introduced, 1789-1986

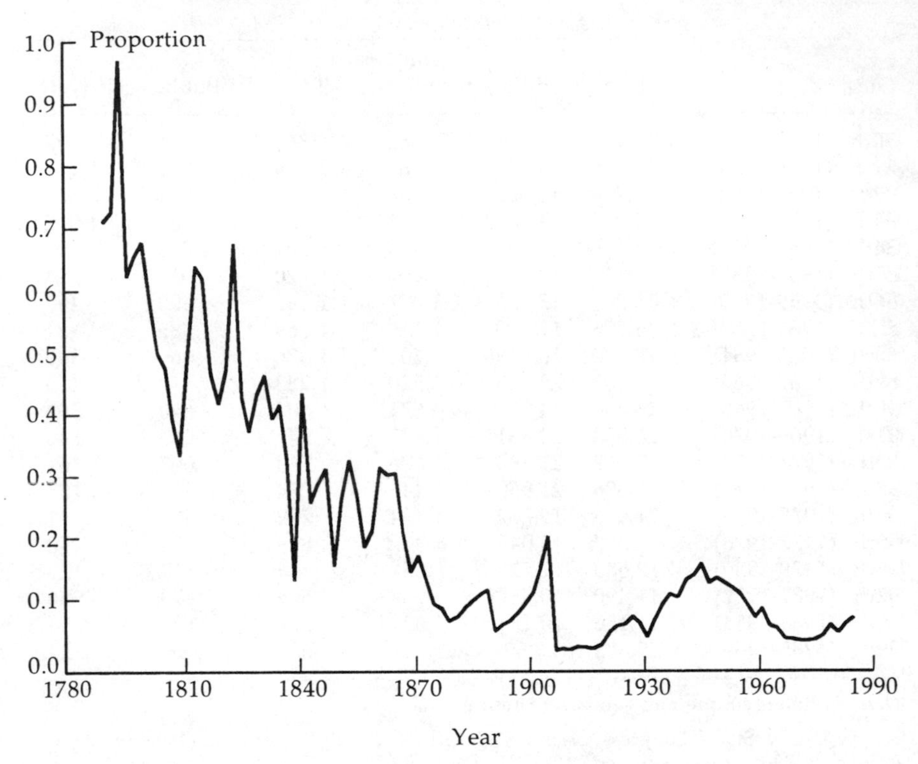

Note: Measures include acts, bills, and joint resolutions. Prior to 1824 only bills and acts are included.

Sources: 1789-1968: *Historical Statistics of the U.S.,* 1081-1082; 1969-1986: *Statistical Abstract of the U.S., 1987,* 235.

Table 7-11 Recorded Votes in the House and the Senate, 1947-1987

Year	*House*	*Senate*
1947	84	138
1948	75	110
1949	121	226
1950	154	229
1951	109	202
1952	72	129
1953	71	89
1954	76	181
1955	73	88
1956	74	136
1957	100	111
1958	93	202
1959	87	215
1960	93	207
1961	116	207
1962	124	227
1963	119	229
1964	113	312
1965	201	259
1966	193	238
1967	245	315
1968	233	280[a]
1969	177	245
1970	266	422
1971	320	423
1972	329	532
1973	541	594
1974	537	544
1975	612	602
1976	661	688
1977	706	635
1978	834	516
1979	672	497
1980	604	531
1981	353	483
1982	459	465
1983	498	381
1984	408	292
1985	439	381
1986	451	359
1987	488	420

[a] Does not include one "yea-and-nay" vote that was ruled invalid for lack of a quorum.

Sources: 1947-1986: Ornstein, *Vital Statistics on Congress, 1987-1988,* 168; 1987: *Congressional Quarterly Weekly Report* (1988), 101, 102.

Table 7-12 Number of Committees and Majority Party Chairmanships, 1955-1988

Congress	*Number of committees*[a]	*Party in majority*	*Number of majority party members*	*Number of majority party members chairing standing committees and subcommittees*	*Percentage of majority party members chairing standing committees and subcommittees*	*Number of majority party members chairing all committees and subcommittees*	*Percentage of majority party members chairing all committees and subcommittees*
House							
84th (1955-1956)	130	D	232	63	27.2	75	32.3
90th (1967-1968)	185	D	247	111	44.9	117	47.4
92d (1971-1972)	175	D	254	120	47.2	131	51.6
94th (1975-1976)	204	D	289	142	49.1	150	51.9
96th (1979-1980)	193	D	276	144	52.2	149	54.0
97th (1981-1982)	174	D	243	121	49.8	125	51.4
98th (1983-1984)	172	D	267	124	46.4	127	47.6
99th (1985-1986)	191	D	253	129	51.0	131	51.8
100th (1987-1988)	192	D	258	128	49.6	132	51.2
Senate							
84th (1955-1956)	133	D	48	42	87.5	42	87.5
90th (1967-1968)	155	D	64	55	85.9	58	90.6
92d (1971-1972)	181	D	55[b]	51	92.7	52	94.5
94th (1975-1976)	205	D	62[b]	57	91.9	57	91.9
96th (1979-1980)	130	D	59[b]	58	98.3	58	98.3
97th (1981-1982)	136	R	53	51	96.2	52	98.1
98th (1983-1984)	137	R	54	52	96.3	52	96.3
99th (1985-1986)	120	R	53	49	92.4	49	92.4
100th (1987-1988)	118	D	54	47	87.0	47	87.0

[a] Includes standing committees, subcommittees of standing committees, select and special committees, subcommittees of select and special committees, joint committees, and subcommittees of joint committees.
[b] Includes Harry Byrd, Jr. (I-Va.), elected as independent.

Source: Ornstein, *Vital Statistics on Congress, 1987-1988*, 127, 131, 132.

Table 7-13 The 100th Congress: House of Representatives

District/representative	Party	Year first elected	Year born	Percentage of 1986 vote		Campaign expenditures (1986)	Voting ratings[a]						
				Primary	General		PS	PU	CC	ADA	ACU	AFL-CIO	CCUS
Alabama													
1. Callahan	R	1984	1932	U	100	$144,314	73	75	98	0	95	29	89
2. Dickinson	R	1964	1925	U	67	245,555	71	78	88	15	86	38	73
3. Nichols	D	1966	1918	U	81	110,555	49	36	80	10	63	46	73
4. Bevill	D	1966	1921	U	78	149,263	40	67	82	40	50	79	29
5. Flippo	D	1976	1937	90	79	172,356	33	64	60	40	33	77	29
6. Erdreich	D	1982	1938	U	73	216,526	40	67	82	55	52	92	50
7. Harris	D	1986	1940	60	60	485,560	-	-	-	-	-	-	-
Alaska													
AL Young	R	1973	1933	92	57	487,261	61	63	90	20	65	62	56
Arizona													
1. Rhodes III	R	1986	1943	44	71	493,182	-	-	-	-	-	-	-
2. Udall	D	1961	1922	73	73	447,112	19	89	18	85	5	86	13
3. Stump	R	1976	1927	U	100	135,636	88	92	92	0	100	8	100
4. Kyl	R	1986	1942	59	65	1,010,199	-	-	-	-	-	-	-
5. Kolbe	R	1984	1942	U	65	618,796	69	84	88	20	73	7	88
Arkansas													
1. Alexander	D	1968	1934	52	64	703,571	22	80	58	75	24	100	29
2. Robinson	D	1984	1942	U	76	685,296	46	54	94	25	68	86	44
3. Hammerschmidt	R	1966	1922	U	80	63,341	69	69	90	5	82	14	78
4. Anthony, Jr.	D	1978	1938	U	78	179,169	27	78	62	50	30	54	40

(Table continues)

Table 7-13 *(Continued)*

District/representative	Party	Year first elected	Year born	Percentage of 1986 vote: Primary	Percentage of 1986 vote: General	Campaign expenditures (1986)	Voting ratings[a]: PS	PU	CC	ADA	ACU	AFL-CIO	CCUS
California													
1. Bosco	D	1982	1946	75	68	213,608	21	78	36	70	15	100	23
2. Herger	R	1986	1945	72	58	628,361	-	-	-	-	-	-	-
3. Matsui	D	1978	1941	U	76	563,150	20	94	18	95	5	79	17
4. Fazio	D	1978	1942	U	70	386,346	20	93	30	80	9	93	24
5. Pelosi	D	1987	1940	36	63	1,033,511	-	-	-	-	-	-	-
6. Boxer	D	1982	1940	90	74	279,727	13	84	12	90	5	100	13
7. Miller	D	1974	1945	U	67	312,522	14	84	8	90	6	91	15
8. Dellums	D	1970	1935	82	60	1,223,490	12	89	2	100	0	86	12
9. Stark	D	1972	1931	89	70	533,314	18	86	4	95	5	77	12
10. Edwards	D	1962	1915	U	71	156,410	16	95	4[b]	100	0	93	12
11. Lantos	D	1980	1928	U	74	325,435	23	89	40	70	18	100	31
12. Konnyu	R	1986	1937	53	60	897,205	-	-	-	-	-	-	-
13. Mineta	D	1974	1931	U	70	443,822	22	95	20	95	5	79	18
14. Shumway	R	1978	1934	U	72	257,431	86	82	90	0	95	7	94
15. Coelho	D	1978	1942	U	71	655,211	21	87	40	70	14	100	14
16. Panetta	D	1976	1938	94	78	115,446	20	87	30	85	11	85	31
17. Pashayan, Jr.	R	1978	1941	U	60	304,194	58	62	84	25	64	77	56
18. Lehman	D	1982	1948	U	71	292,626	20	87	26	75	10	100	25
19. Lagomarsino	R	1974	1926	U	72	289,255	80	92	88	5	86	7	89
20. Thomas	R	1978	1941	U	73	255,261	76	82	84	10	85	21	93
21. Gallegly	R	1986	1944	50	68	591,018	-	-	-	-	-	-	-
22. Moorhead	R	1972	1922	U	74	144,132	82	92	96	0	95	7	100
23. Beilenson	D	1976	1932	88	66	215,076	18	89	20	80	9	50	18
24. Waxman	D	1974	1939	U	88	136,807	12	87	2	95	5	92	20

25. Roybal	D	1962	1916	89	76	63,996	16	88	16	95	5	85	19
26. Berman	D	1982	1941	U	65	272,956	18	89	12	95	5	92	19
27. Levine	D	1982	1943	U	64	498,833	16	92	6	85	5	75	15
28. Dixon	D	1978	1934	93	76	103,442	13	80	12	85	0	100	25
29. Hawkins	D	1962	1907	93	85	34,061	19	77	6	85	0	92	16
30. Martinez	D	1982	1929	81	63	135,854	18	82	16	85	10	100	7
31. Dymally	D	1980	1926	85	70	385,063	13	92	8	100	0	93	19
32. Anderson	D	1968	1913	91	69	417,066	22	84	32	75	23	79	28
33. Dreier	R	1980	1952	U	72	148,242	83	95	94	0	95	0	100
34. Torres	D	1982	1930	U	60	111,685	18	91	10	90	5	93	18
35. Lewis	R	1978	1931	U	77	91,355	63	63	56	0	88	15	64
36. Brown, Jr.	D	1962	1920	U	57	511,240	18	82	16	95	0	92	21
37. McCandless	R	1982	1927	85	64	127,793	77	84	94	5	95	7	94
38. Dornan	R	1976	1933	U	55	1,174,637	80	82	88	5	95	8	81
39. Dannemeyer	R	1978	1929	U	75	260,009	81	90	88	5	95	0	87
40. Badham	R	1976	1929	66	60	418,975	64	73	86	0	89	8	100
41. Lowery	R	1980	1947	U	68	401,730	76	68	80	5	74	8	75
42. Lungren	R	1978	1946	U	73	215,940	86	87	80	0	95	7	100
43. Packard	R	1982	1931	U	73	132,967	83	79	88	5	91	7	94
44. Bates	D	1982	1941	U	64	410,017	19	83	24	90	0	86	44
45. Hunter	R	1980	1948	U	77	400,612	78	85	90	0	82	29	100
Colorado													
1. Schroeder	D	1972	1940	U	68	156,237	19	66	14	95	5	86	29
2. Skaggs	D	1986	1943	58	51	512,029	-	-	-	-	-	-	-
3. Nighthorse-Campbell	D	1986	1933	U	52	386,149	-	-	-	-	-	-	-
4. Brown	R	1980	1940	U	70	212,172	67	92	84	10	77	0	94
5. Hefley	R	1986	1935	57	70	283,404	-	-	-	-	-	-	-
6. Schaefer	R	1983	1936	U	65	125,435	76	84	90	0	95	15	88

(Table continues)

Table 7-13 *(Continued)*

District/representative	Party	Year first elected	Year born	Percentage of 1986 vote		Campaign expenditures (1986)	Voting ratings[a]						
				Primary	General		PS	PU	CC	ADA	ACU	AFL-CIO	CCUS
Connecticut													
1. Kennelly	D	1982	1936	U	74	388,045	20	91	20	85	0	93	35
2. Gejdenson	D	1980	1948	U	67	987,167	13	96	12	95	0	100	41
3. Morrison	D	1982	1944	U	70	567,868	16	81	8	80	0	93	27
4. Shays	R	1987	1946	39	57	-	-	-	-	-	-	-	-
5. Rowland	R	1984	1957	U	61	425,611	61	59	82	35	64	79	72
6. Johnson	R	1982	1935	U	64	425,553	52	38	68	40	55	79	72
Delaware													
AL Carper	D	1982	1947	U	66	307,300	30	78	54	55	27	86	50
Florida													
1. Hutto	D	1978	1926	U	64	134,745	57	51	92	5	82	29	89
2. Grant	D	1986	1943	51	99	266,068	-	-	-	-	-	-	-
3. Bennett	D	1948	1910	U	U	19,564	33	82	50	55	27	64	50
4. Chappell, Jr.	D	1968	1922	U	U	135,758	43	65	72	30	52	64	31
5. McCollum	R	1980	1944	U	U	121,052	84	81	96	0	82	7	82
6. MacKay	D	1982	1933	85	70	462,732	29	72	60	55	36	43	61
7. Gibbons	D	1962	1920	U	U	563,509	33	71	56	50	45	31	57
8. Young	R	1970	1930	U	U	96,142	72	75	84	5	95	8	67
9. Bilirakis	R	1982	1930	U	71	509,321	77	88	96	15	86	29	67
10. Ireland	R	1976	1930	U	71	402,873	74	87	86	0	80	8	100
11. Nelson	D	1978	1942	U	73	235,594	43	69	94	15	77	43	61
12. Lewis	R	1982	1924	U	99	285,685	71	82	86	15	70	21	76
13. Mack III	R	1982	1940	U	75	313,639	86	94	98	0	100	7	100
14. Mica	D	1978	1944	U	74	386,905	26	82	60	55	32	64	47

15. Shaw, Jr.	R	1980	1939	U	U	102,671	79	86	90	5	82	7	87
16. Smith	D	1982	1941	U	70	804,568	27	88	38	65	24	100	27
17. Lehman	D	1972	1913	U	U	172,800	20[b]	92	18	100	0	83	20
18. Pepper	D	1962	1900	U	74	1,395,549	30	80	46	70	16	100	25
19. Fascell	D	1954	1917	U	69	293,227	28	88	36	70	23	93	24
Georgia													
1. Thomas	D	1982	1943	U	100	201,603	47	72	96	25	68	43	61
2. Hatcher	D	1980	1939	U	100	140,185	34	67	78	30	56	64	69
3. Ray	D	1982	1927	U	100	150,796	56	50	82	10	71	21	88
4. Swindall	R	1984	1950	U	53	627,655	82	94	98	0	91	14	94
5. Lewis	D	1986	1940	52	75	380,314	-	-	-	-	-	-	-
6. Gingrich	R	1978	1943	U	60	733,438	72	85	80	0	81	14	94
7. Darden	D	1983	1943	U	66	534,239	49	60	80	10	79	31	82
8. Rowland	D	1982	1926	U	86	150,139	44	73	88	40	55	50	56
9. Jenkins	D	1976	1933	88	100	144,641	41	65	70	35	58	36	53
10. Barnard, Jr.	D	1976	1922	U	67	210,274	54	52	70	25	72	23	79
Hawaii													
1. Saiki	R	1986	1930	U	59	528,307	-	-	-	-	-	-	-
2. Akaka	D	1976	1924	U	76	110,490	18	89	28	90	9	86	18
Idaho													
1. Craig	R	1980	1945	U	65	310,471	75	89	92	5	86	21	100
2. Stallings	D	1984	1940	U	54	470,363	42	62	72	45	32	57	71
Illinois													
1. Hayes	D	1983	1918	93	96	113,459	13	89	4	95	0	100	6
2. Savage	D	1980	1925	52	84	150,979	14	79	2	95	0	100	7
3. Russo	D	1974	1944	91	66	483,102	18	81	26	65	9	86	38
4. Davis	R	1986	1935	U	52	272,420	-	-	-	-	-	-	-
5. Lipinski	D	1982	1937	U	70	152,573	42	74	52	45	45	92	27
6. Hyde	R	1974	1924	U	75	229,898	76	75	80	5	90	7	75

(Table continues)

Table 7-13 *(Continued)*

District/representative	Party	Year first elected	Year born	Percentage of 1986 vote: Primary	Percentage of 1986 vote: General	Campaign expenditures (1986)	Voting ratings[a]: PS	PU	CC	ADA	ACU	AFL-CIO	CCUS
Illinois *(continued)*													
7. Collins	D	1973	1931	60	80	233,583	12	78	6	95	0	100	13
8. Rostenkowski	D	1958	1928	87	79	240,208	19	84	36	65	15	86	35
9. Yates	D	1948	1909	84	72	97,479	18	88	2	90	0	85	12
10. Porter	R	1980	1935	U	75	176,228	59	68	68	15	64	7	94
11. Annunzio	D	1964	1915	85	71	171,298	23	90	32	70	5	93	39
12. Crane	R	1969	1930	U	78	365,682	82	87	90	0	100	0	93
13. Fawell	R	1984	1929	U	73	193,882	69	83	78	20	73	14	89
14. Hastert	R	1986	1942	U	52	327,219	-	-	-	-	-	-	-
15. Madigan	R	1972	1936	U	100	209,409	67	70	82	0	76	25	79
16. Martin	R	1980	1939	U	67	239,059	74	81	80	15	68	38	94
17. Evans	D	1982	1951	U	56	620,183	13	95	6	100	0	93	11
18. Michel	R	1956	1923	U	63	639,765	74	73	76	5	86	8	88
19. Bruce	D	1984	1944	U	66	278,421	20	88	34	80	9	100	33
20. Durbin	D	1982	1944	U	68	289,085	17	90	22	85	14	93	22
21. Price	D	1944	1905	52	50	143,009	27	91	44	65	18	100	29
22. Gray	D	1984	1924	U	53	304,950	28	84	48	65	18	100	35
Indiana													
1. Visclosky	D	1984	1949	57	73	163,283	19	93	20	90	0	93	33
2. Sharp	D	1974	1942	94	62	384,009	24	81	42	65	10	86	41
3. Hiler	R	1980	1953	U	50	336,768	78	89	88	0	86	0	94
4. Coats	R	1980	1943	U	70	225,157	70	84	84	10	82	14	94
5. Jontz	D	1986	1951	U	51	462,970	-	-	-	-	-	-	-
6. Burton	R	1982	1938	93	68	215,790	81	94	96	5	100	21	89
7. Myers	R	1966	1927	88	67	161,277	67	54	82	20	91	36	50
8. McCloskey	D	1982	1939	89	53	625,188	24	84	52	55	18	86	50

9. Hamilton	D	1964	1931	92	72	306,485	33	83	48	55	23	57	56
10. Jacobs, Jr.	D	1964	1932	95	58	40,577	17	61	26	85	0	79	50
Iowa													
1. Leach	R	1976	1942	U	66	231,937	47	58	37[b]	55	32	21	61
2. Tauke	R	1978	1950	U	61	387,840	53	71	58	30	43	21	88
3. Nagle	D	1986	1943	50	55	294,811	-	-	-	-	-	-	-
4. Smith	D	1958	1920	89	68	100,675	22	80	44	70	14	83	22
5. Lightfoot	R	1984	1939	U	59	474,179	70	83	84	10	64	14	94
6. Grandy	R	1986	1948	68	51	677,082	-	-	-	-	-	-	-
Kansas													
1. Roberts	R	1980	1936	U	77	87,221	69	87	90	0	82	7	94
2. Slattery	D	1982	1948	U	71	359,251	34	68	62	45	27	57	56
3. Meyers	R	1984	1928	U	100	139,791	59	73	70	25	55	14	78
4. Glickman	D	1976	1944	93	65	523,533	28	76	60	55	32	64	50
5. Whittaker	R	1978	1939	U	71	97,850	67	83	90	10	91	15	94
Kentucky													
1. Hubbard, Jr.	D	1974	1937	81	100	237,748	52	49	94	35	59	86	50
2. Natcher	D	1953	1909	79	100	5,714	29	89	58	65	23	93	28
3. Mazzoli	D	1970	1932	U	73	125,577	40	78	62	50	32	64	24
4. Bunning	R	1986	1931	U	55	895,709	-	-	-	-	-	-	-
5. Rogers	R	1980	1937	U	100	172,875	70	76	92	10	86	43	67
6. Hopkins	R	1978	1933	U	74	160,669	72	82	96	10	73	21	94
7. Perkins	D	1984	1954	U	80	240,757	22	89	40	80	9	93	17
Louisiana													
1. Livingston	R	1977	1943	U	-	151,033	76	71	92	0	82	21	78
2. Boggs	D	1973	1916	91[c]	-	261,984	22	85	48	80	18	100	25
3. Tauzin	D	1980	1943	U	-	329,823	49	56	98	20	64	50	72
4. Roemer	D	1980	1943	U	-	136,735	50	40	82	35	60	43	61
5. Huckaby	D	1976	1941	68[c]	-	326,332	41	53	80	20	65	31	73

(Table continues)

Table 7-13 *(Continued)*

District/representative	Party	Year first elected	Year born	Percentage of 1986 vote		Campaign expenditures (1986)	Voting ratings[a]						
				Primary	General		PS	PU	CC	ADA	ACU	AFL-CIO	CCUS
Louisiana *(continued)*													
6. Baker	R	1986	1948	51[c]	-	433,281	-	-	-	-	-	-	-
7. Hayes	D	1986	1946	30	57	846,953	-	-	-	-	-	-	-
8. Holloway	R	1986	1943	23	51	454,661	-	-	-	-	-	-	-
Maine													
1. Brennan	D	1986	1934	U	53	287,691	-	-	-	-	-	-	-
2. Snowe	R	1978	1947	U	77	215,659	44	53	64	50	48	64	61
Maryland													
1. Dyson	D	1980	1948	89	67	354,240	53	57	88	30	64	69	50
2. Delich-Bentley	R	1984	1923	U	59	1,070,161	57	60	80	15	62	67	63
3. Cardin	D	1986	1943	82	79	487,797	-	-	-	-	-	-	-
4. McMillen	D	1986	1952	65	50	796,344	-	-	-	-	-	-	-
5. Hoyer	D	1981	1939	91	82	368,388	21	95	26	95	5	93	22
6. Byron	D	1978	1932	84	72	206,120	50	55	78	20	71	46	63
7. Mfume	D	1986	1948	44	87	104,550	-	-	-	-	-	-	-
8. Morella	R	1986	1931	68	53	630,317	-	-	-	-	-	-	-
Massachusetts													
1. Conte	R	1958	1921	U	78	204,921	27	25	22	75	14	100	22
2. Boland	D	1952	1911	U	66	281,963	20	82	22	70	5	100	17
3. Early	D	1974	1933	U	100	186,651	13	80	16	85	14	93	20
4. Frank	D	1980	1940	90	89	213,909	18	91	12	100	0	86	17
5. Atkins	D	1984	1948	U	100	557,531	18	86	10	90	0	92	25
6. Mavroules	D	1978	1928	U	100	184,485	19	87	18	85	5	93	24
7. Markey	D	1976	1946	U	100	314,056	11	86	8	95	0	85	13
8. Kennedy II	D	1986	1952	53	72	1,800,781	-	-	-	-	-	-	-

9. Moakley	D	1972	1927	90	84	314,452	16	87	16	85	5	100	18
10. Studds	D	1972	1937	81	65	396,216	16	93	6	95	0	86	19
11. Donnelly	D	1978	1946	88	100	46,171	18	86	18	75	14	93	29
Michigan													
1. Conyers, Jr.	D	1964	1929	89	89	163,360	11	71	4	85	0	92	9
2. Pursell	R	1976	1932	U	59	140,396	51	50	74	45	55	43	76
3. Wolpe	D	1978	1939	U	60	852,746	16	91	10	90	5	93	33
4. Upton	R	1986	1953	55	62	382,663	-	-	-	-	-	-	-
5. Henry	R	1984	1942	U	71	304,765	43	67	66	40	45	43	89
6. Carr	D	1974	1943	94	57	692,787	21	75	56	70	24	86	33
7. Kildee	D	1976	1929	94	80	101,545	13	97	6	95	0	100	17
8. Traxler	D	1974	1931	93	73	98,670	19	79	34	80	9	100	29
9. Vander Jagt	R	1966	1931	U	64	398,996	62	76	76	0	79	14	89
10. Schuette	R	1984	1953	U	51	897,820	60	76	82	10	76	23	73
11. Davis	R	1978	1932	U	63	207,080	39	36	76	35	60	92	57
12. Bonior	D	1976	1945	90	66	283,904	16	90	6	95	0	100	6
13. Crockett, Jr.	D	1980	1909	80	85	56,271	12	77	2	95	0	92	15
14. Hertel	D	1980	1948	96	73	172,835	14	90	10	85	9	93	19
15. Ford	D	1964	1927	91	75	306,543	18	84	12	80	5	93	6
16. Dingell	D	1955	1926	92	78	483,019	24	80	32	75	19	92	6
17. Levin	D	1982	1931	94	76	134,327	19	97	12	85	0	100	33
18. Broomfield	R	1956	1922	U	74	68,497	70	69	72	5	73	7	100
Minnesota													
1. Penny	D	1982	1951	93	72	334,484	34	61	48	75	18	64	50
2. Weber	R	1980	1952	U	52	909,607	69	80	80	15	73	21	72
3. Frenzel	R	1970	1928	U	70	323,232	66	74	66	25	64	0	81
4. Vento	D	1976	1940	89	73	197,906	19	94	6	90	0	93	28
5. Sabo	D	1978	1938	91	73	208,043	20	95	12	95	0	93	11
6. Sikorski	D	1982	1948	U	66	492,385	17	79	22	85	5	100	33
7. Stangeland	R	1977	1930	U	50	547,810	68	71	84	10	80	21	59
8. Oberstar	D	1974	1934	U	73	156,186	18	92	18	85	5	93	6

(Table continues)

Table 7-13 *(Continued)*

District/representative	Party	Year first elected	Year born	Percentage of 1986 vote: Primary	Percentage of 1986 vote: General	Campaign expenditures (1986)	Voting ratings[a]: PS	PU	CC	ADA	ACU	AFL-CIO	CCUS
Mississippi													
1. Whitten	D	1941	1910	77	66	170,878	30	76	60	55	16	69	31
2. Espy	D	1986	1953	50	52	591,002	-	-	-	-	-	-	-
3. Montgomery	D	1966	1920	U	100	70,580	58	53	92	5	86	29	76
4. Dowdy	D	1981	1943	86	72	325,665	29	68	74	45	32	77	29
5. Lott	R	1972	1941	U	82	264,822	78	79	84	5	95	23	86
Missouri													
1. Clay	D	1968	1931	80	66	191,113	8	71	2	75	0	100	15
2. Buechner	R	1986	1940	72	52	326,375	-	-	-	-	-	-	-
3. Gephardt	D	1976	1941	U	69	881,325	16	69	18	70	0	100	18
4. Skelton	D	1976	1931	U	100	183,973	48	66	76	35	55	86	22
5. Wheat	D	1982	1951	U	71	196,612	14	96	12	95	0	86	47
6. Coleman	R	1976	1943	U	57	250,606	67	76	82	5	75	21	75
7. Taylor	R	1972	1928	U	67	143,284	68	65	82	5	90	21	71
8. Emerson	R	1980	1938	U	53	598,090	69	82	92	10	77	29	72
9. Volkmer	D	1976	1931	U	57	383,791	33	79	60	45	32	79	33
Montana													
1. Williams	D	1978	1937	U	62	229,170	12	76	18	85	5	92	20
2. Marlenee	R	1976	1935	U	53	251,163	74	80	82	0	95	7	82
Nebraska													
1. Berenter	R	1978	1939	91	64	227,910	58	73	78	15	59	21	72
2. Daub	R	1980	1941	U	59	509,019	78	89	90	5	86	7	78
3. Smith	R	1974	1911	U	70	253,292	64	62	78	10	71	8	81

Nevada													
1. Bilbray	D	1986	1938	36	54	387,717	-	-	-	-	-	-	-
2. Vucanovich	R	1982	1921	U	58	367,044	69	84	90	0	86	7	89
New Hampshire													
1. Smith	R	1984	1941	77	56	387,532	82	96	94	0	91	14	100
2. Gregg	R	1980	1947	U	74	138,713	74	85	84	20	80	21	88
New Jersey													
1. Florio	D	1974	1937	96	76	322,534	19	87	28	70	10	100	15
2. Hughes	D	1974	1932	95	68	241,948	28	78	32	75	9	79	22
3. Howard	D	1964	1927	95	59	540,240	21	93	20	85	5	100	18
4. Smith	R	1980	1953	U	61	338,224	46	32	60	45	45	93	33
5. Roukema	R	1980	1929	75	75	304,786	56	62	64	30	36	43	78
6. Dwyer	D	1980	1921	U	69	115,192	19	95	22	80	9	100	22
7. Rinaldo	R	1972	1931	U	79	387,616	40	34	60	45	55	100	28
8. Roe	D	1969	1924	96	63	211,235	22	89	28	75	10	100	18
9. Torricelli	D	1982	1951	96	69	408,779	19	85	20	70	9	100	13
10. Rodino, Jr.	D	1948	1909	60	96	407,220	16	84	10	100	0	100	19
11. Gallo	R	1984	1935	87	68	660,059	70	71	86	35	68	57	61
12. Courter	R	1978	1941	U	63	779,078	69	75	84	25	64	57	61
13. Saxton	R	1984	1943	U	65	325,522	64	67	68	30	64	57	56
14. Guarini	D	1978	1924	87	71	305,003	22	89	28	80	14	93	17
New Mexico													
1. Lujan, Jr.	R	1968	1928	U	71	243,695	57	60	82	5	68	18	80
2. Skeen	R	1980	1927	U	63	293,428	68	79	94	10	82	7	67
3. Richardson	D	1982	1947	U	71	354,849	24	90	52	75	18	100	41
New York													
1. Hochbrueckner	D	1986	1938	U	51	416,332	-	-	-	-	-	-	-
2. Downey	D	1974	1949	U	64	739,062	18	91	16	95	5	79	17
3. Mrazek	D	1982	1945	U	56	646,610	17	86	16	80	5	85	31

(Table continues)

Table 7-13 *(Continued)*

District/representative	Party	Year first elected	Year born	Percentage of 1986 vote		Campaign expenditures (1986)	Voting ratings[a]						
				Primary	General		PS	PU	CC	ADA	ACU	AFL-CIO	CCUS
New York *(continued)*													
4. Lent	R	1970	1931	U	65	337,118	61	65	72	20	64	46	64
5. McGarth	R	1980	1942	U	65	294,365	60	61	70	20	55	43	69
6. Flake	D	1986	1945	49	68	359,382	-	-	-	-	-	-	-
7. Ackerman	D	1983	1942	U	77	116,950	12	91	4	85	0	100	13
8. Scheuer	D	1964	1920	U	90	65,543	18	88	8	95	0	100	18
9. Manton	D	1984	1932	U	69	416,151	18	88	30	75	9	100	29
10. Schumer	D	1980	1950	U	93	95,951	17	88	14	85	5	86	29
11. Towns	D	1982	1934	U	89	185,565	14	81	8	95	0	100	15
12. Owens	D	1982	1936	78	92	167,617	11	89	6	95	0	93	20
13. Solarz	D	1974	1940	U	82	417,975	18	89	16	90	5	86	20
14. Molinari	R	1980	1928	U	69	152,312	69	75	76	15	59	36	72
15. Green	R	1978	1929	U	58	709,384	38	26	36	70	18	64	39
16. Rangel	D	1970	1930	U	96	375,344	17	89	4	100	0	93	11
17. Weiss	D	1976	1927	83	86	242,860	12	81	4	95	0	79	25
18. Garcia	D	1978	1933	U	94	314,485	13	83	2	95	0	100	17
19. Biaggi	D	1968	1917	U	90	252,790	27	82	36	65	18	100	21
20. DioGuardi	R	1984	1940	U	54	1,264,167	57	55	74	35	55	64	78
21. Fish, Jr.	R	1968	1926	U	77	217,637	40	33	56	45	32	57	44
22. Gilman	R	1972	1922	U	70	305,258	43	31	66	40	55	92	28
23. Stratton	D	1958	1916	U	96	38,035	50	60	62	45	42	86	29
24. Solomon	R	1978	1930	U	70	153,651	79	84	92	0	81	21	83
25. Boehlert	R	1982	1936	67	69	268,122	46	53	66	50	41	93	56
26. Martin	R	1980	1944	U	100	76,301	53	56[b]	86	15	74	42	79
27. Wortley	R	1980	1926	U	50	697,045	63	53	82	20	60	57	65
28. McHugh	D	1974	1938	U	68	287,080	23	91	18	80	9	71	17

29. Horton	R	1962	1919	U	71	96,489	27	18	48	75	10	100	31
30. Slaughter	D	1986	1929	81	51	553,072	-	-	-	-	-	-	-
31. Kemp	R	1970	1935	U	57	2,613,605	69	52	72	15	89	31	58
32. LaFalce	D	1974	1939	91	91	108,258	19	80	20	85	10	83	25
33. Nowak	D	1974	1935	U	85	76,902	18	92	16	95	5	100	28
34. Houghton	R	1986	1926	U	60	720,843	-	-	-	-	-	-	-
North Carolina													
1. Jones	D	1966	1913	U	70	87,114	27	76	56	55	22	77	40
2. Valentine	D	1982	1926	U	75	164,680	41	67	90	30	55	43	65
3. Lancaster	D	1986	1943	44	64	439,725	-	-	-	-	-	-	-
4. Price	D	1986	1940	48	56	854,616	-	-	-	-	-	-	-
5. Neal	D	1974	1934	U	54	494,014	28	75	54	65	29	71	50
6. Coble	R	1984	1931	U	50	585,245	66	84	92	10	81	36	89
7. Rose	D	1972	1939	U	64	302,654	29	78	54	55	37	67	44
8. Hefner	D	1974	1930	U	58	157,576	30	80	64	50	36	57	40
9. McMillan	R	1984	1932	U	51	877,235	66	69	94	10	82	36	100
10. Ballenger	R	1986	1926	53	57	462,333	-	-	-	-	-	-	-
11. Clarke	D	1986	1917	75	51	435,435	-	-	-	-	-	-	-
North Dakota													
AL Dorgan	D	1980	1942	U	76	391,909	26	82	44	70	27	71	29
Ohio													
1. Luken	D	1976	1925	88	62	261,455	21	84	34	80	19	86	25
2. Gradison	R	1974	1928	U	71	68,473	61	59	60	15	59	7	94
3. Hall	D	1978	1942	92	74	76,558	14	78	20	65	9	64	44
4. Oxley	R	1981	1944	U	75	184,379	80	85	86	0	95	7	100
5. Latta	R	1958	1920	85	65	268,667	63	71	88	5	91	27	86
6. McEwen	R	1980	1950	U	70	247,971	67	63	84	5	86	31	79
7. DeWine	R	1982	1947	U	100	140,405	75	85	82	0	91	14	94
8. Lukens	R	1986	1931	U	68	218,387	-	-	-	-	-	-	-
9. Kaptur	D	1982	1946	U	78	317,798	17	84	24	75	5	93	33

(Table continues)

Table 7-13 *(Continued)*

District/representative	Party	Year first elected	Year born	Percentage of 1986 vote		Campaign expenditures (1986)	Voting ratings[a]						
				Primary	General		PS	PU	CC	ADA	ACU	AFL-CIO	CCUS
Ohio *(continued)*													
10. Miller	R	1966	1917	U	70	67,073	77	83	86	5	86	14	78
11. Eckart	D	1980	1950	92	72	348,552	21	87	40	65	14	86	22
12. Kasich	R	1982	1952	U	73	424,678	70	75	88	10	82	29	89
13. Pease	D	1976	1931	77	63	415,486	26	92	32	75	18	79	77
14. Sawyer	D	1986	1945	49	54	480,813	-	-	-	-	-	-	-
15. Wylie	R	1966	1920	U	64	338,230	63	58	76	15	64	31	71
16. Regula	R	1972	1924	U	76	103,471	56	56	80	15	45	71	61
17. Traficant, Jr.	D	1984	1941	76	72	91,338	10	87	24	95	9	100	28
18. Applegate	D	1976	1928	91	100	83,591	24	75	50	65	23	93	35
19. Feighan	D	1982	1947	87	55	630,326	17	90	14	95	0	100	33
20. Oakar	D	1976	1940	94	85	378,170	16	92	8	95	5	93	12
21. Stokes	D	1968	1925	U	82	154,321	11	87	2	100	0	93	12
Oklahoma													
1. Inhofe	R	1986	1934	54	55	410,286	-	-	-	-	-	-	-
2. Synar	D	1978	1950	84	73	286,491	24	83	24	70	15	57	22
3. Watkins	D	1976	1938	85	78	210,936	32	75	66	40	41	64	29
4. McCurdy	D	1980	1950	81	76	176,096	31	70	72	35	38	42	80
5. Edwards	R	1976	1937	U	71	284,473	71	72	82	5	85	14	81
6. English	D	1974	1940	U	U	149,998	43	63	82	35	48	50	61
Oregon													
1. AuCoin	D	1974	1942	88	62	946,767	29	82	36	90	9	86	33
2. Smith	R	1982	1931	U	60	323,210	66	82	86	5	82	14	100
3. Wyden	D	1980	1949	95	86	242,600	23	89	38	80	14	79	28
4. DeFazio	D	1986	1947	34	54	295,654	-	-	-	-	-	-	-

5. Smith	R	1980	1938	89	60	312,236	74	86	90	0	95	15	88
Pennsylvania													
1. Foglietta	D	1980	1928	60	75	427,561	16	79	10	90	5	100	14
2. Gray III	D	1978	1941	97	98	551,836	13	88	8	80	5	92	33
3. Borski	D	1982	1948	96	62	391,980	20	93	94	75	10	100	33
4. Kolter	D	1982	1926	81	60	249,885	26	83	54	70	14	100	33
5. Schulze	R	1974	1929	U	66	320,232	58	60	60	15	58	46	81
6. Yatron	D	1968	1927	U	69	97,114	22	80	48	65	27	100	38
7. Weldon	R	1986	1947	U	61	617,063	-	-	-	-	-	-	-
8. Kostmayer	D	1976	1946	91	55	651,526	17	87	24	90	5	100	39
9. Shuster	R	1972	1932	U	100	276,463	77	85	90	5	90	29	94
10. McDade	R	1962	1931	U	75	291,757	49	31	66	45	63	93	35
11. Kanjorski	D	1984	1937	94	71	713,740	22	83	54	65	32	93	28
12. Murtha	D	1974	1932	81	67	272,436	42	76	68	40	52	93	25
13. Coughlin	R	1968	1929	U	59	702,834	48	51	58	45	41	71	61
14. Coyne	D	1980	1936	86	90	60,903	17	95	0	100	6	100	22
15. Ritter	R	1978	1940	U	57	440,370	70	65	88	10	90	57	94
16. Walker	R	1976	1942	U	75	75,730	82	96	94	0	86	14	94
17. Gekas	R	1982	1930	U	74	90,963	76	83	92	10	73	36	83
18. Walgren	D	1976	1940	U	63	557,031	13	83	24	85	14	86	41
19. Goodling	R	1974	1927	U	73	46,813	60	69	76	25	55	43	88
20. Gaydos	D	1968	1926	87	99	119,321	33	73	62	55	44	100	31
21. Ridge	R	1982	1945	U	81	267,525	47	59	68	35	41	64	61
22. Murphy	D	1976	1927	88	100	118,557	21	75	50	70	19	93	33
23. Clinger, Jr.	R	1978	1929	U	55	695,266	52	48	84	50	45	86	44
Rhode Island													
1. St Germain	D	1960	1928	U	58	798,700	21	87	20	80	5	100	35
2. Schneider	R	1980	1947	U	72	325,052	31	29	34	80	5	100	47
South Carolina													
1. Ravenal, Jr.	R	1986	1927	57	52	265,574	-	-	-	-	-	-	-

(Table continues)

Table 7-13 *(Continued)*

District/representative	*Party*	*Year first elected*	*Year born*	*Percentage of 1986 vote*		*Campaign expenditures (1986)*	*Voting ratings*[a]						
				Primary	General		PS	PU	CC	ADA	ACU	AFL-CIO	CCUS
South Carolina *(continued)*													
2. Spence	R	1970	1928	U	54	294,665	69	75	94	10	77	43	76
3. Derrick	D	1974	1936	U	68	177,714	28	81	52	55	26	57	44
4. Patterson	D	1986	1939	U	51	594,026	-	-	-	-	-	-	-
5. Spratt, Jr.	D	1982	1942	U	100	66,944	28	84	54	60	33	64	59
6. Tallon	D	1982	1946	U	76	269,708	40	59	86	40	57	71	44
South Dakota													
AL Johnson	D	1986	1946	48	59	430,806	-	-	-	-	-	-	-
Tennessee													
1. Quillen	R	1962	1916	88	69	459,119	62	49	82	20	77	38	60
2. Duncan	R	1964	1919	U	76	328,413	69	62	94	10	62	21	72
3. Lloyd	D	1974	1929	U	54	637,887	53	39	92	20	62	50	53
4. Cooper	D	1982	1954	U	100	127,108	31	80	52	70	14	64	53
5. Boner	D	1978	1945	58	58	909,521	30	70	60	50	30	100	18
6. Gordon	D	1984	1949	U	77	253,689	27	83	56	75	9	86	39
7. Sundquist	R	1982	1936	U	72	281,817	74	86	92	5	82	14	72
8. Jones	D	1969	1912	U	80	108,957	29	69	68	45	29	62	40
9. Ford	D	1974	1945	73	83	320,227	16	71	12	100	0	91	8
Texas													
1. Chapman	D	1985	1945	U	100	837,817	37	69	86	40	38	69	50
2. Wilson	D	1972	1933	U	66	339,873	38	61	72	35	50	92	27
3. Bartlett	R	1982	1947	U	94	592,304	77	91	94	5	95	7	94
4. Hall	D	1980	1923	U	72	269,676	56	38	88	10	80	33	80
5. Bryant	D	1982	1947	U	59	994,285	18	84	54	65	23	93	44
6. Barton	R	1984	1949	U	56	1,034,515	76	93	92	0	95	7	94

7. Archer	R	1970	1928	U	87	152,779	82	81	98	0	95	0	94
8. Fields	R	1980	1952	U	68	574,657	79	95	98	5	95	0	94
9. Brooks	D	1952	1922	U	62	400,038	21	76	50	70	9	100	33
10. Pickle	D	1963	1913	81	72	1,369,912	39	63	80	40	38	43	44
11. Leath	D	1978	1931	U	100	84,296	53	55	82	45	57	50	50
12. Wright	D	1954	1922	91	69	1,081,252	19	83	40	80	14	100	31
13. Boulter	R	1984	1942	U	65	744,332	66	85	86	5	90	14	89
14. Sweeney	R	1984	1955	U	52	883,081	67	70	94	5	86	23	94
15. de la Garza	D	1964	1927	U	100	141,973	27	72	64	55	27	85	39
16. Coleman	D	1982	1941	U	66	511,094	29	81	64	70	35	86	56
17. Stenholm	D	1978	1938	U	100	217,744	66	32	88	5	81	21	78
18. Leland	D	1978	1944	91	90	207,419	9	88	2	100	0	93	12
19. Combest	R	1984	1945	U	62	317,265	78	82	100	5	91	21	94
20. Gonzalez	D	1961	1916	U	100	133,055	17	90	10	95	0	93	17
21. Smith	R	1986	1947	31	61	1,043,325	-	-	-	-	-	-	-
22. DeLay	R	1984	1947	U	72	294,850	83	91	100	0	100	7	94
23. Bustamante	D	1984	1935	U	91	190,891	32	82	58	50	33	100	20
24. Frost	D	1978	1942	93	67	709,864	23	74	52	45	26	73	43
25. Andrews	D	1982	1944	94	100	133,817	37	72	96	50	45	64	61
26. Armey	R	1984	1940	85	68	558,559	82	97	100	0	100	7	100
27. Ortiz	D	1982	1937	85	100	127,793	36	78	70	45	40	85	29
Utah													
1. Hansen	R	1980	1932	U	52	419,959	79	80	84	0	91	0	93
2. Owens	D	1986	1937	U	55	704,609	-	-	-	-	-	-	-
3. Nielson	R	1982	1924	U	67	104,844	74	84	84	5	95	14	89
Vermont													
AL Jeffords	R	1974	1934	U	89	86,917	41	29	44	60	14	71	56
Virginia													
1. Bateman	R	1982	1928	U	56	602,251	69	64	88	0	68	7	78
2. Pickett	D	1986	1930	U	49	607,558	-	-	-	-	-	-	-

(Table continues)

Table 7-13 *(Continued)*

District/representative	Party	Year first elected	Year born	Percentage of 1986 vote		Campaign expenditures (1986)	Voting ratings[a]						
				Primary	General		PS	PU	CC	ADA	ACU	AFL-CIO	CCUS
Virginia *(continued)*													
3. Bliley, Jr.	R	1980	1932	U	67	816,159	69	82	94	5	73	14	88
4. Sisisky[d]	D	1982	1927	U	100	53,807	35	79	70	45	48	57	56
5. Daniel	D	1968	1914	U	82	124,348	61	44	80	5	86	23	88
6. Olin	D	1982	1920	U	70	356,857	36	71	66	55	14	57	56
7. Slaughter, Jr.	R	1984	1925	U	98	208,448	80	86	86	0	91	21	94
8. Parris	R	1980	1929	U	62	428,788	70	71	76	5	83	25	71
9. Boucher	D	1982	1946	U	99	262,606	23	83	36	70	6	86	20
10. Wolf	R	1980	1939	U	60	1,124,866	67	74	78	5	86	21	67
Washington													
1. Miller	R	1984	1938	U	51	592,313	56	60	58	40	55	36	67
2. Swift	D	1978	1935	U	72	239,341	19	93	22	90	9	79	18
3. Bonker	D	1974	1937	U	74	195,212	23	80	34	70	11	79	40
4. Morrison	R	1980	1933	U	72	105,513	59	56	80	25	73	38	67
5. Foley	D	1964	1929	U	75	421,477	23	91	40	75	14	86	33
6. Dicks	D	1976	1940	U	71	229,634	27	90	46	70	23	79	28
7. Lowry	D	1978	1939	U	73	170,979	17	88	6	95	5	71	6
8. Chandler	R	1982	1942	U	65	210,373	56	66	74	20	71	21	71
West Virginia													
1. Mollohan	D	1982	1943	U	100	216,378	36	79	70	50	35	100	24
2. Staggers, Jr.	D	1982	1951	86	69	136,766	18	89	32	80	5	100	28
3. Wise	D	1982	1948	U	65	138,732	23	88	40	75	5	93	22
4. Rahall II	D	1976	1949	U	71	68,970	21	90	34	90	9	93	17

Wisconsin													
1. Aspin	D	1970	1938	U	74	497,588	28	83	42	50	24	80	42
2. Kastenmeier	D	1958	1924	U	56	385,947	16	92	4	100	0	86	17
3. Gunderson	R	1980	1951	U	64	311,707	52	66	78	40	45	67	72
4. Kleczka	D	1984	1943	U	100	93,749	24	85	28	75	9	86	25
5. Moody	D	1982	1935	U	99	302,442	18	87	16	90	5	86	18
6. Petri	R	1979	1940	U	97	106,394	73	74	76	5	73	0	94
7. Obey	D	1969	1938	U	62	462,535	19	92	20	85	10	93	12
8. Roth	R	1978	1938	U	67	284,287	68	79	88	0	82	8	81
9. Sensenbrenner, Jr.	R	1978	1943	U	78	178,698	73	89	80	0	77	7	89
Wyoming													
AL Cheney	R	1978	1941	87	69	161,591	81	81	92	0	100	7	100

Note: "-" indicates a newly elected representative (no basis for rating votes). "AL" indicates at large, "R" indicates Republican, "D" indicates Democrat, "U" indicates unopposed.

[a] "PS" indicates presidential support score (percentage of the votes on which the president took a position that a member of Congress supported the president). "PU" indicates party unity score (percentage of the votes on which a member of Congress supported his or her party when a majority of voting Democrats opposed a majority of voting Republicans). "CC" indicates conservative coalition score (percentage of the votes on which a member of Congress voted in agreement with majorities of voting Republicans and southern Democrats against a majority of nonsouthern Democrats). Group ratings indicate the percentage of the time a member of Congress has supported the group-preferred position on votes the group selects. ADA (Americans for Democratic Action) is a liberal group, ACU (American Conservative Union) is a conservative group, AFL-CIO (American Federation of Labor-Congress of Industrial Organizations) is a labor group, and CCUS (Chamber of Commerce of the United States) is a business group.

[b] Not eligible for all recorded votes.

[c] Declared elected with more than 50.1 percent of the vote in an open primary.

[d] Deceased, January 23, 1988.

Sources: Congressional Quarterly, *Politics in America,* passim; *Congressional Quarterly Weekly Report* (1987), 1673, 1950.

Table 7-14 The 100th Congress: Senate

State/senator	Party	Year first elected	Year born	Percentage of vote in last election		Campaign expenditures (most recent election)	Voting Ratings[a]						
				Primary	General		PS	PU	CC	ADA	ACU	AFL-CIO	CCUS
Alabama													
Heflin	D	1978	1921	83	63	$1,917,493	76	42	84	25	65	53	58
Shelby	D	1986	1934	51	50	2,259,167	44	58	84	40	55	93	39
Alaska													
Stevens	R	1970	1923	U	71	1,195,616	83	83[b]	88	15	71	33	74
Murkowski	R	1980	1933	U	54	1,387,756	80	81	88	20	78	36	65
Arizona													
DeConcini	D	1976	1937	U	57	1,907,358	43	62	61	45	52	60	35
McCain	R	1986	1936	U	61	2,189,510	68	67	76	10	73	14	60
Arkansas													
Bumpers	D	1974	1925	U	62	1,672,432	39	77	49	70	22	64	47
Pryor	D	1978	1934	U	57	1,761,115	35	70	55	60	33	40	53
California													
Cranston	D	1968	1914	81	49	11,037,707	20	85	9	95	10	87	32
Wilson	R	1982	1933	38	52	7,082,651	82	88[b]	93	5	83	7	89
Colorado													
Armstrong	R	1978	1937	U	64	2,993,045	94	89[b]	91	0	96	0	100
Wirth	D	1986	1939	U	50	3,787,202	27	76	24	75	14	92	54
Connecticut													
Weicker, Jr.	R	1970	1931	U	50	2,306,119	45	47	46	80	14	62	50
Dodd	D	1980	1944	U	65	2,276,764	25	71	29	85	17	73	44
Delaware													
Roth, Jr.	R	1970	1921	U	55	794,210	83	83	80	15	78	13	82
Biden, Jr.	D	1972	1942	U	60	1,439,310	27	83	25	80	5	87	38

Florida													
Chiles	D	1970	1930	U	62	806,629	57	56	76	40	52	47	58
Graham	D	1986	1936	85	55	6,173,663	-	-	-	-	-	-	-
Georgia													
Nunn	D	1972	1938	90	80	729,843	58	50	75	30	55	47	50
Fowler, Jr.	D	1986	1940	50	51	2,779,297	17	30	24	15	44	43	50
Hawaii													
Inouye	D	1962	1924	U	74	1,039,418	17	72	18	90	5	100	38
Matsunaga	D	1976	1916	U	80	561,388	25	77	28	85	13	73	39
Idaho													
McClure	R	1972	1924	U	72	958,225	92	87	93	0	100	0	95
Symms	R	1980	1938	U	52	3,229,939	86	84	88	0	100	0	100
Illinois													
Dixon	D	1980	1927	85	65	1,928,750	51	62	59	65	43	80	58
Simon	D	1984	1928	36	50	4,578,703	19	89	13	80	9	80	32
Indiana													
Lugar	R	1976	1932	U	54	2,973,791	88	89	88	10	78	0	89
Quayle	R	1980	1947	U	61	1,979,561	90	94	95	5	82	0	89
Iowa													
Grassley	R	1980	1933	U	66	2,513,319	67	72	82	30	70	27	74
Harkin	D	1984	1939	U	56	2,843,695	19	91	5	90	14	93	28
Kansas													
Dole	R	1968	1923	84	70	1,517,585	92	92	95	0	91	0	89
Kassebaum	R	1978	1932	U	76	360,964	70	77	80	45	41	21	58
Kentucky													
Ford	D	1974	1924	U	74	1,201,624	34	74	47	55	35	67	53
McConnell	R	1984	1942	79	50	1,776,128	87	90	92	0	83	7	89
Louisiana													
Johnston	D	1972	1932	86[c]	-	1,179,239	58	61	67	50	35	67	44
Breaux	D	1986	1944	44	53	2,948,313	21	24	32	30	63	100	25

(Table continues)

Table 7-14 *(Continued)*

State/senator	Party	Year first elected	Year born	Percentage of vote in last election		Campaign expenditures (most recent election)	Voting Ratings[a]						
				Primary	General		PS	PU	CC	ADA	ACU	AFL-CIO	CCUS
Maine													
Cohen	R	1978	1940	U	73	1,022,134	78	63	74	50	52	20	63
Mitchell	D	1982	1933	U	61	1,208,026	31	84	25	85	14	87	32
Maryland													
Sarbanes	D	1976	1933	81	64	1,612,746	18	96	3	100	0	100	16
Mikulski	D	1986	1936	50	61	2,057,216	11	75	10	90	5	93	20
Massachusetts													
Kennedy	D	1962	1932	U	61	2,470,473	28	79	24	80	10	77	47
Kerry	D	1984	1943	41	55	2,070,000	22	85	16	90	9	93	32
Michigan													
Riegle, Jr.	D	1976	1938	U	58	1,540,563	18	96	5	95	9	93	26
Levin	D	1978	1934	U	52	3,504,962	23	91	11	90	9	87	26
Minnesota													
Durenberger	R	1978	1934	93	53	3,969,408	64	65	66	40	43	40	58
Boschwitz	R	1978	1930	97	58	6,022,365	84	84	84	15	57	13	74
Mississippi													
Stennis	D	1947	1901	U	64	944,054	63	29	75	35	40	50	56
Cochran	R	1978	1937	U	61	2,791,749	88	88	91	5	78	0	89
Missouri													
Danforth	R	1976	1936	74	51	1,806,350	80	77	82	30	57	33	61
Bond	R	1986	1939	89	53	5,376,255[d]	-	-	-	-	-	-	-
Montana													
Melcher	D	1976	1924	68	55	821,011	20	86	14	90	17	86	26
Baucus	D	1978	1941	79	57	1,224,258	30	74	37	80	13	60	37

Nebraska													
Exon	D	1978	1921	U	52	843,393	34	66	45	35	48	53	32
Karnes	R	1987	1948	[e]	[e]	-	-	-	-	-	-	-	-
Nevada													
Hecht	R	1982	1928	39	50	1,352,547	89	95	99	0	96	0	100
Reid	D	1986	1939	83	50	2,055,756	26	84	48	60	32	93	44
New Hampshire													
Humphrey	R	1978	1940	U	59	1,683,536	92	83	86	0	86	0	89
Rudman	R	1980	1930	U	63	831,098	90	89	91	10	83	0	84
New Jersey													
Bradley	D	1978	1943	93	64	4,566,758	51	66	36	85	23	87	31
Lautenberg	D	1982	1924	26	51	6,431,334	30	79	12	85	17	100	22
New Mexico													
Domenici	R	1972	1932	U	72	2,618,105	88	89	95	5	83	13	79
Bingaman	D	1982	1943	54	54	1,586,245	41	70	41	65	35	73	26
New York													
Moynihan	D	1976	1927	85	65	2,708,660	40	72	36	85	13	67	39
D'Amato	R	1980	1937	U	57	8,104,587	77	66	66	35	70	53	56
North Carolina													
Helms	R	1972	1921	91	52	16,499,387	90	95	95	0	100	0	95
Sanford	D	1986	1917	60	52	4,168,509	-	-	-	-	-	-	-
North Dakota													
Burdick	D	1960	1908	U	63	779,859	18	87	20	100	4	93	21
Conrad	D	1986	1948	U	50	908,374	-	-	-	-	-	-	-
Ohio													
Glenn	D	1974	1921	88	62	1,319,026	42	74	29	65	30	87	44
Metzenbaum	D	1976	1917	83	57	2,792,968	24	86	5	100	4	93	21
Oklahoma													
Boren	D	1978	1941	90	76	1,080,008	67	42	92	40	65	27	65
Nickles	R	1980	1948	U	55	3,252,964	86	82	99	0	91	0	79

(Table continues)

Table 7-14 *(Continued)*

State/senator	Party	Year first elected	Year born	Percentage of vote in last election		Campaign expenditures (most recent election)	Voting Ratings[a]						
				Primary	General		PS	PU	CC	ADA	ACU	AFL-CIO	CCUS
Oregon													
Hatfield	R	1966	1922	79	67	605,557	42	54	50	75	30	47	39
Packwood	R	1968	1932	58	63	6,523,492	49	58	63	60	33	40	58
Pennsylvania													
Heinz	R	1976	1938	U	59	2,607,983	69	56	59	55	43	60	50
Specter	R	1980	1930	76	56	5,993,230	31	27	29	75	33	87	44
Rhode Island													
Pell	D	1960	1918	U	73	433,436	30	75	16	80	17	67	42
Chafee	R	1976	1922	U	51	1,019,020	67	64	62	60	35	33	63
South Carolina													
Thurmond	R	1954	1902	94	67	1,638,467	89	91	97	5	91	0	78
Hollings	D	1966	1922	U	63	2,233,843	70	54	74	35	52	73	32
South Dakota													
Pressler	R	1978	1942	U	74	938,709	77	72	82	10	86	33	68
Daschle	D	1986	1947	U	52	3,485,870	20	84	44	80	18	64	22
Tennessee													
Sasser	D	1976	1936	89	62	2,088,483	24	87	37	70	17	87	32
Gore, Jr.	D	1984	1948	U	61	3,180,975	29	83	33	70	9	87	32
Texas													
Bentsen	D	1970	1921	78	59	4,971,342	60	46	87	45	50	33	68
Gramm	R	1984	1942	73	59	9,509,724	99	95	97	0	100	0	89
Utah													
Garn	R	1974	1932	U	72	741,645	80	73	75	0	94	7	100
Hatch	R	1976	1934	U	58	3,736,771	92	92	95	5	96	13	95

Vermont													
Stafford	R	1972	1913	46	50	397,015	55	53	43	60	43	50	25
Leahy	D	1974	1940	U	63	1,705,099	24	83	21	85	9	87	29
Virginia													
Warner	R	1978	1927	U	70	2,786,140	87	86	87	5	73	7	79
Trible, Jr.	R	1982	1946	U	51	2,170,771	83	85	91	5	78	7	79
Washington													
Evans	R	1983	1925	64	55	1,792,036	76	72	76	35	32	29	66
Adams	D	1986	1927	46	51	1,912,307	-	-	-	-	-	-	-
West Virginia													
Byrd	D	1958	1917	U	69	1,762,326	36	84	30	75	26	93	16
Rockefeller IV	D	1984	1937	66	52	12,057,039	31	79	18	75	13	93	32
Wisconsin													
Proxmire	D	1957	1915	86	64	145	28	76	22	60	26	60	37
Kasten	R	1980	1942	U	51	3,433,870	81	74	87	15	83	27	74
Wyoming													
Wallop	R	1976	1933	81	57	1,102,046	93	94	95	0	100	0	95
Simpson	R	1978	1931	88	78	702,643	92	90	92	10	86	0	76

Note: "-" indicates a newly elected senator (no basis for rating votes),"R" indicates Republican, "D" indicates Democrat, "U" indicates unopposed.

[a] "PS" indicates presidential support score (percentage of the votes on which the president took a position that a member of Congress supported the president). "PU" indicates party unity score (percentage of the votes on which a member of Congress supported his or her party when a majority of voting Democrats opposed a majority of voting Republicans). "CC" indicates conservative coalition score (percentage of the votes on which a member of Congress voted in agreement with majorities of voting Republicans and southern Democrats against a majority of nonsouthern Democrats). Group ratings indicate the percentage of the time a member of Congress has supported the group-preferred position on votes the group selects. ADA (Americans for Democratic Action) is a liberal group, ACU (American Conservative Union) is a conservative group, AFL-CIO (American Federation of Labor-Congress of Industrial Organizations) is a labor group, and CCUS (Chamber of Commerce of the United States) is a business group.

[b] Not eligible for all recorded votes.

[c] Declared elected with more than 50.1 percent of the vote in an open primary.

[d] Based on incomplete data.

[e] David Karnes was appointed to replace deceased member Edward Zorinsky.

Source: Congressional Quarterly, *Politics in America,* passim.

Questions

1. Find the 1980 population of the state you are from (Table 1-1). Using the number of representatives from your state (Table 7-1), calculate the apportionment ratio (the number of citizens per House member). Why does it vary from the overall apportionment ratio (Table 7-1)?

2. Describe the changes in the characteristics of congressional representatives between 1971 and now (Table 7-2). Have these changes also occurred in the Senate? Why or why not?

3. There were considerably fewer new House members in 1985 and 1987 than in 1981 and 1983 (Table 7-3). Assuming this is not due to chance, why might this be the case? (Consider Table 7-5 in your answer.)

4. Note the pattern of seat changes for the president's party in midterm House elections (Table 7-4). Why does this pattern exist? An exception occurred in 1934. Why?

5. When a new Congress meets every two years, roughly how many new representatives are there as a percentage of the House? About how many senators are new as a percentage? In each case, base your answer on the last five elections (Table 7-5).

6. In House elections, the number of seats that switch from Democratic to Republican and Republican to Democratic is usually more even in open-seat races (no incumbent running) than in those in which an incumbent is defeated (Table 7-6). For example, in 1954, 86 percent of the seats in which an incumbent was defeated changed from the Republicans to the Democrats, but this was true of only 60 percent of the open seats. Why is this the case? (Hint: think of the kinds of districts in which incumbents are defeated.)

7. Calculate and show the average party unity and polarization scores for each president, making separate calculations for the House and the Senate (Table 7-7). Is there a general decline in the scores in the House (consider Figure 7-2)? In the Senate? Compare the pattern over time here with that for split-ticket voting by the electorate (Table 4-7). How would you interpret this difference?

8. In every instance but one (the Senate in 1957), southern Democrats are lower in party support than Republicans and nonsouthern Democrats (Table 7-8). How do we know from the table that southern Democrats are lower on party unity than nonsouthern Democrats? Why are they less loyal to the party?

9. In the Senate the percentage of Conservative Coalition victories is highest in 1957 and during the Reagan years, 1981-1987 (Table 7-9). Why? (Hint: see Table 3-11.)

10. What was the approximate size of the total congressional staff (House and Senate members' staffs and House and Senate committees) in 1960 (Figure 7-3)? What was the approximate size in 1985? About how many staff members did the average House member have in 1985?

11. Under Ronald Reagan, who argued that more activities ought to be left to private initiatives, the number of measures enacted by Congress was lower than under any other post-World War II president (Table 7-10). Was this due primarily to his ideology? What evidence in the table would support or contradict such an explanation? What light does Figure 7-4 shed on this topic?

12. What modern technological development helps explain the increase in the number of recorded votes in the House in the mid-1970s (Table 7-11)? A larger number of recorded votes could have a number of effects on House members and on voters. What are some of the possible effects?

13. Representative Jack Kemp, R-N.Y., was unopposed in the 1986 primary and won by 57 percent of the general election vote, which was not an especially tight race (Table 7-13). Yet he spent more than any other candidate. Why, under these circumstances, might he have spent so much? Which Senate candidate spent the least on his reelection campaign (Table 7-14)?

14. In both the House and the Senate, those who were rated very favorably (one hundred is the "best" score) by the AFL-CIO also tended to be rated favorably by the ADA (Tables 7-13 and 7-14). Why?

15. Almost all Democratic senators with a presidential support score of more than fifty were from which region of the country (Table 7-14)?

8

The Presidency and the Executive Branch

The presidency poses special problems to those interested in the collection of statistical data. The scope and the variety of data available on the presidency are limited by the singularity of the president and the difference the individual president makes on the office's organization and operation. Moreover, the modern presidency has evolved since Franklin Roosevelt took office in the 1930s. Since then the emergence of the United States as a world power, the expansion of television, the growth of government, and the alteration of the presidential selection process have further changed the demands on and expectations of the presidency. Hence, for data on many points, the recent occupants of the Oval Office are just too few to sustain statistical analysis.

In spite of these seemingly insurmountable handicaps, the visibility of the president provides a considerable amount of relevant data. Of all elected officials, for example, only presidents have public judgments about how well they are doing prominently and repeatedly displayed: the twists and turns in the public approval ratings of a president's job performance are themselves news items. Consequently, in this book a series of figures is devoted to this subject alone—showing overall presidential approval scores for a number of presidents (Figure 8-1), two separate and more detailed ratings of Ronald Reagan (Figures 8-2 and 8-3), and ratings of the economic and foreign policy aspects of his performance (Figures 8-4 and 8-5). But presidents are not judged only by the public or only while they are in office. At various times and in various ways, historians and political scientists have rated all the U.S. presidents (Table 8-2).

Apart from approval ratings (and of course presidential elections), the presidency has not been subjected to extensive statistical scrutiny.

However, perhaps because the number of presidents has now reached thirty-nine individuals, some additional areas are beginning to receive systematic study. The president's relationship with Congress is one such area. Information about presidential "victories" on votes in Congress (Table 8-10), the extent to which the president is supported by his own party and by the other party (Table 8-11), and success in having nominations approved (Table 8-13) are all regularly tabulated and increasingly analyzed.

Media coverage is also beginning to receive systematic study. In part this study results from the extreme visibility of the president and of the federal government in general (Figures 2-1 and 2-3); it is also due to changing relationships between the president and the press, as indicated, for example, by the considerable decline in press conferences since the 1930s (Table 2-4).

Compilations of various presidential characteristics and activities also have become more numerous or more meaningful with the larger number who have served as president. How individuals get to be president, for example, has been a subject of considerable interest (Tables 8-3 and 8-4). Presidential appointments have been checked for their partisan characteristics (Tables 8-14 and 9-3) and increasingly for their racial and gender distributions (Table 9-2).

The executive branch, apart from the president, has been subjected even less to statistical analysis. Yet here, too, there is ample opportunity for meaningful tabulations if not for t-tests and correlations. The tremendous size of the federal government (Table 8-7) necessitates such an interest. The expanded involvement of the government in regulation (Table 8-9), at least until the Reagan administration, also compels attention. But there are other more subtle and more significant messages in these data. For example, the changing emphases of the nation and of the priorities of particular presidents can be seen in such mundane listings as the size and composition of the White House staff (Table 8-6).

Thus, while the presidency provides data for conventional statistical analyses in only a few areas, a generous and increasing amount of numerical data provides considerable insight into what has traditionally been viewed as an office of impressive singularity.

Table 8-1 Presidents and Vice Presidents of the United States

President (political party)	*Born*	*Died*	*Age at inauguration*	*Native of...*	*Elected from...*	*Term of service*	*Vice president*
George Washington (F)	1732	1799	57	Va.	Va.	April 30, 1789-March 4, 1793	John Adams
George Washington (F)			61			March 4, 1793-March 4, 1797	John Adams
John Adams (F)	1735	1826	61	Mass.	Mass.	March 4, 1797-March 4, 1801	Thomas Jefferson
Thomas Jefferson (D-R)	1743	1826	57	Va.	Va.	March 4, 1801-March 4, 1805	Aaron Burr
Thomas Jefferson (D-R)			61			March 4, 1805-March 4, 1809	George Clinton
James Madison (D-R)	1751	1836	57	Va.	Va.	March 4, 1809-March 4, 1813	George Clinton
James Madison (D-R)			61			March 4, 1813-March 4, 1817	Elbridge Gerry
James Monroe (D-R)	1758	1831	58	Va.	Va.	March 4, 1817-March 4, 1821	Daniel D. Tompkins
James Monroe (D-R)			62			March 4, 1821-March 4, 1825	Daniel D. Tompkins
John Q. Adams (N-R)	1767	1848	57	Mass.	Mass.	March 4, 1825-March 4, 1829	John C. Calhoun
Andrew Jackson (D)	1767	1845	61	S.C.	Tenn.	March 4, 1829-March 4, 1833	John C. Calhoun
Andrew Jackson (D)			65			March 4, 1833-March 4, 1837	Martin Van Buren
Martin Van Buren (D)	1782	1862	54	N.Y.	N.Y.	March 4, 1837-March 4, 1841	Richard M. Johnson
W. H. Harrison (W)	1773	1841	68	Va.	Ohio	March 4, 1841-April 4, 1841	John Tyler
John Tyler (W)	1790	1862	51	Va.	Va.	April 6, 1841-March 4, 1845	
James K. Polk (D)	1795	1849	49	N.C.	Tenn.	March 4, 1845-March 4, 1849	George M. Dallas
Zachary Taylor (W)	1784	1850	64	Va.	La.	March 4, 1849-July 9, 1850	Millard Fillmore
Millard Fillmore (W)	1800	1874	50	N.Y.	N.Y.	July 10, 1850-March 4, 1853	
Franklin Pierce (D)	1804	1869	48	N.H.	N.H.	March 4, 1853-March 4, 1857	William R. King
James Buchanan (D)	1791	1868	65	Pa.	Pa.	March 4, 1857-March 4, 1861	John C. Breckinridge
Abraham Lincoln (R)	1809	1865	52	Ky.	Ill.	March 4, 1861-March 4, 1865	Hannibal Hamlin
Abraham Lincoln (R)			56			March 4, 1865-April 15, 1865	Andrew Johnson
Andrew Johnson (R)	1808	1875	56	N.C.	Tenn.	April 15, 1865-March 4, 1869	
Ulysses S. Grant (R)	1822	1885	46	Ohio	Ill.	March 4, 1869-March 4, 1873	Schuyler Colfax
Ulysses S. Grant (R)			50			March 4, 1873-March 4, 1877	Henry Wilson
Rutherford B. Hayes (R)	1822	1893	54	Ohio	Ohio	March 4, 1877-March 4, 1881	William A. Wheeler
James A. Garfield (R)	1831	1881	49	Ohio	Ohio	March 4, 1881-Sept. 19, 1881	Chester A. Arthur
Chester A. Arthur (R)	1830	1886	50	Vt.	N.Y.	Sept. 20, 1881-March 4, 1885	
Grover Cleveland (D)	1837	1908	47	N.J.	N.Y.	March 4, 1885-March 4, 1889	Thomas A. Hendricks
Benjamin Harrison (R)	1833	1901	55	Ohio	Ind.	March 4, 1889-March 4, 1893	Levi P. Morton

Grover Cleveland (D)	1837	1908	55			March 4, 1893-March 4, 1897	Adlai E. Stevenson
William McKinley (R)	1843	1901	54	Ohio	Ohio	March 4, 1897-March 4, 1901	Garret A. Hobart
William McKinley (R)			58			March 4, 1901-Sept. 14, 1901	Theodore Roosevelt
Theodore Roosevelt (R)	1858	1919	42	N.Y.	N.Y.	Sept. 14, 1901-March 4, 1905	
Theodore Roosevelt (R)			46			March 4, 1905-March 4, 1909	Charles W. Fairbanks
William H. Taft (R)	1857	1930	51	Ohio	Ohio	March 4, 1909-March 4, 1913	James S. Sherman
Woodrow Wilson (D)	1856	1924	56	Va.	N.J.	March 4, 1913-March 4, 1917	Thomas R. Marshall
Woodrow Wilson (D)			60			March 4, 1917-March 4, 1921	Thomas R. Marshall
Warren G. Harding (R)	1865	1923	55	Ohio	Ohio	March 4, 1921-Aug. 2, 1923	Calvin Coolidge
Calvin Coolidge (R)	1872	1933	51	Vt.	Mass.	Aug. 3, 1923-March 4, 1925	
Calvin Coolidge (R)			52			March 4, 1925-March 4, 1929	Charles G. Dawes
Herbert Hoover (R)	1874	1964	54	Iowa	Calif.	March 4, 1929-March 4, 1933	Charles Curtis
Franklin D. Roosevelt (D)	1882	1945	51	N.Y.	N.Y.	March 4, 1933-Jan. 20, 1937	John N. Garner
Franklin D. Roosevelt (D)			55			Jan. 20, 1937-Jan. 20, 1941	John N. Garner
Franklin D. Roosevelt (D)			59			Jan. 20, 1941-Jan. 20, 1945	Henry A. Wallace
Franklin D. Roosevelt (D)			63			Jan. 20, 1945-April 12, 1945	Harry S Truman
Harry S Truman (D)	1884	1972	60	Mo.	Mo.	April 12, 1945-Jan. 20, 1949	
Harry S Truman (D)			64			Jan. 20, 1949-Jan. 20, 1953	Alben W. Barkley
Dwight D. Eisenhower (R)	1890	1969	62	Texas	N.Y.	Jan. 20, 1953-Jan. 20, 1957	Richard M. Nixon
Dwight D. Eisenhower (R)			66		Pa.	Jan. 20, 1957-Jan. 20, 1961	Richard M. Nixon
John F. Kennedy (D)	1917	1963	43	Mass.	Mass.	Jan. 20, 1961-Nov. 22, 1963	Lyndon B. Johnson
Lyndon B. Johnson (D)	1906	1973	55	Texas	Texas	Nov. 22, 1963-Jan. 20, 1965	
Lyndon B. Johnson (D)			56			Jan. 20, 1965-Jan. 20, 1969	Hubert H. Humphrey
Richard M. Nixon (R)	1913		56	Calif.	N.Y.	Jan. 20, 1969-Jan. 20, 1973	Spiro T. Agnew
Richard M. Nixon (R)			60		Calif.	Jan. 20, 1973-Aug. 9, 1974	Spiro T. Agnew
							Gerald R. Ford
Gerald R. Ford (R)	1913		61	Neb.	Mich.	Aug. 9, 1974-Jan. 20, 1977	Nelson A. Rockefeller
Jimmy Carter (D)	1924		52	Ga.	Ga.	Jan. 20, 1977-Jan. 20, 1981	Walter F. Mondale
Ronald Reagan (R)	1911		69	Ill.	Calif.	Jan. 20, 1981-Jan. 20, 1985	George Bush
Ronald Reagan (R)			73			Jan. 20, 1985-	George Bush

Note: "D" indicates Democrat, "D-R" indicates Democrat-Republican, "F" indicates Federalist, "N-R" indicates National Republican, "R" indicates Republican, and "W" indicates Whig.

Source: Congressional Quarterly, *Presidential Elections Since 1789*, 4th ed. (Washington, D.C.: Congressional Quarterly, 1987), 4.

Table 8-2 Ratings of U.S. Presidents

Schlesinger poll (1948)	*Schlesinger poll (1962)*	*Dodder poll (1970)*	*DiClerico poll (1977)*	*Tribune poll (1982)*	*Murray poll (1982)*
Great	Great	Accomplishments of administration	Ten greatest presidents	Ten best presidents	Presidential rank
1. Lincoln	1. Lincoln	1. Lincoln	1. Lincoln	1. Lincoln (best)	1. Lincoln
2. Washington	2. Washington	2. F. Roosevelt	2. Washington	2. Washington	2. F. Roosevelt
3. F. Roosevelt	3. F. Roosevelt	3. Washington	3. F. Roosevelt	3. F. Roosevelt	3. Washington
4. Wilson	4. Wilson	4. Jefferson	4. Jefferson	4. T. Roosevelt	4. Jefferson
5. Jefferson	5. Jefferson	5. T. Roosevelt	5. T. Roosevelt	5. Jefferson	5. T. Roosevelt
6. Jackson		6. Truman	6. Wilson	6. Wilson	6. Wilson
		7. Wilson	7. Jackson	7. Jackson	7. Jackson
Near great	Near great	8. Jackson	8. Truman	8. Truman	8. Truman
7. T. Roosevelt	6. Jackson	9. L. Johnson	9. Polk	9. Eisenhower	9. J. Adams
8. Cleveland	7. T. Roosevelt	10. Polk	10. J. Adams	10. Polk (10th best)	10. L. Johnson
9. J. Adams	8. Polk	11. J. Adams			11. Eisenhower
10. Polk	Truman (tie)	12. Kennedy		Ten worst presidents	12. Polk
	9. J. Adams	13. Monroe		1. Harding (worst)	13. Kennedy
	10. Cleveland	14. Cleveland		2. Nixon	14. Madison
Average	Average	15. Madison		3. Buchanan	15. Monroe
11. J. Q. Adams	11. Madison	16. Taft		4. Pierce	16. J. Q. Adams
12. Monroe	12. J. Q. Adams	17. McKinley		5. Grant	17. Cleveland
13. Hayes	13. Hayes	18. J. Q. Adams		6. Fillmore	18. McKinley
14. Madison	14. McKinley	19. Hoover		7. A. Johnson	19. Taft
15. Van Buren	15. Taft	20. Eisenhower		8. Coolidge	20. Van Buren
16. Taft	16. Van Buren	21. A. Johnson		9. Tyler	21. Hoover
17. Arthur	17. Monroe	22. Van Buren		10. Carter (10th worst)	22. Hayes
18. McKinley	18. Hoover	23. Arthur			23. Arthur
19. A. Johnson	19. B. Harrison	24. Hayes			24. Ford
					25. Carter

20. Hoover	20. Arthur	25. Tyler	26. B. Harrison
21. B. Harrison	Eisenhower (tie)	26. B. Harrison	27. Taylor
	21. A. Johnson	27. Taylor	28. Tyler
		28. Buchanan	29. Fillmore
Below average	Below average	29. Fillmore	30. Coolidge
22. Tyler	22. Taylor	30. Coolidge	31. Pierce
23. Coolidge	23. Tyler	31. Pierce	32. A. Johnson
24. Fillmore	24. Fillmore	32. Grant	33. Buchanan
25. Taylor	25. Coolidge	33. Harding	34. Nixon
26. Buchanan	26. Pierce		35. Grant
27. Pierce	27. Buchanan		36. Harding
Failure	Failure		
28. Grant	28. Grant		
29. Harding	29. Harding		

Note: These ratings result from surveys of scholars ranging in number from 55 to 950.

Source: Henry J. Abraham, *Justices and Presidents: Appointments to the Supreme Court*, 2d ed. (New York: Oxford University Press, 1985), 380-383 (copyright © Henry J. Abraham, 1974, 1985, reprinted by permission of Oxford University Press, Inc.); Arthur Murphy, "Evaluating the Presidents of the United States," *Presidential Studies Quarterly* 14 (1984): 117-126.

Table 8-3 Previous Public Positions Held by Presidents

Position	*Number of presidents holding position prior to presidency*	
	Pre-1900 (24)	Post-1900 (15)
Vice president	7	7
Cabinet secretary	7	2
Subcabinet official	1	5
U.S. representative	13	4
U.S. senator	8	5
U.S. Supreme Court justice	0	0
Federal judge	0	1
Governor	11	6
State legislator	17	5
State executive	10	2
State judge	1	3
Mayor	2	1
City government official	1	3
Diplomat, ambassador	7	1
Military general	5	1

Position	*Last public position held before presidency*	
	Pre-1900 (24)	Post-1900 (15)
Vice president		
Succeeded to presidency	4	5
Won presidency in own right	3	1
Congress		
Senate	3	2
House	1	0
Appointive federal office		
Military general	3	1
Cabinet secretary	3	2
Ambassador	2	0
Other civilian	1	0
Governor	4	4

Sources: Previous public positions: Richard M. Pious, *The American Presidency* (New York: Basic Books, 1979), 87, updated by the editors (copyright © 1979 by Richard M. Pious, reprinted by permission of Basic Books, Inc., publishers); last public position: Richard A. Watson and Norman C. Thomas, *The Politics of the Presidency*, 2d ed. (Washington, D.C.: CQ Press, 1988), 122-123.

Table 8-4 Candidates for Presidential Nominations by Latest Public Office Held, 1936-1984

Public office[a]	*Percentage of all persons polling at least 1 percent in Gallup Poll*	*Percentage of all nominees*
Vice president	2	31
U.S. senator	35	19
Governor	23	38
Cabinet officer	17	0
U.S. representative	6	0
Mayor	4	0
Supreme Court justice	2	0
All others	1	0
None	10	12
Total	100 (*N*=109)	100 (*N*=16)

[a] Last or current office at time person first polled at least 1 percent support for presidential nomination among fellow partisans or was first nominated.

Source: William R. Keech and Donald R. Matthews, *The Party's Choice: With an Epilogue on the 1976 Nominations* (Washington, D.C.: Brookings, 1976), 18; updated by the editors.

Table 8-5 The President's Cabinet, 1988

Cabinet office	*Year established*[a]	*Current secretary*[b]	*Date confirmed*	*Number of paid civilian employees* 1980	1987[c]	*Number of non-civil service positions*[c]	*Percentage of all positions*
State	1789	George P. Shultz	7/15/82	23,497	25,410	21,349	84
Treasury	1789	James A. Baker III	1/29/85	124,633	153,136	9,332	6
War	1789[d]						
Navy	1798[d]						
Interior	1849	Donald P. Hodel	2/6/85	77,357	69,956	15,673	22
Justice	1870	Edwin Meese III	2/23/85	56,327	66,721	29,776	45
Post Office	1872[e]						
Agriculture	1889	Richard E. Lyng	3/6/86	129,139	106,101	13,771	13
Commerce and Labor	1903[f]						
Commerce	1913	C. William Verity, Jr.	10/13/87	48,563	34,212	6,529	19
Labor	1913	Ann Dore McLaughlin	12/11/87	23,400	17,626	1,299	7
Defense	1947	Frank C. Carlucci	11/20/87	960,116	1,076,194	180,720	17
Health, Education and Welfare	1953[g]						
Health and Human Services	1979	Otis R. Bowen	12/12/85	155,662	130,453	18,940	15
Housing and Urban Development	1965	Samuel R. Pierce, Jr.	1/22/81	16,964[h]	12,439[h]	875	7
Transportation	1966	James H. Burnley IV	11/30/87	72,361	61,594	2,443	4
Energy	1977	John S. Herrington	2/6/85	21,557	16,480	1,580	10
Education	1979	William J. Bennett	2/6/85	7,364	4,544	726	16

Note: The Cabinet also currently includes Vice President George Bush and nondepartmental secretaries: Chief of Staff Howard Baker, U.S. Trade Representative Clayton Yeutter, Director of the Office of Management and the Budget James Miller, U.N. Ambassador Vernon Walters, and Chairman of the Council of Economic Advisors Beryl Sprinkel.

[a] Dates are when the department achieved cabinet status. Offices of Attorney General and Postmaster General were created in 1789, but executive departments were not created until later. A Department of Agriculture was established in 1862, but the commissioner did not achieve cabinet status until 1889.

[b] As of January 25, 1988.

[c] As of March 1987. Non-civil service positions include excepted and senior executive service.

[d] Incorporated into Defense Department in 1947.

[e] Independent agency as of 1971.

[f] Split into separate departments in 1913.

[g] Split into Health and Human Services and Education in 1979.

[h] Number of civilian employees includes Housing and Home Finance Agency.

Sources: Ronald C. Moe, "The Federal Executive Establishment: Evolution and Trends," prepared for the U.S. Senate Commitee on Government Affairs by the Congressional Research Service (Washington, D.C.: U.S. Government Printing Office, 1980), 26-27; U.S. Bureau of the Census, *Statistical Abstract of the U.S., 1987* (Washington, D.C.: U.S. Government Printing Office, 1986), 312; U.S. Office of Personnel Management, *Federal Civilian Workforce Statistics, Employment and Trends* (March 1987), 30-31.

Table 8-6 White House Staff and the Executive Office of the President, 1943-1987

Year	White House	OMB/ Bureau of Budget[a]	Council of Economic Advisors	National Security Council	Office of Economic Opportunity	Office of Science and Technology	Office of Adminis-tration	Special Representative for Trade Negotiations	Office of Policy Development/ Domestic Council	Total executive office[b]
1943[c]	51	543								703
1944[c]	58	542								683
1945[c]	64	705								820
1946[c]	216	692	26							1,034
1947[c]	228	549	26							1,077
1948[c]	209	521	38	20						1,205
1949	243	517	36	17						1,240
1950	313	509	38	17						1,408
1951	246	518	37	21						1,326
1952	248	470	31	22						1,296
1953	247	417	28	28						1,183
1954	262	430	34	26						1,078
1955	366	422	33	27						1,221
1956	392	443	38	25						1,228
1957	399	441	35	65						1,255
1958	395	424	33	61						2,605
1959	406	432	33	64						2,735
1960	423	441	31	64						2,779
1961	439	456	45	43						1,586
1962	338	465	65	39		63				1,492
1963	376	485	57	43		48		30		1,572
1964	328	493	46	41		57		29		1,478
1965	292	506	45	39	1,768	75		24		3,307

1966	270	592	62	40	2,319	105		26		4,050
1967	271	570	56	38	2,951	58		24		4,747
1968	261	550	74	35	3,211	62		22		4,964
1969	341	576	54	66	2,282	75		22		4,116
1970	491	636	57	82	2,633	77		26	26	4,808
1971	580	717	62	80	2,304	75		33	44	4,809
1972	583	703	58	80	2,066	76		38	53	5,721
1973	528	642	49	85	1,148			39	24	3,877
1974	560	646	46	87	1,090			45	32	2,868
1975	525	664	48	85				56	55	1,801
1976	534	694	39	79		19		55	43	1,796
1977	387	721	36	68		44		52	41	1,637
1978	381	617	35	76		46	197	58	55	1,679
1979	418	638	36	73		44	180	70	60	1,918
1980	426	631	38	74		50	182	131	68	2,013
1981	378	679	38	65		13	190	139	48	1,674
1982	374	617	35	59		20	196	138	46	1,608
1983	376	619	34	61		23	213	139	39	1,622
1984	371	605	28	63		21	196	147	40	1,593
1985	368	568	33	64		17	196	149	32	1,549
1986	360	541	35	66		12	198	143	44	1,525
1987	367	546	32	62		9	199	148	34	1,540

Note: In almost all instances when no figures are shown, the office did not exist as a separate entity. Data as of December of the year indicated, except 1947 (January), 1960 (October), 1985 and 1986 (November), and 1987 (July).

[a] The Bureau of the Budget became the Office of Management and the Budget in 1970.

[b] Includes offices not shown separately.

[c] Total executive office excludes personnel in war establishments or emergency war agencies.

Source: U.S. Office of Personnel Management, *Federal Manpower Statistics, Federal Civilian Workforce Statistics,* monthly release.

Table 8-7 Number of Civilian Federal Government Employees and Percentage Under Merit Civil Service, 1816-1985

Year	*Total number of employees*[a]	*Percentage under merit*	*Year*	*Total number of employees*	*Percentage under merit*
1816	4,837	—	1942	2,296,384	—
1821	6,914	—	1943	3,299,414	—
1831	11,491	—	1944	3,332,356	—
1841	18,038	—	1945	3,816,310	—
1851	26,274	—	1946	2,696,529	—
1861	36,672	—	1947	2,111,001	80.2
1871	51,020	—	1948	2,071,009	82.4
1881	100,020	—	1949	2,102,109	84.3
1891	157,442	21.5	1950	1,960,708	84.5
1901	239,476	44.3	1951	2,482,666	86.4
1908	356,754	57.9	1952	2,600,612	86.4
1909	372,379	63.1	1953	2,558,416	83.6
1910	388,708	57.2	1954	2,407,676	82.7
1911	395,905	57.5	1955	2,397,309	83.6
1912	400,150	54.3	1956	2,398,736	85.1
1913	396,494	71.3	1957	2,417,565	85.5
1914	401,887	72.8	1958	2,382,491	85.3
1915	395,429	73.9	1959	2,382,807	85.7
1916	399,381	74.3	1960	2,398,704	85.5
1917	438,500	74.5	1961	2,435,804	86.1
1918	854,500	75.2	1962	2,514,197	85.9
1919	794,271	86.6	1963	2,527,960	85.6
1920	655,265	75.9	1964	2,500,503	86.1
1921	561,142	79.9	1965	2,527,915	85.2
1922	543,507	77.4	1966	2,759,019	85.8
1923	536,900	76.6	1967	3,002,461	82.8
1924	543,484	76.5	1968	3,055,212	84.1
1925	553,045	76.6	1969	3,076,414	82.9
1926	548,713	77.0	1970	2,981,574	82.3
1927	547,127	77.3	1972[b]	2,608,000	65.6
1928	560,772	77.0	1973	2,667,000	61.6
1929	579,559	88.2	1974	2,724,000	62.6
1930	601,319	87.9	1975	2,741,000	62.5
1931	609,746	76.8	1976	2,725,000	62.0
1932	605,496	77.2	1977	2,724,000	62.6
1933	603,587	75.6	1978	2,752,000	63.5
1934	698,649	64.5	1979	2,763,000	55.7
1935	780,582	58.3	1980	2,772,000	61.0
1936	867,432	57.5	1981	2,722,000	61.1
1937	895,993	59.4	1982	2,733,000	61.3
1938	882,226	63.8	1983	2,754,000	61.2
1939	953,891	69.5	1984	2,824,000	60.1
1940	1,042,420	69.7	1985	2,902,000	58.9
1941	1,437,682	68.9			

(Notes follow)

Table 8-7 *(Continued)*

Note: "—"indicates not available.
[a] Excludes employees of the Central Intelligence Agency and the National Security Agency.
[b] Under Postal Reorganization Act of 1970, U.S. Postal Service employees were changed from competitive (merit) service to excepted service.

Sources: 1816-1970: U.S. Bureau of the Census, *Historical Statistics of the U.S.* (Washington, D.C.: U.S. Government Printing Office, 1975), 1102-1103; 1972-1985: U.S. Bureau of the Census, *Statistical Abstract of the U.S., 1977,* 268, *1980,* 279, *1987,* 309.

Table 8-8 Major Regulatory Agencies

Agency	*Year established*	*Agency head* Number	Title	*Number of employees*[a]
Consumer Product Safety Commission	1972	5	commissioner	551
Environmental Protection Agency	1970	1	administrator	14,696
Equal Employment Opportunity Commission	1965	5	commissioner	3,112
Federal Communications Commission	1934	5	commissioner	1,881
Federal Deposit Insurance Corporation	1933	3	board of director	9,141
Federal Energy Regulatory Commission	1977	5	commissioner	—
Federal Reserve System	1913	7	governor	1,483
Federal Trade Commission	1914	5	commissioner	1,041
Food and Drug Administration	1906	1	commissioner	7,288
Interstate Commerce Commission	1887	5	commissioner	744
National Labor Relations Board	1935	5	board of director	2,305
Occupational Safety and Health Administration	1970	1	assistant secretary	72
Securities and Exchange Commission	1934	5	commissioner	1,926

Note: "—" indicates not available.
[a] As of May 1987.

Sources: Congressional Quarterly, *Federal Regulatory Directory* (Washington, D.C.: Congressional Quarterly, 1986), passim; U.S. Office of Personnel Management, *Federal Civilian Workforce Statistics, Employment and Trends* (May 1987), 11-13, 40.

Table 8-9 Number of Pages in the *Federal Register*, 1936-1986

Year	*Pages*	*Year*	*Pages*
1936	2,355	1975	60,221
1946	14,736	1976	57,072
1956	10,528	1977	63,629
1966	16,850	1978	61,261
1967	21,087	1979	77,497
1968	20,068	1980	87,012
1969	20,464	1981	63,554
1970	20,032	1982	58,493
1971	25,442	1983	57,703
1972	28,920	1984	50,997
1973	35,586	1985	53,479
1974	45,422	1986	47,418

Source: Norman J. Ornstein et al., eds., *Vital Statistics on Congress, 1987-1988* (Washington, D.C.: Congressional Quarterly, 1987), 170.

Table 8-10 Presidential Victories on Votes in Congress, 1953-1987

President/year	*House and Senate*	*House*	*Number of votes*	*Senate*	*Number of votes*
Eisenhower					
1953	89.2%	91.2%	34	87.8%	49
1954	82.8	—	—	—	—
1955	75.3	63.4	41	84.6	52
1956	69.2	73.5	34	67.6	65
1957	68.4	58.3	60	78.9	57
1958	75.7	74.0	50	76.5	98
1959	52.9	55.5	54	50.4	121
1960	65.1	65.0	43	65.1	86
Average	72.2				
Kennedy					
1961	81.5	83.1	65	80.6	124
1962	85.4	85.0	60	85.6	125
1963	87.1	83.1	71	89.6	115
Average	84.6				
Johnson					
1964	87.9	88.5	52	87.6	97
1965	93.1	93.8	112	92.6	162
1966	78.9	91.3	103	68.8	125
1967	78.8	75.6	127	81.2	165
1968	74.5	83.5	103	68.9	164
Average	82.6				

(Table continues)

Table 8-10 *(Continued)*

President/year	*House and Senate*	*House*	*Number of votes*	*Senate*	*Number of votes*
Nixon					
1969	74.8%	72.3%	47	76.4%	72
1970	76.9	84.6	65	71.4	91
1971	74.8	82.5	57	69.5	82
1972	66.3	81.1	37	54.3	46
1973	50.6	48.0	125	52.4	185
1974	59.6	67.9	53	54.2	83
Average	67.2				
Ford					
1974	58.2	59.3	54	57.4	68
1975	61.0	50.6	89	71.0	93
1976	53.8	43.1	51	64.2	53
Average	57.6				
Carter					
1977	75.4	74.7	79	76.1	88
1978	78.3	69.6	112	84.8	151
1979	76.8	71.7	145	81.4	161
1980	75.1	76.9	117	73.3	116
Average	76.4				
Reagan					
1981	82.3	72.4	76	87.3	128
1982	72.4	55.8	77	83.2	119
1983	67.1	47.6	82	85.9	85
1984	65.8	52.2	113	85.7	77
1985	59.9	45.0	80	71.6	102
1986	56.5	34.1	88	81.2	80
1987	43.5	34.3	99	56.4	78
Average	63.9				

Note: "—" indicates not available. Percentages indicate number of congressional votes supporting the president divided by the total number of votes on which the president took a position.

Sources: 1969-1986: Ornstein, *Vital Statistics on Congress, 1987-1988,* 203-204; 1987: *Congressional Quarterly Weekly Report* (1988), 95, 97.

Table 8-11 Congressional Voting in Support of the President's Position, 1954-1987 (percent)

	House			Senate		
President / year	All Demo-crats	Southern Demo-crats	Repub-licans	All Demo-crats	Southern Demo-crats	Repub-licans
Eisenhower						
1954	54	—	—	45	—	82
1955	58	—	67	65	—	85
1956	58	—	79	44	—	80
1957	54	—	60	60	—	80
1958	63	—	65	51	—	77
1959	44	—	76	44	—	80
1960	49	—	63	52	—	76
Kennedy						
1961	81	—	41	73	—	42
1962	83	71	47	76	63	48
1963	84	71	36	77	65	52
Johnson						
1964	84	70	42	73	63	52
1965	83	65	46	75	60	55
1966	81	64	45	71	59	53
1967	80	65	51	73	69	63
1968	77	63	59	64	50	57
Nixon						
1969	56	55	65	55	56	74
1970	64	64	79	56	62	74
1971	53	69	79	48	59	76
1972	56	59	74	52	71	77
1973	39	49	67	42	55	70
1974	52	64	71	44	60	65
Ford						
1974	48	52	59	45	55	67
1975	40	48	67	53	67	76
1976	36	52	70	47	61	73
Carter						
1977	69	58	46	77	71	58
1978	67	54	40	74	61	47
1979	70	58	37	75	66	51
1980	71	63	44	71	69	50
Reagan						
1981	46	60	72	52	63	84
1982	43	55	70	46	57	77
1983	30	45	74	45	46	77
1984	37	47	64	45	58	81
1985	31	43	69	36	46	80
1986	26	37	69	39	56	90
1987	26	37	65	38	43	67

Note: "—" indicates not available. Percentages indicate number of congressional votes supporting the president divided by the total number of votes on which the president took a position. The percentages are calculated to eliminate the effects of absences as follows: support = (support)/(support + opposition).

Sources: Ornstein, *Vital Statistics on Congress, 1987-1988,* 206-207; 1987: *Congressional Quarterly Weekly Report* (1988), 94.

Table 8-12 Presidential Vetoes, 1789-1986

Years	*President*	*Regular vetoes*	*Vetoes overridden*	*Pocket vetoes*	*Total vetoes*
1789-1797	Washington	2	0	0	2
1797-1801	Adams	0	0	0	0
1801-1809	Jefferson	0	0	0	0
1809-1817	Madison	5	0	2	7
1817-1825	Monroe	1	0	0	1
1825-1829	J. Q. Adams	0	0	0	0
1829-1837	Jackson	5	0	7	12
1837-1841	Van Buren	0	0	1	1
1841-1841	Harrison	0	0	0	0
1941-1845	Tyler	6	1	4	10
1845-1849	Polk	2	0	1	3
1849-1850	Taylor	0	0	0	0
1850-1853	Fillmore	0	0	0	0
1853-1857	Pierce	9	5	0	9
1857-1861	Buchanan	4	0	3	7
1861-1865	Lincoln	2	0	5	7
1865-1869	A. Johnson	21	15	8	29
1869-1877	Grant	45	4	48	93
1877-1881	Hayes	12	1	1	13
1881-1881	Garfield	0	0	0	0
1881-1885	Arthur	4	1	8	12
1885-1889	Cleveland	304	2	110	414
1889-1893	Harrison	19	1	25	44
1893-1897	Cleveland	42	5	128	170
1897-1901	McKinley	6	0	36	42
1901-1909	T. Roosevelt	42	1	40	82
1909-1913	Taft	30	1	9	39
1913-1921	Wilson	33	6	11	44
1921-1923	Harding	5	0	1	6
1923-1929	Coolidge	20	4	30	50
1929-1933	Hoover	21	3	16	37
1933-1945	F. Roosevelt	372	9	263	635
1945-1953	Truman	180	12	70	250
1953-1961	Eisenhower	73	2	108	181
1961-1963	Kennedy	12	0	9	21
1963-1969	L. Johnson	16	0	14	30
1969-1974	Nixon	26[a]	7	17	43
1974-1977	Ford	48	12	18	66
1977-1981	Carter	13	2	18	31
1981-1986	Reagan	29	6	28	57
Total		1,409	100	1,039	2,448

[a] Two pocket vetoes, overruled in the courts, are counted here as regular vetoes.

Source: Louis Fisher, *The Politics of Shared Power: Congress and the Executive,* 2d ed. (Washington, D.C.: CQ Press, 1987), 30.

Table 8-13 Senate Action on Nominations, 1929-1986

		Senate action				
Congress		Number received	Confirmed	Withdrawn	Rejected[a]	Unconfirmed
71st	(1929-1931)	17,508	16,905	68	5	530
72d	(1931-1933)	12,716	10,909	19	1	1,787
73d	(1933-1934)	9,094	9,027	17	3	47
74th	(1935-1936)	22,487	22,286	51	15	135
75th	(1937-1938)	15,330	15,193	20	27	90
76th	(1939-1941)	29,072	28,939	16	21	96
77th	(1941-1942)	24,344	24,137	33	5	169
78th	(1943-1944)	21,775	21,371	31	6	367
79th	(1945-1946)	37,022	36,550	17	3	452
80th	(1947-1948)	66,641	54,796	153	0	11,692
81st	(1949-1951)	87,266	86,562	45	6	653
82d	(1951-1952)	46,920	46,504	45	2	369
83d	(1953-1954)	69,458	68,563	43	0	852
84th	(1955-1956)	84,173	82,694	38	3	1,438
85th	(1957-1958)	104,193	103,311	54	0	828
86th	(1959-1960)	91,476	89,900	30	1	1,545
87th	(1961-1962)	102,849	100,741	1,279	0	829
88th	(1963-1964)	122,190	120,201	36	0	1,953
89th	(1965-1966)	123,019	120,865	173	0	1,981
90th	(1967-1968)	120,231	118,231	34	0	1,966
91st	(1969-1971)	134,464	133,797	487	2	178
92d	(1971-1972)	117,053	114,909	11	0	2,133
93d	(1973-1974)[b]	134,384	131,254	15	0	3,069
94th	(1975-1976)	132,151	131,378	6	0	3,801
95th	(1977-1978)	137,504	124,730	66	0	12,713
96th	(1979-1980)	154,797	154,665	18	0	1,458
97th	(1981-1982)	186,264	184,844	55	7	1,346
98th	(1983-1984)	97,893	97,262	4	0	610
99th	(1985-1986)	99,614	95,811	16	0	3,787

[a] Includes only those nominations rejected outright by a vote of the Senate. Most nominations that fail to win approval of the Senate are unfavorably reported by committees and never reach the Senate floor, having been withdrawn. In some cases, the full Senate may vote to recommit a nomination to committee, in effect killing it.
[b] Forty-six nominations were returned to the president during the October-November 1974 recess in accordance with Senate Rule 38, which states: "[I]f the Senate shall adjourn or take a recess for more than thirty days, all nominations pending and not finally acted upon at the time of taking such adjournment or recess shall be returned by the Secretary to the President, and shall not again be considered unless they shall again be made to the Senate by the President."

Source: 1929-1980: Congressional Quarterly, *Congressional Quarterly's Guide to Congress,* 3d ed. (Washington, D.C.: Congressional Quarterly, 1982), 195; 1981-1986: Congressional Record (daily ed.), Daily Digest, "Resume of Congressional Activity," 97th Cong. (1st sess., D1613; 2d sess., D1499); 98th Cong. (2d sess., D 1348); 99th Cong. (1st sess., D1565; 2d sess., D 1343).

Table 8-14 Senate Rejections of Cabinet Nominations

Nominee	*Position*	*President*	*Date*	*Vote*
Roger B. Taney	secretary of treasury	Jackson	6/23/1834	18-28
Caleb Cushing	secretary of treasury	Tyler	3/3/1843	19-27
Caleb Cushing	secretary of treasury	Tyler	3/3/1843	10-27
Caleb Cushing	secretary of treasury	Tyler	3/3/1843	2-29
David Henshaw	secretary of navy	Tyler	1/15/1844	6-34
James M. Porter	secretary of war	Tyler	1/30/1844	3-38
James S. Green	secretary of treasury	Tyler	6/15/1844	[a]
Henry Stanbery	attorney general	A. Johnson	6/2/1868	11-29
Charles B. Warren	attorney general	Coolidge	3/10/1925	39-41
Charles B. Warren	attorney general	Coolidge	3/16/1925	39-46
Lewis L. Strauss	secretary of commerce	Eisenhower	6/19/1959	46-49

[a] Not recorded.

Source: Congressional Quarterly's Guide to Congress, 198.

Table 8-15 Party Affiliation of Major Appointments, 1961-1984

Administration	*Number of appointees*	*Affiliated with president's party*	*Party affiliated*	*Unaffiliated*
Kennedy	430	63%	73%	27%
Johnson	524	47	58	42
Nixon	737	65	73	27
Ford	293	56	64	36
Carter (1977-1978)[a]	402	58	65	35
Reagan (1981-1984)	524	82	85	15

Note: Major appointments include cabinet, subcabinet, and lower policy-level positions in the executive branch, including ambassadorships and positions on various boards and commissions. In the case of some positions, particularly those on independent regulatory commissions, the ratio of party affiliation among appointees is legislatively prescribed. Therefore, these cases were not included in the annual totals. The *Congressional Quarterly Almanac* indicates the party affiliation for every appointee for whom that information is available. When not listed or listed as "independent," the appointee's affiliation was included here as "unaffiliated."

[a] Lists of major presidential appointees confirmed during the years 1979 and 1980 contained a high proportion of names for whom no information on party affiliation was made available by the Carter administration. In 1979, out of a total of 256 appointees listed, only 48 were assigned a party affiliation. For 1980, only 22 of 148 listed included this information.

Source: Roger G. Brown, "Party and Bureaucracy: From Kennedy to Reagan," *Political Science Quarterly* 97 (1982): 283. Data for 1981-1984 have been supplied by Professor Brown. Used by permission of Roger G. Brown, Department of Political Science, University of North Carolina-Charlotte.

Table 8-16 Treaties and Executive Agreements Approved by the United States, 1789-1986

Year	*Number of treaties*	*Number of executive agreements*
1789-1839	60	27
1839-1889	215	238
1889-1929	382	763
1930-1932	49	41
1933-1944 (F. Roosevelt)	131	369
1945-1952 (Truman)	132	1,324
1953-1960 (Eisenhower)	89	1,834
1961-1963 (Kennedy)	36	813
1964-1968 (L. Johnson)	67	1,083
1969-1974 (Nixon)	93	1,317
1975-1976 (Ford)	26	666
1977-1980 (Carter)	79	1,476
1981-1986 (Reagan)	92	2,019

Note: Varying definitions of what comprises an executive agreement and their entry-into-force date make the above numbers approximate.

Sources: 1789-1980: *Congressional Quarterly's Guide to Congress,* 291; 1981-1986: Office of the Assistant Legal Advisor for Treaty Affairs.

Figure 8-1 Presidential Approval, Gallup Poll, 1938-1987

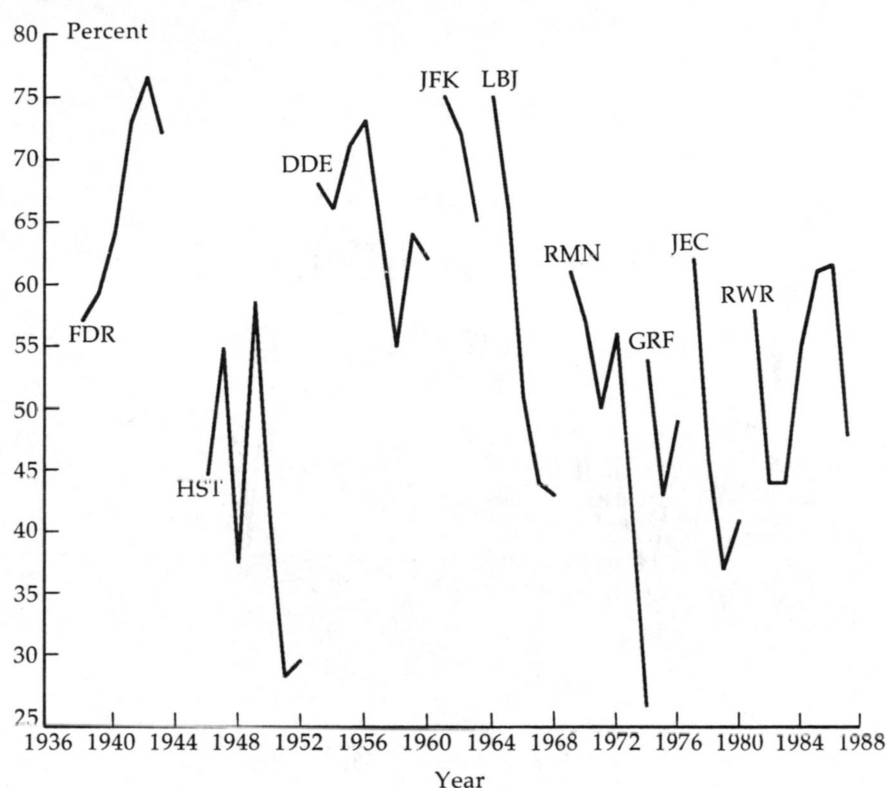

Note: Averaged by year. Question: "Do you approve or disapprove of the way ____ (last name of president) is handling his job as president?"

Sources: 1938-1953: *The Gallup Opinion Index* (October-November 1980), 34-38; 1953-1985: Gallup polls as reported in George C. Edwards III, *Presidential Performance and Public Approval* (Baltimore: Johns Hopkins University Press, forthcoming) (reprinted by permission of The Johns Hopkins University Press); 1986-1987: *The Gallup Report* (May 1987), 11-12, (June 1987), 23.

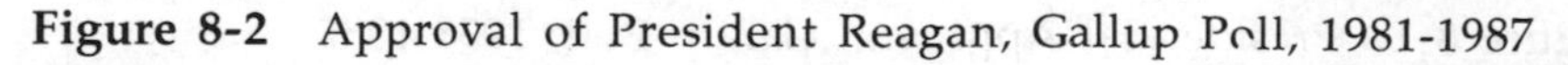

Figure 8-2 Approval of President Reagan, Gallup Poll, 1981-1987

Note: Question: "Do you approve or disapprove of the way Reagan is handling his job as president?"

Source: The Gallup Report (May 1987), 11-12, (June 1987), 23.

Figure 8-3 Approval of President Reagan, *New York Times*/CBS News Poll, 1981-1987

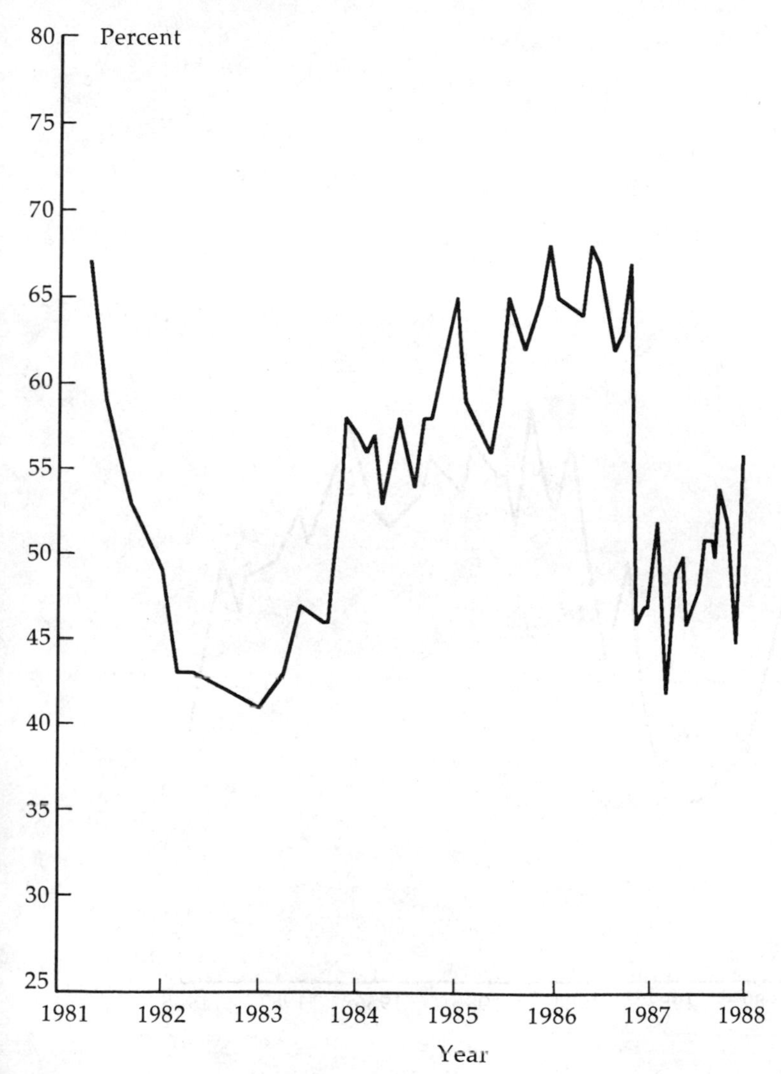

Note: Question: "Do you approve or disapprove of the way Ronald Reagan is handling his job as president?"

Source: New York Times/CBS News Poll.

Figure 8-4 Approval of President Reagan's Economic Policy, *New York Times*/CBS News Poll, 1981-1987

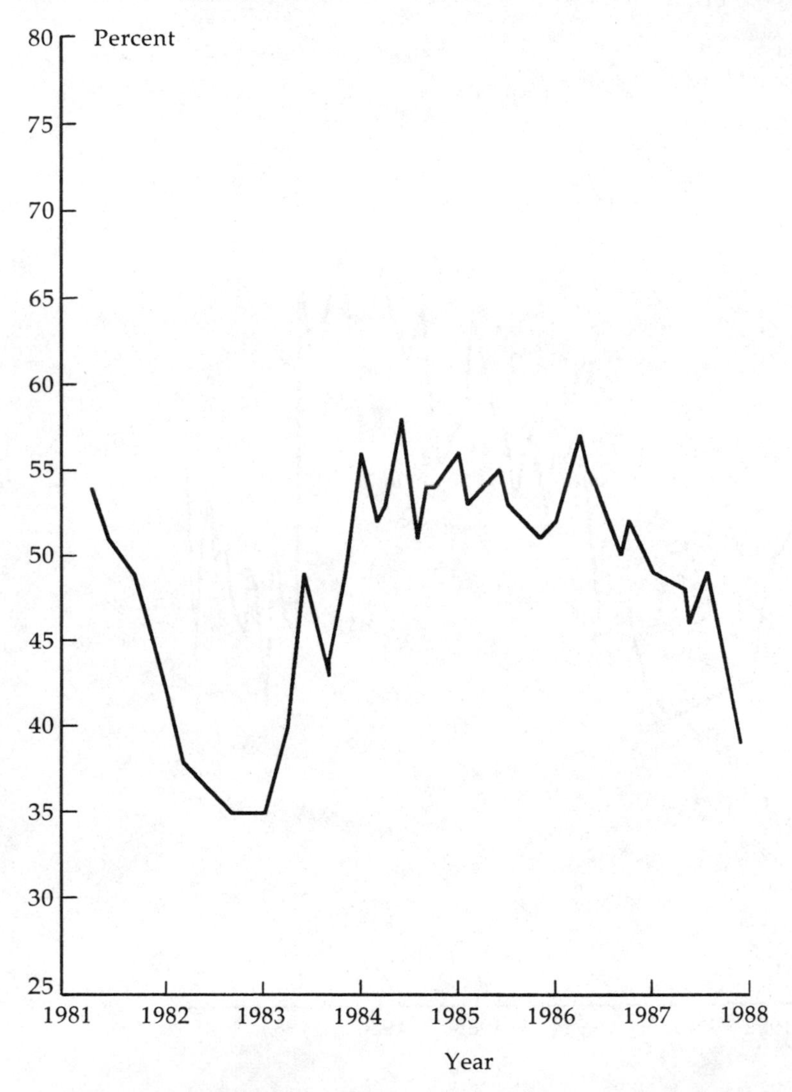

Note: Question: "How about the economy? Do you approve or disapprove of the way Ronald Reagan is handling the economy?"

Source: New York Times/CBS News Poll.

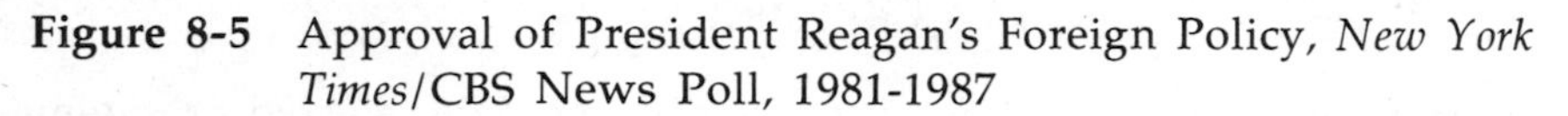

Figure 8-5 Approval of President Reagan's Foreign Policy, *New York Times*/CBS News Poll, 1981-1987

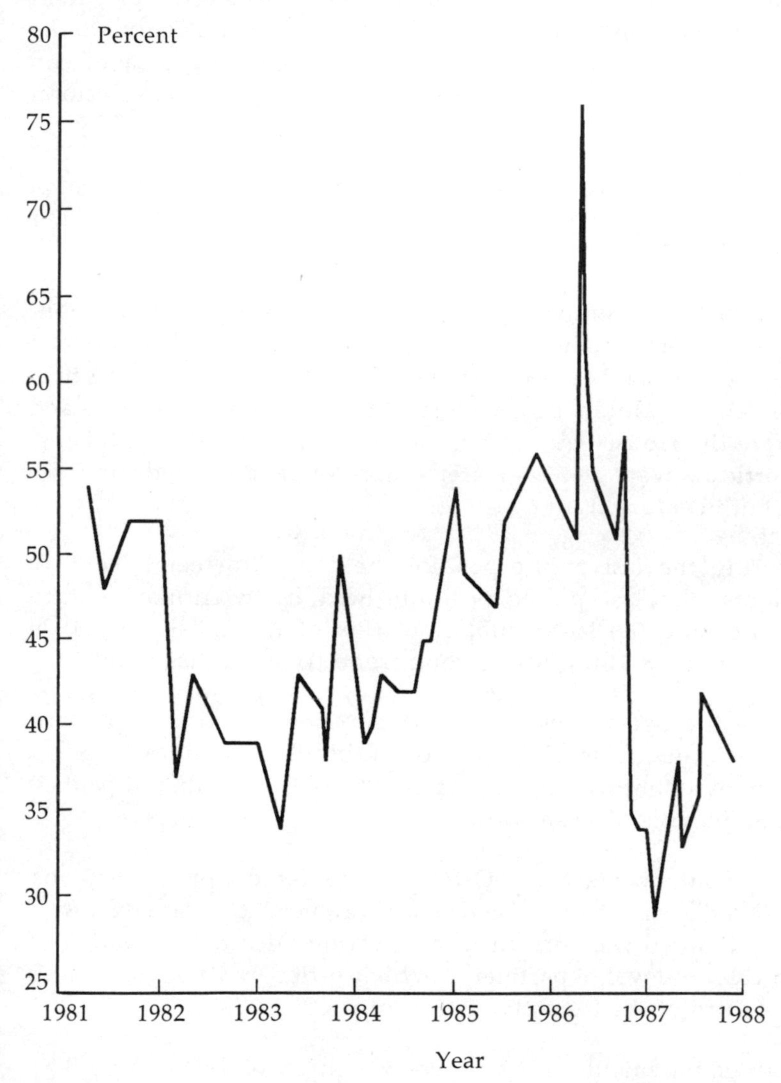

Note: Question: "Do you approve or disapprove of the way Ronald Reagan is handling foreign policy?"

Source: New York Times/CBS News Poll.

Questions

1. How many and which vice presidents were later elected president (Table 8-1)? How many were elected without first succeeding to the presidency because the president died? Most presidents have been elected from large states. Why? (Hint: see the current state electoral votes in Table 3-2.)

2. Evaluations of presidents sometimes change over time. Which recent president "moved up" considerably between 1970 and later polls (Table 8-2)?

3. In the nineteenth century, compared to the twentieth, proportionately more presidents were at one time members of the House of Representatives (Table 8-3). What structural change near the turn of the century (Table 1-3) made the Senate more attractive, and therefore the House less so, as a source of presidential candidates? State officials were also a greater source of candidates during the nineteenth century. Why?

4. Comparing the last public position held by nineteenth century presidents, the last public position held by twentieth century presidents, and the latest public position of nominees since 1936 (Tables 8-3 and 8-4) reveals a strong trend. What is that trend?

5. What are the two newest cabinet departments, and what department were they formerly a part of (Table 8-5)? Besides Defense, which department was the largest in 1987 in the number of paid civilian employees? The smallest?

6. Which president began the Office of Economic Opportunity and what "war" was it associated with (Table 8-6)? The National Security Council was formed in connection with the formation of which cabinet-level department? Which office by itself constitutes about a third of the Executive Office of the President?

7. Civilian employment reached a postwar high in 1969 (Table 8-7). How much lower than the peak was 1985 employment? Did employment rise or fall between 1981, when President Ronald Reagan took office, and 1985? By what percentage?

8. What is the oldest major federal regulatory agency and when was it established (Table 8-8)? Most agencies were formed in response to

crises or major contemporary problems. Briefly, in response to what event or situation were the following formed: EPA, EEOC, FDIC, FERC, NLRB, and SEC?

9. Deregulation under President Reagan was intended to cut government bureaucracy. Based on the number of pages in the *Federal Register*, was it successful (Table 8-9)?

10. Democratic presidents since Dwight Eisenhower have been uniformly more successful than Republican presidents in obtaining legislation they favored (Table 8-10). Why? (Hint: see Table 3-11.) The president is said to enjoy a "honeymoon" period after each election. Does the evidence in Table 8-10 support the hypothesis that such a honeymoon period exists and has an effect on presidential victories on votes in Congress?

11. Which Democratic president received the lowest voting support from members of his own party in the House (Table 8-11)? Did President Jimmy Carter receive more or less support than other Democratic presidents from southern Democrats in the House?

12. Why is it important to distinguish regular vetoes from pocket vetoes (Table 8-12)? Apart from Franklin Roosevelt, who had slightly more than three terms to make his six hundred plus vetoes, which president vetoed the largest number of bills? Which president had the largest percentage of his vetoes overridden by Congress?

13. Over the past three decades, the Senate has rejected fewer than a dozen nominations (Table 8-13). Does this mean that the Senate has abdicated its role in approving or disapproving the president's nominees?

14. Which president has been the most partisan in his appointments (Table 8-15)? Was this president more or less partisan in his appointments to federal courts (Tables 9-2 and 9-3)?

9

The Judiciary

The judiciary, although one of the three "separate but equal" branches of government, is often considered remote from the political push and pull that characterizes the other two. Preoccupation with process, precedent, and the meaning of the law gives the courts a strikingly different appearance. But grappling with the constitutionality of abortion or the death penalty and pouring practical meaning into ambiguous, generally worded statutes enacted by legislatures puts the courts squarely in the midst of the political process.

But even if courts can be considered political, are statistics essential to understanding the courts? They are for two reasons. First, the courts themselves have to deal with statistics. A 1987 Supreme Court decision, for example, considered the question of racially disparate patterns in the imposition of the death penalty—Georgia defendants who killed whites were eleven times more likely to be sentenced to die as those who killed blacks.[1] The Court held that the statistics were not relevant to this particular case. Although the numbers may have been accurate and meaningful, they did not show that there was racial discrimination against this defendant. This case serves as a pointed reminder of the distinction a court draws between general patterns and the facts of the specific case before it.

But this example should not give the impression that courts disdain statistics. In fact, as one federal judge wrote, "In the problem of racial discrimination, statistics often tell much, and Courts listen."[2] Cases often turn on conclusions drawn from numerical data—voting rights (Table 1-17), reapportionment (Table 1-16), and school desegregation (Table 12-11) are but three areas in which this is true.

Statistics also can promote understanding of the courts. A single case does not lend itself to statistical analysis, but the large number, the hierarchy (Figure 9-1), and the geographical spread (Figure 9-2) of the federal courts, and the even greater variety of state courts and appointment methods (Table 9-1) suggest that numerical summarization aids comprehension. In addition, precisely because of the judicial emphasis on precedents, there are perhaps better records of previous activities than in most other areas of government. A lengthy history by itself suggests statistical summation.

The characteristics of those on the federal bench are one area of interest. Although the nature of the courts might suggest that appointments are merely a matter of judicial qualifications, the record indicates otherwise. Federal judicial appointments have always been subject to partisan considerations (Tables 9-3 and 9-5), and other characteristics of federal judges have been shown to vary with the appointing president (Table 9-2). Partisan and ideological differences also explain part of the frustration presidents have encountered with nominations to the Supreme Court (Table 9-4). Nor are more subjective judgments ignored in characterizing court appointees. Just as historians have judged presidents, legal scholars have evaluated Supreme Court justices (Table 9-6).

The growing caseload of the courts has become a major concern in recent years, and, while individual "horror" stories may be more dramatic (when Chief Justice Warren E. Burger retired in 1986 he noted that in a recent week he had worked more than one hundred hours), statistical evidence tells an even more convincing story. The caseload of the courts has indeed climbed dramatically in recent years (Tables 9-7 through 9-10, Figure 9-3). Cases filed in the district courts rose by 59 percent between 1980 and 1985, while the number of judges rose by only 2 percent (Table 9-9).

There is also considerable information on the nature of judicial work. For example, civil rather than criminal cases account for the increased workload (Table 9-10). One can also see from the distribution of types of cases in the federal courts that a district court judge must be prepared to hear and decide cases on a wide range of topics (Table 9-11). Dramatic changes also have occurred in the kinds of cases courts must deal with and in the ways they have responded. Reacting to forces supporting greater judicial activism, the Supreme Court has struck down more federal, state, and local laws on constitutional grounds in this century than in the nineteenth (Table 9-12). During this time, however, doctrinal trends have changed dramatically, and since the 1930s the Court has rejected far fewer economic regulatory laws and has increasingly struck down laws restricting civil liberties (Figure 9-4).

As they are with the executive and the legislature, statistics are a necessary component for understanding the courts and their decisions.

Notes

1. *McCleskey v. Kemp*, 481 U.S. —, decided April 22, 1987.
2. *Alabama v. United States*, 304 F.2d 201 (1961).

Figure 9-1 The United States Federal Court System

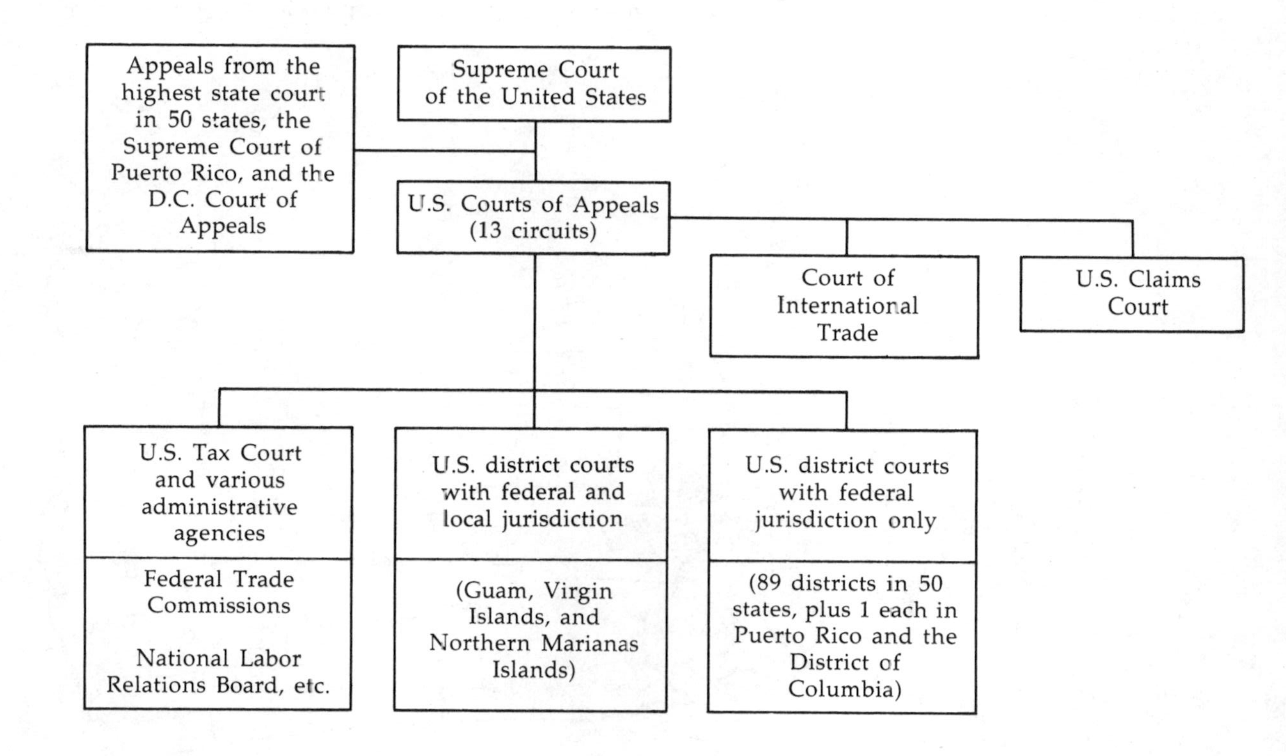

Source: Administrative Office of the United States Courts.

Figure 9-2 The Thirteen Federal Judicial Circuits and Ninety-four U.S. District Courts

Source: Administrative Office of the United States Courts (January 1983).

Note: The remaining two circuit courts, the D.C. Circuit and Federal Circuit, are located in Washington, D.C.

Table 9-1 Principal Methods of Judicial Selection for State Courts

Partisan election	*Nonpartisan election*	*Legislative election*	*Gubernatorial appointment*	*Merit plan*
Alabama[a]	Georgia[a]	Connecticut[a]	California[b]	Alaska
Arkansas	Idaho[a]	Rhode Island[b]	Delaware	Arizona[a]
Illinois[a]	Kentucky[a]	South Carolina[a]	Maine[a]	Colorado[a]
Mississippi[a]	Louisiana	Virginia[a]	Massachusetts[a]	Florida[a,c]
New Mexico	Michigan[a]		New Hampshire	Hawaii
North Carolina	Minnesota		New Jersey[a]	Indiana[a]
Pennsylvania[a]	Montana		New York[a,b]	Iowa[a]
Tennessee[a,c]	Nevada			Kansas[a]
Texas[a]	North Dakota			Maryland
West Virginia	Ohio[a]			Missouri[a]
	Oregon[a]			Nebraska
	Washington[a]			Oklahoma[a,c]
	Wisconsin[a]			South Dakota[a]
				Utah[a]
				Vermont[a]
				Wyoming[a]

[a] Minor court judges chosen by other methods.
[b] Appellate judges only.
[c] Most but not all major judicial positions selected this way.

Source: Council of State Governments, *Book of the States, 1986-87* (Lexington, Ky.: Council of State Governments, 1986), 161-163.

Table 9-2 Characteristics of Federal District and Appellate Court Nominees, Presidents Johnson to Reagan (percent)

	Johnson nominees	*Nixon nominees*	*Ford nominees*	*Carter nominees*	*Reagan nominees*[a]
District courts					
Occupation					
Politics/government	21.3	10.6	21.2	4.4	12.5
Judiciary	31.1	28.5	34.6	44.6	37.5
Large law firm[b]	2.4	11.3	9.7	14.0	14.3
Moderate firm[b]	18.9	27.9	25.0	19.8	20.1
Small/solo firm[b]	23.0	19.0	9.7	23.9	12.1
Other	3.3	2.8	0.0	3.5	3.6
Experience					
Judicial	34.4	35.2	42.3	54.5	48.2
Prosecutorial	45.9	41.9	50.0	38.6	44.2
Neither	33.6	36.3	30.8	28.2	26.3
Political affiliation					
Democrat	94.3	7.3	21.2	92.6	4.9
Republican	5.7	92.7	78.8	4.4	93.8
Independent	0.0	0.0	0.0	2.9	1.3
Past party activism	49.2	48.6	50.0	60.9	60.3
Religion					
Protestant	58.2	73.2	73.1	60.4	61.2
Catholic	31.1	18.4	17.3	27.7	30.4
Jewish	10.7	8.4	9.6	11.9	0.4
Race/ethnicity					
White	93.4	95.5	88.5	78.7	92.9
Black	4.1	3.4	5.8	13.9	1.8
Asian-American	0.0	0.0	3.9	0.5	0.4
Hispanic	2.5	1.1	1.9	6.9	4.9
Gender					
Female	1.6	0.6	1.9	14.4	8.9
Total number of nominees	122	179	52	202	224
Courts of Appeals					
Occupation					
Politics/government	10.0	4.4	8.3	5.4	4.8
Judiciary	57.5	53.3	75.0	46.4	50.8
Large law firm[b]	5.0	4.4	8.3	10.8	14.3
Moderate firm[b]	17.5	22.2	8.3	16.1	11.1
Small/solo firm[b]	7.5	6.7	0.0	5.4	1.6
Other	2.5	8.9	0.0	16.1	17.5
Experience					
Judicial	65.0	57.8	75.0	53.6	70.9
Prosecutorial	47.5	46.7	25.0	32.1	22.2
Neither	20.0	17.8	25.0	37.5	39.7

Table 9-2 *(Continued)*

	Johnson nominees	*Nixon nominees*	*Ford nominees*	*Carter nominees*	*Reagan nominees*[a]
Political affiliation					
Democrat	95.0	6.7	8.3	82.1	0.0
Republican	5.0	93.3	91.7	7.1	98.4
Independent	0.0	0.0	0.0	10.7	1.6
Past party activism	57.5	60.0	58.3	73.2	68.3
Religion					
Protestant	60.0	75.6	58.3	60.7	55.6
Catholic	25.0	15.6	33.3	23.2	31.7
Jewish	15.0	8.9	8.3	16.1	12.7
Race/ethnicity					
White	95.0	97.8	100.0	66.7	96.8
Black	5.0	0.0	0.0	25.0	1.6
Asian-American	0.0	2.2	0.0	8.3	0.0
Hispanic	0.0	0.0	0.0	0.0	1.6
Gender					
Female	2.5	0.0	0.0	0.0	6.3
Total number of appointees	40	45	12	56	63

[a] Reagan appointees through 1986 (99th Congress).
[b] Large: 25 or more partners and associates; moderate: 5-24 partners and associates; small: 2-4 partners and associates.

Source: Sheldon Goldman, "Reagan's Second Term Judicial Appointments: The Battle at Midway," *Judicature* 70 (1987): 324-339.

Table 9-3 Federal Judicial Appointments of Same Party as President, Presidents Cleveland to Reagan

President	*Party*	*Percentage*
Cleveland	Democrat	97.3
Harrison	Republican	87.9
McKinley	Republican	95.7
T. Roosevelt	Republican	95.8
Taft	Republican	82.2
Wilson	Democrat	98.6
Harding	Republican	97.7
Coolidge	Republican	94.1
Hoover	Republican	85.7
F. Roosevelt	Democrat	96.4
Truman	Democrat	93.1
Eisenhower	Republican	95.1
Kennedy	Democrat	90.9
Johnson	Democrat	95.2
Nixon	Republican	93.7
Ford	Republican	81.2
Carter	Democrat	94.8
Reagan	Republican	98.1[a]

[a] As of September 1984.

Source: Henry J. Abraham, *Justices and Presidents: Appointments to the Supreme Court,* 2d ed. (New York: Oxford University Press, 1985), 67 (copyright © Henry J. Abraham, 1974, 1985, reprinted by permission of Oxford University Press, Inc.).

Table 9-4 Supreme Court Nominations that Failed

Nominee	*Year*	*President*	*Action*
William Paterson	1793	Washington	withdrawn
John Rutledge	1795	Washington	rejected, 10-14
Alexander Wolcott	1811	Madison	rejected, 9-24
John Crittenden	1828	J. Q. Adams	postponed
Roger B. Taney	1835	Jackson	postponed
John Spencer	1844	Tyler	rejected, 21-26
R. Walworth	1844	Tyler	withdrawn
Edward King	1844	Tyler	withdrawn
Edward King	1844	Tyler	withdrawn
John Read	1845	Tyler	postponed
G. Woodward	1846	Polk	rejected, 20-29
Edward Bradford	1852	Fillmore	postponed
George Badger	1853	Fillmore	postponed
William Micou	1853	Fillmore	postponed
Jeremiah Black	1861	Buchanan	rejected, 25-26
Henry Stanbery	1866	A. Johnson	postponed
Ebenezer Hoar	1870	Grant	rejected, 24-33
George Williams	1874	Grant	withdrawn
Caleb Cushing	1874	Grant	withdrawn
Stanley Matteys	1881	Hayes	postponed
W. B. Hornblower	1894	Cleveland	rejected, 24-30
Wheeler H. Peckham	1894	Cleveland	rejected, 32-41
John J. Parker	1930	Hoover	rejected, 39-41
Abe Fortas[a]	1968	L. Johnson	withdrawn
Homer Thornberry	1968	L. Johnson	withdrawn
C. Haynsworth	1969	Nixon	rejected, 45-55
G. H. Carswell	1970	Nixon	rejected, 45-51
Robert Bork	1987	Reagan	rejected, 42-58
Douglas Ginsburg	1987	Reagan	not submitted[b]

Note: Twenty-nine of the 145 presidential nominations have failed to obtain Senate confirmation. However, 5 nominees declined appointment after having been nominated (Harrison, 1789; W. Cushing, 1796; Jay, 1800; Lincoln, 1811; Adams, 1811) and 2 withdrew after being confirmed (W. Smith, 1837; Conkling, 1882).

[a] In 1968, Fortas, an associate justice, was nominated for chief justice.

[b] Publicly announced but withdrawn before the president formally submitted his nomination to the Senate.

Source: Congressional Quarterly, *Congressional Quarterly's Guide to Congress,* 3d ed. (Washington, D.C.: Congressional Quarterly, 1982), 786-788.

Table 9-5 Characteristics of Supreme Court Justices

Seat number and justice	*Party*	*Home state*	*Years on Court*	*Age at nomination*	*Years of previous judicial experience*
Washington appointees					
1 John Jay	Federalist	New York	1789-1795	44	2
2 John Rutledge	Federalist	South Carolina	1789-1791	50	6
3 William Cushing	Federalist	Massachusetts	1789-1810[a]	57	29
4 James Wilson	Federalist	Pennsylvania	1789-1798[a]	47	0
5 John Blair, Jr.	Federalist	Virginia	1789-1796	57	11
6 James Iredell	Federalist	North Carolina	1790-1799[a]	38	0.5
2 Thomas Johnson	Federalist	Maryland	1791-1793	59	1.5
2 William Paterson	Federalist	New Jersey	1793-1806[a]	47	0
1 John Rutledge	Federalist	South Carolina	1795	55	6[b]
5 Samuel Chase	Federalist	Maryland	1796-1811[a]	55	8
1 Oliver Ellsworth	Federalist	Connecticut	1796-1800	51	5
J. Adams appointees					
4 Bushrod Washington	Federalist	Virginia	1798-1829[a]	36	0
6 Alfred Moore	Federalist	North Carolina	1799-1804	44	1
1 John Marshall	Federalist	Virginia	1801-1835[a]	45	3
Jefferson appointees					
6 William Johnson	Jeffersonian	South Carolina	1804-1834[a]	32	6
2 H. Brockholst Livingston	Jeffersonian	New York	1806-1823[a]	49	0
7 Thomas Todd	Jeffersonian	Kentucky	1807-1826[a]	42	6
Madison appointees					
5 Gabriel Duvall	Jeffersonian	Maryland	1811-1835	58	6
3 Joseph Story	Jeffersonian	Massachusetts	1811-1845[a]	32	0
Monroe appointee					
2 Smith Thompson	Jeffersonian	New York	1823-1843[a]	55	16

J. Q. Adams appointee					
7 Robert Trimble	Jeffersonian	Kentucky	1826-1828[a]	49	11
Jackson appointees (first term)					
7 John McLean	Democrat	Ohio	1829-1861[a]	44	6
4 Henry Baldwin	Democrat	Pennsylvania	1830-1844[a]	50	0
Jackson appointees (second term)					
6 James Wayne	Democrat	Georgia	1835-1867[a]	45	5
1 Roger B. Taney	Democrat	Maryland	1836-1864[a]	59	0
5 Philip P. Barbour	Democrat	Virginia	1836-1841[a]	52	8
Van Buren appointees					
8 John Catron	Democrat	Tennessee	1837-1865[a]	51	10
9 John McKinley	Democrat	Alabama	1837-1852[a]	57	0
5 Peter V. Daniel	Democrat	Virginia	1841-1860[a]	57	0
Tyler appointee					
2 Samuel Nelson	Democrat	New York	1845-1872	52	22
Polk appointees					
3 Levi Woodbury	Democrat	New Hampshire	1845-1851[a]	55	6
4 Robert C. Grier	Democrat	Pennsylvania	1846-1870	52	13
Fillmore appointee					
3 Benjamin R. Curtis	Whig	Massachusetts	1851-1857	41	0
Pierce appointee					
9 John A. Campbell	Democrat	Alabama	1853-1861	41	0
Buchanan appointee					
3 Nathan Clifford	Democrat	Maine	1858-1881[a]	54	0
Lincoln appointees					
7 Noah H. Swayne	Republican	Ohio	1862-1881	57	0
5 Samuel F. Miller	Republican	Iowa	1862-1890[a]	46	0

(Table continues)

Table 9-5 *(Continued)*

Seat number and justice	*Party*	*Home state*	*Years on Court*	*Age at nomination*	*Years of previous judicial experience*
Lincoln appointees *(continued)*					
9 David Davis	Republican	Illinois	1862-1877	47	14
10 Stephen J. Field	Democrat	California	1863-1897	46	6
1 Salmon P. Chase	Republican	Ohio	1864-1873[a]	56	0
Grant appointees (first term)					
4 William Strong	Republican	Pennsylvania	1870-1880	61	11
6 Joseph P. Bradley	Republican	New Jersey	1870-1892[a]	56	0
2 Ward Hunt	Republican	New York	1873-1882	62	8
Grant appointee (second term)					
1 Morrison R. Waite	Republican	Ohio	1874-1888[a]	57	0
Hayes appointees					
9 John M. Harlan	Republican	Kentucky	1877-1911[a]	44	1
4 William B. Woods	Republican	Georgia	1880-1887[a]	56	12
Garfield appointee					
7 Stanley Matthews	Republican	Ohio	1881-1889[a]	56	4
Arthur appointees					
3 Horace Gray	Republican	Massachusetts	1881-1902	53	18
2 Samuel Blatchford	Republican	New York	1882-1893[a]	62	15
Cleveland appointees (first term)					
4 Lucius Q. C. Lamar	Democrat	Mississippi	1883-1893[a]	62	0
1 Melville W. Fuller	Democrat	Illinois	1888-1910[a]	55	0
Harrison appointees					
7 David J. Brewer	Republican	Kansas	1889-1910[a]	52	19
5 Henry B. Brown	Republican	Michigan	1891-1906	54	16

6 George Shiras, Jr.	Republican	Pennsylvania	1892-1903	60	0
4 Howell E. Jackson	Democrat	Tennessee	1893-1895[a]	60	7
Cleveland appointees (second term)					
2 Edward D. White	Democrat	Louisiana	1894-1910[a]	48	1.5
4 Rufus W. Peckham	Democrat	New York	1895-1909[a]	57	9
McKinley appointee					
8 Joseph McKenna	Republican	California	1898-1925	54	5
T. Roosevelt appointees					
3 Oliver W. Holmes	Republican	Massachusetts	1902-1932	61	20
6 William R. Day	Republican	Ohio	1903-1922	53	7
5 William H. Moody	Republican	Massachusetts	1906-1910	52	0
Taft appointees					
4 Horace H. Lurton	Democrat	Tennessee	1909-1914[a]	65	26
7 Charles E. Hughes	Republican	New York	1910-1916	48	0
1 Edward D. White	Democrat	Louisiana	1910-1921[a]	65	1.5[b]
2 Willis Van Devanter	Republican	Wyoming	1910-1937	51	8
5 Joseph R. Lamar	Democrat	Georgia	1910-1916[a]	53	2
9 Mahlon Pitney	Republican	New Jersey	1912-1922	54	11
Wilson appointees					
4 James C. McReynolds	Democrat	Tennessee	1914-1941	52	0
5 Louis D. Brandeis	Republican	Massachusetts	1916-1939	59	0
7 John H. Clarke	Democrat	Ohio	1916-1922	59	2
Harding appointees					
1 William H. Taft	Republican	Ohio	1921-1930	63	13
7 George Sutherland	Republican	Utah	1922-1938	60	0
6 Pierce Butler	Democrat	Minnesota	1923-1939[a]	56	0
9 Edward T. Sanford	Republican	Tennessee	1923-1930[a]	57	14

(Table continues)

Table 9-5 *(Continued)*

Seat number and justice	*Party*	*Home state*	*Years on Court*	*Age at nomination*	*Years of previous judicial experience*
Coolidge appointee					
8 Harlan Fiske Stone	Republican	New York	1925-1941	52	0
Hoover appointees					
1 Charles E. Hughes	Republican	New York	1930-1941	67	0
9 Owens J. Roberts	Republican	Pennsylvania	1930-1945	55	0
3 Benjamin N. Cardozo	Democrat	New York	1932-1938[a]	61	18
F. Roosevelt appointees					
2 Hugo L. Black	Democrat	Alabama	1937-1971[a]	51	1.5
7 Stanley F. Reed	Democrat	Kentucky	1938-1957	53	0
3 Felix Frankfurter	Independent	Massachusetts	1939-1962	56	0
5 William O. Douglas	Democrat	Connecticut	1939-1975	40	0
6 Frank Murphy	Democrat	Michigan	1940-1949[a]	49	7
4 James F. Byrnes	Democrat	South Carolina	1941-1942	62	0
1 Harlan Fiske Stone	Republican	New York	1941-1946[a]	68	0[b]
9 Robert H. Jackson	Democrat	New York	1941-1954[a]	49	0
4 Wiley B. Rutledge	Democrat	Iowa	1943-1949[a]	48	4
Truman appointees					
9 Harold H. Burton	Republican	Ohio	1945-1958	57	0
1 Fred M. Vinson	Democrat	Kentucky	1946-1953[a]	56	5
6 Tom C. Clark	Democrat	Texas	1949-1967	49	0
4 Sherman Minton	Democrat	Indiana	1949-1956	58	8
Eisenhower appointees					
1 Earl Warren	Republican	California	1953-1969	62	0
8 John M. Harlan	Republican	New York	1955-1971	55	1
4 William J. Brennan	Democrat	New Jersey	1956-	50	7

7 Charles E. Whittaker	Republican	Missouri	1957-1962	56	3
9 Potter Stewart	Republican	Ohio	1958-1981	43	4
Kennedy appointees					
7 Byron R. White	Democrat	Colorado	1962-	44	0
3 Arthur J. Goldberg	Democrat	Illinois	1962-1965	54	0
L. Johnson appointees					
3 Abe Fortas	Democrat	Tennessee	1965-1969	55	0
6 Thurgood Marshall	Democrat	New York	1967-	59	4
Nixon appointees					
1 Warren E. Burger	Republican	Minnesota	1969-1986	61	13
3 Harry A. Blackmun	Republican	Minnesota	1970-	61	11
2 Lewis F. Powell, Jr.	Democrat	Virginia	1971-1987	64	0
8 William H. Rehnquist	Republican	Arizona	1971-1986	47	0
Ford appointee					
5 John Paul Stevens	Republican	Illinois	1976-	55	5
Reagan appointees					
9 Sandra Day O'Connor	Republican	Arizona	1981-	51	6.5
1 William H. Rehnquist	Republican	Arizona	1986-	61	0[b]
8 Antonin Scalia	Republican	Illinois	1986-	50	4
2 Anthony Kennedy	Republican	California	1988-	51	12

Note: Seat number 1 always held by the chief justice of the United States.

[a] Died in office.

[b] Prior to appointment to associate justice.

Sources: Sheldon Goldman, *Constitutional Law: Cases and Essays* (New York: Harper and Row, 1987); previous judicial experience: Abraham, *Justices and Presidents,* 56-58 (copyright © Henry J. Abraham, 1974, 1985, reprinted by permission of Oxford University Press, Inc.); *Congressional Quarterly's Guide to Congress,* 786-788; updated by the editors.

Table 9-6 Ratings of Supreme Court Justices

Great	*Near great*	*Average*			*Below average*	*Failure*
J. Marshal	W. Johnson	Jay	McKinley	Shiras	T. Johnson	Van Devanter
Story	Curtis	J. Rutledge	Daniel	Peckham	Moore	McReynolds
Taney	Miller	Cushing	Nelson	McKenna	Trimble	Butler
Harlan I	Field	Wilson	Woodbury	Day	Barbour	Byrnes
Holmes	Bradley	Blair	Grier	Moody	Woods	Burton
Hughes	Waite	Iredell	Campbell	Lurton	H. E. Jackson	Vinson
Brandeis	E. D. White	Paterson	Clifford	J. R. Lamar		Minton
Stone	Taft	S. Chase	Swayne	Pitney		Whittaker
Cardozo	Sutherland	Ellsworth	Davis	J. H. Clarke		
Black	Douglas	Washington	S. P. Chase	Sanford		
Frankfurter	R. H. Jackson	Livingston	Strong	Roberts		
Warren	W. B. Rutledge	Todd	Hunt	Reed		
		Harlan II	Duvall	Matthews		
		Brennan	Thompson	Gray		
		Fortas	McLean	Blatchford		
		Murphy	Brewer	Baldwin		
		T. C. Clark	B. R. White	Wayne		
		Stewart	Goldberg	Catron		
		L. Q. C. Lamar	T. Marshall	Brown		
		Fuller				

Note: Ratings reflect evaluations made in June 1970 by 65 law school deans and professors of law, history, and political science with expertise in the judicial process.

Source: Albert P. Blaustein and Roy M. Mersky, *The First One Hundred Justices: Statistical Studies on the Supreme Court of the United States* (Hamden, Conn.: Shoe String Press, Archon Books, 1978), 37-40.

Table 9-7 Caseload of the U.S. Supreme Court, 1970-1986

Action	*1970*	*1971*	*1972*	*1973*	*1974*	*1975*	*1976*	*1977*	*1978*	*1979*	*1980*	*1981*	*1982*	*1983*	*1984*	*1985*	*1986*
Appellate cases on docket	1,903	2,070	2,183	2,480	2.308	2,352	2,324	2,341	2,383	2,509	2,749	2,935	2,710	2,688	2,575	2,571	2,547
From prior term	325	362	442	412	540	431	452	472	434	425	527	522	545	520	539	400	476
Docketed during present term	1,578	1,708	1,741	2,068	1.768	1,921	1,872	1,869	1,949	2,084	2,222	2,413	2,165	2,168	2,036	2,171	2,071
Cases acted upon	1,613	1,752	1,834	1,948	1.967	1,900	2,019	1,979	2,023	2,050	2,324[a]	2,513[a]	2,279[a]	2,220[a]	2,253[a]	2,185[a]	—
Granted review	214	238	217	229	235	244	237	224	210	199	167	203	169	140	167	166	—
Denied, dismissed, or withdrawn	1,285	1,409	1,397	1,572	1,594	1,538	1,620	1,676	1,734	1,776	1,999	2,100	1,892	1,902	1,953	1,863	—
Summarily decided	114	105	220	147	138	118	162	79	79	75	90	114	113	71	59	78	—
Cases not acted upon	290	318	349	532	341	452	305	362	360	459	425	422	413	468	322	386	—
Pauper cases on docket	2,289	2,445	2,436	2,585	2,348	2,395	2,398	2,349	2,331	2,249	2,371	2,354	2,352	2,394	2,416	2,577	2,564
Cases acted upon	1,802	2,023	1,982	2,013	1,976	1,997	2,083	1,960	1,996	1,838	2,027[a]	2,039[a]	2,013[a]	1,992[a]	2,067[a]	2,189[a]	—
Granted review	41	61	35	30	28	28	30	24	27	32	17	7	10	9	18	20	—
Denied, dismissed, or withdrawn	1,683	1,781	1,902	1,942	1,914	1,903	2,013	1,899	1,938	1,757	1,968	2,014	1,995	1,968	2,050	2,136	—
Summarily decided	78	181	45	41	34	66	40	37	31	49	32	12	6	10	14	24	—
Cases not acted upon	487	422	454	572	372	398	315	389	335	411	344	315	339	402	329	388	—
Original cases on docket	20	18	21	14	12	14	8	14	17	23	24	22	17	18	15	10	12
Cases disposed of during term	7	8	8	4	4	7	2	3	0	1	7	6	3	7	8	2	1
Total cases available for argument	267	280	256	261	278	280	269	260	249	238	264	318	312	269	271	276	91
Cases disposed of	160	181	180	172	178	181	181	185	170	160	162	192	199	189	184	175	—
Cases argued	151	176	177	170	175	179	176	172	168	156	154	184	183	184	175	171	—
Cases dismissed or remanded without argument	9	5	3	2	3	2	5	13	2	4	8	8	16	5	9	4	—
Cases remaining	107	99	76	89	100	99	88	75	79	78	102	126	113	80	87	101	—
Cases decided by signed opinion	126	143	159	161	144	160	154	153	153	143	144	170	174	174	159	161	164
Cases decided per curiam opinion	22	24	18	8	20	16	22	8	3	12	8	10	6	6	11	10	10
Number of signed opinions	109	129	140	140	123	138	126	129	130	130	123	141	151	151	139	146	145
Total cases on docket	4,212	4,533	4,640	5,079	4,668	4,761	4,731	4,704	4,731	4,781	5,144	5,311	5,079	5,100	5,006	5,158	5,123

Note: "—" indicates not available.

[a] Includes cases granted review and carried over to next term, not shown separately.

Sources: U.S. Bureau of the Census, *Statistical Abstract of the U.S., 1977* (Washington, D.C.: U.S. Government Printing Office, 1976), 184, *1979*, 191, *1987*, 168; 1986: Office of the Clerk, Supreme Court of the United States, unpublished data.

Figure 9-3 Cases Filed in the U.S. Supreme Court, 1938-1986

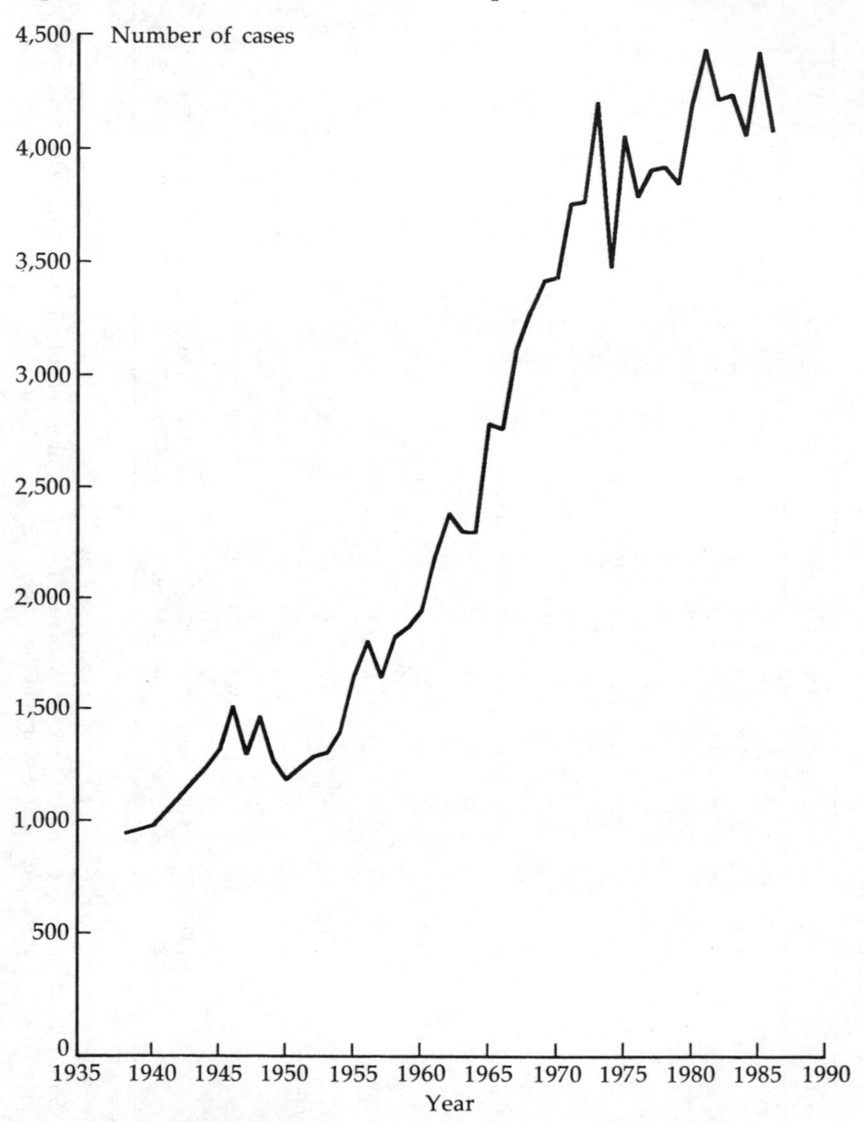

Sources: 1938-1969: successive volumes of the *Statistical Abstract of the U.S.;* 1970-1986: Office of the Clerk of the Supreme Court.

Table 9-8 Caseloads of U.S. Courts of Appeals, 1980-1985

	1980	*1981*	*1982*	*1983*	*1984*	*1985*
Number of judgeships	132	132	132	132	132	156
Number of sitting senior judges	42	39	47	50	50	45
Number of vacant judgeship months	217.1	89.2	103.1	53.3	23.9	275.0
Appeals filed						
Prisoner	3,704	4,311	4,834	5,327	5,964	6,532
All other civil	12,141	13,874	15,227	16,444	17,600	18,660
Criminal	4,405	4,377	4,767	4,790	4,881	4,989
Administrative	2,950	3,800	3,118	3,069	3,045	3,179
Total	23,200	26,362	27,946	29,630	31,490	33,360
Appeals terminated						
Consolidations and cross appeals	2,704	3,538	4,204	4,180	3,953	2,669
Procedural	6,170	9,360	11,060	11,263	12,905	12,349
On the merits						
Prisoner	2,267	1,541	1,838	2,052	2,163	2,835
Other civil	5,861	6,671	6,934	7,014	7,916	9,208
Criminal	2,718	2,618	2,541	2,859	2,927	3,070
Administrative	1,167	1,338	1,407	1,292	1,321	1,256
Total on the merits	12,013	12,168	12,720	13,217	14,327	16,369
Total	20,887	25,066	27,984	28,660	31,185	31,387
Pending appeals	20,252	21,548	21,510	22,480	22,785	24,758
Per active judge[a]						
Termination on the merits	227	231	237	238	276	308
Procedural terminations	—	—	—	100	116	103

Note: "—" indicates not available.

[a] Includes only judges active during the entire twelve-month period.

Source: Director of the Administrative Office of United States Courts, *Federal Court Management Statistics* (Washington, D.C.: U.S. Government Printing Office, 1985), 29-30.

Table 9-9 Caseloads of U.S. District Courts, 1980-1985

	1980	*1981*	*1982*	*1983*	*1984*	*1985*
Overall						
Filings	188,487	201,387	228,489	266,440	285,563	299,164
Terminations	180,245	198,172	210,878	238,675	266,304	293,545
Pending	199,019	202,283	219,872	247,708	267,020	272,636
Number (and percentage) of civil cases over three years old	20,592 (11.7)	15,275 (8.4)	13,979 (7.0)	14,554 (6.4)	15,646 (6.3)	16,726 (6.6)
Number of judgeships	516	516	515	515	515	525
Vacant judgeship months	956.2	414.5	424.9	287.8	246.8	889.8
Per judgeship						
Civil filings	327	350	400	470	508	476
Criminal felony filings	38	40	44	47	46	44
Total filings	365	390	444	517	554	520
Pending cases	386	392	427	481	518	474
Terminations	349	384	409	463	517	511
Trials completed	38	41	42	41	40	36
Median time from filing to disposition (months)						
Criminal felony	3.7	3.3	3.4	3.4	3.5	3.7
Civil	8	9	7	7	7	7
Median time from issue to trial (months)						
Civil only[a]	15	14	14	14	14	14

[a] Time is computed from the date that the answer or response is filed to the date trial begins.

Source: Federal Court Management Statistics, 167.

Table 9-10 Number of Civil and Criminal Cases Filed in U.S. District Courts, 1950-1986

	Civil cases		*Criminal cases*	
Year	Commenced	Terminated	Commenced	Terminated
1950	44,454	42,482	36,383	37,675
1955	48,308	47,959	35,310	38,990
1960	49,852	48,847	28,137	30,512
1965	67,678	63,137	31,569	33,718
1970	87,321	79,466	38,102	36,356
1975	117,320	103,787	41,108	49,212
1980	168,789	160,481	28,932	29,297
1981	180,576	177,975	31,328	30,221
1982	206,193	189,473	32,682	31,889
1983	241,842	215,356	35,913	33,985
1984	261,485	243,113	36,845	35,494
1985	273,670	269,848	39,500	37,139
1986	254,828	266,765	41,490	39,328

Source: Statistical Abstract of the U.S., 1971, 152, *1976,* 168, *1987,* 169.

Table 9-11 Types of Civil and Criminal Cases in the Federal District Courts, 1986

Civil cases	*Percentage*	*Criminal cases*	*Percentage*
Contract actions	34.7	Embezzlement and fraud	21.2
Recovery of overpayments and enforcement of judgments	(16.0)	Drunk driving and traffic	18.2
Other contract actions	(18.7)	Narcotics	11.6
Liability	16.6	Larceny and theft	8.9
Product liability	(4.9)	Marijuana	6.0
Motor vehicle personal injury	(2.7)	Forgery and counterfeiting	5.9
Marine personal injury	(1.6)	Homicide, robbery, assault, and burglary	5.2
Other personal injury	(5.8)	Immigration	5.0
Personal property damage	(1.6)	Weapons and firearms	4.7
Statutory	44.5	Controlled substances	1.9
State prisoner petitions	(11.5)	Escape	1.9
Civil rights	(7.9)	Auto theft	0.8
Social security	(5.7)	All other	8.7
Labor laws	(5.0)	Total number of criminal cases	40,427
Federal prisoner petitions	(1.7)		
Tax suits	(1.1)		
Antitrust	(0.3)		
Other statutory	(11.3)		
Real property	4.2		
Total number of civil cases	254,828		

Source: Director of the Administrative Office of the United States Courts, *Annual Report of the Director of the Administrative Office of the United States Courts* (Washington, D.C.: U.S. Government Printing Office, 1986), 13, 17.

Table 9-12 Federal, State, and Local Laws Declared Unconstitutional by the Supreme Court by Decade, 1789-1983

Years	*Federal*	*State and local*
1789-1799	0	0
1800-1809	1	1
1810-1819	0	7
1820-1829	0	8
1830-1839	0	3
1840-1849	0	9
1850-1859	1	7
1860-1869	4	23
1870-1879	8	37
1880-1889	4	45
1890-1899	5	36
1900-1909	9	40
1910-1919	5	118
1920-1929	15	139
1930-1939	13	93
1940-1949	2	58
1950-1959	4	68
1960-1969	16	140
1970-1979	19	193
1980-1983	8	63
Total	114	1,088

Source: Lawrence Baum, *The Supreme Court*, 2d ed. (Washington, D.C.: CQ Press, 1985), 171, 173.

Figure 9-4 Economic and Civil Liberties Laws Overturned by the Supreme Court, 1900-1979

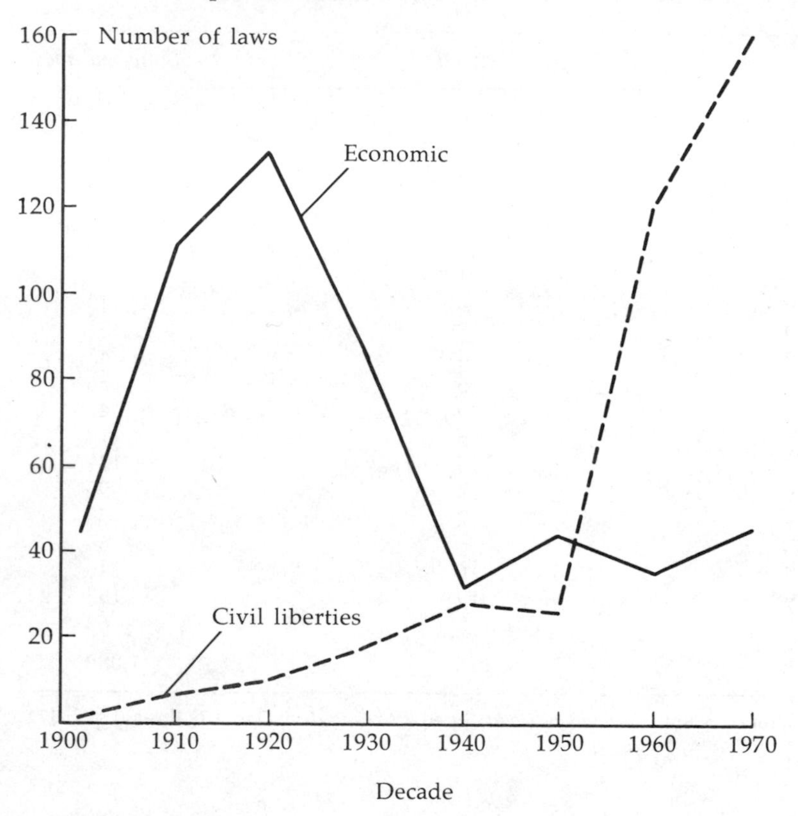

Note: Civil liberties category does not include laws supportive of civil liberties. Laws include federal, state, and local.

Source: Baum, *The Supreme Court,* 182.

Questions

1. Generally, cases can be appealed to the Supreme Court only after they have been heard by one of two other high-level courts. What are these kinds of courts (Figure 9-1)?

2. Six of the ten youngest states use a merit plan to elect most of their judges for state courts (Table 9-1 and Table 1-1). This would suggest that as states update their constitutions, many might adopt this method. Is this true? Use the states that have adopted new constitutions since 1945 (Table 1-2).

3. Are district and appellate court judges chosen on a nonpartisan basis (Tables 9-2 and 9-3)? Is the proportion of blacks, Hispanics, and women steadily rising?

4. Using the ratings in the 1982 *Tribune* poll (Table 8-2), ascertain whether the worst presidents had more trouble with their Supreme Court nominees than the best presidents. A historical curiosity: two people were rejected for positions both in the cabinet (Table 8-14) and on the Supreme Court (Table 9-4). Who were they? Which of them subsequently served for nearly thirty years as chief justice?

5. Who were the youngest appointees to the Supreme Court (Table 9-5)? Who was the oldest? The one with the longest previous judicial experience? The first from west of the Mississippi?

6. Ratings of the sort in Table 9-6 are a subjective and imperfect guide. Looking at the year of appointment of the Supreme Court justices (Table 9-5) rated as "great" and as "failures," state a hypothesis about why these justices stand out as especially good or bad. Evaluate the following: the great justices compared to those below average and failures: (1) were more often chief justice; (2) had, on average, more years of previous judicial experience; (3) served longer on the Court.

7. Warren E. Burger, former chief justice of the United States, argued frequently that the caseload of the Supreme Court was too great and that some intermediate court needs to be established to deal with the overload. Drawing on Table 9-7 and Figure 9-3, construct an argument to support Burger's contention that the Court is overburdened. If an intermediate court is not established, how else could the Court reduce its load?

8. What happens to most cases that reach the Supreme Court (Table 9-7)? How can there be more cases decided by signed opinion than there are signed opinions, something that has happened every year since 1970?

9. With the increase in the number of judges in 1985, how many authorized judgeships are there per circuit in the U.S. courts of appeals (Table 9-8)? Per district in the ninety-four district courts (Table 9-9)?

10. What kinds of cases—civil or criminal—account for the considerable increase in the caseload of district courts and courts of appeals (Tables 9-8 through 9-10)? Has the time taken to dispose of cases increased in the past six years (Table 9-9)?

11. From Table 9-12 and Figure 9-4, are you able to determine the subject matter of most laws declared unconstitutional in this century? If so, what are they?

12. The note to Figure 9-4 seems almost self-contradictory at first reading. What kinds of civil liberties laws were in fact overturned? Since most civil liberties laws were overturned in the 1950s, 1960s, and 1970s, what is likely to have been the subject matter of many of these laws?

10

Federalism

From a statistical point of view, a major problem in studying American government below the federal level is that there are fifty state governments and thousands of local governmental units (Table 10-1). Among other things, this often makes it difficult to get accurate, up-to-date information about all relevant jurisdictions. Even for state-level data, a researcher often must turn to each of the fifty state capitals, or to fifty-one units if data about the District of Columbia are needed, or even more if Puerto Rico and areas such as the Northern Marianas Islands are included, as might be necessary for studying delegates to the national party conventions. If the researcher's interest is in counties, cities, school districts, and the like, the data collection task can be enormous—well beyond the capacity of one person.

Fortunately, organizations and publications devoted to data collection have stepped to the fore. Some, such as the Council of State Governments and the International City Management Association, are well established. The former has published the *Book of the States* since 1935, and the latter the *Municipal Year Book* since 1934. Other sources are brand new, such as Congressional Quarterly's magazine *Governing*, which began publishing in 1987. The U.S. Census Bureau also offers systematic collections of data covering increasingly longer spans. Two examples are the *State and Metropolitan Area Data Book* (published biennially since 1980) and the *County and City Data Book* (published, though with varying frequency, since 1952). Such groups and publications make data collection far easier, more systematic, and ensure higher quality than in the past.

Even when data are available, a researcher still can be frustrated by the inevitable variety that occurs across units. Simple tables or one-sentence summaries are often inadequate. Table 6-8, which concerns financing state election campaigns, for example, shows enormous variation among states. Similarly, the listing of state fiscal discipline measures (Table 10-9) notes that provisions for overriding gubernatorial vetoes vary, without giving the exact requirement in each state. So much variation exists on this single point—a two-thirds majority of the legislators present and voting, two-thirds of the total number of legislators, 60 percent of the legislators present, and so on—that this book leaves it to the original sources to present the particulars.

Therefore, in studying state and local governments, their interrelationships, and their relations with the federal government, a researcher must pay attention to details. Even more than usual it is essential to read footnotes and check several sources. Differences in data collection procedures, the timing of data collection, and variations in detail of reports all become important. The user must also keep in mind the purpose for examining the data. It takes a careful researcher to know when variations can be ignored and when they become so frequent or so large that they must be an explicit part of the analysis.

Despite improvements in data collection, it is still necessary to go directly to states and localities for some information. Fortunately, this too has become easier. Publications such as the *National Directory of State Agencies* and the *State Information Book* give names and titles of specific individuals and offices, typically with addresses and phone numbers. While this will still not make a project involving twenty-five or fifty states easy, at least one can gather missing information or exact details about specific states and localities.

The recent surge in availability of information has now made possible a serious look at cities, counties, states, regions, and the relationships among all of these governments. The tables in this book emphasize three topics. First, data are provided about states and localities as a whole and how they differ from the federal government and from each other (Tables 10-1 and 10-3, Figure 10-1). Second, information is given about specific states, often with an eye toward how states rank relative to one another (Tables 10-2 and 10-12). Third, considerable emphasis is given to intergovernmental relationships because of the growing fiscal interdependence between federal and state governments, state and local units, and even directly between federal and local governments (Tables 10-4 through 10-8).

As amply demonstrated by these tables, students as well as professionals now have access to systematic information about all fifty states and increasingly about localities. Although users may have to make extra effort to absorb all the details provided by these tables, they are rewarded by the new possibilities for research and understanding.

Table 10-1 Federal, State, and Local Governmental Units, Number and Employees, 1942-1985

Year	*Federal*	*State*	*Local government*						*Total*
			County	Municipal	School district	Township and town	Special district[a]	Total	
1942									
Number	1	48	3,050	16,220	108,579	18,919	8,299	155,067	155,116
Employees (thousands)	2,664	503[b]	333[b]	872[b]	—	223[b,c]	[c]	1,428[b]	5,915
1952[d]									
Number	1	50	3,052	16,807	67,355	17,202	12,340	116,756	116,807
Employees (thousands)	2,583	1,060	573	1,341	1,234	312[c]	[c]	3,461	7,105
1957[d]									
Number	1	50	3,050	17,215	50,454	17,198	14,424	102,341	102,392
Employees (thousands)[e]	2,439	1,300	726	1,539	1,651	394[c]	[c]	4,307	8,047
1962									
Number	1	50	3,043	18,000	34,678	17,142	18,323	91,186	91,237
Employees (thousands)	2,539	1,680	862	1,696	2,161	449[c]	[c]	5,169	9,388
1967									
Number	1	50	3,049	18,048	21,781	17,105	21,264	81,248	81,299
Employees (thousands)	2,993	2,335	1,077	1,993	2,919	549[c]	[c]	6,539	11,867
1972									
Number	1	50	3,044	18,517	15,781	16,991	23,885	78,218	78,269
Employees (thousands)	2,795	2,957	—	—	—	—	—	8,007	13,759
1977									
Number	1	50	3,042	18,862	15,174	16,822	25,962	79,862	79,913
Employees (thousands)	2,848	3,491	1,761	2,469	4,127	361	402	9,120	15,459

(Table continues)

Table 10-1 *(Continued)*

			Local government						
Year	*Federal*	*State*	County	Municipal	School district	Township and town	Special district[a]	Total	*Total*
1982									
Number	1	50	3,041	19,076	14,851	16,734	28,588	82,290	82,341
Employees (thousands)	2,848	3,744	1,824	2,397	4,194	356	478	9,249	15,841
1985									
Number	1	50	—	—	—	—	—	—	—
Employees (thousands)	3,021	3,984	1,891	2,467	4,416	392	519	9,685	16,690

Note: "—" indicates not available.

[a] Special districts include independent public housing authorities, local irrigation units, power authorities, and other such bodies.

[b] Employees in other than education.

[c] Townships and special districts are combined.

[d] Adjusted to include units in Alaska and Hawaii, which adopted statehood in 1959.

[e] As of April 30. Others as of Oct. 6.

Sources: U.S. Bureau of the Census, *Statistical Abstract of the U.S., 1987* (Washington, D.C.: U.S. Government Printing Office, 1986), 249, 280, *1977*, 306; U.S. Bureau of the Census, *Historical Statistics of the U.S.* (Washington, D.C.: U.S. Government Printing Office, 1975), 1, 100.

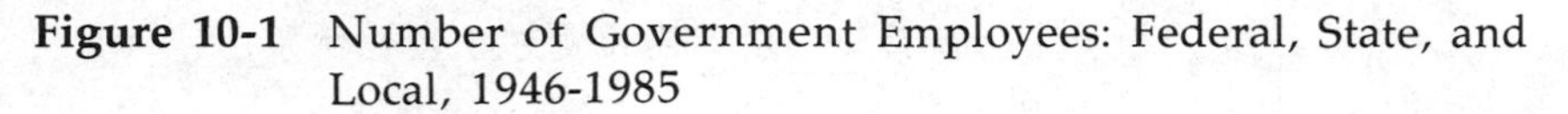

Figure 10-1 Number of Government Employees: Federal, State, and Local, 1946-1985

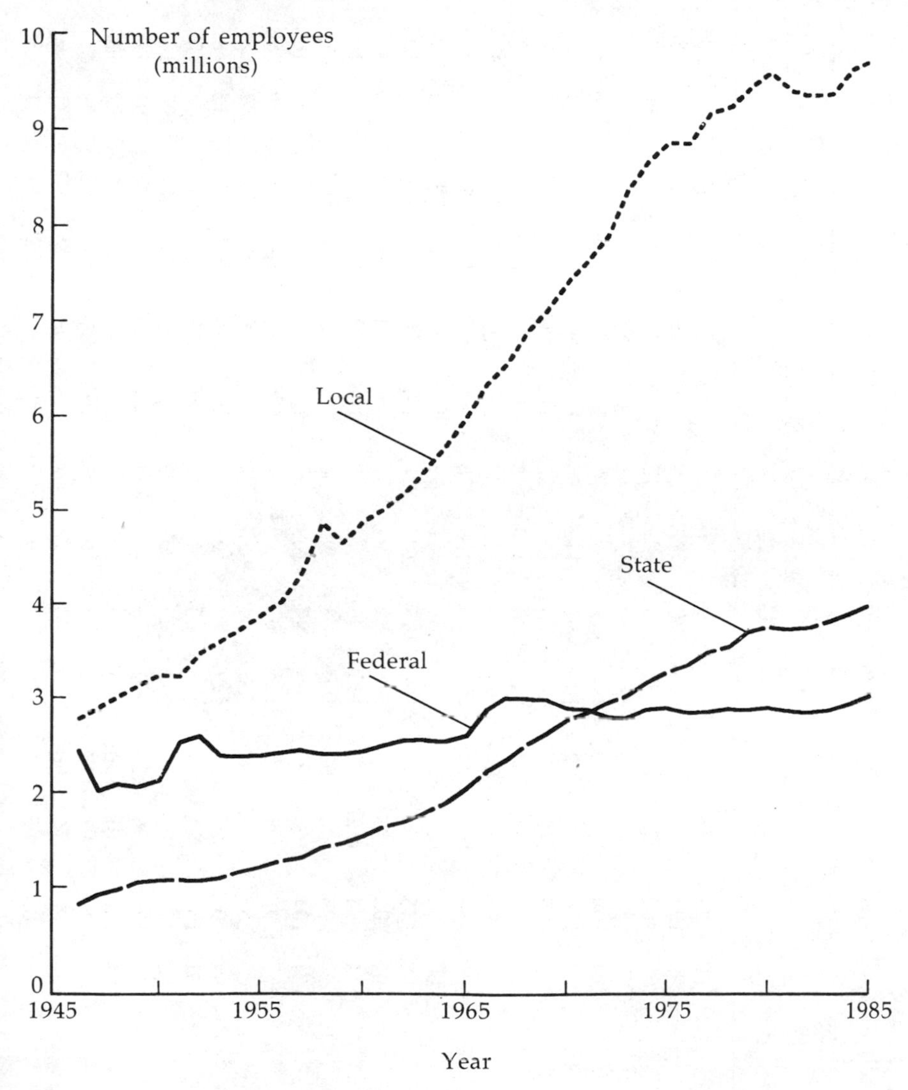

Sources: 1946-1970: *Historical Statistics of the U.S.*, 1, 100; 1971-1984: U.S. Advisory Commission on Intergovernmental Relations, *Significant Features of Fiscal Federalism, 1985-1986* (Washington, D.C.: U.S. Advisory Commission on Intergovernmental Relations, 1986), 132; *Statistical Abstract of the U.S., 1987*, 280.

Table 10-2 Tax Capacity and Tax Efforts of the States, 1967-1983

State	1967		1975		1977		1979		1980		1981		1982		1983	
	TC	TE	TC	TE	TC	TE	TC	TE	TC	TE	TC	TE	TC	TE	TC	TE
Alabama	70	89	77	79	77	79	76	86	76	85	74	91	74	87	75	87
Alaska	99	104	155	76	158	130	217	129	260	166	324	184	313	180	272	166
Arizona	95	109	92	108	89	110	91	115	89	117	89	106	96	92	97	91
Arkansas	77	83	78	78	78	78	77	81	79	86	82	79	79	81	78	83
California	124	108	110	119	114	117	116	95	117	102	115	100	116	99	119	92
Colorado	104	106	106	90	107	95	110	96	113	90	113	84	121	81	122	79
Connecticut	117	93	110	99	112	103	109	102	112	100	110	103	117	99	124	96
Delaware	123	90	124	84	120	80	110	96	111	89	111	87	115	84	118	82
District of Columbia	121	90	118	94	123	118	110	132	111	131	111	145	115	145	117	146
Florida	104	84	102	74	101	73	100	78	100	74	101	73	104	72	103	75
Georgia	80	92	86	89	84	89	81	96	82	96	81	97	84	96	87	93
Hawaii	99	135	109	119	107	115	103	128	107	124	105	126	117	105	114	108
Idaho	91	105	89	90	88	89	91	90	87	88	87	87	86	85	83	87
Illinois	114	84	112	99	112	96	112	99	108	102	104	105	99	107	98	107
Indiana	99	95	98	92	100	83	98	84	92	84	91	88	89	88	86	89
Iowa	104	104	106	93	105	90	108	93	105	96	102	98	96	105	91	109
Kansas	105	96	109	85	105	89	109	87	109	88	109	87	106	88	102	92
Kentucky	80	85	85	84	83	84	85	87	83	89	82	88	82	88	79	91
Louisiana	94	90	97	87	99	79	104	82	109	78	117	77	113	82	107	81
Maine	81	105	84	104	82	100	80	110	80	111	79	113	84	107	90	100
Maryland	101	103	101	106	101	105	99	109	99	109	98	107	100	106	99	107
Massachusetts	98	121	98	129	95	133	93	144	96	135	96	134	101	119	107	112
Michigan	104	100	101	106	103	109	104	113	97	116	96	116	93	120	90	128
Minnesota	95	119	97	117	100	112	105	115	102	111	100	109	99	111	97	124
Mississippi	64	98	70	96	70	94	70	97	69	96	72	95	71	92	68	95
Missouri	97	86	96	84	96	80	97	82	94	84	92	81	91	82	89	87

Montana	105	93	103	92	103	94	113	88	112	92	114	92	110	97	105	94
Nebraska	110	78	106	85	101	98	100	98	97	102	97	95	97	93	101	94
Nevada	171	71	145	70	143	62	154	65	154	60	148	62	151	63	147	64
New Hampshire	110	81	102	75	102	73	96	78	97	75	95	74	100	75	108	69
New Jersey	107	97	109	103	106	113	102	118	105	112	105	112	106	113	112	109
New Mexico	94	92	97	85	98	77	103	85	107	83	114	89	115	82	108	79
New York	108	138	98	160	94	168	89	171	90	167	89	171	92	170	95	163
North Carolina	78	94	85	86	83	87	82	91	80	97	80	95	82	94	87	88
North Dakota	92	97	101	92	99	88	109	78	108	79	123	74	115	83	111	81
Ohio	100	82	104	80	104	78	101	86	97	87	94	89	92	94	89	103
Oklahoma	102	80	98	73	101	72	108	74	117	72	127	73	126	78	115	80
Oregon	106	101	100	96	104	92	106	93	103	93	99	101	99	95	95	103
Pennsylvania	91	99	98	93	99	94	93	105	93	104	90	105	89	106	88	105
Rhode Island	91	105	88	112	87	114	84	121	84	123	80	130	81	133	86	126
South Carolina	64	97	77	85	77	86	76	91	75	95	75	95	74	96	76	96
South Dakota	91	107	94	87	91	87	95	84	90	88	86	93	87	91	87	85
Tennessee	78	87	84	79	83	82	81	87	79	84	79	87	77	86	80	82
Texas	98	75	111	68	112	68	117	64	124	65	132	65	130	66	124	67
Utah	87	111	86	89	88	91	87	99	86	101	86	97	86	97	82	98
Vermont	88	119	94	108	93	104	85	110	84	104	84	105	89	102	94	95
Virginia	86	90	93	87	91	88	93	88	95	88	94	90	94	90	96	89
Washington	112	106	98	101	100	94	103	96	103	94	99	92	102	93	101	104
West Virginia	75	96	89	85	90	80	92	82	94	82	90	83	92	86	87	88
Wisconsin	94	124	98	115	99	113	100	118	95	116	91	120	87	128	87	137
Wyoming	141	79	154	70	154	82	173	83	196	74	216	73	201	105	182	113

Note: Tax capacity (TC) measures a state's underlying economic resources and speaks to the ability to raise revenue. The tax capacity is the amount of revenue each state would raise if it applied a national average set of tax rates for 26 commonly used tax bases. The index above is the per capita tax capacity divided by the per capita average for all states, with the index for the average set at 100. Tax effort (TE) is the ratio of a state's actual tax collections to its tax capacity. The relative index of tax effort is created by dividing each state's tax effort by the average for all states. One hundred is the index for the U.S. average. For a more complete explanation, see the source.

Source: U.S. Advisory Commission on Intergovernmental Relations, *Significant Features of Fiscal Federalism 1985-86* (Washington, D.C.: U.S. Advisory Commission on Intergovernmental Relations, 1986), 130-131.

Table 10-3 Federal, State, and Local Taxes by Source, 1948-1985 (percent)

Jurisdiction/ year	*Personal income*	*Corporate income*	*Personal and corporate income*	*General and selective sales*[a]	*Property*	*Other*
Federal						
1948	51.0	25.3		20.2		3.3
1950	44.7	29.8		22.3		3.2
1955	49.9	31.0		16.6		2.4
1960	52.9	27.9		16.4		2.8
1965	52.1	27.2		16.8		3.9
1970	61.9	22.5		12.5		3.1
1975	64.4	21.4		11.1		3.1
1976	65.3	20.6		10.8		3.3
1977	64.3	22.5		9.5		3.7
1978	65.9	21.8		9.3		3.0
1979	68.3	20.6		8.4		2.7
1980	69.6	18.4		9.1		2.9
1981	70.4	15.1		12.0		2.6
1982	73.6	12.1		11.3		3.0
1983	75.8	9.7		11.7		2.8
1984	71.3	13.7		11.9		3.0
1985[b]	72.5	13.5		10.8		2.9
State						
1948	7.4	8.7		59.9		24.0
1950	9.1	7.4		58.9		24.6
1955	9.4	6.4		59.2		25.0
1960	12.2	6.5		58.3		22.9
1965	14.0	7.4		57.6		21.0
1970	19.1	7.8		56.8		16.2
1975	23.5	8.3		54.1		14.2
1976	24.0	8.1		53.1		14.7
1977	25.2	9.1		51.8		13.9
1978	25.7	9.5		51.4		13.4
1979	26.1	9.7		51.0		13.2
1980	27.1	9.7		49.5		13.7
1981	27.3	9.4		48.6		14.7
1982	28.1	8.6		48.5		14.8
1983	29.0	7.7		48.9		14.4
1984	30.0	7.9		48.7		13.5
1985[b]	29.9	8.4		48.6		13.1

Table 10-3 *(Continued)*

Jurisdiction/ year	*Personal income*	*Corporate income*	*Personal and corporate income*	*General and selective sales*[a]	*Property*	*Other*
Local						
1948			0.67	6.1	88.6	4.6
1950			0.80	6.1	88.2	4.9
1955			1.2	6.6	86.9	5.4
1960			1.4	7.4	87.4	3.8
1965			1.7	8.2	86.9	3.2
1970			4.2	7.9	84.9	3.0
1975			4.3	10.5	81.6	3.5
1976			4.6	10.6	81.2	3.5
1977			5.0	11.1	80.5	3.4
1978			5.1	11.6	79.7	3.6
1979			5.3	13.1	77.5	4.1
1980			5.8	14.0	75.9	4.3
1981			5.8	13.9	76.0	4.2
1982			5.9	14.3	76.0	3.8
1983			5.7	14.5	76.0	3.9
1984			5.8[c]	14.8	75.0	4.3
1985[b]			5.3	15.9	75.0	3.8

[a] Includes customs taxes for federal government.
[b] Estimates by the Treasury department for the federal government, Advisory Commission on Intergovernmental Relations for state and local.
[c] For 1984 local personal income tax revenues were $5,680 million and corporate income tax revenues were $1,535 million. Nearly all local corporation income taxes are raised by two localities: New York and Washington, D.C.

Source: U.S. Advisory Commission on Intergovernmental Relations, *Significant Features of Fiscal Federalism 1985-86,* 40.

Table 10-4 Flow of Federal Funds to and from the States, 1965-1984

State	*1965-1967*	*1969-1971*	*1974-1976*	*1982-1984*
Alabama	1.52	1.49	1.31	1.29
Alaska	1.01	2.76	1.82	1.01
Arizona	1.33	1.19	1.18	1.14
Arkansas	1.29	1.20	1.19	1.27
California	1.32	1.24	1.15	1.09
Colorado	1.33	1.24	1.05	0.91
Connecticut	0.92	0.88	0.92	1.02
Delaware	0.54	0.60	0.71	0.83
District of Columbia	2.16	2.99	3.23	—
Florida	1.15	1.09	0.96	1.09
Georgia	1.52	1.29	1.08	1.09
Hawaii	1.38	1.53	1.56	1.38
Idaho	1.15	0.96	1.03	1.13
Illinois	0.59	0.63	0.70	0.70
Indiana	0.75	0.81	0.74	0.83
Iowa	1.00	0.83	0.81	0.80
Kansas	1.44	1.14	0.96	1.02
Kentucky	1.32	1.14	1.17	1.10
Louisiana	1.33	1.19	1.07	0.90
Maine	1.14	1.04	1.19	1.30
Maryland	1.34	1.39	1.31	1.27
Massachusetts	0.90	0.95	1.04	1.10
Michigan	0.58	0.61	0.76	0.78
Minnesota	0.93	0.89	0.87	0.85
Mississippi	1.68	1.73	1.65	1.61
Missouri	1.09	1.10	1.12	1.43
Montana	1.53	1.18	1.17	1.07
Nebraska	1.26	0.91	0.91	0.95
Nevada	0.86	0.75	0.85	0.92
New Hampshire	0.83	0.97	0.90	0.98
New Jersey	0.71	0.75	0.79	0.70
New Mexico	1.68	1.67	1.47	1.80
New York	0.62	0.78	0.93	0.92
North Carolina	1.21	0.99	1.00	0.95
North Dakota	2.04	1.51	1.32	1.06
Ohio	0.70	0.75	0.76	0.85
Oklahoma	1.36	1.35	1.23	0.88
Oregon	0.80	0.84	0.91	0.89
Pennsylvania	0.71	0.85	0.95	0.96
Rhode Island	1.17	1.14	1.07	1.05
South Carolina	1.58	1.25	1.22	1.25
South Dakota	1.67	1.26	1.33	1.24
Tennessee	1.12	1.01	0.98	1.20

Table 10-4 *(Continued)*

State	*1965-1967*	*1969-1971*	*1974-1976*	*1982-1984*
Texas	1.35	1.31	0.96	0.78
Utah	1.32	1.53	1.28	1.27
Vermont	1.11	1.02	1.16	1.10
Virginia	1.73	1.68	1.46	1.52
Washington	1.24	1.10	1.20	1.09
West Virginia	1.02	1.09	1.21	1.07
Wisconsin	0.67	0.71	0.76	0.82
Wyoming	1.50	1.10	1.00	0.75

Note: "—" indicates not available. Numbers are the estimated amount of federal expenditures in each state for each $100 of federal taxes paid by residents of each state. Includes all federal expenditures that can be allocated by state. All figures adjusted proportionally so that overall there is $1.00 of revenue for each $1.00 of expenditure. Three-year averages for expenditures and revenue were used to ensure that unusually high or low figures in a particular state in any single year would not unduly influence the flow-of-fund ratios.

Source: U.S. Advisory Commission on Intergovernmental Relations, *Significant Features of Fiscal Federalism 1985-86,* 178.

Table 10-5 Federal Grants-in-Aid Outlays, 1950-1992

		Federal grants as a percentage of			
		Federal outlays[a]		State and local expendi- tures[c]	Gross national product
Year	*Total grants- in-aid (billions)*	*Total*	*Domestic programs*[b]		
1950	$ 2.3	5.3	11.6	10.4	0.8
1955	3.2	4.7	17.2	10.1	0.8
1960	7.0	7.6	20.6	14.6	1.4
1965	10.9	9.2	20.3	15.2	1.6
1970	24.1	12.3	25.3	19.2	2.4
1975	49.8	15.0	23.1	22.7	3.3
1980	91.5	15.5	23.3	25.8	3.4
1981	94.8	14.0	21.6	24.6	3.2
1982	88.2	11.8	19.0	21.6	2.8
1983	92.5	11.4	18.6	21.3	2.8
1984	97.6	11.5	19.6	21.1	2.6
1985	105.9	11.2	19.3	21.0	2.7
1986	112.4	11.4	19.8	20.6	2.7
1987 est.	109.9	10.8	18.9	—	2.5
1988 est.	106.3	10.4	18.6	—	2.2
1989 est.	106.5	10.0	17.8	—	2.1
1990 est.	107.9	9.7	17.4	—	2.0
1991 est.	109.2	9.5	17.0	—	1.9
1992 est.	110.6	9.4	16.6	—	1.8

Note: "—" indicates not available. Fiscal years.

[a] Includes off-budget outlays; all grants are on-budget.

[b] Excludes outlays for national defense, international affairs, and net interest.

[c] As defined in the national income and product accounts.

Source: Office of Management and Budget, *Budget of the United States Government, Fiscal Year 1988, Special Analyses* (Washington, D.C.: U.S. Government Printing Office, 1987), Table H-6.

Table 10-6 Fiscal Dependency of Lower Levels on Higher Levels of Government, 1955-1984 (percent)

	Intergovernmental revenue as a percentage of general revenue from own sources		
Year	State from federal	Local from federal[a]	Local from state[b]
1955	20.9	2.5	40.6
1960[c]	31.0	2.6	41.6
1965[c]	32.3	3.6	43.3
1970[c]	33.5	5.1	52.4
1972	37.9	7.1	54.5
1974	35.5	13.3	58.1
1975	37.3	12.9	60.5
1976	39.1	14.6	60.3
1977	37.9	16.3	59.1
1978	37.0	17.5	58.4
1979	36.1	17.6	63.3
1980	36.6	16.3	62.5
1981	36.2	15.4	61.1
1982	32.1	12.8	58.2
1983	31.7	11.7	54.9
1984	30.5	10.6	53.9

[a] Local governments include townships and special districts.
[b] Includes indirect federal aid passed through the states; duplicate intergovernmental transfers are excluded.
[c] Partially estimated.

Source: U.S. Advisory Commission on Intergovernmental Relations, *Significant Features of Fiscal Federalism 1985-86*, 59.

Table 10-7 Variations in Local Dependency on State Aid, 1984-1985, (percent)

State	*Percentage*	*State*	*Percentage*
1. New Mexico	50.2	26. Virginia	32.0
2. California	43.2	27. Wyoming	31.3
3. Delaware	43.1	28. Louisiana	31.0
4. Wisconsin	42.7	29. Pennsylvania	30.6
5. Alaska	42.2	30. Maine	30.4
6. North Dakota	41.6	31. Michigan	29.6
7. Washington	41.0	32. Utah	29.4
8. Mississippi	40.8	33. Maryland	28.8
9. North Carolina	40.1	34. Florida	28.7
10. Kentucky	40.4	35. Rhode Island	27.4
11. Arkansas	38.9	36. Tennessee	26.8
12. Idaho	38.9	37. Texas	26.7
13. Minnesota	38.8	38. Georgia	26.3
14. West Virginia	38.8	39. Missouri	25.3
15. Arizona	38.0	40. Illinois	25.2
16. South Carolina	37.9	41. Connecticut	24.5
17. Indiana	37.8	42. Colorado	24.4
18. Massachusetts	36.3	43. Vermont	24.0
19. Alabama	35.1	44. Oregon	23.9
20. New York	34.8	45. Montana	23.7
21. New Jersey	34.5	46. Kansas	23.2
22. Ohio	34.2	47. South Dakota	20.8
23. Iowa	34.0	48. Nebraska	20.6
24. Nevada	33.8	49. New Hampshire	11.9
25. Oklahoma	33.5	50. Hawaii	6.7
		Total	33.4

Note: Percentages reflect state transfers (including "pull-through" monies from the federal government) as a percentage of total local revenues.

Source: U.S. Bureau of the Census, *Governmental Finances in 1984-1985* (Washington, D.C.: U.S. Government Printing Office, 1986), 22-23.

Table 10-8 Federal Grants-in-Aid to State and Local Governments by Function, 1960-1992 (percent)

Function	*1960*	*1970*	*1980*	*1986*	*1988 (est.)*	*1990 (est.)*	*1992 (est.)*
Health	3	16	17	24	27	29	31
Income security	38	24	20	26	28	27	27
Education, training, employment, and social services	7	27	24	17	18	19	18
Transportation	43	19	14	16	16	16	16
Natural resources and environment	2	2	6	4	3	3	3
Community and regional development	2	7	7	4	4	3	3
General purpose fiscal assistance	2	2	9	6	1	1	2
Agriculture	3	3	1	2	2	1	1
Other	-	1	1	1	1	1	1
Total	100	100	100	100	100	100	100

Note: "-" indicates 0.5 percent or less.

Source: Office of Management and Budget, *Budget of the U.S. Government, Fiscal Year 1988, Special Analyses,* Table H-4.

Table 10-9 State Fiscal Discipline Measures

State	*Tax and expenditure limitations*	*Balanced budget requirement*	*Require super-majority vote to pass tax*	*Index income tax*	*Gubernatorial line-item veto*	*Fiscal note review procedure*	*Program evaluation and sunset*	*"Rainy day" funds*
Alabama		x			x	x	x	
Alaska	x	x			x		x	x
Arizona	x	x		x	x	x	x	
Arkansas		x	x		x	x		
California	x	x	x	x	x	x		x
Colorado	x	x		x	x	x	x	x
Connecticut		x			x	x	x	x
Delaware		x	x		x		x	x
Florida		x	x		x	x		x
Georgia		x			x	x	x	x
Hawaii	x	x			x		x	
Idaho	x	x			x	x		x
Illinois		x			x	x	x	
Indiana		x				x	x	x
Iowa		x		x	x	x		x
Kansas		x			x	x	x	
Kentucky		x			x	x		x
Louisiana	x	x	x		x	x	x	
Maine		x		x			x	
Maryland		x			x	x	x	
Massachusetts		x			x	x		
Michigan	x	x			x	x		x
Minnesota		x		x	x			x
Mississippi		x	x		x	x		x
Missouri	x	x			x	x		
Montana	x	x		x	x	x	x	

	(1)	(2)	(3)	(4)	(5)	(6)	(7)	(8)
Nebraska		x			x	x		x
Nevada	x	x				x		
New Hampshire		x				x	x	
New Jersey		x			x	x		
New Mexico		x			x	x	x	x
New York		x			x			x
North Carolina		x				x		
North Dakota		x			x			
Ohio		x			x	x		x
Oklahoma		x			x		x	
Oregon	x	x		x	x	x	x	
Pennsylvania		x			x	x	x	
Rhode Island	x	x				x	x	x
South Carolina	x	x		x	x	x	x	x
South Dakota		x	x		x	x		
Tennessee	x	x			x	x	x	x
Texas	x	x			x	x	x	
Utah	x	x			x	x	x	
Vermont							x	
Virginia		x			x	x		x
Washington	x	x			x	x	x	x
West Virginia		x		x	x	x	x	
Wisconsin		x			x	x		
Wyoming		x			x	x	x	x
Total	18	49	7	10	43	41	29	24

Note: Considerable detail about each mechanism can be found in the source.

Source: U.S. Advisory Commission on Intergovernmental Relations, *Significant Features of Fiscal Federalism 1985-86*, 145.

Table 10-10 State Lottery Revenues, 1980 and 1984

State/year	*Date established*	*Gross revenue (millions)*	*Net proceeds (millions)*	*Net proceeds as a percentage of state revenue*[a]	*Annual bet per capita*
Arizona	July 1981				
1980		—	—	—	—
1984		$ 59.3	$20.0	0.6	$ 19.42
Colorado	January 1983				
1980		—	—	—	—
1984		110.5	37.7	1.3	34.78
Connecticut	February 1972				
1980		129.9	60.8	2.6	41.80
1984		240.7	97.0	2.4	76.30
Delaware	November 1975				
1980		15.9	6.3	0.9	26.79
1984		30.3	13.0	1.2	49.51
Illinois	July 1974				
1980		91.0	35.8	0.4	7.97
1984		826.5	378.0	3.5	71.80
Maine	June 1974				
1980		6.0	0.7	[b]	5.36
1984		16.0	4.6	0.4	13.81
Maryland	May 1973				
1980		372.3	185.4	5.1	88.32
1984		515.4	216.9	4.2	118.52
Massachusetts	March 1972				
1980		192.5	92.5	2.0	33.55
1984		331.0	106.5	1.5	57.08
Michigan	November 1972				
1980		487.9	236.0	3.2	52.70
1984		544.2	229.7	2.1	59.97
New Hampshire	March 1964				
1980		9.0	3.7	0.9	9.72
1984		17.1	5.5	0.8	17.47
New Jersey	January 1971				
1980		331.9	142.4	2.7	45.07
1984		800.4	356.1	3.8	106.57
New York	1967-1975, September 1976				
1980		182.8	83.3	0.6	10.41
1984		797.6	380.8	1.7	44.97
Ohio	August 1974				
1980		57.2	35.7	0.6	5.30
1984		572.0	244.6	2.4	53.20

Table 10-10 *(Continued)*

State/year	*Date established*	*Gross revenue (millions)*	*Net proceeds (millions)*	*Net proceeds as a percentage of state revenue*[a]	*Annual bet per capita*
Pennsylvania	March 1972				
1980		$ 194.7	$158.0	1.9	$ 16.40
1984		1,152.8	514.8	4.4	96.87
Rhode Island	May 1974				
1980		33.4	16.6	2.0	35.24
1984		46.6	17.4	1.4	48.46
Vermont	February 1978				
1980		2.9	0.2	[b]	5.58
1984		4.5	1.2	0.2	8.49
Washington	November 1982				
1980		—	—	—	—
1984		171.7	60.7	1.1	39.47

Note: "—" indicates not available. In addition to the states listed above, in which lotteries were in operation in 1984, California, Florida, Idaho, Iowa, Kansas, Missouri, Montana, Oregon, South Dakota, Virginia, West Virginia, Wisconsin, and the District of Columbia have adopted lotteries.

[a] Excludes federal grants-in-aid.

[b] Less than one-tenth.

Source: U.S. Advisory Commission on Intergovernmental Relations, *Significant Features of Fiscal Federalism 1985-86,* 126.

Figure 10-2 Government Spending as a Percentage of GNP, 1929-1986

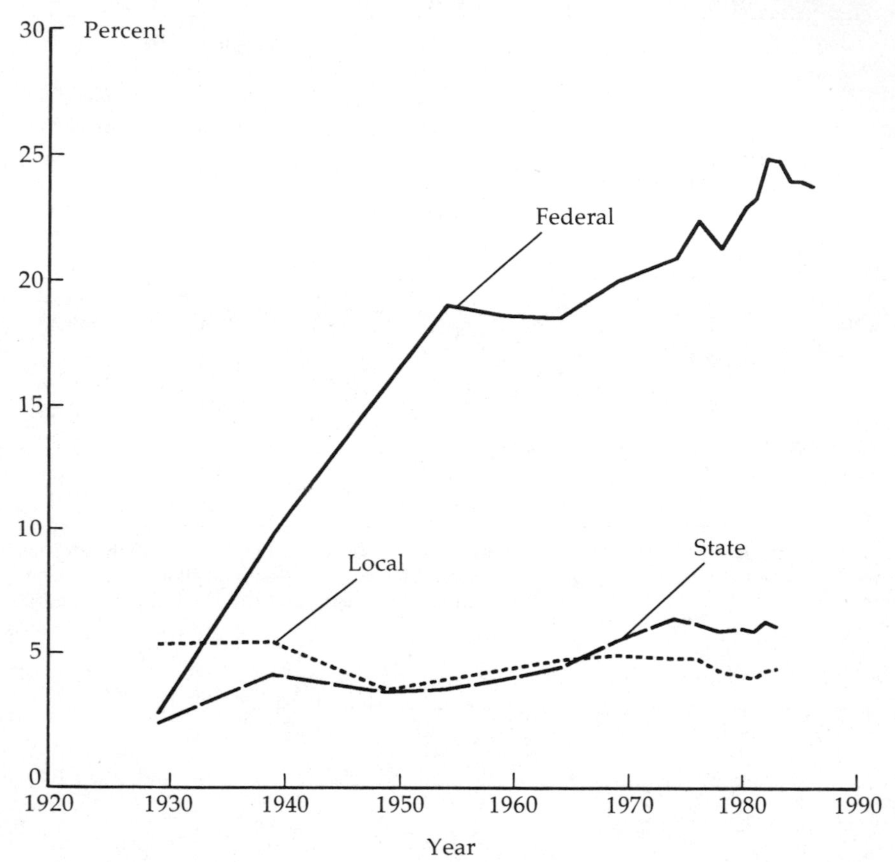

Note: State and local figures unavailable for 1984-1986.

Sources: 1929-1984: U.S. Advisory Commission on Intergovernmental Relations, *Significant Features of Fiscal Federalism, 1985-1986,* 6; 1985-1986: Office of Management and Budget, *Budget of the U.S. Government, Fiscal Year 1988, Historical Tables,* Table 15.2.

Table 10-11 State and Local Government Expenditures by Function, 1902-1984 (percent)

Function	*1902*	*1940*	*1952*	*1962*	*1970*	*1980*	*1984*
Education	23.3	23.5	27.0	31.5	35.6	30.8	29.4
Highways	16.0	14.0	15.1	14.7	11.1	7.7	6.6
Public welfare	3.4	10.3	9.0	7.2	9.9	10.5	10.8
Health	1.6	1.4	1.4	0.9	1.2	1.9	2.0
Hospitals	3.9	4.0	5.7	5.2	5.3	5.5	5.7
Police protection	4.6	3.2	3.0	3.0	3.0	3.1	3.2
Fire protection	3.7	2.1	1.9	1.6	1.4	1.3	1.4
Natural resources	0.8	1.9	2.5	1.9	1.8	1.3	1.2
Corrections	—	—	1.1	1.1	—	—	—
Sanitation and sewerage	4.7	1.8	3.2	2.8	2.3	3.1	2.7
Housing and urban renewal	—	2.0	2.5	1.6	1.4	1.4	1.5
Parks and recreation	2.6	1.4	1.0	1.3	1.3	1.5	1.4
Financial administration	12.9	5.0	3.9	1.5	1.4	1.6	1.6
Other government administration				1.8	1.8	2.0	2.2
Social insurance administration	—	0.6	0.6	0.6	—	—	—
Interest on general debt	6.2	5.8	1.8	2.9	3.0	3.4	4.8
Utility and liquor store[a]	7.5	11.8	9.9	7.7	6.4	8.4	9.2
Insurance trust expenditure[b]	—	6.1	5.5	6.9	4.9	6.7	6.8
Other	8.9	5.0	4.2	4.8	8.2	9.8	9.5
Total direct expenditure (millions)	$1,095	$11,240	$30,863	$70,547	$148,052	$432,328	$598,945

Note: "—" indicates not available. For 1902-1952, financial administration includes other government administration. For 1970-1984, other government administration is referred to as general control.

[a] Utility systems—water, electric, and gas—accounted for 6.6 percent of direct expenditure in the 1983-1984 fiscal year, transit systems another 2.2 percent, and liquor stores 0.5 percent.

[b] Employee retirement accounted for 3.7 percent of direct expenditure in the 1983-1984 fiscal year, unemployment compensation another 2.3 percent.

Sources: 1970-1984: *Statistical Abstract of the U.S., 1987,* 257; 1902-1952: U.S. Bureau of the Census, *Census of Governments, 1982* (Washington, D.C.: U.S. Government Printing Office, 1985), 33.

Figure 10-3 Surpluses and Deficits in Government Finances, 1947-1986

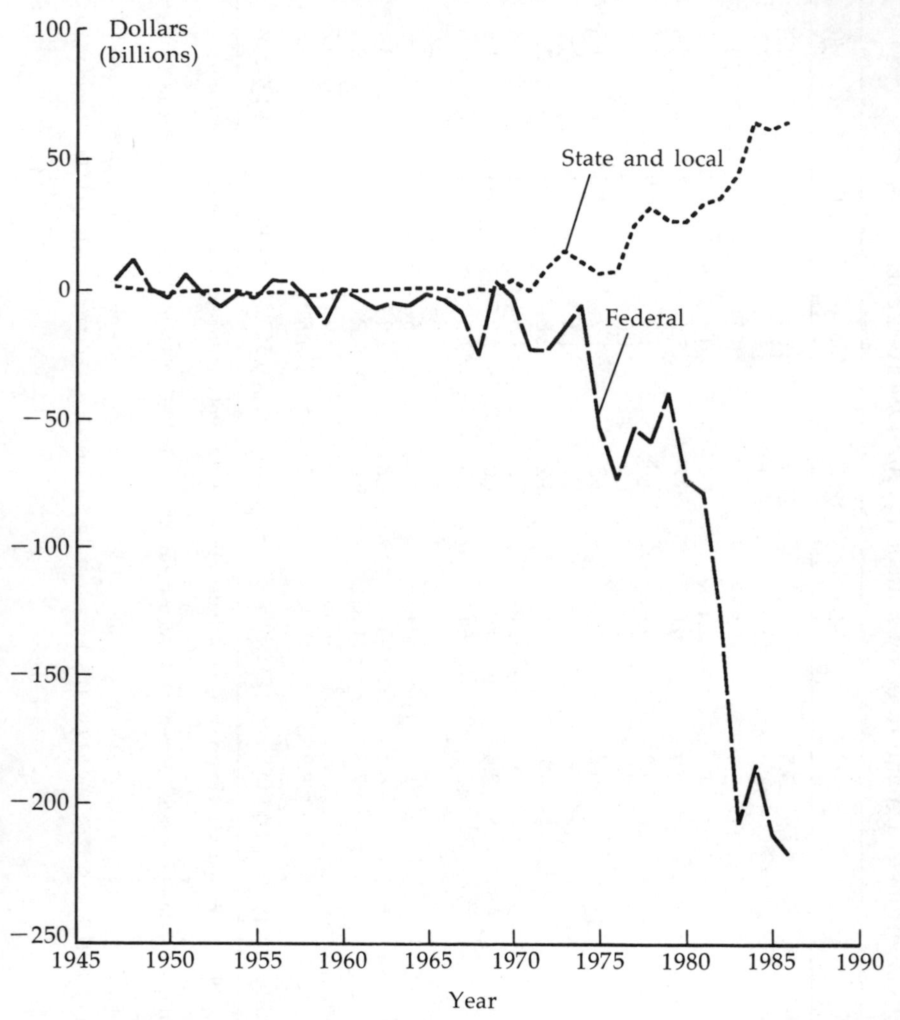

Source: Office of Management and Budget, *Budget of the U.S. Government, Fiscal Year 1988, Historical Tables,* Table 15.6.

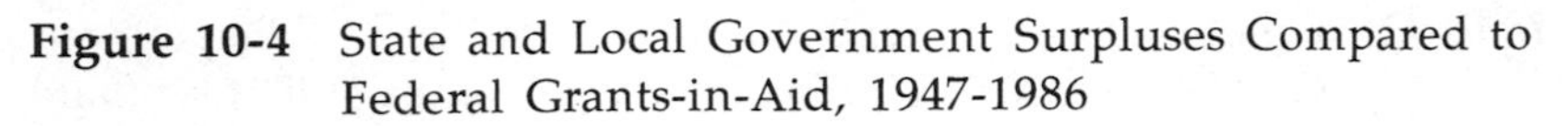

Figure 10-4 State and Local Government Surpluses Compared to Federal Grants-in-Aid, 1947-1986

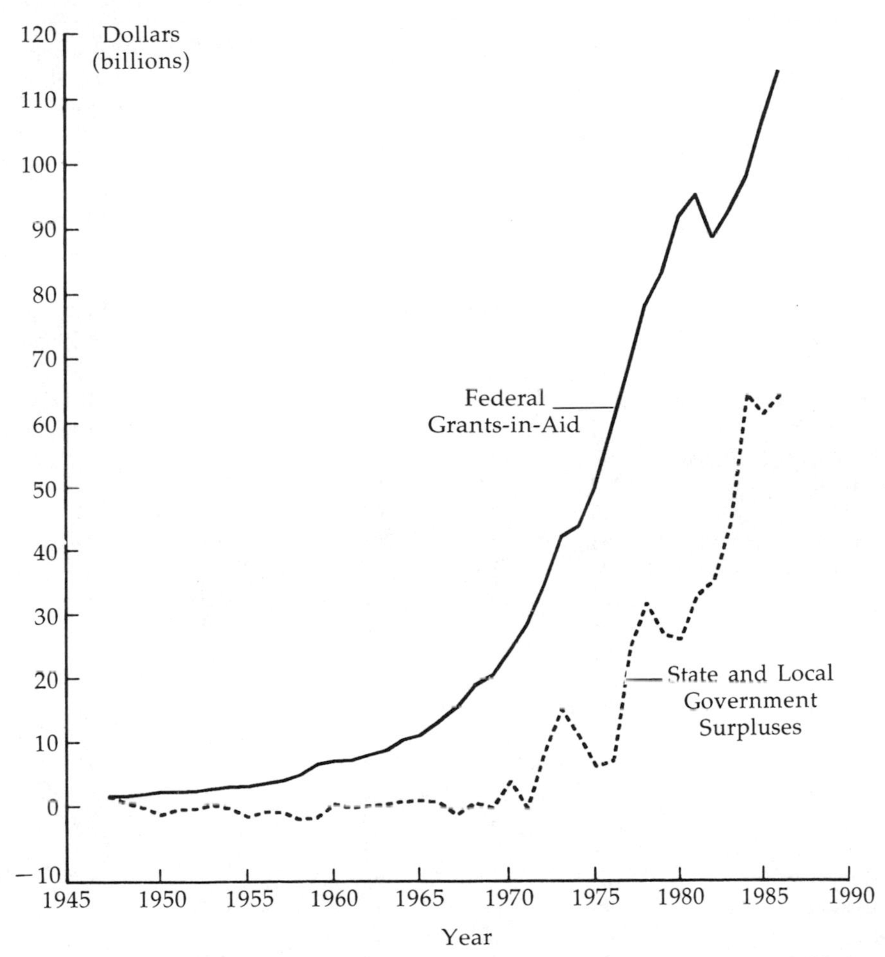

Source: Office of Management and Budget, *Budget of the U.S. Government, Fiscal Year 1988, Historical Tables,* Table 12.1 (grants-in-aid), Table 15.6 (surpluses).

Table 10-12 Benefits and Recipients of Aid to Families with Dependent Children (AFDC) (1985) and Food Stamps (1984) by State

State	*Maximum AFDC grant (per month)*[a]	*Food stamp benefit (per month)*	*Combined benefits as a percentage of 1984 poverty threshold*[b]	*Public aid recipients (percentage of population)*	*Food stamp recipients (percentage of population)*
Alabama	$118	$208	47	7.0	15.1
Alaska	719	192	106	3.9	3.4
Arizona	233	206	64	3.3	7.0
Arkansas	164	208	54	5.8	11.2
California	555	110	96	8.7	6.2
Colorado	346	172	75	3.3	5.2
Connecticut	546	112	95	4.6	4.7
Delaware	287	190	69	5.0	6.4
District of Columbia	327	178	73	11.8	12.2
Florida	240	204	64	4.0	5.6
Georgia	208	208	60	6.5	9.7
Hawaii	468	276	94	5.8	9.6
Idaho	304	185	71	2.5	5.6
Illinois	302	186	71	7.5	9.6
Indiana	256	199	66	3.9	7.3
Iowa	360	168	77	5.2	6.5
Kansas	373	164	78	3.6	4.8
Kentucky	197	208	59	6.9	15.0
Louisiana	190	208	58	8.0	14.0
Maine	370	165	78	7.0	9.7
Maryland	313	195	74	5.5	6.9
Massachusetts	396	157	80	5.9	5.9
Michigan	417[c]	173	86	8.9	11.2
Minnesota	524	119	93	4.2	5.4
Mississippi	96	208	44	10.2	19.0
Missouri	263	197	67	5.5	7.4
Montana	332	177	74	3.8	6.7
Nebraska	350	171	76	3.7	5.4
Nevada	233	206	64	2.3	3.4
New Hampshire	378	163	78	2.0	3.0
New Jersey	385	161	79	6.0	6.4
New Mexico	258	199	66	5.2	10.7

Table 10-12 *(Continued)*

State	*Maximum AFDC grant (per month)*[a]	*Food stamp benefit (per month)*	*Combined benefits as a percentage of 1984 poverty threshold*[b]	*Public aid recipients (percentage of population)*	*Food stamp recipients (percentage of population)*
New York	$474[d]	$143	89	8.2	10.4
North Carolina	223	208	62	4.9	7.5
North Dakota	371	165	78	2.7	3.9
Ohio	290	189	69	7.4	10.5
Oklahoma	282	192	69	4.3	7.8
Oregon	386	196	84	3.8	8.0
Pennsylvania	364	167	77	6.1	9.0
Rhode Island	479	171	94	6.2	7.4
South Carolina	187	208	57	6.2	11.2
South Dakota	329	178	73	3.6	6.4
Tennessee	138	208	50	5.9	11.0
Texas	167	208	54	3.8	7.5
Utah	363	167	77	2.8	4.4
Vermont	558	109	97	6.0	8.5
Virginia	327	178	73	4.1	6.5
Washington	476	143	90	5.2	6.1
West Virginia	206	208	60	7.5	13.6
Wisconsin	533	116	94	7.5	7.4
Wyoming	265	197	67	2.6	4.3

Note: The first two columns are maximum potential AFDC and food stamp benefits for a one-parent family of three persons. In most states the AFDC and food stamps amounts apply also to two-parent families of three (where the second parent is incapacitated or, as permitted in almost half the states, unemployed). Some, however, increase benefits for such families.

[a] In states with area differentials, figure shown is for areas with highest benefit.

[b] Based on the Census Bureau's 1984 poverty threshold for a family of three persons, $8,280, converted to a monthly rate of $690. For Alaska, this threshold was increased by 25 percent; for Hawaii, by 15 percent, following the practice of the Office of Management and Budget.

[c] Wayne County only.

[d] New York City only.

Sources: U.S. Advisory Commission on Intergovernmental Relations, *Significant Features of Fiscal Federalism 1985-86*, 177; *Statistical Abstract of the U.S., 1986*, 939, *1987*, 364.

Questions

1. Which component of local government accounts for the largest decline in the number of governments between 1942 and 1982 (Table 10-1)? Federal, state, local—which level had the greatest numerical increase in employees from 1982 to 1985 (Figure 10-1)? The greatest percentage increase?

2. Surely Wyoming cannot raise more revenue than large states such as California and New York. Yet Wyoming consistently has one of the greatest tax capacities of the fifty states (Table 10-2). How do you explain this apparent anomaly? (Hint: read footnote a.) Do tax capacity and tax effort "go together"; specifically, for 1983 where do the five highest states in tax capacity rank in terms of tax effort?

3. Describe the differences in the sources of federal, state, and local taxes (Table 10-3). How has the source of state taxes changed over the period shown?

4. Which state received the most federal funds relative to federal taxes in 1982-1984 (Table 10-4)? The least? Find the states with a value of 1.5 or more in 1965-1967. What happened to their value in 1982-1984? What about states with a value of .75 or below? What could account for this pattern?

5. From 1983 to 1984 and from 1985 to 1986, federal grants went up as a percentage of federal outlays but went down as a percentage of state and local expenditures (Table 10-5). What does this imply about federal versus state and local expenditures?

6. There has been great growth in intergovernmental revenue since 1955 (despite the decline since the mid- to late-1970s (Table 10-6). Say in different words what this growth means. What social or political implications might follow from this growth?

7. Are states in which localities are most dependent on state aid (Table 10-7) typically those states making the greatest tax effort (Table 10-2)?

8. In which function has there been the largest increase in federal grants-in-aid (Table 10-8)?

9. How many states have all of the fiscal discipline mechanisms listed in Table 10-9? How many states have none? Indexing income taxes means that as prices go up, tax brackets change so that individuals whose income goes up only as much as prices will not pay any more in taxes. In what way is this a fiscal discipline measure?

10. What is the highest percentage of state revenue raised by lottery proceeds (Table 10-10)? In what state and year was this? Are lotteries becoming more or less successful as fund raisers? Explain your reasoning.

11. Of the "program" expenditures (education through parks and recreation) for which function was the ratio of 1984 to 1962 expenditures the greatest (Table 10-11)? Between 1984 and 1902? Which function saw the biggest decline between 1902 and 1984?

12. Do the farm belt states of Illinois, Iowa, Minnesota, Kansas, Nebraska, South Dakota, and North Dakota have lower percentages of food stamp recipients than other states do (Table 10-12)? Which farm state has the higher percentage of food stamp recipients? Why?

11

Foreign and Military Policy

Even if one sought to understand only U.S. domestic politics, data on international relations would be essential. In the 1960 presidential campaign, for example, John Kennedy made the "missile gap" a major issue: the United States was falling behind the Soviet Union in its missile arsenal, and this imperiled the defense of the free world. The actual existence of that missile gap has been disputed, but the charge fit in with Kennedy's pledge to get the country moving again and played well to the public in the aftermath of Sputnik and the U-2 incident. Similarly, Ronald Reagan made increased military spending a cornerstone of his campaign platform in 1980.

One might think that statistics relating to foreign policy, especially the military aspects, are difficult or impossible to find, that secrecy prevents publication of important information about our defense capabilities. There are instances in which this is the case. There are reports, for example, of a U.S. "stealth" bomber, a plane designed to be almost impossible to detect by radar. Even when a prototype evidently crashed in California, the plane's existence was officially denied. There are also secret diplomatic and military initiatives undertaken by the Central Intelligence Agency and other organizations that the public learns about only when something goes wrong. The sale of weapons to Iran while the United States was publicly declaring that it would have nothing to do with that country, and the use of profits from these sales to support the Nicaraguan contras, is a case in point.

Despite these examples and the obvious need for secrecy in defense-related areas, a surprisingly wide array of data is available, in part because details about military hardware are not the only kinds of relevant information. In fact, the first table in this chapter deals with public opinion data. As was evident during the 1960s, public opinion about foreign policy is extraordinarily relevant and powerful information. Public opinion on U.S involvement in Vietnam reveals a great deal about why President Lyndon Johnson declined to run for reelection in 1968 and why U.S. forces began tc withdraw from Vietnam shortly thereafter (Figure 11-1). Public opinion on defense spending has been politically relevant, although the pattern of changes in the late 1970s and 1980s suggests that Ronald Reagan was leading as well as responding to changes in public sentiments (Table 11-11).

A great deal of other information closely relates to both defense and domestic policy, and this kind of data is emphasized here. Defense spending, for example, involves more than whether the United States has spent enough to defend itself. Elementary economics courses use the phrase "guns or butter" to express the tradeoff between defense spending and nondefense spending. Every dollar spent for weaponry means a dollar less that can be spent for social programs, tax reductions, and other politically worthy causes. Therefore information on defense spending (Table 11-10) is doubly relevant.

In presenting information about defense spending, two elements arise. The first is the concept of "constant" versus "current" dollars. Current dollars are what people deal with every day. The price asked for goods is the price paid; whether the price has gone up more or less than other prices is not especially relevant. People may be aware that prices of some goods have gone up (e.g., oil and gasoline in the 1970s) or down (e.g., many electronic products) more than others, but the price quoted is what is most significant. Constant dollars, in contrast, take into account what has happened to prices more generally (see Table 13-2 for the Consumer Price Index). Thus, for example, most food clearly costs more in current dollars than it did years ago; in the 1960s one never heard of a loaf of bread that cost $1.00. Yet relative to other prices, the cost of bread has been reduced. Its price may have only doubled in a given period of time while other prices have tripled. In a very meaningful sense, therefore, bread and other foods are cheaper than they used to be; the "real" cost of bread has been reduced.

Another, perhaps simpler, way to express this is to say that constant dollar calculations take inflation into account. For defense spending, therefore, the question is: after taking inflation into account, has spending increased? If spending has risen only as fast as inflation, the new budget will buy only as much as the previous budget, even though nominally, that is, in current dollars, it is larger. Because this issue of real versus current dollars is so significant, Table 11-10 and many of the tables in Chapter 13 express expenditures both ways.

The second new element in presenting information about defense spending is that it is especially relevant to see what other countries are doing as well. Whether the United States is spending a lot or a little is a relative question. If other countries raise their spending, then perhaps the United States must do the same. As a consequence, information is presented on worldwide military expenditures (Table 11-12) even though the focus in this volume is on the United States.

Economic and social dimensions are also relevant to U.S. foreign and military policy, and data about these are widely available. The slippage of the U.S. trade balance (Table 11-16) and the increasing foreign investment in the United States and U.S. investment abroad (Table 11-15) are two aspects of the economic context of recent foreign policy discussions. Foreign aid, whether in the form of military (Table 11-13) or nonmilitary (Table 11-14) assistance, is another part of economic foreign policy. Immigration policy has social and economic implications, and changes in the flow of immigrants, along with future prospects, make it a most significant aspect of U.S. foreign relations (Table 11-17).

The statistical picture would be incomplete without information about military weapons and forces. Here, too, information is needed about more than just the United States. Therefore, one of many possible comparisons between Soviet and American military strength is presented (Table 11-5) as well as existing bilateral and multilateral arms control agreements (Table 11-4). In both a contemporary and historical vein, information is given about military conflicts and personnel. Even here, however, it is impossible to avoid domestic aspects of these data. One of the tables on military personnel reports information by sex, race, and Hispanic origin (Table 11-9). This classification of personnel is obviously more relevant to U.S. domestic policy than to the question of whether the country is sufficiently prepared to meet a challenge from abroad.

The emergence of the United States as a world power in the twentieth century has elevated the political significance of international relations so that no overview of American politics would be complete without a look at foreign and military policy. Foreign policy has often proved critical in domestic politics, and that accounts for the array of numbers presented here.

Table 11-1 Public Opinion on U.S. Involvement in World Affairs, 1945-1986 (percent)

Date	*Active part*	*Stay out*	*No opinion*
October 1945	70	19	11
September 1947	65	26	9
September 1949	67	25	8
November 1950	64	25	11
December 1950	66	25	9
October 1952	68	23	9
February 1953	73	22	5
September 1953	71	21	8
April 1954	69	25	6
March 1955	72	21	7
November 1956	71	25	4
June 1965	79	16	5
March 1973	66	31	3
March 1975	61	36	4
March 1976	63	32	5
March 1978	64	32	4
December 1978	59	29	12
March 1982	61	34	5
November 1982	53	35	12
March 1983	65	31	4
March 1984	65	29	6
March 1985	70	27	2
March 1986	65	32	4

Note: Question: "Do you think it would be best for the future of this country if we take an active part in world affairs, or if we stay out of world affairs?"

Sources: 1945, 1947, November 1950, December 1978, November 1982: Gallup surveys; 1949, December 1950, 1952-1965: National Opinion Research Center; all others: General Social Survey, National Opinion Research Center, University of Chicago.

Table 11-2 U.S. Diplomatic and Consular Posts, 1781-1987

Year	*Diplomatic*	*Consular*
1781	4	3
1790	2	10
1800	6	52
1810	4	60
1820	7	83
1830	15	141
1840	20	152
1850	27	197
1860	33	282
1870	36	318
1880	35	303
1890	41	323
1900	41	318
1910	48	324
1920	45	368
1930	57	299
1940	58	264
1950	74	179
1960	99	166
1970	117	122
1980	133	100
1987	168	102

Note: 1987 figure is as of September. For that year, diplomatic posts include embassies, countries with ambassadors without physical missions, branch offices, missions, and interest sections. Consular posts include consulates general and consulates.

Source: U.S. Department of State, Office of Public Communication, *A Short History of the U.S. Department of State 1781-1981* (Washington, D.C.: U.S. Government Printing Office, 1981), 35. Updated from U.S. Department of State, *Key Officers of Foreign Service Posts* (Washington, D.C.: U.S. Government Printing Office, September 1987), vii.

Table 11-3 U.S.-Soviet Summit Meetings, 1945-1987

Date	*Location*	*Leaders*	*Topic*
July-August 1945	Potsdam	President Harry S Truman, Soviet leader Josef Stalin, British prime ministers Winston Churchill and Clement R. Attlee	Partition and control of Germany
July 1955	Geneva	President Dwight D. Eisenhower, Soviet leader Nikolai A. Bulganin, British prime minister Anthony Eden, French premier Edgar Faure	Reunification of Germany, disarmament, European security
September 1959	Camp David, Md.	President Dwight D. Eisenhower, Soviet leader Nikita S. Khruschev	Berlin problem
May 1960	Paris	President Dwight D. Eisenhower, Soviet leader Nikita S. Khrushchev, French president Charles de Gaulle, British prime minister Harold Macmillan	U-2 incident
June 1961	Vienna	President John F. Kennedy, Soviet leader Nikita S. Khruschev	Berlin problem
June 1967	Glassboro, N.J.	President Lyndon B. Johnson, Soviet leader Aleksei N. Kosygin	Middle East
May 1972	Moscow	President Richard M. Nixon, Soviet leader Leonid I. Brezhnev	SALT I, antiballistic missile limitations
June 1973	Washington, D.C.	President Richard M. Nixon, Soviet leader Leonid I. Brezhnev	Détente
June-July 1974	Moscow and Yalta	President Richard M. Nixon, Soviet leader Leonid I. Brezhnev	Arms control
November 1974	Vladivostok	President Gerald R. Ford, Soviet leader Leonid I. Brezhnev	Arms control
June 1979	Vienna	President Jimmy Carter, Soviet leader Leonid I. Brezhnev	SALT II

(Table continues)

Table 11-3 *(Continued)*

Date	*Location*	*Leaders*	*Topic*
November 1985	Geneva	President Ronald Reagan, Soviet leader Mikhail Gorbachev	Arms control
October 1986	Reykjavik	President Ronald Reagan, Soviet leader Mikhail Gorbachev	Arms control
December 1987	Washington, D.C.	President Ronald Reagan, Soviet leader Mikhail Gorbachev	Arms control

Source: Congressional Quarterly Weekly Report (1987), 667; updated by the editors.

Table 11-4 Arms Control and Disarmament Agreements

Issue	*Participants*
Nuclear weapons	
To prevent the spread of nuclear weapons	
Antarctic Treaty, 1959	32 states[a]
Outer Space Treaty, 1967	125 states[a]
Latin American Nuclear-Free Zone Treaty, 1967	31 states[a]
Nonproliferation Treaty, 1968	136 states[a]
Seabed Treaty, 1971	108 states[a]
To reduce the risk of nuclear war	
Hot Line and Modernization Agreements, 1963	United States and Soviet Union
Accidents Measures Agreement, 1971	United States and Soviet Union
Prevention of Nuclear War Agreement, 1973	United States and Soviet Union
To limit nuclear testing	
Limited Test Ban Treaty, 1963	127 states[a]
Threshold Test Ban Treaty, 1974[b]	United States and Soviet Union
Peaceful Nuclear Explosions Treaty, 1976[b]	United States and Soviet Union
To limit nuclear weapons	
ABM Treaty (SALT I) and Protocol, 1972	United States and Soviet Union
SALT I Interim Agreement, 1972[c]	United States and Soviet Union
SALT II, 1979[d]	United States and Soviet Union
Intermediate Range Missiles Treaty, 1987	United States and Soviet Union
Other Weapons	
To prohibit use of gas	
Geneva Protocol, 1925	130 states
To prohibit biological weapons	
Biological Weapons Convention, 1972	131 states
To prohibit techniques changing the environment	
Environmental Modification Convention, 1977	73 states
To control use of inhumane weapons	
Inhumane Weapons Convention, 1981	22 states[e]
To reduce risk of war	
Notification of Military Activities, 1986	35 states

[a] Number of parties and signatories as of December 1986.
[b] Not yet ratified.
[c] Expired by its terms on October 3, 1977.
[d] Never ratified. If the treaty had entered into force, it would have expired by its terms on December 31, 1985.
[e] Convention entered into force December 1983. The United States is not a signatory.

Source: U.S. Arms Control and Disarmament Agency, *World Military Expenditures and Arms Transfers* (Washington, D.C.: U.S. Government Printing Office, 1983), 28, and unpublished data from Arms Control and Disarmament Agency.

Table 11-5 Strategic Offensive Forces of the Superpowers, 1986

	United States		*Soviet Union*	
Classification	Weapon	Number	Weapon	Number
ICBMs	Titan	7	SS-11	448
	Minuteman II	450	SS-13	60
	Minuteman III	547	SS-17	150
	Peacekeeper	2	SS-18	308
			SS-19	360
			SS-25	72
Total		1,006		1,398
SLBMs	Poseidon (C-3)	256	SS-N-5	39
	Trident 1(C-4)[a]	384	SS-N-6	304
			SS-N-8	292
			SS-N-17	12
			SS-N-18	224
			SS-N-20[a]	80
			SS-N-23[a]	48
Total		640		999
Bombers	B-526	167	Bear	150
	B-52H	96	Bison	15
	FB-111	61	Backfire	275
	B-1B	18		
Total		342		440
Delivery vehicles				
	Missiles	1,646	Missiles	2,397
	Bombers	342	Bombers	440
Total		1,988		2,837

Note: Data as of September 30, 1986. "ICBM" refers to intercontinental ballistic missile, "SLBM" refers to submarine-launched ballistic missile.

[a] Includes SLBMs potentially carried on U.S. Trident and on Soviet Typhoon and Delta-IV submarines on sea trials.

Source: Joint Chiefs of Staff, *Military Posture for Fiscal Year 1988* (Washington, D.C.: U.S. Government Printing Office, 1987), 33.

Table 11-6 U.S. Personnel in Major Military Conflicts

Item	*Civil War*[a]	*Spanish-American War*	*World War I*	*World War II*	*Korean conflict*	*Vietnam conflict*
Personnel serving (thousands)	2,213	307[b]	4,744	16,354[c]	5,764[d]	8,811[e]
Average duration of service (months)	20	8	12	33	19	23
Casualties (thousands)						
Battle deaths	140	[f]	53	292	34	47[g]
Wounds not mortal	282	2	204	671	103	304[g]
Draftees: classified (thousands)	777	0	24,234	36,677	9,123	75,717[e]
Examined	522	0	3,764	17,955	3,685	8,611[e]
Rejected	160	0	803	6,420	1,189	3,880[e]
Inducted	46	0	2,820	10,022	1,560	1,759[e]
Cost (millions)[h]						
Current	$2,300	$ 270	$ 32,700	$360,000	$50,000	$140,600
Constant (1967)	8,500	1,100	100,000	816,300	69,300	148,800

Note: For Revolutionary War, number of personnel serving not known, but estimates range from 184,000 to 250,000; for War of 1812, 286,730 served; for Mexican War, 78,718 served. Dates of the major conflicts may differ from those specified in various laws providing benefits for veterans.

[a] Union forces only. Estimates of the number serving in Confederate forces range from 600,000 to 1.5 million; cost for the Confederacy estimated at $1 million (current dollars) and $3.7 million (constant dollars).

[b] Covers April 21, 1898, to August 13, 1898.

[c] Covers December 1, 1941, to December 31, 1946.

[d] Covers June 25, 1950, to July 27, 1953.

[e] Covers August 4, 1964, to January 27, 1973.

[f] Fewer than 500.

[g] Covers Jan. 1, 1961, to Jan. 27, 1973.

[h] Original direct costs only. Excludes service-connected veterans' benefits and interest payments on war loans.

Source: U.S. Bureau of the Census, *Statistical Abstract of the U.S., 1987* (Washington, D.C.: U.S. Government Printing Office, 1986), 323, 328.

Table 11-7 U.S. Military Forces and Casualities in Vietnam, 1959-1984

		Battle deaths				Wounded, nonfatal[a]	
Year	*Military forces (thousands)*	Total[a]	Killed	Died of wounds	Died while missing[b]	Hospital care (thousands)	No hospital care (thousands)
1959-1964	23.3[c]	269	187	10	72	0.8	0.8
1965	184.3	1,427	1,119	111	197	3.3	2.8
1966	385.3	5,036	4,131	579	326	16.5	13.6
1967	485.6	9,461	7,524	978	959	32.4	29.7
1968	536.1	14,617	12,618	1,598	401	46.8	46.0
1969	475.2	9,416	8,107	1,168	141	32.9	37.3
1970	234.6	4,230	3,486	555	189	15.2	15.4
1971	156.8	1,373	1,079	160	134	4.8	4.2
1972	24.2	360	204	28	128	0.6	0.6
1973-1984	0.0	1,139	26	8	1,105	[d]	[d]
Total	[e]	47,328	38,481	5,195	3,652	153.3	150.3

Note: Military forces as of December 31. All U.S. forces withdrawn by January 27, 1973.

[a] Casualties from enemy action. Deaths excludes 10,449 servicemen who died in accidents or from disease.

[b] Includes servicemen who died while captured.

[c] For 1964 only.

[d] Fewer than 50.

[e] Not applicable.

Source: Statistical Abstract of the U.S., 1987, 328.

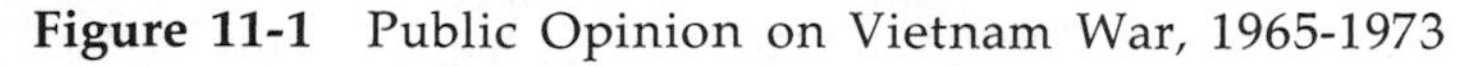

Figure 11-1 Public Opinion on Vietnam War, 1965-1973

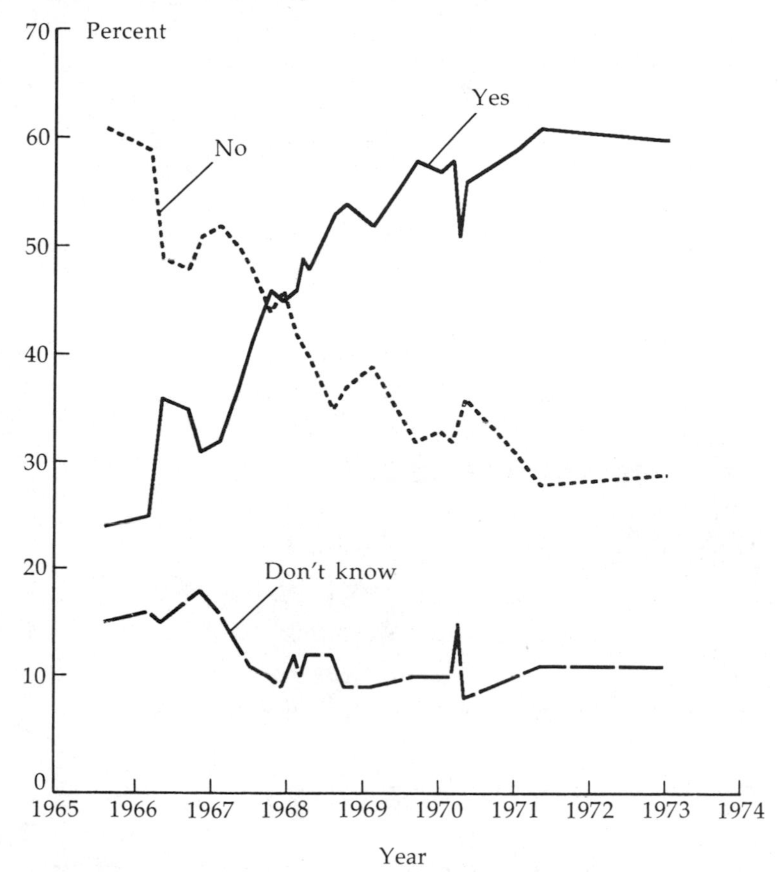

Note: Question: "In view of the developments since we entered the fighting in Vietnam, do you think the United States made a mistake sending troops to fight in Vietnam?"

Sources: Gallup polls as cited in John E. Mueller, *War, Presidents and Public Opinion* (New York: Wiley, 1973), 54-55 (reprinted in 1985 by University Press of America, Lanham, Md.); *The Gallup Poll*, 1972-1975, vol. I (Wilmington, Del.: Scholarly Resources Inc., 1977), 87.

Table 11-8 U.S. Military Personnel Abroad or Afloat by Country, 1972-1985 (thousands)

Country	*1972*	*1973*	*1974*	*1975*	*1976*	*1977*	*1978*	*1979*	*1980*	*1981*	*1982*	*1983*	*1984*	*1985*
Outside United States[a]	628	585	519	517	464	483	494	481	502	502	528	520	511	515
Europe[b]	298	319	297	314	297	313	330	325	332	337	356	342	352	358
Germany, Federal Republic	210	229	208	220	209	224	234	239	244	248	256	254	254	247
Greece	3	5	4	4	3	3	4	3	4	3	4	4	4	4
Iceland	3	3	3	3	3	3	3	3	3	3	3	3	3	4
Italy	10	10	12	12	12	10	12	12	12	12	13	14	15	15
Spain	9	9	10	9	9	9	9	9	9	9	9	9	9	9
Turkey	7	7	6	7	4	5	5	5	5	5	5	5	5	5
United Kingdom	22	21	21	21	20	21	22	23	24	25	26	28	29	30
Other countries	8	6	6	7	6	6	6	6	7	7	7	7	8	9
Afloat	28	26	26	30	29	32	35	25	22	25	33	18	25	36
Asia and Pacific	275	199	169	156	123	130	129	122	115	125	139	137	121	125
Japan[c]	65	57	58	48	45	46	46	46	46	46	51	49	46	47
Philippines	17	16	17	15	15	14	14	14	13	15	14	15	15	15
South Korea	41	42	38	42	40	40	42	39	39	38	39	39	41	42
Taiwan	8	9	5	4	2	1	1	[d]	[d]	[d]	[d]	[d]	[d]	[d]
Thailand	47	42	31	20	1	[d]	[d]	[d]	[d]	[d]	[d]	[d]	[d]	[d]
South Vietnam	47	[d]	[d]	0	0	0	0	0	0	0	0	0	0	0
Afloat	51	33	20	28	19	29	26	22	16	25	33	34	18	20
U.S. outlying areas[e]	29	33	26	25	24	23	22	22	2	13	13	13	13	14
Troop dependents	342	341	347	365	334	322	318	383	369	347	368	386	399	385

Note: As of September 30.

[a] Includes troops in countries not shown.

[b] Western Europe and related areas.

[c] Includes Okinawa.

[d] Fewer than 500.

[e] Primarily Guam, Panama Canal Zone, Puerto Rico, and Midway Islands.

Sources: Statistical Abstract of the U.S., 1977, 370, *1981,* 364, *1982-1983,* 361, *1986,* 343, *1987,* 328.

Table 11-9 U.S. Active Duty Forces by Sex, Race, and Hispanic Origin, 1965-1985

	Female			*Black*			*Hispanic*[a]			*Total*[b]	
Year	Officers	Enlisted	Total	Officers	Enlisted	Total	Officers	Enlisted	Total	Officers (thousands)	Enlisted (thousands)
1965	3.1%	0.9%	1.2%	1.9%	10.5%	9.5%	—	—	—	339	2,317
1966	3.2	0.8	1.1	—	—	—	—	—	—	349	2,745
1967	3.3	0.8	1.0	2.1	9.9	8.9	—	—	—	385	2,992
1968	3.2	0.8	1.1	2.1	10.2	9.2	—	—	—	416	2,132
1969	3.1	0.9	1.1	2.1	9.6	8.7	—	—	—	419	3,041
1970	3.3	1.1	1.4	2.2	11.0	9.8	—	—	—	402	2,664
1971	3.5	1.3	1.6	2.3	12.1	10.7	1.3%	3.4%	3.1%[c]	371	2,329
1972	3.8	1.6	1.9	2.4	13.5	11.9	1.2	4.0	3.6	336	1,987
1973	4.0	2.2	2.5	2.7	14.9	13.2	1.2	4.5	4.0	321	1,932
1974	4.3	3.3	3.5	3.0	16.2	14.4	1.3	4.5	3.9	303	1,860
1975	4.6	4.5	4.6	3.2	16.2	14.4	1.4	4.6	4.2	292	1,836
1976	5.0	5.3	5.2	3.6	17.1	15.2	1.3	4.6	4.2	281	1,801
1977	5.4	5.8	5.7	3.9	17.4	15.6	1.5	4.5	4.1	276	1,798
1978	6.2	6.5	6.5	4.3	19.3	17.3	1.6	4.5	4.1	274	1,788
1979	6.9	7.5	7.4	4.7	21.2	19.0	1.6	4.4	3.8	274	1,753
1980	7.7	8.5	8.4	5.0	21.9	19.6	1.2	4.0	3.6	278	1,759
1981	8.1	9.0	8.9	5.3	22.1	19.8	1.2	4.1	3.7	285	1,783
1982	8.6	9.0	9.0	5.3	22.0	19.7	1.2	4.1	3.7	292	1,804
1983	9.0	9.3	9.3	5.8	21.6	19.4	1.4	4.1	3.7	301	1,811
1984	9.4	9.5	9.5	6.2	21.1	19.0	1.4	3.9	3.6	304	1,820
1985	9.8	9.8	9.8	6.4	21.1	18.9	1.5	3.9	3.6	309	1,828

Note: "—" indicates not available.

[a] Hispanics may be of any race.

[b] Includes other races not shown separately.

[c] Data on percent Hispanic origin from 1971-1979 is based on male armed forces members only.

Sources: Statistical Abstract of the U.S., 1976, 336, *1980,* 375-376, *1984,* 353, *1986,* 341, *1987,* 327.

Table 11-10 U.S. Defense Spending, 1955-1986

Year	*Average annual percentage change*[a]		*Defense outlays as a percentage of*	
	Current dollars	Constant dollars	Federal outlays	Gross national product
1955	−25.5	−20.3	62.4	11.0
1960	2.4	−1.9	52.2	9.5
1962	4.3	2.6	49.0	9.4
1963	2.0	−2.5	48.0	9.1
1964	2.5	0.9	46.2	8.7
1965	−7.6	−8.8	42.8	7.5
1966	14.8	9.1	43.2	7.8
1967	22.9	18.8	45.4	9.0
1968	14.7	8.4	46.0	9.6
1969	0.7	−4.5	44.9	8.9
1970	−1.0	−7.3	41.8	8.2
1971	−3.5	−10.2	37.5	7.5
1972	0.4	−5.8	34.3	6.9
1973	−3.1	−8.3	31.2	6.0
1974	3.5	−6.7	29.5	5.6
1975	9.0	−2.1	26.0	5.7
1976	3.6	−3.9	24.1	5.3
1976[b]	[c]	[c]	23.2	5.0
1977	8.5	0.5	23.8	5.0
1978	7.5	0.5	22.8	4.8
1979	11.3	2.6	23.1	4.7
1980	15.2	3.1	22.7	5.0
1981	17.5	4.5	23.2	5.3
1982	17.6	8.1	24.9	5.9
1983	13.3	8.4	26.0	6.3
1984	8.3	4.8	26.7	6.2
1985	11.1	7.7	26.7	6.4
1986 est.	5.2	2.3	27.1	6.3

Note: For actual dollar amounts of defense spending (current and constant), see Table 13-3.
[a] Change from prior year shown; for 1955, change from 1950.
[b] Transition quarter, July-September.
[c] Not applicable.

Source: Statistical Abstract of the U.S., 1987, 317.

Table 11-11 Public Opinion on U.S. Defense Spending, 1960-1987 (percent)

Year	*Too much*	*About right*	*Too little*	*No opinion*
1960	18	45	21	16
1969	52	31	8	9
1971	50	31	11	8
1973	46	30	13	11
1974	44	32	12	12
1976	36	32	22	10
1977	23	40	27	10
1979	21	33	34	12
1980	14	24	49	13
1981	15	22	51	12
1982	41	31	16	12
1983	37	36	21	6
1985	46	36	11	7
1986	47	36	13	4
1987	44	36	14	6

Note: Question: "There is much discussion as to the amount of money the government in Washington should spend for national defense and military purposes. How do you feel about this? Do you think we are spending too little, too much, or about the right amount?"

Sources: Gallup Opinion Index (February 1980), 10; *The Gallup Report* (March 1985), 4, (April 1986), 15, and (May 1987), 3.

Table 11-12 Worldwide Military Expenditures, 1973-1983

Country group	*1973*	*1974*	*1975*	*1976*	*1977*	*1978*	*1979*	*1980*	*1981*	*1982*	*1983*	*Per capita (dollars)* 1980	1983
Current dollars (billions)													
Worldwide, total[a]	$288.0	$330.3	$374.2	$405.0	$435.6	$477.2	$529.4	$600.8	$682.0	$762.4	$811.9	135	174
NATO countries[b]	120.0	132.8	142.6	146.9	161.3	175.8	195.8	226.7	261.9	297.4	325.1	391	550
United States	78.4	85.9	90.9	91.0	100.9	109.2	123.3	144.0	169.9	196.4	217.2	632	926
Percentage of total	27.2	26.0	24.3	22.5	23.2	22.9	23.1	24.0	24.9	25.8	26.8	-	-
Warsaw Pact countries[c]	113.7	129.9	147.1	161.6	172.8	188.4	207.8	232.0	257.4	284.2	299.8	619	782
Soviet Union	96.4	110.6	125.4	138.4	148.1	161.9	179.2	200.3	222.6	243.6	258.0	755	947
Percentage of total	33.5	33.5	33.5	34.2	34.0	33.9	33.8	33.3	32.6	32.0	31.8	-	-
Constant (1982) dollars (billions)													
Worldwide, total[a]	564.9	595.7	618.9	633.7	643.8	656.8	671.7	699.7	726.6	762.6	778.9	156	166
NATO countries[b]	235.3	239.6	235.8	229.9	238.4	242.0	248.4	264.0	279.0	297.4	311.9	455	527
United States	153.7	154.9	150.4	142.4	149.2	150.3	155.1	167.7	181.0	196.4	208.3	736	888
Warsaw Pact[c] countries	223.0	234.3	243.3	252.8	255.4	259.3	263.7	270.1	274.2	284.2	287.6	720	750
Soviet Union	189.1	199.5	207.4	216.5	218.9	222.8	227.4	233.3	237.1	243.8	247.5	878	908

Percentage of GNP[d]													
Worldwide, total[a]	5.7	5.9	6.0	5.9	5.7	5.6	5.6	5.7	5.8	6.1	6.1	-	-
United States	5.9	6.0	5.8	5.3	5.2	5.1	5.1	5.5	5.8	6.4	6.6	-	-
NATO countries[b]	4.7	4.8	4.8	4.4	4.4	4.3	4.3	4.5	4.7	5.1	5.2	-	-
Warsaw Pact countries[c]	11.4	11.6	11.6	11.7	11.5	11.3	11.4	11.6	11.6	11.8	11.7	-	-
Soviet Union	13.7	14.0	14.1	14.3	14.0	13.8	13.9	14.1	14.1	14.2	14.0	-	-

Note: "-" indicates not applicable.

[a] Includes countries not shown separately.

[b] Current members of NATO (North Atlantic Treaty Organization) are Belgium, Canada, Denmark, France, Iceland, Great Britain, Greece, Italy, Luxembourg, The Netherlands, Norway, Portugal, Spain, Turkey, the United States, and West Germany.

[c] The Warsaw Pact countries include Bulgaria, Czechoslovakia, East Germany, Hungary, Poland, Romania, and the Soviet Union.

[d] The meaning of military expenditures as a percentage of GNP differs between most Communist countries and non-Communist countries because of different estimating procedures.

Source: Statistical Abstract of the U.S., 1987, 321.

Table 11-13 U.S. Military Sales and Military Assistance to Foreign Governments, Principal Recipients, 1950-1985 (millions)

	Military sales					*Military assistance*				
Country	1950-1981	1982	1983	1984	1985	1950-1981	1982	1983	1984	1985
Australia	$ 1,988.9	$ 127.4	$ 326.1	$ 472.9	$ 493.4	$ 0.0	$ 0.0	$ 0.0	$ 0.0	$ 0.0
Belgium	894.9	296.2	273.0	196.0	127.6	1,203.8	0.0	0.0	0.0	0.0
Cambodia	0.0	0.0	0.0	0.0	0.0	1,177.2	0.0	0.0	0.0	0.0
Canada	1,473.3	116.3	110.6	139.4	75.1	0.0	0.0	0.0	0.0	0.0
China (Taiwan)	1,578.6	389.8	405.9	300.0	375.7	2,554.5	2.0	0.0	0.0	0.0
France	388.5	15.5	14.1	47.3	47.4	4,045.1	0.0	0.0	0.0	0.0
Germany, Federal Republic	6,725.8	419.4	322.9	342.5	233.3	884.8	0.0	0.0	0.0	0.0
Greece	1,461.1	133.9	157.8	111.2	144.2	1,612.6	22.2	34.6	1.0	2.0
Iran	10,827.1	0.0	0.0	0.0	0.0	766.7	0.0	0.0	0.0	0.0
Israel	7,199.5	864.6	265.5	220.7	531.7	0.0	0.0	0.0	0.0	0.0
Italy	780.5	24.7	28.3	56.8	58.9	2,243.7	0.0	0.0	0.0	0.0
Korea	1,825.6	217.4	298.6	260.5	266.8	5,330.4	139.0	0.7	1.3	0.3
Laos	0.0	0.0	0.0	0.0	0.0	1,460.1	0.0	0.0	0.0	0.0
The Netherlands	1,044.4	471.7	516.7	432.6	403.2	1,178.1	0.0	0.0	0.0	0.0
Saudi Arabia	14,119.1	3,848.4	6,014.0	3,420.8	2,805.3	23.9	0.0	0.0	0.0	0.0
Thailand	724.0	149.0	165.9	170.8	127.9	1,161.9	3.4	2.3	0.9	0.2
Turkey	791.0	187.6	150.4	306.2	396.4	3,119.7	10.1	4.3	3.1	0.6
United Kingdom	2,785.7	336.9	478.4	462.0	386.0	1,012.9	0.0	0.0	0.0	0.0
Vietnam	1.2	0.0	0.0	0.0	0.0	14,773.9	0.0	0.0	0.0	0.0
Total	$65,112.6	$10,591.7	$13,164.7	$9,816.8	$9,567.7	$53,803.5	$420.5	$173.9	$129.7	$32.9

Note: Figures exclude training.

Source: Statistical Abstract of the U.S., 1987, 324.

Table 11-14 U.S. Foreign Aid, Principal Recipients, 1962-1985 (millions)

Region/country	*1962-1981*	*1982*	*1983*	*1984*	*1985*
Near East and South Asia[a]	$20,928	$2,307	$2,400	$2,474	$3,867
Egypt	5,134	771	750	853	1,065
India	3,349	99	89	0	0
Israel	5,269	806	785	910	1,950
Jordan	995	15	10	20	100
Pakistan	2,041	100	200	225	250
Turkey	1,559	300	285	139	175
East Asia[a]	9,225	219	216	230	313
Indonesia	1,119	68	72	75	72
Korea	1,080	0	0	0	0
Philippines	603	89	87	84	183
Vietnam	4,490	0	0	0	0
Europe	726	99	45	62	94
Latin America[a]	7,901	614	842	912	1,506
Brazil	1,480	0	0	0	0
Costa Rica	161	32	184	146	196
Dominican Republic	454	60	35	64	126
El Salvador	243	155	199	161	376
Honduras	260	68	87	71	205
Jamaica	151	119	82	88	115
ROCAP[b]	293	13	19	16	107
Africa[a]	4,688	643	636	728	900
Sudan	230	125	115	146	149
Total	$53,649	$4,990	$5,244	$5,684	$8,132

[a] Includes countries not shown separately.
[b] Regional programs covering Costa Rica, El Salvador, Guatemala, Honduras, Nicaragua, and Panama.

Sources: Statistical Abstract of the U.S., 1987, 788, *1985*, 812, *1984*, 830.

Table 11-15 Foreign Investment in the United States and U.S. Investment Abroad (millions)

Year	*All areas*	*Canada*	*Europe*	*Japan*
Foreign direct investment in the United States				
1960	$ 6,910	$ 1,934	$ 4,707	$ 88
1970	13,270	3,117	9,554	229
1980	83,046	12,162	54,688	4,723
1981	108,714	12,116	72,377	7,697
1982	124,677	11,708	83,193	9,677
1983	137,061	11,434	92,936	11,336
1984	164,583	15,286	108,211	16,044
1985	182,951	16,678	120,906	19,116
U.S. investment abroad				
1970	75,480	21,015	25,255	1,482
1977	145,990	35,052	62,552	4,593
1978	162,727	36,396	70,647	5,406
1979	187,858	40,662	83,056	6,180
1980	215,375	45,119	96,287	6,225
1981	228,348	47,073	101,601	6,762
1982	221,843	46,190	99,525	6,407
1983	226,962	47,553	102,689	7,661
1984	233,412	50,467	103,663	8,374

Sources: U.S. Department of Commerce, *Survey of Current Business* (Washington, D.C.: U.S. Government Printing Office, August 1985), 36; *Statistical Abstract of the U.S., 1981,* 836-837, *1982-1983,* 824, 826, *1987,* 780, 782.

Table 11-16 U.S. Balance of Trade, 1946-1985 (millions)

Year	*Merchandise trade balance*[a]	*Balance on current account*[b]
1946	$ 6,697	$ 4,885
1947	10,124	8,992
1948	5,708	2,417
1949	5,339	873
1950	1,122	−1,840
1951	3,067	884
1952	2,611	614
1953	1,437	−1,286
1954	2,576	219
1955	2,897	430
1956	4,753	2,730
1957	6,271	4,762
1958	3,462	784
1959	1,148	−1,282
1960	4,892	2,824
1961	5,571	3,822
1962	4,521	3,387
1963	5,224	4,414
1964	6,801	6,823
1965	4,951	5,431
1966	3,817	3,031
1967	3,800	2,583
1968	635	611
1969	607	399
1970	2,603	2,331
1971	−2,260	−1,433
1972	−6,416	−5,795
1973	911	7,140
1974	−5,505	1,962
1975	8,903	18,116
1976	−9,483	4,207
1977	−31,091	−14,511
1978	−33,947	−15,427
1979	−27,536	−991
1980	−25,480	1,873
1981	−27,978	6,339
1982	−36,444	−9,131
1983	−67,080	−46,604
1984	−112,522	−106,466
1985	−124,439	−117,677

[a] "Merchandise trade balance" measures the difference between the value of goods the United States imports and the goods the United States exports.
[b] "Balance on current account" is the broadest trade gauge, measuring the difference in imports and exports of merchandise trade and trade in services; also includes certain one-way flows of money into the United States, such as pension payments.

Source: U.S. President, *The Economic Report of the President* (Washington, D.C.: U.S. Government Printing Office, 1987), 358.

Table 11-17 Immigrants by Country, 1820-1985

Year	*Europe*				*Asia*[e]	*Canada*	*Other western hemisphere*[f]	*All other*[g]	*Total number (thousands)*
	North-western[a]	Central[b]	Southern[c]	Eastern[d]					
1820-1830	62.8%	5.1%	2.1%	0.1%	-	1.6%	6.2%	22.0%	151.8
1831-1840	56.3	25.5	1.0	-	-	2.3	3.3	11.7	599.1
1841-1850	67.6	25.4	0.3	-	-	2.4	1.2	3.1	1,713.3
1851-1860	56.9	36.7	0.8	-	1.6%	2.3	0.6	1.1	2,598.2
1861-1870	53.7	34.4	0.9	0.1	2.8	6.6	0.5	0.8	2,314.8
1871-1880	48.1	28.6	2.7	1.4	4.4	13.6	0.7	0.4	2,812.2
1881-1890	44.3	35.4	6.3	4.2	1.3	7.5	0.6	0.3	5,246.6
1891-1900	30.9	32.4	19.1	14.2	1.9	0.1	1.0	0.5	3,687.6
1901-1910	17.8	28.2	26.4	20.1	2.8	2.0	2.1	0.2	8,795.4
1911-1920	14.9	18.3	25.5	17.7	3.4	12.9	7.0	0.4	5,735.8
1921-1930	21.2	20.8	14.0	4.3	2.4	22.5	14.4	0.4	4,107.2
1931-1940	15.8	30.5	16.5	2.4	3.0	20.3	9.7	0.8	533.4
1941-1950	25.4	26.3	7.7	0.6	3.5	16.6	17.7	2.1	1,035.0
1951-1960	17.7	26.0	10.6	2.9	6.1	10.9	22.5	3.1	2,515.5
1961-1970	12.2	11.2	12.2	1.3	13.2	8.6	38.9	2.3	3,321.7
1971-1980	4.3	4.0	8.0	1.8	35.9	2.6	40.4	3.1	4,493.3
1981-1985	3.8	3.1	2.2	2.4	47.7	1.9	35.4	3.5	2,864.4

Note: "-" indicates less than 0.1 percent.

[a]Great Britain, Ireland, Norway, Sweden, Denmark, Iceland, Netherlands, Belgium, Luxembourg, Switzerland, and France.

[b]Germany, Poland, Czechoslovakia, Yugoslavia, Hungary, and Austria.

[c] Italy, Spain, Portugal, and Greece.

[d] USSR, Finland, Romania, Bulgaria, and Turkey.

[e] Cambodia, China, Taiwan, Hong Kong, India, Iran, Iraq, Israel, Japan, Jordan, Korea, Laos, Lebanon, Pakistan, Philippines, Thailand, and Vietnam.

[f] Mexico, Caribbean, Central and South America.

[g] Africa, Australia, New Zealand.

Sources: U.S. Bureau of the Census, *Historical Statistics of the U.S.* (Washington, D.C.: U.S. Government Printing Office, 1975), 105-109; *Statistical Abstract of the U.S., 1987*, 11, *1984*, 92.

Questions

1. Although the change has been small and possibly has run its course, there seems to have been a shift away from public support for active U.S. involvement in world affairs (Table 11-1). Based on its timing, why do you think this change occurred?

2. A considerable increase in the number of countries in the world accounts for the rise in the number of diplomatic posts (Table 11-2). Yet the number of consular posts has dropped sharply. Why?

3. How many of the eight U.S. postwar presidents have held a summit meeting with the Soviet leader (Table 11-3)? What was the topic of four of the first five meetings? Of most of the meetings since 1972?

4. When was the first multinational arms control agreement reached (Table 11-4)? What was it about?

5. Does the United States or the Soviet Union have the greater number of weapons (Table 11-5)? The number of weapons alone does not determine the balance of power. Why not?

6. Which U.S. war cost the most lives (Table 11-6)? The second most? In which war was the casualty rate (battle deaths per person served) the greatest?

7. What feature of public opinion about the Vietnam War (Figure 11-1) coincided almost perfectly with the maximum number of battle deaths in Vietnam?

8. As of 1985 about how many military personnel were overseas or on board ship (Table 11-8)? Where were most of these troops stationed? Of our Asian and Pacific troops, where were most of these stationed? Altogether, how many Americans were living abroad as a result of military deployments?

9. Between 1965 and 1985, the number of females and blacks in the armed forces increased (Table 11-9), tripling the proportion of females and doubling the proportion of blacks. However, these increases differed in important respects. Based on information in the table, how did the increases of females and blacks differ?

10. The defense budget has changed dramatically at times (Table 11-10). How much are the biggest increase and decrease (in percentage of constant dollars) and when did they occur? Apart from the buildup for the war in Vietnam (1966-1968), in what year was the increase the greatest?

11. In 1980 Ronald Reagan campaigned in part on the theme that the United States was spending too little on national defense. Based on Table 11-11, do you think he was following or leading public opinion? Throughout his terms, President Reagan continued to support a defense buildup, and in fact spending increased (Table 11-10). Did he continue to follow or lead public opinion?

12. Which defense group—NATO or the Warsaw Pact—has higher military expenditures in actual dollars (Table 11-12)? Which in terms of spending as a percentage of GNP? In constant dollars, which group or country (NATO, the United States, the Warsaw Pact, the Soviet Union) increased its spending by the largest percentage between 1982 and 1983? What was the percentage?

13. Since 1982 which country has been the principal recipient of U.S. military sales (Table 11-13)? Another country among the top buyers of military materiel was also the largest recipient of U.S. foreign aid (Table 11-14). What was that country?

14. What region of the world has had the largest increase in U.S. foreign aid since 1982 (Table 11-14)? Why is this?

15. By what percentage did U.S. investment abroad grow between 1980 and 1984 (Table 11-15)? By what percentage did foreign investment in the United States grow during the same period?

16. What was the first year in which the United States imported more goods than it exported (Table 11-16)? What was the most recent year in which the United States exported more goods than it imported?

17. Only one area—Central Europe—has sent a large, steady stream of immigrants to the United States. All other groups came in waves (Table 11-17). Describe when and where these waves came from. Note that 22 percent came from "all other" areas of the world in the 1820s. Who were they? Make and justify a projected distribution of immigrants for the 1990s.

12

Social Policy

The study of social policies might fairly be described as controversies informed by, but not settled by, statistics. No matter what the area, those on all sides of an issue try to support their arguments with relevant data.

The data are of many kinds and can be characterized in a variety of ways. First, there is factual information showing, for example, how many whites, blacks, and Hispanics are below the poverty line (Table 12-2), how much money is spent on social welfare (Tables 12-4 and 12-5), and how many crimes were committed in a given year (Table 12-19). Second, there are data about public opinion and social policy. Social policy concerns not only the actual crime rate but what people think about crime—for example, whether the courts are too easy on criminals (Table 12-21) and whether the death penalty is acceptable and desirable (Table 1-11). It matters not only what abortion rates are (Table 1-12) but also what people think and say about abortion (Table 1-13). One might also distinguish between data about the past or present and projections about the future. Much of the concern about Social Security payments and about health care costs are not about present payments but about what to expect in the future (Tables 12-6 and 12-7).

Social policies are inherently controversial, and so too are data relevant to such policies. Often, for example, analysts agree on a set of facts but disagree on the relevance of the material and on its interpretation. Information about numbers of people on welfare (Table 12-8), about the proportion of women and minorities elected to political office (Table 12-16), about the extent of crime and the cost of prisons (Tables 12-19 and 12-20), and so on, do not automatically answer causal questions (why the situation is as it is) any more than they answer normative questions (whether the existing situation is good and what should be done). Moreover, the importance of future projections often leads to special problems of inference. Any projection must be based on assumptions about what the future will be like. A footnote in Table 12-7, for example, should underscore the fact that no one can be certain in 1988 what health or Social Security costs will be in 2065.

In the face of enormous problems of inference, of controversy about almost every fact, and of the need to deal with future unknowns, one might well ask whether all these numbers are useful or necessary when discussing social policies. There are at least two answers to this question. The first is highly pragmatic. Some analysts will surely have factual information at their disposal; those who do not or cannot understand data and are unable or unwilling to provide any of their own will be hostage to others' information and interpretations.

From a more theoretical perspective, one can note that although data are always subject to some error and interpretation, people often do agree on the facts and on roughly how they should be interpreted. There is no disagreement, for example, that—barring major unforseen catastrophes or extremely large and unlikely changes in immigration—there will be a considerably smaller ratio of young people to old people in the first half of the next century. Knowing this does not solve the problems implicit in this fact, but it tells analysts that there will be problems and that the country needs to be thinking of solutions. It also suggests possible solutions—raising the retirement age, lowering Social Security payments or raising Social Security taxes, encouraging private pension plans so that the elderly need less government support, and so on.

In the area of social policy, then, as in other areas, data do not speak for themselves. They must be analyzed and interpreted. The facts alone will settle few arguments about causality or about normative questions. Still, data and an ability to interpret them are an essential ingredient in the arsenal of any well-educated social analyst, commentator, or student.

Figure 12-1 U.S. Population: Total, Urban, and Rural, 1790-2020

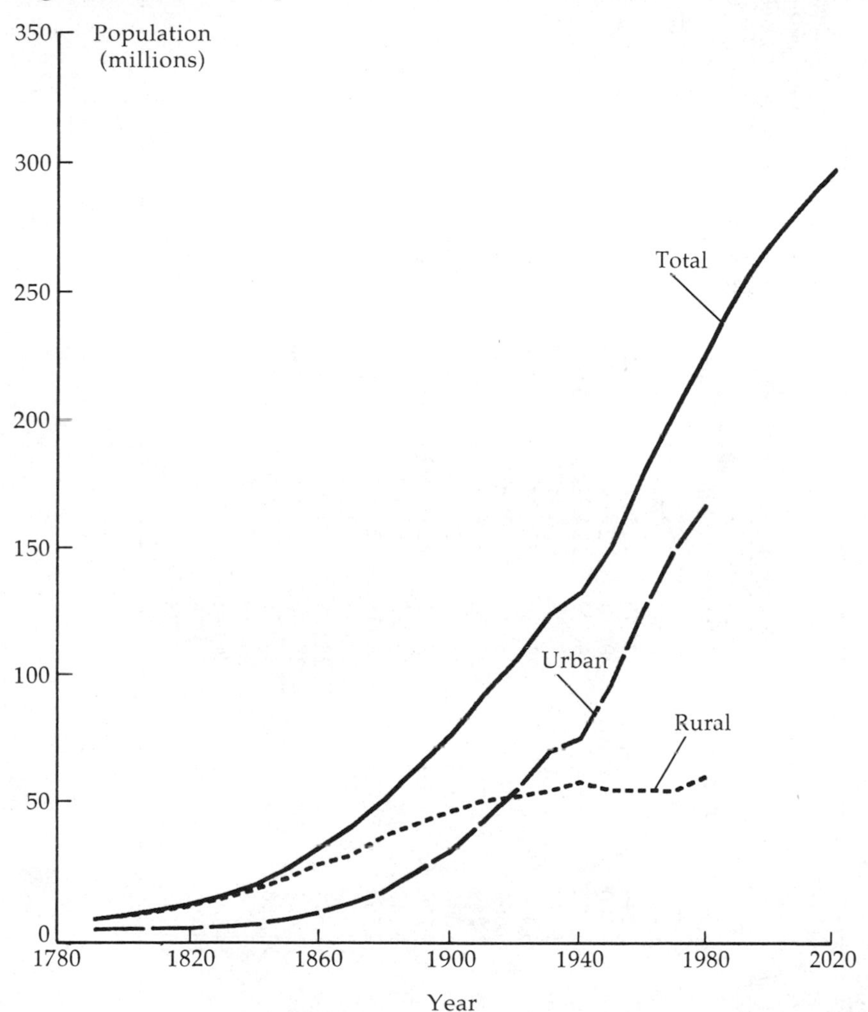

Note: Urban places, in general, are those with a population of 2,500 or more. A change in definition in 1950 resulted in about 5 percent more individuals being classified as urban than under the old definition. For details on definitions and projections, see sources.

Sources: Total population: U.S. Bureau of the Census, *Statistical Abstract of the U.S., 1987* (Washington, D.C.: U.S. Government Printing Office, 1986), 8, 15; urban and rural populations: U.S. Bureau of the Census, *Historical Statistics of the United States* (Washington, D.C.: U.S. Government Printing Office, 1975), 11.

Table 12-1 Median Family Income by Race and Hispanic Origin, 1950-1985

	Median income in current dollars				*Median income in constant (1985) dollars*				*Annual percentage change in median income of all families*	
Year	All families[a]	White	Black	Hispanic origin[b]	All families[a]	White	Black	Hispanic origin[b]	Current dollars	Constant dollars
1950	3,319	3,445	1,869[c]	—	14,832	15,395	8,352	—	3.1[d]	0.6[d]
1955	4,418	4,613	2,544[c]	—	17,749	18,533	10,220	—	5.9	3.7
1960	5,620	5,835	3,230[c]	—	20,414	21,195	11,733	—	4.9	2.8
1965	6,957	7,251	3,993[c]	—	23,720	24,722	13,614	—	4.4	3.1
1970	9,867	10,236	6,279	—	27,336	28,358	17,395	—	7.2	2.9
1971	10,285	10,672	6,440	—	27,319	28,347	17,106	—	4.2	−0.1
1972	11,116	11,549	6,864	8,183	28,584	29,697	17,650	21,042	8.1	4.6
1973	12,051	12,595	7,269	8,715	29,172	30,489	17,596	21,097	8.4	2.1
1974	12,902	13,408	8,006	9,540	28,145	29,249	17,465	20,811	7.1	−3.5
1975	13,719	14,268	8,779	9,551	27,421	28,518	17,547	19,090	6.3	−2.6
1976	14,958	15,537	9,242	10,259	28,267	29,361	17,465	19,387	9.0	3.1
1977	16,009	16,740	9,563	11,421	28,419	29,717	16,976	20,275	7.0	0.5
1978	17,640	18,368	10,879	12,566	29,087	30,287	17,939	20,720	10.2	2.4
1979	19,587	20,439	11,574	14,169	23,029	30,292	17,153	20,999	11.0	−0.2
1980	21,023	21,904	12,674	14,716	27,446	28,596	16,546	19,212	7.3	−5.5
1981	22,388	23,517	13,266	16,401	26,481	27,816	15,691	19,399	6.5	−3.5
1982	23,433	24,603	13,598	16,227	26,116	27,420	15,155	18,085	4.7	−1.4
1983	24,674	25,837	14,561	16,930	26,642	27,898	15,722	18,280	5.3	2.0
1984	26,433	27,686	15,432	18,833	27,376	28,674	15,982	19,505	7.1	2.8
1985	27,735	29,152	16,786	19,027	27,735	29,152	16,786	19,027	4.9	1.3

Note: "—" indicates not available.
[a] Includes other races not shown separately.
[b] Persons of Hispanic origin may be of any race.
[c] For 1950-1965, black and other races.
[d] Change from 1947.

Source: Statistical Abstract of the U.S., 1987, 436.

Table 12-2 Percentage Below the Poverty Level by Race and Hispanic Origin, 1959-1985

Year	*White*	*Black*	*Hispanic origin*[a]	*Total*[b]
1959	18.1	55.1	—	22.4
1960	17.8	—	—	22.2
1966	12.2	41.8	—	14.7
1969	9.5	32.2	—	12.1
1970	9.9	33.5	—	12.6
1971	9.9	32.5	—	12.5
1972	9.0	33.3	22.8	11.9
1973	8.4	31.4	21.9	11.1
1974	8.6	30.3	23.0	11.2
1975	9.7	31.3	26.9	12.3
1976	9.1	31.1	24.7	11.8
1977	8.9	31.3	22.4	11.6
1978	8.7	30.6	21.6	11.4
1979[c]	8.9	30.9	21.6	11.6
1979[d]	9.0	31.0	21.8	11.7
1980	10.2	32.5	25.7	13.0
1981[e]	11.1	34.2	26.5	14.0
1982[e]	12.0	35.6	29.9	15.0
1983[e]	12.2	35.7	28.1	15.3
1984[e]	11.5	33.8	28.4	14.4
1985[e]	11.4	31.3	29.0	14.0

Note: "—" indicates not available.
[a] Persons of Hispanic origin may be of any race.
[b] Includes other races not shown separately.
[c] Population controls based on 1970 census.
[d] Population controls based on 1980 census.
[e] Data based on revised poverty definition.

Source: Statistical Abstract of the U.S., 1987, 442.

Table 12-3 Persons and Families Below the Poverty Line, 1986

Group	*Percentage of group that is poor*	*Group as a percentage of all poor people*
Race/ethnicity		
White	11.0	68.5
Black	31.1	27.8
Hispanic origin[a]	27.3	18.6
Family status		
Married couple families[b]	6.1	44.4
Families with male head and no wife present[b]	11.4	4.1
Families with female head and no husband present[b]	34.6	51.4
Age		
Under 15	21.2	34.0
65 or over	12.4	10.7
Dwelling		
Metropolitan residents	12.3	70.0
Nonmetropolitan residents	18.1	30.0
Region		
Northeast	10.5	16.1
Midwest	13.0	23.6
South	16.1	40.5
West	13.2	19.8

[a] Persons of Hispanic origin may be of any race.
[b] Percentages based on number of families.

Source: U.S. Bureau of the Census, Current Population Reports, "Money Income and Poverty Status of Families and Persons in the United States: 1986" (Washington, D.C.: U.S. Government Printing Office, 1987), series P-60, no. 157, 23.

Table 12-4 Social Welfare Expenditures, 1960-1984

	Federal		*State and local*		*Total expenditures*	
Year	Total (billions)	Percentage of total federal outlays	Total (billions)	Percentage of total state and local outlays	Total (billions)	Percentage of total GNP
1960	$ 25.0	28.1	$ 27.3	60.1	$ 52.3	10.3
1965	37.7	32.6	39.5	60.4	77.2	11.2
1970	77.3	40.1	68.5	64.0	145.9	14.7
1971	92.6	44.9	79.3	64.0	171.9	16.0
1972	106.3	47.4	85.0	63.8	191.4	16.1
1973	122.6	50.5	91.4	64.9	213.9	16.1
1974	137.2	52.3	102.2	64.1	239.4	16.7
1975	167.4	53.8	122.7	63.5	290.1	18.7
1976	197.1	57.0	135.0	65.1	332.1	19.3
1977	218.4	56.3	142.2	64.5	360.6	18.8
1978	240.0	55.3	154.6	64.7	394.6	18.2
1979	263.2	54.9	166.6	63.8	429.8	17.8
1980	302.8	54.4	189.7	64.4	492.5	18.7
1981	344.1	53.9	206.2	62.1	550.3	18.4
1982	367.7	52.6	227.1	60.0	594.8	19.0
1983	398.8	51.9	243.3	60.0	642.1	19.3
1984[a]	419.3	50.2	252.7	58.9	672.0	18.2

[a] Preliminary.

Source: Statistical Abstract of the U.S., 1987, 342, *1985,* 355.

Table 12-5 Social Welfare Expenditures By Category, 1960-1984

Year	*Social insurance*	*Public aid*	*Health and medical programs*[a]	*Veterans programs*	*Education*	*Housing*	*Other social welfare*	*All health and medical care*[b]	*Total social welfare outlays*
Federal (millions)									
1960	$14,307	$ 2,117	$ 1,737	$ 5,367	$ 868	$ 144	$ 417	$ 2,918	$24,957
1965	21,807	3,594	2,781	6,011	2,470	238	812	4,625	37,712
1970	45,246	9,649	4,775	8,952	5,876	582	2,259	16,600	77,337
1975	99,715	27,186	8,521	16,570	8,629	2,541	4,264	34,100	167,426
1980	191,162	48,666	12,688	21,254	13,452	6,608	8,786	68,786	302,616
1984[c]	289,884	57,666	16,496	25,822	12,979	9,068	7,349	108,603	419,264
State and local (millions)									
1960	4,999	1,984	2,727	112	16,758	33	723	3,478	27,337
1965	6,316	2,690	3,466	20	25,638	80	1,254	4,911	39,464
1970	9,446	6,839	5,132	127	44,970	120	1,886	8,791	68,519
1975	23,298	14,122	9,267	449	72,205	631	2,683	18,248	122,654
1980	38,592	23,133	15,231	212	107,597	601	4,813	31,777	190,180
1984[c]	52,381	32,206	21,368	305	139,046	1,306	6,096	46,490	252,707
Total (millions)									
1960	19,307	4,101	4,464	5,479	17,626	177	1,139	6,395	52,293
1965	28,123	6,283	6,246	6,031	28,108	318	2,066	9,535	77,175
1970	54,691	16,488	9,907	9,078	50,845	701	4,145	25,391	145,856
1975	123,013	41,308	17,788	17,019	80,834	3,172	6,947	52,348	290,084
1980	229,754	71,799	27,919	21,466	121,050	7,210	13,599	100,563	492,797
1984[c]	342,264	89,871	37,864	26,127	152,025	10,374	13,445	155,092	671,972

Percentage of total expenditures									
1960	36.9	7.8	8.5	10.5	33.7	0.3	2.2	12.2	100.0
1965	36.4	8.1	8.1	7.8	36.4	0.4	2.7	12.4	100.0
1970	37.5	11.3	6.8	6.2	34.9	0.5	2.8	17.4	100.0
1975	42.4	14.2	6.1	5.9	27.9	1.1	2.4	18.0	100.0
1980	46.6	14.6	5.7	4.4	24.5	1.5	2.8	20.5	100.0
1984[c]	50.9	13.4	5.6	3.9	22.6	1.5	2.0	23.1	100.0
Percentage federal of total									
1960	74.1	51.6	33.9	98.0	4.9	81.4	36.6	45.6	47.7
1965	77.5	57.2	44.5	99.7	8.8	74.8	39.3	48.5	48.9
1970	82.7	58.5	48.2	98.6	11.6	83.0	54.5	65.4	53.0
1975	81.1	65.8	47.9	97.4	10.7	80.1	61.4	65.1	57.7
1980	83.2	67.8	44.9	99.0	11.1	91.7	64.6	68.1	61.4
1984[c]	84.7	64.2	43.6	99.0	8.5	87.4	54.7	70.0	62.4

Note: Figures for fiscal years ending in year shown.

[a] Excludes medical services parts of social insurance, public aid, veterans, and other social welfare.

[b] Combines health and medical programs with medical services included in social insurance, public aid, veterans, vocational rehabilitation, and antipoverty programs.

[c] Preliminary figures.

Source: Statistical Abstract of the U.S., 1987, 340.

Table 12-6 Federal Pension and Health Spending as a Percentage of GNP and the Budget, 1965-2040

Year	*Pension spending as a percentage of GNP*[a]	*Health spending as a percentage of GNP*[a]	*Total as a percent of GNP*[a]	*Total as a percentage of budget*[b]
1965	4.1	0.3	4.4	24.9
1970	4.7	1.4	6.1	30.0
1975	6.4	2.0	8.4	37.1
1980	6.5	2.3	8.8	38.2
1982	7.1	2.7	9.7	39.6
1984	7.0	2.8	9.8	39.7
1986	6.6	3.0	9.6	39.4
1988	6.4	3.2	9.6	39.4
1990	6.6	3.1	9.7	40.4
1995	6.2	3.7	9.9	41.3
2000	5.8	4.0	9.8	40.8
2005	5.6	4.4	10.0	41.7
2010	6.0	4.7	10.7	44.6
2015	6.0	5.0	11.0	45.8
2020	6.5	5.4	11.9	49.6
2025	7.0	5.9	12.9	53.9
2030	7.1	6.4	13.5	56.3
2035	7.1	7.0	14.1	58.8
2040	7.0	7.5	14.5	60.4

[a] Estimates for 1984-1988 are based on Congressional Budget Office baseline assumptions (August 1983); forecasts for 1990 and beyond are based on intermediate assumptions of the Social Security and Medicare actuaries.
[b] Forecasts for 1990 and beyond are based on the assumption that the budget accounts for 24 percent of GNP.

Source: United States, Congress, Senate, Special Committee on Aging, "Developments in Aging: 1986," 100th Cong., 1st sess., S. Rep. 100-4, vol. 3, February 27, 1987, 107.

Table 12-7 Social Security (OASDI) Covered Workers and Beneficiaries, 1945-2065

Year	*Covered workers (thousands)*[a]	*Beneficiaries*[b] OASI	DI	Total	*Covered workers per OASDI beneficiary*	*Beneficiaries per 100 covered workers*
1945	46,390	1,106	—	1,106	41.9	2
1950	48,280	2,930	—	2,930	16.5	6
1955	65,200	7,563	—	7,563	8.6	12
1960	72,530	13,740	522	14,262	5.1	20
1965	80,680	18,509	1,648	20,157	4.0	25
1970	93,090	22,618	2,568	25,186	3.7	27
1975	100,200	26,998	4,125	31,123	3.2	31
1980	113,000	30,385	4,734	35,119	3.2	31
1985	121,830[c]	32,776	3,874	36,650	3.3[c]	30[c]
1986	124,200[c]	33,349	3,972	37,321	3.3[c]	30[c]
1987	125,476	33,959	4,051	38,010	3.3	30
1990	130,452	35,784	4,172	39,956	3.3	31
1995	137,880	38,119	4,536	42,655	3.2	31
2000	142,820	38,627	5,168	43,795	3.3	31
2005	146,468	40,965	6,081	47,046	3.1	32
2010	148,276	43,636	7,112	50,748	2.9	34
2015	148,375	49,122	7,686	56,808	2.6	38
2020	147,055	55,771	8,011	63,782	2.3	43
2025	145,658	61,209	8,372	69,581	2.1	48
2030	145,277	66,954	8,252	75,206	1.9	52
2035	145,689	68,621	8,063	76,684	1.9	53
2040	146,043	69,820	8,053	77,873	1.9	53
2045	146,200	70,071	8,289	78,360	1.9	54
2050	146,292	70,217	8,399	78,616	1.9	54
2055	146,610	70,643	8,388	79,031	1.9	54
2060	147,320	71,104	8,358	79,462	1.9	54
2065	148,013	71,407	8,414	79,821	1.9	54

Note: "—" indicates not available; "OASI" indicates Old-Age and Survivors' Insurance; "DI" indicates Disability Insurance. Projections (1987-2065) are the so-called Alternative II-B projections. See source for further reference.

[a] Workers who pay OASDI taxes at some time during the year.

[b] Beneficiaries with monthly benefits in current-payment status as of June 30.

[c] Preliminary.

Source: U.S. Congress, House, House Committee on Ways and Means, *1987 Annual Report of the Board of Trustees of the Fededral Old-Age and Survivors Insurance and Disability Insurance Trust Funds,* 100th Cong., 1st sess., H. Doc. 100-55, March 31, 1987, 72-73.

Table 12-8 Recipients of Social Insurance Programs, 1984

Program	*Number of recipients (thousands)*	*Percentage of population*
Nonmeans-tested		
Social Security (OASDI)	36,241.0	15.3
Medicare (hospital insurance)[a]	29,996.0	12.7
Veterans programs	4,142.0	1.7
Railroad retirement	1,001.0	0.4
State unemployment insurance	2,167.0	0.9
State temporary disability	191.4	0.1
Means-tested		
Medicaid	21,557.0	9.1
Supplemental Security Income[b]	4,093.9	1.7
Aid to Families with Dependent Children[c]	10,830.5	4.6
Food Stamps[d]	20,858.0	8.8
General Assistance[c]	1,364.0	0.6

Note: "Means-tested" refers to the requirement of demonstration of financial need based on income and assets. People may receive benefits from more than one program. In 1984 17 percent of U.S. households received one or more means-tested benefits; in addition to the programs listed above, these include free or reduced-price school lunches and publicly owned or subsidized housing.

[a] Number of enrollees on July 1.

[b] Number of persons receiving payments in December 1984.

[c] Average monthly number of recipients.

[d] Average number of persons participating during year.

Sources: U.S. Department of Health and Human Services, Social Security Administration, *Social Security Bulletin, Annual Statistical Supplement 1986* (Washington, D.C.: U.S. Government Printing Office, 1987), 234, 248, 253, 268, 283-284, 289; *Statistical Abstract of the United States, 1987*, 8; U.S. Bureau of the Census, Current Population Reports, "Characteristics of Households and Persons Receiving Selected Noncash Benefits: 1984" (Washington, D.C.: U.S. Government Printing Office, 1985), series P-60, no. 150, 2, 4.

Table 12-9 Aid to Families with Dependent Children versus the Poverty Line, 1959-1984

Year	*Average monthly benefit*	*Yearly benefit*	*Average poverty threshold*
1959	$103.70	$1,244.40	$2,973
1960	108.35	1,300.20	3,022
1961	114.65	1,375.80	3,054
1962	119.10	1,429.20	3,089
1963	122.40	1,468.80	3,128
1964	131.30	1,575.60	3,169
1965	136.95	1,643.40	3,223
1966	150.10	1,801.20	3,317
1967	161.70	1,940.40	3,410
1968	168.15	2,017.80	3,553
1969	176.05	2,113.20	3,743
1970	187.95	2,255.40	3,968
1971	191.00	—	4,137
1972	192.00	2,304.00	4,275
1973	195.00	2,340.00	4,540
1974	216.00	2,592.00	5,038
1975	229.00	2,748.00	5,500
1976	242.00	2,904.00	5,815
1977	250.00	3,000.00	6,191
1978	256.00	3,072.00	6,662
1979	271.00	3,252.00	7,412
1980	288.00	3,456.00	8,414
1981	301.00	3,612.00	9,287
1982	310.00	3,720.00	9,862
1983	313.00	3,756.00	10,178
1984	325.00	3,900.00	10,609

Note: "—" indicates not available. Average AFDC benefits are per three to four member families. Poverty threshold is for a family of four persons.

Sources: Statistical Abstract of the U.S., 1976, 316, *1977,* 345, *1978,* 356, *1982-1983,* 340, *1984,* 393, *1987,* 365; U.S. Bureau of the Census, *Historical Statistics of the U.S.* (Washington, D.C.: U.S. Government Printing Office, 1975), 356; U.S. Bureau of the Census, *Current Population Reports,* "Characteristics of the Population Below the Poverty Level: 1984," series P-60, no. 152, 121.

Table 12-10 Years of School Completed by Age and Race, 1940-1985

Age/year	*Median school years completed by all persons*	*Median school years completed by black persons*
25 years and over		
1940	8.6	5.7
1950	9.3	6.8
1960	10.6	8.0
1970	12.1	9.8
1980	12.5	12.0
1985	12.6	12.3
25-29 years		
1940	10.3	7.0
1950	12.0	8.6
1960	12.3	9.9
1970	12.6	12.1
1980	12.9	12.6
1985	12.9	12.7

Source: Statistical Abstract of the U.S., 1987, 121.

Table 12-11 School Desegregation by Region, 1968-1984

Region/year	*Percentage of black students in schools with more than half minority students*	*Percentage of Hispanic students in schools with more than half minority students*	*Percentage of white students in schools 90-100 percent white*
South			
1968	80.9	69.6	70.6
1972	55.3	69.9	38.0
1976	54.9	70.9	34.6
1980	57.1	76.0	35.0
1984	56.9	75.4	—
Change 1968 to 1984[a]	− 24.0	+5.8	− 35.6
Border			
1968	71.6	—	80.0
1972	67.2	—	75.9
1976	60.1	—	64.8
1980	59.2	—	64.1
1984	62.5	—	—
Change 1968 to 1984[a]	− 9.1	—	− 15.9

Table 12-11 *(Continued)*

Region/year	*Percentage of black students in schools with more than half minority students*	*Percentage of Hispanic students in schools with more than half minority students*	*Percentage of white students in schools 90-100 percent white*
Northeast			
1968	66.8	74.8	83.0
1972	69.9	74.4	82.9
1976	72.5	74.9	81.4
1980	79.9	76.3	80.2
1984	73.1	77.5	—
Change 1968 to 1984[a]	+6.3	+2.7	− 2.8
Midwest			
1968	77.3	31.8	89.4
1972	75.3	34.4	87.5
1976	70.3	39.3	84.7
1980	69.5	46.6	81.2
1984	70.7	53.9	—
Change 1968 to 1984[a]	− 6.6	+22.1	− 8.2
West			
1968	72.2	42.4	63.0
1972	68.1	44.7	56.0
1976	67.4	52.7	49.9
1980	66.8	63.5	43.3
1984	66.9	68.4	—
Change 1968 to 1984[a]	− 5.3	+26.0	− 19.7
Total			
1968	76.6	54.8	78.4
1972	63.6	56.6	68.9
1976	62.4	60.8	64.9
1980	62.9	68.1	61.2
1984	63.5	70.6	—
Change 1968 to 1984[a]	−13.1	+15.8	− 17.2

Note: "—" indicates not available. For composition of regions, see Appendix Table A-4.
[a] To 1980 for whites.

Sources: 1968-1980: Gary Orfield, testimony before the House Subcommittee on Civil and Constitutional Rights, *Civil Rights Implications of the Education Block Grant Program,* September 9, 1982, 67-72; 1984: Gary Orfield and Franklin Monfort, "Are American Schools Resegregating in the Reagan Era? A Statistical Analysis of Segregation Levels from 1980-1984," Paper no. 14, National School Desegregation Project Working Papers (Chicago: no date).

Table 12-12 Public Opinion of Whites on School Integration, 1942-1985 (percent)

	Blacks and whites should attend		
Date	Same schools	Separate schools	Don't know
June 1942	30	66	4
April 1956	49	47	4
June 1956	49	49	2
September 1956	48	49	3
May 1963	63	32	5
December 1963	65	29	6
June 1964	62	32	5
October 1964	64	34	2
June 1965	67	30	3
October 1965	68	28	4
April 1970	74	24	3
March 1972	85	14	2
November 1972	80	15	5
March 1976	83	15	3
March 1977	85	14	2
March 1980	86	12	2
March 1982	88	9	2
March 1984	90	8	2
March 1985	92	7	1

Note: Questions: "Do you think white students and (Negro/black) students should go to the same schools or to separate schools?" (October 1964): "Do you think white children and Negro children should go to the same schools or to separate but equal schools?" Questions asked of whites only.

Sources: 1942-1970, November 1972: National Opinion Research Center; March 1972, 1976-1985: General Social Survey, National Opinion Research Center, University of Chicago.

Table 12-13 Public Opinion on School Integration by Racial Composition of School, 1958-1986 (percent)

	Object to own children attending school with		
Date	A few blacks	Half blacks	More than half blacks
September 1958	25	53	70
February 1959	20	47	71
May 1963	25	52	75
April 1965	16	42	67
June 1965	20	44	68
May 1966	11	41	67
July 1969	11	38	66
March 1970	8	32	66
April 1970	10	34	63
March 1972	6	25	55
August 1973	9	36	67
March 1974	4	33	67
March 1975	6	38	66
September 1975	7	35	62
March 1977	7	26	64
March 1978	4	24	61
July 1978	7	36	67
December 1980	6	28	62
March 1982	4	21	54
March 1983	3	25	65
March 1985	4	22	60
March 1986	4	24	64

Note: Question: "Would you, yourself, have any objection to sending your children to a school where a few of the children are (Negroes/blacks)?" If no: "Where half of the children are (Negroes/blacks)?" If no: "Where more than half of the children are (Negroes/blacks)?" Those saying "don't know" were assumed to have expressed some objection. Question asked of whites with school-age children only.

Sources: 1958-1970, 1973, September 1975, 1978, 1980: Gallup surveys; other years: General Social Survey.

Table 12-14 Black Elected Officials by Category of Office, 1970-1987

Year	*Federal*	*State*	*Substate/ regional*	*County*	*Municipal*	*Judicial, law enforcement*	*Education*	*Total*
1970	10	169	—	92	623	213	362	1,469
1971	14	202	—	120	785	274	465	1,860
1972	14	210	—	176	932	263	669	2,264
1973	16	240	—	211	1,053	334	767	2,621
1974	17	239	—	241	1,360	340	793	2,991
1975	18	281	—	305	1,573	387	939	3,503
1976	18	281	30	355	1,889	412	994	3,979
1977	17	299	33	381	2,083	447	1,051	4,311
1978	17	299	26	410	2,159	454	1,138	4,503
1979	17	313	25	398	2,224	486	1,144	4,607
1980	17	323	25	451	2,356	526	1,214	4,912
1981	18	341	30	449	2,384	549	1,267	5,038
1982	18	336	35	465	2,477	563	1,266	5,160
1983	21	379	29	496	2,697	607	1,377	5,606
1984[a]	21	389	30	518	2,735	636	1,371	5,700
1985	20	396	32	611	2,898	661	1,438	6,056
1986	20	400	31	681	3,112	676	1,504	6,424
1987	23	417	23	724	3,219	728	1,547	6,681

Note: "—" indicates not available.

[a] The 1984 figures reflect blacks who took office during the seven-month period between July 1, 1983 and January 30, 1984.

Source: Joint Center for Political Studies, *Black Elected Officials: A National Roster* (Washington, D.C.: Joint Center for Political Studies, 1987), 10.

Table 12-15 Black Elected Officials and Black Voting-Age Population (VAP) by State, 1986

State	*Number of black elected officials*	*Total number of elected officials*	*Percentage of black elected officials*	*Percentage black VAP*	*Ratio of black elected officials to black VAP*[a]
Alabama	403	4,160	9.7	22.9	0.423
Alaska	4	1,365	-	3.3	0.089
Arizona	12	2,412	0.5	3.1	0.160
Arkansas	315	10,692	3.0	13.6	0.217
California	287	18,135	1.6	7.5	0.211
Colorado	14	7,801	-	3.4	0.053
Connecticut	67	7,920	0.8	6.2	0.136
Delaware	19	999	1.9	14.7	0.129
District of Columbia	251	370	67.8	66.6	1.019
Florida	178	4,902	3.6	10.8	0.336
Georgia	417	6,672	6.3	24.9	0.251
Hawaii	1	176	0.6	2.1	0.271
Idaho	0	4,183	-	-	b
Illinois	426	40,422	1.0	13.6	0.077
Indiana	70	11,029	0.6	7.1	0.089
Iowa	9	17,730	-	1.2	0.042
Kansas	28	17,070	-	4.9	0.033
Kentucky	46	7,013	0.7	6.7	0.098
Louisiana	488	4,720	10.3	26.6	0.389
Maine	3	5,885	-	-	b
Maryland	108	2,172	5.0	22.5	0.221
Massachusetts	35	11,605	-	3.7	0.082
Michigan	314	19,403	1.6	12.3	0.132
Minnesota	9	19,153	-	1.2	0.039
Mississippi	521	5,278	9.9	30.8	0.320
Missouri	161	17,802	0.9	9.5	0.095
Montana	0	4,335	-	-	b
Nebraska	4	15,747	-	2.7	0.009
Nevada	9	1,145	0.8	5.5	0.143
New Hampshire	0	5,991	-	-	b
New Jersey	200	9,431	2.1	11.7	0.181
New Mexico	5	2,052	-	1.7	0.143
New York	248	24,112	1.0	13.1	0.079
North Carolina	311	5,308	5.9	20.7	0.283
North Dakota	0	18,045	-	-	b
Ohio	209	19,913	1.0	9.6	0.109
Oklahoma	116	9,018	1.3	6.1	0.211

(Table continues)

Table 12-15 *(Continued)*

State	*Number of black elected officials*	*Total number of elected officials*	*Percentage of black elected officials*	*Percentage black (VAP)*	*Ratio of black elected officials to black VAP*[a]
Oregon	10	7,880	-	1.2	0.106
Pennsylvania	134	28,928	0.5	8.2	0.056
Rhode Island	8	1,107	0.7	2.4	0.301
South Carolina	329	3,233	10.2	27.7	0.367
South Dakota	3	9,191	-	-	[b]
Tennessee	142	7,256	2.0	14.4	0.136
Texas	281	24,757	1.1	11.0	0.103
Utah	1	2,363	-	-	[b]
Vermont	1	7,323	-	-	[b]
Virginia	125	3,053	4.1	17.9	0.229
Washington	17	7,467	-	2.5	0.091
West Virginia	20	2,899	0.7	3.0	0.230
Wisconsin	22	18,973	-	3.4	0.034
Wyoming	3	2,174	-	-	[b]
Total	6,384	490,770	1.3	10.8	0.120

Note: "-" indicates less than 0.5 percent. Data are as of January.

[a] Ratios calculated before rounding.

[b] Ratios not calculated when black voting-age population is below 0.5 percent.

Source: Joint Center for Political Studies, *Black Elected Officials* (1986), 10-11.

Table 12-16 Blacks, Hispanics, and Women as a Percentage of State Legislators and State Population

		Blacks				*Hispanics*				*Women*			
		Legislators		Percentage of state		Legislators		Percentage of state		Legislators		Percentage of state	
State	*Total number of legislators*	*Number*	*Percentage*	population	Ratio[a]	*Number*	*Percentage*	population	Ratio[a]	*Number*	*Percentage*	population	Ratio[a]
Alabama	140	24	17.1	25.6	.670	0	0.0	0.9	.000	9	6.4	51.9	.124
Alaska	60	1	1.7	3.4	.487	0	0.0	2.3	.000	11	18.3	47.0	.390
Arizona	90	2	2.2	2.7	.814	12	13.3	16.3	.816	18	20.0	50.8	.394
Arkansas	135	5	3.7	16.3	.227	0	0.0	0.7	.000	10	7.4	51.7	.143
California	120	8	6.7	7.7	.868	7	5.8	19.2	.304	15	12.5	50.7	.246
Colorado	100	3	3.0	3.5	.852	9	9.0	11.8	.762	24	24.0	50.4	.476
Connecticut	187	10	5.3	7.0	.767	1	0.5	4.0	.133	41	21.9	51.8	.423
Delaware	62	3	4.8	16.2	.299	0	0.0	1.6	.000	10	16.1	51.8	.311
Florida	160	12	7.5	13.8	.544	7	4.4	8.8	.497	31	19.4	52.0	.372
Georgia	236	27	11.4	26.8	.427	0	0.0	1.1	.000	23	9.7	51.7	.189
Hawaii	76	0	0.0	1.8	.000	1	1.3	7.4	.178	14	18.4	48.7	.378
Idaho	126	0	0.0	0.3	.000	0	0.0	3.9	.000	24	19.0	50.1	.380
Illinois	177	20	11.3	14.6	.771	2	1.1	5.5	.204	30	16.9	51.5	.329
Indiana	150	8	5.3	7.5	.706	1	0.7	1.6	.422	19	12.7	51.4	.246
Iowa	150	1	0.7	1.4	.460	0	0.0	0.9	.000	22	14.7	51.4	.285
Kansas	165	4	2.4	5.3	.453	3	1.8	2.6	.686	30	18.2	51.0	.356
Kentucky	138	2	1.4	7.1	.205	0	0.0	0.7	.000	9	6.5	51.1	.128
Louisiana	144	18	12.5	29.4	.424	1	0.7	2.4	.293	5	3.5	51.5	.067
Maine	186	0	0.0	0.3	.000	0	0.0	0.5	.000	44	23.7	51.4	.460
Maryland	188	24	12.8	22.7	.562	0	0.0	1.5	.000	36	19.1	51.5	.371
Massachusetts	200	6	3.0	3.8	.779	0	0.0	2.5	.000	33	16.5	52.4	.315
Michigan	148	17	11.5	12.9	.888	0	0.0	1.7	.000	16	10.8	51.2	.211
Minnesota	201	1	0.5	1.3	.389	1	0.5	0.8	.630	29	14.4	51.0	.283
Mississippi	174	20	11.5	35.2	.327	0	0.0	1.0	.000	4	2.3	51.8	.044
Missouri	197	15	7.6	10.4	.729	0	0.0	1.0	.000	26	13.2	51.9	.254
Montana	150	0	0.0	0.2	.000	2	1.3	1.3	1.042	22	14.7	50.1	.293
Nebraska	49	1	2.0	3.0	.669	0	0.0	1.8	.000	8	16.3	51.2	.319
Nevada	63	3	4.8	6.4	.744	0	0.0	6.8	.000	10	15.9	49.4	.321

(Table continues)

Table 12-16 *(Continued)*

State	Total number of legislators	Blacks				Hispanics				Women			
		Legislators		Percentage of state population	Ratio[a]	Legislators		Percentage of state population	Ratio[a]	Legislators		Percentage of state population	Ratio[a]
		Number	Percentage			Number	Percentage			Number	Percentage		
New Hampshire	424	0	0.0	0.5	.000	0	0.0	0.6	.000	140	33.0	51.3	.644
New Jersey	120	7	5.8	12.6	.464	2	1.7	6.7	.248	12	10.0	52.0	.192
New Mexico	112	0	0.0	1.8	.000	34	30.4	36.6	.829	13	11.6	50.7	.229
New York	210	20	9.5	13.7	.695	7	3.3	9.5	.352	23	11.0	52.5	.209
North Carolina	170	16	9.4	22.4	.420	0	0.0	0.9	.000	20	11.8	51.5	.229
North Dakota	150	0	0.0	0.4	.000	0	0.0	0.5	.000	18	12.0	49.7	.242
Ohio	132	12	9.1	10.0	.912	0	0.0	1.1	.000	12	9.1	51.7	.176
Oklahoma	149	5	3.4	6.8	.496	0	0.0	1.9	.000	13	8.7	51.2	.170
Oregon	90	3	3.3	1.4	2.347	0	0.0	2.5	.000	18	20.0	50.8	.394
Pennsylvania	253	18	7.1	8.8	.808	1	0.4	1.3	.306	13	5.1	52.1	.099
Rhode Island	150	4	2.7	2.9	.923	1	0.7	2.0	.333	23	15.3	52.4	.293
South Carolina	170	20	11.8	30.4	.387	0	0.0	1.1	.000	10	5.9	51.4	.115
South Dakota	105	0	0.0	0.3	.000	0	0.0	0.5	.000	15	14.3	50.7	.282
Tennessee	132	13	9.8	15.8	.624	0	0.0	0.7	.000	11	8.3	51.7	.161
Texas	181	14	7.7	12.0	.646	23	12.7	21.0	.606	16	8.8	50.8	.174
Utah	104	1	1.0	0.7	1.457	0	0.0	1.4	.000	7	6.7	50.4	.134
Vermont	180	1	0.6	0.2	2.415	0	0.0	0.7	.000	47	26.1	51.3	.509
Virginia	140	9	6.4	18.9	.341	0	0.0	1.5	.000	10	7.1	51.0	.140
Washington	147	3	2.0	2.6	.797	0	0.0	2.9	.000	35	23.8	50.3	.473
West Virginia	134	1	0.7	3.3	.223	0	0.0	0.7	.000	23	17.2	51.5	.333
Wisconsin	132	4	3.0	3.9	.779	0	0.0	1.3	.000	25	18.9	51.0	.371
Wyoming	94	1	1.1	0.7	1.520	0	0.0	5.2	.000	24	25.5	48.8	.523
Total	7,466	396	5.3	11.7	.454	115	1.5	6.4	.239	1,101	14.7	51.4	.287

Note: Hispanics may be of any race. Data for Hispanics are from 1985; data for blacks and women are from 1986; population data are from 1980.
[a] The ratio between the percentage minority of state legislators and the percentage minority of the state population. Ratios calculated before rounding.

Sources: Joint Center for Political Studies, *Black Elected Officials* (1986), 20-21; *Statistical Abstract of the U.S., 1987*, 241; U.S. Bureau of the Census, *County and City Data Book* (Washington, D.C.: U.S. Government Printing Office, 1983), 2.

Table 12-17 State and Local Government Employment and Salary by Sex, Race, and Hispanic Origin, 1973-1984 (thousands)

	Employment							Median annual salary						
					Minority							Minority		
Year	Total	Male	Female	White	*Total*[a]	*Black*	*Hispanic*[b]	Total	Male	Female	White	*Total*[a]	*Black*	*Hispanic*[b]
1973	3,809	2,486	1,322	3,115	693	523	125	$ 8.6	$ 9.6	$ 7.0	$ 8.8	$ 7.5	$ 7.4	$ 7.4
1975	3,899	2,436	1,464	3,102	797	602	147	9.8	11.3	8.2	10.2	8.8	8.6	8.9
1977	4,415	2,737	1,678	3,480	935	705	175	10.9	12.4	9.1	11.3	9.7	9.5	9.9
1978	4,447	2,711	1,736	3,481	966	723	181	11.7	13.3	9.7	12.0	10.4	10.1	10.7
1979	4,576	2,761	1,816	3,568	1,008	751	192	12.3	14.1	10.4	12.8	10.9	10.6	11.4
1980	3,987	2,350	1,637	3,146	842	619	163	13.3	15.2	11.4	13.8	11.8	11.5	12.3
1981	4,665	2,740	1,925	3,591	1,074	780	205	15.6	17.7	13.1	16.1	13.5	13.3	14.7
1983	4,492	2,674	1,818	3,423	1,069	768	219	18.0	20.1	15.3	18.5	15.9	15.6	17.3
1984	4,580	2,700	1,880	3,458	1,121	799	233	19.1	21.4	16.2	19.6	17.4	16.5	18.4

Note: Full-time employment as of June 30, excludes school systems and educational institutions. Based on reports from state governments (44 in 1973, 48 in 1975, 47 in 1977, 45 in 1979, 43 in 1979, 42 in 1980, 49 in 1981, 47 in 1983, and 50 in 1984) and a sample of county, municipal, township, and special district jurisdictions employing 15 or more nonelected, nonappointed full-time employees.

[a] Includes other minority groups, not shown separately.

[b] Prior to 1977, this ethnic group was classified as "Spanish-surnamed American."

Source: Statistical Abstract of the U.S., 1987, 281.

Table 12-18 Federal Employment by GS Salary Level, by Race/Ethnic Group, and Sex, 1984

Government service (GS) salary level		*Total number*	*Percentage black*	*Percentage Hispanic*	*Percentage female*
GS-01	$ 9,023-11,283	5,850	35.3	9.2	72.5
GS-02	$10,146-12,764	19,694	29.8	7.0	72.2
GS-03	$11,070-14,391	90,009	25.1	6.1	76.4
GS-04	$12,427-16,153	175,800	23.4	5.3	76.6
GS-05	$13,903-18,070	203,803	20.9	4.9	71.5
GS-06	$15,497-20,150	92,867	22.0	4.4	74.6
GS-07	$17,221-22,387	140,467	17.1	4.8	57.4
GS-08	$19,073-24,797	30,606	20.0	3.3	55.1
GS-09	$21,066-27,384	160,173	12.2	4.9	43.1
GS-10	$23,199-30,156	29,163	12.2	5.1	45.1
GS-11	$25,489-33,139	184,713	9.9	3.8	32.2
GS-12	$30,549-39,711	179,007	7.9	2.8	19.8
GS-13	$36,327-47,266	112,297	6.1	2.2	13.5
GS-14	$42,928-55,807	62,716	5.0	1.7	10.0
GS-15	$50,495-65,642	38,049	3.6	2.1	8.5
Total, all pay plans		2,023,333	15.7	4.7	40.0
Total, GS and equivalent		1,525,214	15.2	4.2	48.3

Sources: Office of Personnel Management, *Affirmative Employment Statistics* (Washington, D.C.: U.S. Government Printing Office, 1984), 32, 38; Office of Personnel Management, *Pay Structure of the Federal Civil Service* (Washington, D.C.: U.S. Government Printing Office, March 31, 1984), 51.

Table 12-19 Crime Rates, 1960-1985

	Violent crime					*Property crime*				
Year	Murder	Forcible rape	Robbery	Aggravated assault	Total	Burglary	Larceny theft	Vehicle theft	Total	*Total*
1960	5.1	9.6	60	86	161	509	1,035	183	1,729	1,887
1965	5.1	12.1	72	111	200	663	1,329	257	2,249	2,249
1968	6.9	15.9	132	144	298	932	1,747	393	3,072	3,370
1969	7.3	18.5	148	155	329	984	1,931	436	3,351	3,680
1970	7.9	18.7	172	165	364	1,085	2,079	457	3,621	3,985
1971	8.6	20.5	188	179	396	1,164	2,146	460	3,769	4,165
1972	9.0	22.5	181	189	401	1,141	1,994	426	3,560	3,961
1973	9.4	24.5	183	201	417	1,223	2,072	443	3,737	4,154
1974	9.8	26.2	209	216	461	1,438	2,490	462	4,389	4,850
1975	9.6	26.3	218	227	482	1,526	2,805	469	4,800	5,282
1976	8.8	26.6	199	233	468	1,448	2,921	450	4,820	5,287
1977	8.8	29.4	191	247	476	1,420	2,730	452	4,602	5,078
1978	9.0	31.0	196	262	498	1,435	2,747	461	4,643	5,140
1979	9.7	34.7	218	286	549	1,512	2,999	506	5,017	5,566
1980	10.2	36.8	251	299	597	1,684	3,167	502	5,353	5,950
1981	9.8	36.0	259	290	594	1,650	3,140	475	5,264	5,858
1982	9.1	34.0	239	289	571	1,489	3,085	459	5,033	5,604
1983	8.3	33.7	217	279	538	1,338	2,869	431	4,637	5,175
1984	7.9	35.7	205	290	539	1,264	2,791	437	4,492	5,031
1985	7.9	36.6	209	303	556	1,287	2,901	462	4,651	5,207

Note: Figures are rates per 100,000 inhabitants. For definitions of crimes, see the source.

Source: Statistical Abstract of the U.S., 1976, 153, *1987,* 155.

Table 12-20 Number of Federal and State Prisoners and Cost per Inmate per Year, 1950-1986

	Number of inmates		*Cost per inmate per year*	
Year	Federal	State	Federal	State[a]
1950	17,134	148,989	—	—
1960	23,218	189,735	—	—
1965	21,040	189,855	—	—
1970	20,038	176,391	—	—
1975	24,131	216,462	—	—
1980	20,611	295,363	$13,505	$10,354
1981	22,169	331,505	14,758	13,572
1982	23,652	371,864	14,508	15,829
1983	26,331	393,390	20,826	16,245
1984	27,602	417,797	16,858	17,324
1985	32,695	450,358	14,520	14,591
1986	40,828	481,916	13,162	15,220

Note: "—" indicates not available. Excludes state institutions in Alaska prior to 1970 and those in Hawaii for 1950. Beginning in 1980, figures include all persons under jurisdiction of federal and state authorities rather than those in the custody of such authorities. Represents inmates sentenced to maximum term of more than one year.
[a] Average for all states.

Sources: 1950-1985: *Statistical Abstract of the U.S., 1984,* 194, *1987,* 172; 1986 and costs: Criminal Justice Institute, *The Corrections Yearbook* (New York: Criminal Justice Institute), annual volumes, 1981-1987.

Table 12-21 Public Opinion on the Courts, 1965-1986

Date	*Too harsh*	*About right*	*Not harsh enough*	*Don't know*
April 1965	2	34	48	16
August 1965	2	27	60	12
February 1968	2	19	63	16
January 1969	2	13	74	10
March 1972	7	16	66	11
December 1972	4	13	74	8
March 1973	5	13	73	9
March 1974[a]	5	6	60	29
March 1974	6	10	78	7
March 1975	4	10	79	7
March 1976	3	10	81	6
March 1977	3	8	83	6
March 1978	3	7	85	5
March 1980	3	8	83	6
January 1981	3	13	77	7
March 1982[a]	4	5	76	14
March 1982	3	8	86	4
March 1983	4	6	85	4
March 1984	3	11	82	4
March 1985	3	9	84	3
March 1986	3	8	85	4

Note: Question: "In general, do you think the courts in this area deal too harshly or not harshly enough with criminals?"

[a] In 1974 and 1982 half of the General Social Survey sample was asked the question as noted above and half the sample was asked the same question but with the phrase "or don't you have enough information about the courts to say" added at the end. The "don't know" column for these rows includes those saying "not enough information."

Sources: 1965-1969, December 1972: Gallup survey; 1981: *Los Angeles Times* survey (copyright © 1981, *Los Angeles Times,* reprinted by permission); others: General Social Survey.

Questions

1. In 1950 black family income was 54.3 percent of white family income (Table 12-1). Had the gap narrowed significantly by the mid-1980s?

2. In the 1970s and 1980s, when the proportion of whites and blacks below the poverty level was stable or rose very slightly, the proportion of those of Hispanic origin below the poverty level increased by about 6.7 percent (Table 12-2). State two hypotheses that might explain this result.

3. Which group is poorer, as measured by the percentage below the poverty line—the young or the elderly (Table 12-3)? If white income is so much higher than black income (Table 12-1), how can it be that more than two-thirds of the poor people are white (Table 12-3)?

4. State and local social welfare expenditures (as a percentage of total outlays) have been steady since 1960 (Table 12-4). What is there about state and local expenditures that kept them steady when total expenditures were increasing rapidly? (Hint: look at Table 12-5.)

5. If you add the expenditures under each category (for a given row), the amount exceeds the "total" column (Table 12-5). Similarly, if you add the percentages in a row of the next to last panel they total more than 100 percent. Why? (Hint: read carefully the explanatory material of the table—the heading, labels, footnotes.)

6. Why are pension and health spending likely to rise substantially in the late twentieth century and into the twenty-first century (Table 12-6)? (Hint: see Table 12-7.) What can be done to keep these costs down?

7. Apart from the early increases due to the expansion of Social Security to more types of workers, in what twenty-year period will the ratio of beneficiaries to covered workers increase the most (Table 12-7)? Why?

8. What are some of the assumptions that must go into projections of the sort shown in Table 12-7? Which of these assumptions do you think is the weakest? Why?

9. On the basis of the percentages in the body of Table 12-8, what is the minimum proportion of the population that could be covered by one or more means-tested programs? The maximum proportion? How many in fact are covered by one or more means-tested benefits?

10. Have AFDC benefits increased or decreased since 1959 in relation to the poverty threshold (Table 12-9)? By how much? What has been the average under Democratic administrations? Republican administrations?

11. Combining information in Table 3-1 and Table 12-10, explain why the difference between black and white turnout rates is declining.

12. In what region, in 1968, was the greatest percentage of black students attending schools with more than half minority students (Table 12-11)? In 1984? In each of these years, which region had the smallest percentage of black students in minority-dominated schools? Which region, in 1980, had the fewest white students in almost totally white schools? Based on these data, which region currently appears to have the most segregated schools? The least segregated?

13. What conclusion would you draw about current attitudes on school integration from Table 12-12? Would you modify these conclusions in light of Table 12-13?

14. The District of Columbia is the only "state" in which the ratio of black elected officials to voting age population is higher than .50, and there it is higher than 1.0 (Table 12-15). Why is it so high by comparison with the fifty states? Aside from D.C., Alabama has the largest ratio of elected officials to voting age population. Does this mean that Alabama elects a larger percentage of black officials than any other state? If not, what does it mean?

15. Many of the ratios in Table 12-15 don't seem quite correct. For example, for Alabama:

    $$9.7/22.9 = .424$$

    and for Arkansas:

    $$3.0/13.6 = .221$$

Why don't these values match those in the table?

16. The percentage of blacks in the state population (Table 12-16) is almost always larger than the percentage of blacks in the voting age population (Table 12-15). Why?

17. Which region (using the Census Bureau definition given in Table A-1 in the Appendix) has the lowest ratio of female legislators to population (Table 12-16)? There is less variation in the ratios for women (.044 to .644) than for blacks (.100 to 2.415) or for Hispanics (.000 to 1.042). Why?

18. Women in state and local government earned less than men in 1973 (Table 12-17). Eleven years later, how much of the gap had they made up? What about blacks versus whites? How might the employment figures on the left side of the table help explain what you found for females' and blacks' earnings ratios? Insofar as the pattern at the federal level mirrors the state and local situation, how might Table 12-18 help explain the gap in earnings ratios?

19. Which category, violent crimes or property crimes, increased at a faster rate between 1960 and 1985 (Table 12-19)? Among violent crimes, forcible rapes evidently increased the most. Could changes in willingness to report rapes partially explain this result? Why?

20. A comparison of endpoints—the first and last entries of a table or figure—sometimes masks part of the story. In Table 12-20, what is revealed about the change in the number of federal and state inmates if one looks at the years between 1950 and 1986?

21. There are at least two kinds of opinion change occurring in Table 12-21. Describe them.

13

Economic Policy

Economic policy makers labor under the burden of an overabundance of numbers. Statistics recording various aspects of the economy's performance appear regularly—often monthly. These statistics are important, not simply because of the conditions they report, but for the way they filter into economic calculations: expectations and reactions to indicators of past performance are critical determinants of how the economy performs in the future. Moreover, there is a direct link to politics because the public's perceptions of economic performance help shape choices in the voting booth: properly or not, presidents often get blamed when the economy turns down, and (less often) praised when it recovers. President Ronald Reagan's public approval ratings plummeted as an economic downturn continued through 1982 (Figures 8-3 and 8-4). The subsequent economic recovery played a substantial role in shaping the mood of the voters to secure Reagan's 1984 reelection in a landslide.

When one turns to even simple economic matters, fundamental issues and terms arise that distinguish the discourse from that in other areas of politics. One is the overall size of the economy, usually measured by the gross national product or GNP (Table 13-1). Knowing what the GNP is and what it means are important to even a minimal understanding of economic statistics and policy. Without some sense of the size of the economy, it is impossible to make informed judgments about economic matters. For example, a trillion dollar national debt is unquestionably large, but many argue that it is not overburdening because it in fact represents the same proportion of the total economy as numerically smaller deficits did in earlier years (Figure 13-2).

A second key concept is that of constant dollars, which is explained in the introduction to Chapter 11, in connection with defense spending. A few additional points are appropriate here. Note that the basis for many constant dollar calculations is the Consumer Price Index or CPI (Table 13-2). One can see from this index that a marketbasket of goods that cost $100 in 1967 would have cost $328.40 in 1986. Unfortunately, while 1967 is the base year for this index, other tabulations, such as those in Table 13-1, use another year as the base. This makes it more difficult to compare the data. However, the concept of a constant dollar is unchanged by which year is used as the base. (The CPI is not always used as the basis for such adjustments, and here it is not possible to move precisely from the figures in Table 13-2 to those in 13-1.)

During Ronald Reagan's presidency, economic news was dominated by the deficit. The growth in the federal deficit (Table 13-6) helped focus public attention on government spending and taxing, as politicians and economists alike tried to assess ways of reducing the gap between income and expenditures. Economic growth could provide the basis for greater tax revenues to balance the budget and reduce the deficit ("Grow our way out," as Reagan insisted). But as the national debt has continued to mount in relation to GNP (Figure 13-2), the political and economic demands for reduction of the debt have constrained government spending and compelled consideration of additional revenue sources. Tax increases are one means of reducing the federal deficit: Table 13-7 displays the revenue loss to the federal government from selected tax breaks, some of which have already been curtailed to raise revenue.

Cutting spending is another means of deficit reduction. Although federal budget outlays by function (Table 13-4) may give the impression of vast sums and a variety of programs suitable for cuts, Table 13-5 shows that barely a quarter of federal budget outlays can be changed by presidential decision. An increasing proportion of the federal budget has become relatively uncontrollable from the president's standpoint. Reducing spending in the relatively uncontrollable category would require that Congress rewrite laws affecting payments to which beneficiaries are entitled on the basis of past commitments. Programs that fall under this heading, such as Social Security, are referred to as entitlement programs.

It should come as no surprise to the reader that public opinion data are relevant to economic policy or that such data must be interpreted with care. A plurality of the public who claim knowledge about the issue favor a constitutional amendment requiring a balanced federal budget (Table 13-8). In some respects this tells us very little; a majority of the public is not in favor of spending cuts or tax increases, but at the same time it is in favor of balancing the budget. Despite these contradictory sentiments, feelings expressed in polls are closely watched by politicians. Questions about who has what sort of opinion as well as changes in opinions over time are important to the determination of future policies.

Unemployment and inflation are two other noteworthy features of the economic landscape that merit inclusion when considering politics. The large-scale entry of women into the labor force since World War II (Table 13-9), the fluctuations in the annual unemployment rate since 1929 (Table 13-10), and the relatively high unemployment rates among black teenagers (Table 13-11) document critical economic trends with political ramifications.

Because economic issues are an important aspect of political policy making and because economic conditions affect voter choices, economic data rank among the most vital of vital statistics on American politics.

Table 13-1 Gross National Product, 1929-1986 (billions)

Year	*Current dollars*	*Annual percentage change*	*Constant (1982) dollars*	*Annual percentage change*
1929	103.9		709.6	
1930	91.1	−12.3	642.8	−9.4
1931	76.4	−16.2	588.1	−8.5
1932	58.5	−23.4	509.2	−13.4
1933	56.0	−4.2	498.5	−2.1
1934	65.6	17.0	536.7	7.7
1935	72.8	11.0	580.2	8.1
1936	83.1	14.1	662.2	14.1
1937	91.3	9.8	695.3	5.0
1938	85.4	−6.5	664.2	−4.5
1939	91.3	7.0	716.6	7.9
1940	100.4	10.0	772.9	7.8
1941	125.5	25.0	909.4	17.7
1942	159.0	26.6	1,080.3	18.8
1943	192.7	21.2	1,276.2	18.1
1944	211.4	9.7	1,380.6	8.2
1945	213.4	0.9	1,354.8	−1.9
1946	212.4	−0.5	1,096.9	−19.0
1947	235.2	10.8	1,066.7	−2.8
1948	261.6	11.2	1,108.7	3.9
1949	260.4	−0.5	1,109.0	0.0
1950	288.3	10.7	1,203.7	8.5
1951	333.4	15.7	1,328.2	10.3
1952	351.6	5.5	1,380.0	3.9
1953	371.6	5.7	1,435.3	4.0
1954	372.5	0.2	1,416.2	−1.3
1955	405.9	9.0	1,494.9	5.6
1956	428.2	5.5	1,525.6	2.1
1957	451.0	5.3	1,551.1	1.7
1958	456.8	1.3	1,539.2	−0.8
1959	495.8	8.5	1,629.1	5.8
1960	515.3	3.9	1,665.3	2.2
1961	533.8	3.6	1,708.7	2.6
1962	574.6	7.6	1,799.4	5.3
1963	606.9	5.6	1,873.3	4.1
1964	649.8	7.1	1,973.3	5.3
1965	705.1	8.5	2,087.6	5.8
1966	772.0	9.5	2,208.3	5.8
1967	816.4	5.8	2,271.4	2.9
1968	892.7	9.3	2,365.6	4.1
1969	963.9	8.0	2,423.3	2.4

Table 13-1 *(Continued)*

Year	*Current dollars*	*Annual percentage change*	*Constant (1982) dollars*	*Annual percentage change*
1970	1,015.5	5.4	2,416.2	−0.3
1971	1,102.7	8.6	2,484.8	2.8
1972	1,212.8	10.0	2,608.5	5.0
1973	1,359.3	12.1	2,744.1	5.2
1974	1,472.8	8.3	2,729.3	−0.5
1975	1,598.4	8.5	2,695.0	−1.3
1976	1,782.8	11.7	2,826.7	4.9
1977	1,990.5	11.7	2,958.6	4.7
1978	2,249.7	13.0	3,115.2	5.3
1979	2,508.2	11.5	3,192.4	2.5
1980	2,732.0	8.9	3,187.1	−0.2
1981	3,052.6	11.7	3,248.8	1.9
1982	3,166.0	3.7	3,166.0	−2.5
1983	3,405.7	7.6	3,279.1	3.6
1984	3,765.0	10.5	3,489.9	6.4
1985	3,998.1	6.2	3,585.2	2.7
1986	4,206.1	5.2	3,674.9	2.5

Source: U.S. Department of Commerce, *Survey of Current Business* (Washington, D.C.: U.S. Government Printing Office, September 1986), 64, 66.

Table 13-2 Consumer Price Index, 1950-1986

Year	All items	Food	Shelter	Fuel, oil, and coal	Gas and electricity	Apparel and upkeep	Transportation		Medical care	All commodities	All services
							Private	Public			
1950	72.1	74.5	—	72.7	81.2	79.0	72.5	48.9	53.7	78.8	58.7
1951	77.8	82.9	—	76.5	81.5	86.1	75.8	54.0	56.3	85.9	61.9
1952	79.5	84.3	—	78.0	82.6	85.3	80.8	57.5	59.3	87.0	64.5
1953	80.1	83.0	76.5	81.5	84.2	84.6	82.4	61.3	61.4	86.7	67.3
1954	80.5	82.8	78.2	81.2	85.3	84.5	80.3	65.5	63.4	85.9	69.5
1955	80.2	81.6	79.1	82.3	87.5	84.1	78.9	67.4	64.8	85.1	70.9
1956	81.4	82.2	80.4	85.9	88.4	85.8	80.1	70.0	67.2	85.9	72.7
1957	84.3	84.9	83.4	90.3	89.3	87.3	84.7	72.7	69.9	88.6	75.6
1958	86.6	85.5	85.1	88.7	92.4	87.5	87.4	76.1	73.2	90.6	78.5
1959	87.3	87.1	86.0	89.8	94.7	88.2	91.1	78.3	76.4	90.7	80.8
1960	88.7	88.0	87.8	89.2	98.6	89.6	90.6	81.0	79.1	91.5	83.5
1961	89.6	89.1	88.5	91.0	99.4	90.4	91.3	84.6	81.4	92.0	85.2
1962	90.6	89.9	89.6	91.5	99.4	90.9	93.0	87.4	83.5	92.8	86.8
1963	91.7	91.2	90.7	93.2	99.4	91.9	93.4	88.5	85.6	93.6	88.5
1964	92.9	92.4	92.2	92.7	99.4	92.7	94.7	90.1	87.3	94.6	90.2
1965	94.5	94.4	93.8	94.6	99.4	93.7	96.3	91.9	89.5	95.7	92.2
1966	97.2	99.1	96.8	97.0	99.6	96.1	97.5	95.2	93.4	98.2	95.8
1967	100.0	100.0	100.0	100.0	100.0	100.0	100.0	100.0	100.0	100.0	100.0
1968	104.2	103.6	104.8	103.1	100.9	105.4	103.0	104.6	106.1	103.7	105.2
1969	109.8	108.9	113.3	105.6	102.8	111.5	106.5	112.7	113.4	108.4	112.5
1970	116.3	114.9	123.6	110.1	107.3	116.1	111.1	128.5	120.6	113.5	121.6
1971	121.3	118.4	128.8	117.5	114.7	119.8	116.6	137.7	128.4	117.4	128.4
1972	125.3	123.5	134.5	118.5	120.5	122.3	117.5	143.4	132.5	120.9	133.3
1973	133.1	141.4	140.7	136.0	126.4	126.6	121.5	144.8	137.7	129.9	139.1
1974	147.7	161.7	154.4	214.6	145.8	136.2	136.6	148.0	150.5	145.5	152.1

1975	161.2	175.4	169.7	235.3	169.6	142.3	149.8	158.6	168.6	158.4	166.6
1976	170.5	180.8	179.0	250.8	189.0	147.6	164.6	174.2	184.7	165.2	180.4
1977	181.5	192.2	191.1	283.4	213.4	154.2	176.6	182.4	202.4	174.7	194.3
1978	195.4	211.4	210.4	298.3	232.6	159.6	185.0	187.8	219.4	187.1	210.9
1979	217.4	234.5	239.7	403.1	257.8	166.6	212.3	200.3	239.7	208.4	234.2
1980	246.8	254.6	281.7	556.0	301.8	178.4	249.2	251.6	265.9	233.9	270.3
1981	272.4	274.6	314.7	675.9	345.9	186.9	277.5	312.6	294.5	253.6	305.7
1982	289.1	285.7	337.0	667.9	393.8	191.8	287.5	346.0	328.7	263.8	333.3
1983	298.4	291.7	334.8	628.0	428.7	196.5	293.9	362.6	357.3	271.5	344.9
1984	311.1	302.9	361.7	641.8	445.2	200.2	306.6	385.2	379.5	280.7	363.0
1985	322.2	309.8	382.0	619.5	452.7	206.0	314.2	402.8	403.1	286.7	381.5
1986	328.4	319.7	402.9	501.5	446.7	207.8	299.5	426.4	433.5	283.9	400.5

Note: "—" indicates not available. 1967 equals 100. Annual averages of monthly figures. Prior to 1965, excludes Alaska and Hawaii. Through 1977 represents buying patterns of wage earners and clerical workers; beginning 1978, reflects buying patterns of all urban consumers in the 1970s.

Sources: 1950-1985: U.S. Bureau of the Census, *Statistical Abstract of the U.S., 1987* (Washington, D.C.: U.S. Government Printing Office, 1986), 463; 1986: U.S. President, *Economic Report of the President* (Washington, D.C.: U.S. Government Printing Office, 1987), 307-310.

Table 13-3 Federal Budget: Total, Defense, and Nondefense Expenditures, 1940-1992 (billions)

	Current dollars			*Constant (1982) dollars*		
Year	National defense	Non-defense	Total	National defense	Non-defense	Total
1940	1.7	7.8	9.5	15.1	68.1	83.2
1941	6.4	7.2	13.7	51.2	61.3	112.6
1942	25.7	9.5	35.1	174.7	85.9	260.5
1943	66.7	11.9	78.6	414.8	115.2	530.1
1944	79.1	12.2	91.3	522.1	116.0	638.0
1945	83.0	9.7	92.7	591.3	77.6	668.9
1946	42.7	12.6	55.2	339.8	75.4	415.3
1947	12.8	21.7	34.5	89.9	122.9	212.8
1948	9.1	20.7	29.8	55.8	102.4	158.2
1949	13.2	25.7	38.8	77.4	125.0	202.5
1950	13.7	28.8	42.6	83.9	136.5	220.5
1951	23.6	21.9	45.5	150.3	100.4	250.6
1952	46.1	21.6	67.9	258.9	90.5	349.3
1953	52.8	23.3	76.1	271.5	95.8	367.5
1954	49.3	21.6	70.9	250.0	81.0	330.9
1955	42.7	25.7	68.4	211.0	100.1	311.1
1956	42.5	28.1	70.6	198.5	107.6	306.2
1957	45.4	31.1	76.6	203.5	115.3	318.8
1958	46.8	35.6	82.4	198.3	124.4	322.8
1959	49.0	43.1	92.1	196.0	150.9	346.9
1960	48.1	44.1	92.2	192.1	148.4	340.4
1961	49.6	48.1	97.7	195.2	159.8	355.0
1962	52.3	54.5	106.8	202.2	181.9	384.1
1963	53.4	57.9	111.3	197.1	187.8	384.9
1964	54.8	63.8	118.5	198.8	204.4	403.2
1965	50.6	67.6	118.2	181.4	213.5	394.9
1966	58.1	76.4	134.5	197.9	233.6	431.5
1967	71.4	86.0	157.5	235.1	253.7	488.7
1968	81.9	96.2	178.1	254.8	270.9	525.8
1969	82.5	101.1	183.6	243.4	267.0	510.4
1970	81.7	114.0	195.6	225.6	283.8	509.4
1971	78.9	131.3	210.2	202.7	306.7	509.4
1972	79.2	151.5	230.7	190.9	336.7	527.6
1973	76.7	169.0	245.7	175.1	352.4	527.5
1974	79.3	190.0	269.4	163.3	365.3	528.7
1975	86.5	245.8	332.3	159.8	426.2	586.0
1976	89.6	282.2	371.8	153.6	456.2	609.8
TQ[a]	22.3	73.7	96.0	37.1	115.3	152.4
1977	97.2	312.0	409.2	154.3	468.3	622.6
1978	104.5	354.2	458.7	155.0	497.1	652.2

Table 13-3 *(Continued)*

Year	Current dollars: National defense	Current dollars: Non-defense	Current dollars: Total	Constant (1982) dollars: National defense	Constant (1982) dollars: Non-defense	Constant (1982) dollars: Total
1979	116.3	387.1	503.5	159.1	501.0	660.2
1980	134.0	456.9	590.9	164.0	535.1	699.1
1981	157.5	520.7	678.2	171.4	555.2	726.5
1982	185.3	560.4	745.8	185.3	560.4	745.8
1983	209.9	599.6	809.5	201.3	576.2	777.6
1984	227.4	624.4	851.8	211.5	578.4	789.9
1985	252.7	693.6	946.3	228.7	619.3	848.0
1986	273.4	716.4	989.8	242.1	624.1	866.2
1987 est.	282.2	733.3	1,015.6	242.6	619.7	862.3
1988 est.	297.6	726.8	1,024.3	246.9	592.5	839.3
1989 est.	312.2	756.8	1,069.0	250.2	596.4	846.6
1990 est.	330.0	777.8	1,107.8	256.0	592.6	848.6
1991 est.	349.5	794.9	1,144.4	263.6	588.6	852.2
1992 est.	370.9	808.1	1,178.9	273.2	584.6	857.8

[a] Transitional quarter when fiscal year start was shifted from July 1 to October 1.

Source: Office of Management and Budget, *Budget of the United States Government, Fiscal Year 1988, Historical Tables* (Washington, D.C.: U.S. Government Printing Office, 1987), Table 6-1.

Table 13-4 Federal Budget Outlays by Function, 1960-1986

Function	*1960*	*1965*	*1970*	*1975*	*1978*	*1979*	*1980*	*1981*	*1982*	*1983*	*1984*	*1985*	*1986*
Outlays (billions)													
National defense	$48.1	$50.6	$81.7	$86.5	$104.5	$116.3	$134.0	$157.5	$185.3	$209.9	$227.4	$252.7	$273.4
Human resources	26.2	36.8	75.3	173.0	242.1	267.1	312.1	359.2	387.2	425.6	442.1	471.8	481.6
Income security	7.4	10.0	15.6	50.2	61.5	66.4	86.4	99.2	107.0	122.2	112.7	128.2	119.8
Health	0.8	1.8	5.9	12.9	18.5	20.5	23.1	26.9	27.4	28.7	30.4	33.5	35.9
Veterans benefits and services	5.4	5.7	8.7	16.6	19.0	19.9	21.2	23.0	24.0	24.8	25.6	26.4	26.4
Education, training, employment[a]	1.0	2.1	8.6	15.9	26.5	29.9	30.8	31.4	26.3	26.6	27.6	29.3	30.6
Social security and medicare	11.6	175.0	36.5	77.5	116.6	130.6	150.6	178.7	202.5	223.3	235.8	254.4	268.9
Other nondefense	17.9	31.0	38.7	64.7	101.8	107.6	130.6	140.5	155.9	160.5	192.4	222.0	244.9
Commerce and housing credit	1.6	1.2	2.1	5.6	3.3	2.6	7.8	3.9	3.9	4.4	6.9	4.2	4.4
Transportation	4.1	5.7	7.0	10.4	15.4	17.5	21.1	23.4	20.6	21.4	23.7	25.8	28.1
Natural resources and environment	1.6	2.5	3.1	7.3	10.9	12.1	13.8	13.6	13.0	12.7	12.6	13.4	13.6
Energy	0.5	0.7	1.0	2.2	5.8	6.9	6.3	10.3	4.7	4.0	7.1	5.7	4.7
Community, regional development	0.2	1.1	2.4	3.7	11.1	9.5	10.1	9.4	7.2	6.9	7.7	7.7	7.2
Agriculture	2.6	4.0	5.2	1.7	7.7	6.2	4.8	5.5	14.9	22.2	13.6	25.6	31.4
Net interest	6.9	8.6	14.4	23.2	35.4	42.6	52.5	68.7	85.0	89.8	111.1	129.4	136.0
Revenue sharing[b]	0.2	0.2	0.5	7.2	9.6	8.4	8.6	6.9	6.4	6.4	6.7	6.7	6.4
International affairs	3.0	5.2	4.4	7.1	6.1	6.3	10.9	11.2	10.1	9.0	15.9	16.2	14.1
General science, space, technology	0.6	5.8	4.5	4.0	4.7	5.0	5.7	6.4	7.1	7.7	8.3	8.6	9.0
General government	1.0	1.2	1.7	2.9	3.4	3.9	4.1	4.4	4.4	4.8	5.1	5.2	6.1
Administration of justice	0.4	0.5	1.0	2.9	3.8	4.2	4.6	4.8	4.7	5.1	5.7	6.3	16.8
Undistributed offsetting receipts	−4.8	−5.9	−8.6	−13.6	−15.7	−17.5	−19.9	−28.0	−26.1	−34.0	−32.0	−32.8	−33.0
Total outlays	$92.2	$118.4	$195.7	$324.2	$448.4	$491.0	$576.7	$657.2	$728.4	$796.0	$851.8	$946.3	$989.8

Percentage distribution													
National defense	52.2%	42.7%	41.7%	26.7%	23.3%	23.7%	23.2%	24.0%	25.4%	26.4%	26.7%	26.7%	27.6%
Income security	8.0	8.4	8.0	15.5	13.7	13.5	15.0	15.1	14.7	15.4	13.2	13.5	12.1
Health	0.9	1.5	3.0	4.0	4.1	4.2	4.0	4.1	3.8	3.6	3.6	3.5	3.6
Veterans benefits and services	5.9	4.8	4.4	5.1	4.2	4.1	3.7	3.5	3.3	3.1	3.0	2.8	2.7
Education, training, employment[a]	1.0	1.8	4.4	4.9	5.9	6.0	5.3	4.8	3.6	3.3	3.2	3.1	3.1
Social security and medicare	12.6	14.8	18.6	23.9	26.0	26.6	26.1	27.2	27.8	28.0	27.7	26.9	27.2
Commerce and housing credit	1.8	1.0	1.1	1.7	0.7	0.5	1.4	0.6	0.5	0.6	0.8	0.4	0.4
Transportation	4.5	4.9	3.6	3.2	3.4	3.6	3.7	3.6	2.8	2.7	2.8	2.7	2.8
Natural resources and environment	1.7	2.1	1.6	2.3	2.4	2.5	2.4	2.1	1.8	1.6	1.5	1.4	1.4
Energy	0.5	0.6	0.5	0.7	1.3	1.4	1.1	1.6	0.6	0.5	0.8	0.6	0.5
Community and regional development	0.2	0.9	1.2	1.2	2.5	1.9	1.7	1.4	1.0	0.9	0.9	0.8	0.7
Agriculture	2.8	3.4	2.6	0.5	1.7	1.3	0.8	0.8	2.0	2.8	1.6	2.7	3.2
Net interest	7.5	7.2	7.3	7.2	7.9	8.7	9.1	10.5	11.7	11.3	13.0	13.7	13.7
Revenue sharing[b]	0.2	0.2	0.3	2.2	2.1	1.7	1.5	1.0	0.9	0.8	0.8	0.7	0.6
International affairs	3.2	4.4	2.2	2.2	1.3	1.3	1.9	1.7	1.4	1.1	1.9	1.7	1.4
General science, space, technology	0.6	4.9	2.3	1.2	1.1	1.0	1.0	1.0	1.0	1.0	1.0	0.9	0.9
General government	1.1	1.0	0.9	0.9	0.8	0.8	0.7	0.7	0.6	0.6	0.6	0.5	0.6
Administration of justice	0.4	0.4	0.5	0.9	0.8	0.8	0.8	0.7	0.6	0.6	0.7	0.7	1.7
Undistributed offsetting receipts	−5.2	−5.0	−4.4	−4.2	−3.5	−3.6	−3.4	−4.3	−3.6	−4.3	−3.8	−3.5	−3.3
Percentage distribution, total outlays	100.0%	100.0%	100.0%	100.0%	100.0%	100.0%	100.0%	100.0%	100.0%	100.0%	100.0%	100.0%	100.0%

Note: For 1960-1975 ending June 30. Beginning 1978, ending September 30.

[a] Includes social services.

[b] Includes general purpose fiscal assistance.

Sources: Statistical Abstract of the U.S., 1985, 309, *1987,* 293-294; 1986: Office of Management and the Budget, *Budget of the U.S. Government, Fiscal Year 1988, Historical Tables,* Tables 3-1, 3-2.

Figure 13-1 Federal Outlays as a Percentage of GNP, 1869-1986

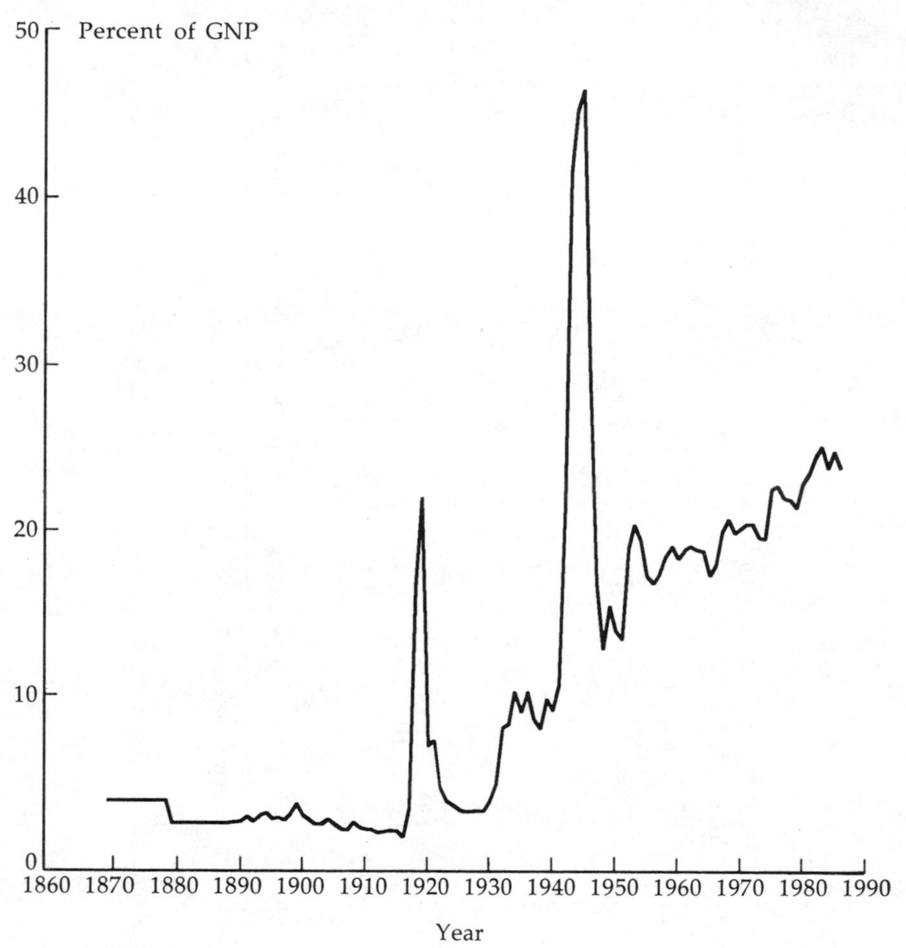

Note: Averaged by decade for 1869-1888. 1971-1986 data are based on fiscal rather than calendar year GNP.

Sources: 1869-1970: U.S. Bureau of the Census, *Historical Statistics of the United States* (Washington, D.C.: U.S. Government Printing Office, 1975), 224, 1114; 1971-1984: *Statistical Abstract of the U.S., 1986,* 305; 1985-1986: Office of Management and Budget, *Budget of the U.S. Government, Fiscal Year 1988, Historical Tables.*

Table 13-5 Executive Controllability of Federal Budget Outlays, 1970-1986

Outlays	*1970*	*1975*	*1979*	*1980*	*1981*	*1982*	*1983*	*1984*	*1985*	*1986 est.*
Relatively uncontrollable outlays (billions)	$120.3	$222.2	$345.3	$413.8	$476.4	$541.4	$593.5	$624.1	$689.5	$742.2
Open-ended programs and fixed costs[a]	78.3	168.9	259.9	310.7	367.8	419.9	464.8	478.8	527.3	560.5
Payments for individuals[a]	60.1	139.5	209.5	246.6	287.6	320.1	353.8	357.4	380.5	399.8
Social Security and railroad retirement	30.7	67.3	105.0	120.0	141.2	157.4	171.8	179.3	189.9	200.9
Medical care	9.4	20.6	39.9	47.2	57.2	65.6	73.5	79.9	91.0	96.2
Federal employees' retirement and insurance[b]	8.7	18.4	29.9	34.7	40.5	44.4	47.3	49.0	49.8	53.0
Food and nutrition assistance	—	1.6	3.0	3.5	3.5	3.0	3.3	3.6	3.7	3.9
Public assistance and related programs	6.4	12.2	15.5	17.5	19.3	19.5	20.9	21.0	22.2	23.3
Unemployment assistance	3.1	12.3	9.7	16.8	18.2	22.1	29.7	16.9	16.1	15.0
Net interest	14.4	23.2	42.6	52.5	68.7	85.0	89.8	111.1	129.4	141.5
Farm price supports[c]	3.8	0.6	3.6	2.8	4.0	11.7	18.9	7.3	17.7	20.3
Prior-year contracts and obligations[d]	41.9	53.3	85.3	103.2	108.6	121.5	128.7	145.3	162.2	181.6
Relatively controllable outlays (billions)	83.8	113.2	159.9	178.7	198.7	206.8	266.0	243.0	284.1	266.9
National defense	57.6	64.2	85.3	97.4	115.9	128.2	141.4	147.8	160.5	162.0
Civilian programs	26.3	49.1	74.6	81.3	82.8	78.6	84.5	95.2	123.6	104.8
Undistributed employer share, employee retirement (billions)	−8.4	−11.2	−14.2	−15.8	−17.9	−19.8	−23.5	−25.3	−27.2	−29.1
Total outlays	$195.6	$332.3	$503.5	$590.9	$678.2	$745.7	$808.3	$851.8	$946.3	$979.9
Relatively uncontrollable outlays as a percentage of total outlays	61.5%	66.9%	68.6%	70.0%	70.2%	72.6%	73.4%	73.3%	72.9%	75.7%

Note: "—" indicates not available.

[a] Includes other outlays not shown separately.

[b] Includes items previously classified in the veterans' benefits grouping.

[c] Prices from Commodity Credit Corporation.

[d] Excludes prior year contracts and obligations for items under open-ended programs and fixed costs.

Source: Statistical Abstract of the U.S., 1987, 296.

Table 13-6 The National Debt, 1940-1992

Year	*Debt held by the public (millions)*	*As a percentage of GNP*
1940	$ 42,772	44.6
1941	48,223	42.7
1942	67,753	47.6
1943	127,766	72.7
1944	184,796	91.5
1945	235,182	110.7
1946	241,861	113.6
1947	224,339	100.3
1948	216,270	87.3
1949	214,322	81.2
1950	219,023	82.1
1951	214,326	68.0
1952	214,758	62.7
1953	218,383	59.7
1954	224,499	60.8
1955	226,616	58.6
1956	222,226	53.2
1957	219,421	49.8
1958	226,363	50.3
1959	235,003	48.8
1960	237,177	46.8
1961	238,604	46.0
1962	248,373	44.5
1963	254,461	43.3
1964	257,553	40.9
1965	261,614	38.9
1966	264,690	35.8
1967	267,529	33.7
1968	290,629	34.2
1969	279,483	30.1
1970	284,880	28.8
1971	304,328	28.8
1972	323,770	28.1
1973	343,045	26.8
1974	346,053	24.4
1975	396,906	26.1
1976	480,300	28.3
TQ[a]	498,327	27.8
1977	551,843	28.5
1978	610,948	28.1
1979	644,589	26.3
1980	715,105	26.8

Table 13-6 *(Continued)*

Year	*Debt held by the public (millions)*	*As a percentage of GNP*
1981	$ 794,434	26.6
1982	929,427	29.6
1983	1,141,771	34.4
1984	1,312,589	35.6
1985	1,509,857	38.3
1986	1,746,141	41.9
1987 est.	1,908,389	43.2
1988 est.	2,015,110	42.6
1989 est.	2,107,457	41.5
1990 est.	2,166,527	39.9
1991 est.	2,187,386	37.8
1992 est.	2,174,679	35.5

[a] Transitional quarter when fiscal year start was shifted from July 1 to October 1.

Source: Office of Management and the Budget, *Budget of the U.S. Government, Fiscal Year 1988, Historical Tables,* Table 7-1.

Figure 13-2 The National Debt as a Percentage of GNP, 1940-1992

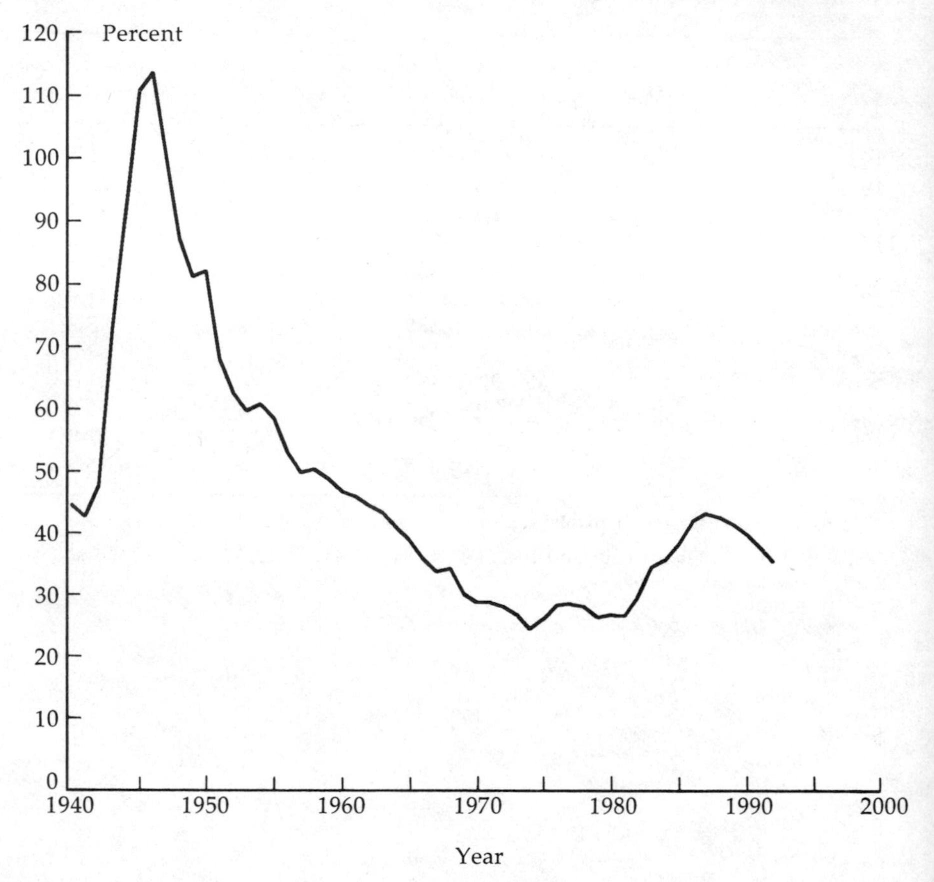

Note: 1987-1992 percentages are estimates. Figures reflect debt held by the public and do not include debt held by federal government accounts.

Source: Office of Management and Budget, *Budget of the U.S. Government, Fiscal Year 1988, Historical Tables,* Table 7.1.

Table 13-7 Revenue Loss Estimates for Selected Tax Expenditures, 1986 (millions)

Type of tax expenditure	*Loss*
Energy	
Expense of exploration and development costs	$ 555
Natural resources and environment	
Tax incentives for preservation of historic structures	570
Commerce and housing credit	
Deductibility of interest on consumer credit	17,600
Deductibility of mortgage interest on owner-occupied homes	29,920
Deductibility of property tax on owner-occupied homes	10,060
Capital gains (other than agriculture, timber, iron ore, and coal)	28,860
Investment credit, other than employee stock ownership plans, rehabilitation of structures, energy property, and reforestation expenditures	25,525
Accelerated depreciation of machinery and equipment	23,025
Education, training, employment, and social services	
Exclusion of scholarship and fellowship income	960
Parental personal exemption for students age 19 or over	1,215
Deductibility of charitable contributions (education)	1,570
Deductibility of charitable contributions, other than education and health	12,275
Health	
Exclusion of employer contributions for medical insurance premiums and medical care	23,510
Social Security and medicare	
OASI benefits for retired workers	13,515
Income security	
Exclusion of public assistance benefits	580
Net exclusion of pension contributions and earnings	
Employer plans	53,365
Individual Retirement Accounts	14,365
Interest	
Deferral of interest on savings bonds	710

Note: Tax expenditures are defined as revenue losses attributable to provisions of the federal tax laws which allow a special exclusion, exemption, or deduction from gross income or which provide a special credit, a preferential rate of tax, or a deferral of liability. The Internal Revenue Service collected slightly under $500 billion in 1985 through individual and corporate income taxes.

Source: Statistical Abstract of the U.S., 1987, 297.

Table 13-8 Public Opinion on the Budget-Balancing Amendment, Cross Section, 1985 (percent)

	Heard/read about amendment				
	Yes	No	*Favor*	*Oppose*	*No opinion*
Sex					
Male	64	36	55	28	17
Female	51	49	44	26	30
Race/ethnicity					
White	59	41	50	26	24
Nonwhite	45	55	44	33	23
Black	48	52	44	35	21
Education					
Less than high school	44	56	39	28	33
High school	45	55	47	28	25
College	78	22	59	27	14
Income					
Under $10,000	46	54	38	27	35
$10,000-14,999	45	55	36	29	35
$15,000-24,999	57	43	51	31	18
$25,000 and over	67	33	59	25	16
Political affiliation					
Democrat	54	46	44	36	20
Independent	60	40	51	25	24
Republican	60	40	55	22	23
National	57	43	49	27	24

Note: Question: "Have you heard or read about a proposal for a constitutional amendment that would require the federal government to balance the national budget each year? Under the proposed amendment, any federal budget passed by Congress would have projected tax revenues that are equal to projected government spending unless a three-fifths majority of Congress voted not to do so. Would you favor or oppose this amendment to the Constitution?"

Source: The Gallup Report (September 1985), 10-11.

Table 13-9 Civilian Labor Force Participation Rate Overall and by Sex and Race, 1948-1986 (percent)

Year	*Total*	*Male*	*Female*	*White and other nonblack*	*Black*
1948	58.8	86.6	32.7	—	—
1949	58.9	86.4	33.1	—	—
1950	59.2	86.4	33.9	—	—
1951	59.2	86.3	34.6	—	—
1952	59.0	86.3	34.7	—	—
1953	58.9	86.0	34.4	—	—
1954	58.8	85.5	34.6	58.2	64.0
1955	59.3	85.4	35.7	58.7	64.2
1956	60.0	85.5	36.9	59.4	64.9
1957	59.6	84.8	36.9	59.1	64.4
1958	59.5	84.2	37.1	58.9	64.8
1959	59.3	83.7	37.1	58.7	64.3
1960	59.4	83.3	37.7	58.8	64.5
1961	59.3	82.9	38.1	58.8	64.1
1962	58.8	82.0	37.9	58.3	63.2
1963	58.7	81.4	38.3	58.2	63.0
1964	58.7	81.0	38.7	58.2	63.1
1965	58.9	80.7	39.3	58.4	62.9
1966	59.2	80.4	40.3	58.7	63.0
1967	59.6	80.4	41.1	59.2	62.8
1968	59.6	80.1	41.6	59.3	62.2
1969	60.1	79.8	42.7	59.9	62.1
1970	60.4	79.7	43.3	60.2	61.8
1971	60.2	79.1	43.4	60.1	60.9
1972	60.4	78.9	43.9	60.4	60.2
1973	60.8	78.8	44.7	60.8	60.5
1974	61.3	78.7	45.7	61.4	60.3
1975	61.2	77.9	46.3	61.5	59.6
1976	61.6	77.5	47.3	61.8	59.8
1977	62.3	77.7	48.4	62.5	60.4
1978	63.2	77.9	50.0	63.3	62.2
1979	63.7	77.8	50.9	63.9	62.2
1980	63.8	77.4	51.5	64.1	61.7
1981	63.9	77.0	52.1	64.3	61.3
1982	64.0	76.6	52.6	64.3	61.6
1983	64.0	76.4	52.9	64.3	62.1
1984	64.4	76.4	53.6	64.6	62.6
1985	64.8	76.3	54.5	65.0	63.3
1986	65.3	76.3	55.3	65.5	63.7

Note: "—" indicates not available. Figures are for persons 16 years and over. The participation rate is the percentage of adults considered to be in the labor force. It is roughly those persons who are working, temporarily laid off, or looking for work. For details, see *Statistical Abstract of the United States 1987*, 372.

Source: U.S. President, *Economic Report of the President*, (1987), 289.

Table 13-10 Unemployment Rate Overall, 1929-1986, and by Sex and Race, 1948-1986 (percent)

Year	*Civilian workers*	*Male*	*Female*	*White*	*Nonwhite*
1929	3.2	—	—	—	—
1933	24.9	—	—	—	—
1939	17.2	—	—	—	—
1940	14.6	—	—	—	—
1941	9.9	—	—	—	—
1942	4.7	—	—	—	—
1943	1.9	—	—	—	—
1944	1.2	—	—	—	—
1945	1.9	—	—	—	—
1946	3.9	—	—	—	—
1947	3.9	—	—	—	—
1948	3.8	3.6	4.1	3.5	5.9
1949	5.9	5.9	6.0	5.6	8.9
1950	5.3	5.1	5.7	4.9	9.0
1951	3.3	2.8	4.4	3.1	5.3
1952	3.0	2.8	3.6	2.8	5.4
1953	2.9	2.8	3.3	2.7	4.5
1954	5.5	5.3	6.0	5.0	9.9
1955	4.4	4.2	4.9	3.9	8.7
1956	4.1	3.8	4.8	3.6	8.3
1957	4.3	4.1	4.7	3.8	7.9
1958	6.8	6.8	6.8	6.1	12.6
1959	5.5	5.2	5.9	4.8	10.7
1960	5.5	5.4	5.9	5.0	10.2
1961	6.7	6.4	7.2	6.0	12.4
1962	5.5	5.2	6.2	4.9	10.9
1963	5.7	5.2	6.5	5.0	10.8
1964	5.2	4.6	6.2	4.6	9.6
1965	4.5	4.0	5.5	4.1	8.1
1966	3.8	3.2	4.8	3.4	7.3
1967	3.8	3.1	5.2	3.4	7.4
1968	3.6	2.9	4.8	3.2	6.7
1969	3.5	2.8	4.7	3.1	6.4
1970	4.9	4.4	5.9	4.5	8.2
1971	5.9	5.3	6.9	5.4	9.9
1972	5.6	5.0	6.6	5.1	10.0
1973	4.9	4.2	6.0	4.3	9.0
1974	5.6	4.9	6.7	5.0	9.9
1975	8.5	7.9	9.3	7.8	13.8
1976	7.7	7.1	8.6	7.0	13.1
1977	7.1	6.3	8.2	6.2	13.1
1978	6.1	5.3	7.2	5.2	11.9
1979	5.8	5.1	6.8	5.1	11.3
1980	7.1	6.9	7.4	6.3	13.1

Table 13-10 *(Continued)*

Year	*Civilian workers*	*Male*	*Female*	*White*	*Nonwhite*
1981	7.6	7.4	7.9	6.7	14.2
1982	9.7	9.9	9.4	8.6	17.3
1983	9.6	9.9	9.2	8.4	17.8
1984	7.5	7.4	7.6	6.5	14.4
1985	7.2	7.0	7.4	6.2	13.7
1986	7.0	6.9	7.1	6.0	13.1

Note: "—" indicates not available. 1929-1947 figures are for persons 14 years of age and over. 1948-1986 figures are for persons 16 years of age and over.

Source: U.S. President, *Economic Report of the President* (1987), 285.

Table 13-11 Teenage Unemployment by Race and Sex, 1972-1986 (percent)

	White				*Black*			
	Male		Female		Male		Female	
Year	*16-19*	*20 and over*	*16-19*	*20 and over*	*16-19*	*20 and over*	*16-19*	*20 and over*
1972	14.2	3.6	14.2	4.9	31.7	7.0	40.5	9.0
1973	12.3	3.0	13.0	4.3	27.8	6.0	36.1	8.6
1974	13.5	3.5	14.5	5.1	33.1	7.4	37.4	8.8
1975	18.3	6.2	17.4	7.5	38.1	12.5	41.0	12.2
1976	17.3	5.4	16.4	6.8	37.5	11.4	41.6	11.7
1977	15.0	4.7	15.9	6.2	39.2	10.7	43.4	12.3
1978	13.5	3.7	14.4	5.2	36.7	9.3	40.8	11.2
1979	13.9	3.6	14.0	5.0	34.2	9.3	39.1	10.9
1980	16.2	5.3	14.8	5.6	37.5	12.4	39.8	11.9
1981	17.9	5.6	16.6	5.9	40.7	13.5	42.2	13.4
1982	21.7	7.8	19.0	7.3	48.9	17.8	47.1	15.4
1983	20.2	7.9	18.3	6.9	48.8	18.1	48.2	16.5
1984	16.8	5.7	15.2	5.8	42.7	14.3	42.6	13.5
1985	16.5	5.4	14.8	5.7	41.0	13.2	39.2	13.1
1986	16.3	5.3	14.9	5.4	39.3	12.9	39.2	12.4

Source: U.S. President, *Economic Report of the President* (1987), 288.

Questions

1. How can it happen, as it did in 1945, 1954, and other years, that the gross national product increases in current dollars but declines in constant dollars (Table 13-1)? What accounts for the greatest increase in GNP when measured in constant dollars? The biggest decrease in current GNP? In GNP in constant dollars? Do the biggest increases and decreases in current GNP coincide with the biggest increases and decreases in GNP in constant dollars? Why or why not?

2. Which component of the Consumer Price Index increased the most between 1967 and 1980 (Table 13-2)? What has happened to this component since 1980? Has inflation for all items been negative in any year since 1950?

3. Employee A got a job in 1967 for $8,000 per year. Twelve years later employee B got the same kind of job with an annual salary of $16,000. Using Table 13-2 and the numbers for "all items" in those years, decide whether starting salaries had increased or decreased in constant terms? If a basket of food cost $32.50 in 1960, what would the same food cost in 1986?

4. Ronald Reagan made the charge in 1980 that an increase in defense spending was overdue because spending had been reduced under President Jimmy Carter. Was Reagan correct (Table 13-3)? Did President Reagan increase military spending? Which increased more under Carter (1977-1980), defense spending or nondefense spending? Under Reagan (1981-1988)? Apart from the anticipated decrease in total (constant) spending in 1987, when was the last time the total federal budget declined and how much did it decline?

5. Of the relatively large categories of expenditures (say over 3 percent of total outlays in 1960), only three categories were a larger percentage of the budget in 1986 than in 1960 (Table 13-4). What were they? In which category was the increase greatest? In constant dollars (using the CPI for "all items" from Table 13-2), did outlays for agriculture increase between 1960 and 1986?

6. What does it mean to say that Social Security, medical care, farm price supports, and so forth are relatively uncontrollable outlays

(Table 13-5)? Table 13-5 indicates why it is increasingly difficult to reduce the federal budget deficit. What is that reason?

7. What milestone in the size of the national debt was passed in 1983 (Table 13-6)? Some people argue that the national debt is not a big problem despite its tremendous size. On what basis could one possibly make that argument (Table 13-6 and Figure 13-2)?

8. Based on the list in Table 13-7, do you personally benefit from any exclusions, exemptions, or deductions? Do your parents? How? (There is no single right and wrong answer.) There is at least one benefit that students certainly benefit from indirectly, more or less depending on whether they attend a public or a private school. What is this benefit?

9. Assuming that the proportions who favor, oppose, and have no opinion are the same for those who have heard or read about the budget-balancing amendment and those who have not, what proportion of the sample heard or read about the amendment and favored it (Table 13-8)? Is this assumption likely to be correct? Why or why not? Is there any evidence in the rest of the table that supports your reasoning?

10. Among the groups shown in Tables 13-10 and 13-11, which had the highest unemployment rate through 1981? Since 1982?

11. For all sets of teenagers, unemployment since 1982 declined considerably faster than unemployment among those aged twenty and over (Table 13-11). Why? (Hint: the same factor explains why it was easier for students today to get into their chosen college than for those who graduated just a few years ago.)

Appendix

Table A-1 Regions as Defined by the U.S. Census Bureau

Northeast	*Midwest*	*South*	*West*
New England	East north central	South Atlantic	Mountain
Connecticut	Illinois	Delaware	Arizona
New Hampshire	Indiana	District of Columbia	Colorado
Maine	Michigan	Florida	Idaho
Massachusetts	Ohio	Georgia	Montana
Rhode Island	Wisconsin	Maryland	Nevada
Vermont	West north central	North Carolina	New Mexico
Middle Atlantic	Iowa	South Carolina	Utah
New Jersey	Kansas	Virginia	Wyoming
New York	Minnesota	West Virginia	Pacific
Pennsylvania	Missouri	East south central	Alaska
	Nebraska	Alabama	California
	North Dakota	Kentucky	Hawaii
	South Dakota	Mississippi	Oregon
		Tennessee	Washington
		West south central	
		Arkansas	
		Louisiana	
		Oklahoma	
		Texas	

Source: U.S. Bureau of the Census, *Statistical Abstract of the U.S., 1987* (Washington,D.C.: U.S. Government Printing Office, 1986), Figure I.

Table A-2 Regions as Defined by the Gallup Poll and Congressional Quarterly

East	*Midwest*	*South*	*West*
Connecticut	Illinois	Alabama	Alaska
Delaware	Indiana	Arkansas	Arizona
District of Columbia	Iowa	Florida	California
Maine	Kansas	Georgia	Colorado
Maryland	Michigan	Kentucky	Hawaii
Massachusetts	Minnesota	Louisiana	Idaho
New Hampshire	Missouri	Mississippi	Montana
New Jersey	Nebraska	North Carolina	Nevada
New York	North Dakota	Oklahoma	New Mexico
Pennsylvania	Ohio	South Carolina	Oregon
Rhode Island	South Dakota	Tennessee	Utah
Vermont	Wisconsin	Texas	Washington
West Virginia		Virginia	Wyoming

Source: The Gallup Report (November 1984), 30; *Congressional Quarterly Weekly Report* (1988), 112.

Table A-3 Regions for Partisan Competition Table

New England	*Middle Atlantic*	*Midwest*	*Plains*
Connecticut	Delaware	Illinois	Iowa
Maine	New Jersey	Indiana	Kansas
Massachusetts	New York	Michigan	Minnesota
New Hampshire	Pennsylvania	Ohio	Nebraska
Rhode Island		Wisconsin	North Dakota
Vermont			South Dakota
South	*Border*	*Rocky Mountain*	*Pacific Coast*
Alabama	District of Columbia	Arizona	Alaska
Arkansas	Kentucky	Colorado	California
Florida	Maryland	Idaho	Hawaii
Georgia	Missouri	Montana	Oregon
Louisiana	Oklahoma	Nevada	Washington
Mississippi	West Virginia	New Mexico	
North Carolina		Utah	
South Carolina		Wyoming	
Tennessee			
Texas			
Virginia			

Table A-4 Regions for Orfield Desegregation Table

South	*Border*	*Northeast*	*Midwest*	*West*	*Excluded*
Alabama	Delaware	Connecticut	Illinois	Arizona	Alaska
Arkansas	District of Columbia	Maine	Indiana	California	Hawaii
Florida	Kentucky	Massachusetts	Iowa	Colorado	
Georgia	Maryland	New Hampshire	Kansas	Idaho	
Louisiana	Missouri	New Jersey	Michigan	Montana	
Mississippi	Oklahoma	New York	Minnesota	Nevada	
North Carolina	West Virginia	Pennsylvania	Nebraska	New Mexico	
South Carolina		Rhode Island	North Dakota	Oregon	
Tennessee		Vermont	Ohio	Utah	
Texas			South Dakota	Washington	
Virginia			Wisconsin	Wyoming	

Source: Gary Orfield, testimony before the House Subcommittee on Civil and Constitutional Rights, *Civil Rights Implications of the Education Block Grant Program,* September 9, 1982, 67-72.

Guide to References for Political Statistics

General

Austin, Erik W., and Jerome M. Clubb. *Political Facts of the United States Since 1789.*
Convenient one-volume compilation of otherwise all-too-often elusive data on politics in the nation; one strength is the long time series.

Congressional Information Service. *American Statistics Index: A Comprehensive Guide and Index to the Statistical Publications of the U.S. Government.*
Definitive guide, multiply indexed, to statistics "of probable research significance" in government publications; 1974 "Annual and Retrospective Edition" includes not only items in print but also significant items published over the preceding decade.

Congressional Information Service. *Statistical Reference Index: A Selective Guide to American Statistical Publications from Sources Other than the U.S. Government.*
A complement to *American Statistics Index,* indexes statistics from private and public sources other than the U.S. federal government.

Congressional Quarterly Weekly Report.
Newsweekly covering political developments in Congress, the presidency, the Supreme Court, and national politics; individual voting records on all roll-call votes in the House and Senate; texts of presidential press conferences and major statements.

National Journal.
Newsweekly about government; reviews recent actions and features analyses of policy and political issues.

U.S. Bureau of the Census. *Historical Statistics of the United States, Colonial Times to 1970.*
Invaluable, broad-ranging collection of over 12,000 time series covering

the nation's history; often the series can be updated by the annual *Statistical Abstract of the United States (see below).*

U.S. Bureau of the Census. *Statistical Abstract of the U.S.*
Strong, indispensable collection of nationally significant statistics from public and private sources on economics, politics, and society; generally worth checking first; also a useful guide to sources for additional statistics; indicates which time series update those in *Historical Statistics* (see above).

The Constitution

Balinski, Michel, and H. P. Young. *Fair Representation.*
Analysis of statistical methods of apportionment of representatives among the states.

Congressional Research Service. *The Constitution of the United States: Analysis and Interpretation.*
Not statistics laden, but the essential document with commentary and annotations of cases decided by the Supreme Court; handy tables on proposed constitutional amendments pending and unratified, laws (congressional, state, or local) held unconstitutional by the Supreme Court, and Supreme Court decisions overruled by subsequent decisions; U.S. law requires a new edition every ten years with biennial supplements between editions to keep this work current.

Dixon, Robert G., Jr. *Democratic Representation: Reapportionment in Law and Politics.*
A comprehensive early account of districting theory and practice, with a strong statistical base.

U.S. Congress. House. *Constitution, Jefferson's Manual, and Rules of the House of Representatives of the United States.*
Handy reference for the Constitution containing complete notes of all ratifications; indexed.

The Mass Media

Broadcasting Publications. *Broadcasting Cablecasting Yearbook.*
International directory of radio, television, and cable industries as well as related fields; presents some statistical overviews.

Editor & Publisher—The Fourth Estate.
Weekly periodical covering the media.

Magazine Index.
Indexes a long list of magazines, including a number of political news magazines.

National Newspaper Index.
Indexes major national newspapers. The current list includes the *New York Times, Wall Street Journal, Christian Science Monitor, Los Angeles Times,* and the *Washington Post.* The *New York Times* has its own longstanding index.

Sterling, Christopher H. *Electronic Media: A Guide to Trends in Broadcasting and Newer Technologies: 1920-1983.*
Data on growth, ownership, economics, employment and training, contents, audience and regulation of radio, television, and cable; strong on trends and time series.

Television Digest. *Cable and Station Coverage Atlas.*
Data on television stations and the growing reach of cable systems.

Television Digest. *Television and Cable Factbook.*
Data on cable, television, and related industries; published in two volumes: "Stations" and "Cable and Services."

Elections and Campaigns

Alexander, Herbert E., and Brian A. Haggerty. *Financing the 1984 Election.*
Detailed statistical coverage of fund-raising and spending in all phases of the presidential campaign; continues a series of books by Alexander on financing presidential campaigns since 1960.

Bartley, Numan V., and Hugh D. Graham. *Southern Elections: County and Precinct Data, 1950-1972.*
Gubernatorial and senatorial contests, meaningful primaries, and referenda in eleven southern states; some socioeconomic and geographic analysis of the pattern of the votes.

Congressional Quarterly. *Congressional Quarterly's Guide to U.S. Elections.*
Superb collection of vote returns for presidential, gubernatorial, and House elections since 1824, electoral college votes since 1789, senatorial elections since 1913, presidential primaries since 1912, and primaries for governor and senator since 1956 (in southern states since 1919); general and candidate indexes; biographies of presidential and vice-presidential candidates; lists of governors and senators since 1789; discussions of and data on political parties and presidential nominating conventions throughout the nation's history.

Federal Election Commission. *Annual Report.*
Cumulative figures since the mid-1970s on contributions and spending in federal election campaigns; also information on political action committee (PAC) growth and activities.

Federal Election Commission. *Reports on Financial Activity.*
Multi-volume work reporting revenues and spending in congressional and presidential campaigns by candidates, party, and nonparty political committees (PACs); reports typically cover a two-year campaign cycle (for example, 1985-1986).

Glashan, Roy R. *American Governors and Gubernatorial Elections, 1775-1978.*
Details about state governors (such as birthdates, party affiliations, principal occupations, terms of office) and election data.

Heard, Alexander E. *The Costs of Democracy.*
A classic work, published in 1960 when hard data on campaign contributions and spending were hard to secure.

Kallenbach, Joseph E., and Jessamine S. Kallenbach. *American State Governors, 1776-1976.*
Election results and biographical data on governors.

Mullaney, Marie. *American Governors and Gubernatorial Elections, 1978-1987: A Statistical Compilation.*
Details about state governors (such as birth dates, party affiliations, principal occupations, terms of office) and election data.

Scammon, Richard M., and Alice V. McGillivray, eds. *America at the Polls: A Handbook of American Presidential Election Statistics.*
Two volumes span 1920-1984, providing popular votes (state and county) for president as well as state presidential primary results.

Scammon, Richard M., and Alice V. McGillivray, eds. *America Votes: A Handbook of Contemporary American Election Statistics.*
Convenient compilation of vote totals and statistics by state for general elections and primaries for president, governor, senator, principally since 1945 (comparable district-level data for members of Congress); county-level totals and statistics for most recent general election for president, governor, and senator; state maps with county and congressional districts boundaries.

U.S. Bureau of the Census. Current Population Reports. Population Characteristics, series P-20. *Voter Participation.*
Survey results on voter registration and turnout in presidential and midterm general elections for the nation and regions (and sometimes states and metropolitan areas) for various groups.

U.S. Congress. Secretary of the U.S. Senate. *Nomination and Election of the President and Vice President of the United States Including the Manner of Selecting Delegates to National Political Conventions.*
Account of variations among the states in laws and rules concerning presidential elections and convention delegate selection procedures.

Political Parties

Bain, Richard C., and Judith H. Parris. *Convention Decisions and Voting Records.*
Pulls together data on convention actions over the years; now slightly dated (1973).

Congressional Quarterly. *National Party Conventions, 1831-1984.*
Summarizes each convention, giving results of ballots, nominees, and profiles of the parties.

David, Paul T. *Party Strength in the United States 1872-1970.*
Measures of party competition in the states covering several offices and an admirably lengthy historical span.

Public Opinion

Converse, Philip E., Jean D. Dotson, Wendy J. Hoag, and William H. McGee III. *American Social Attitudes Data Sourcebook 1947-1978.*
Compendium of national polling data from the Survey Research Center at the University of Michigan, ranging across major social issues.

The Gallup Poll: Public Opinion.
Poll data from thousands of Gallup surveys since 1935 on then-current topics, presented chronologically.

The Gallup Report: Political, Social and Economic Trends.
Monthly compilation of recent Gallup public opinion data on political and social issues, often presented with historical trends.

Miller, Warren E., Arthur H. Miller, and Edward J. Schneider. *American National Election Studies Data Sourcebook, 1952-1978.*
Compendium of national polling data from the National Election Studies covering presidential and congressional election years.

Opinion Research Service. *American Public Opinion Index.*
Indexes scientifically drawn samples of national, state, and local universes.

Public Opinion.
Analysis of public opinion about current issues and trends; regular "Opinion Roundup" section presents poll data from several sources on selected topics.

Public Opinion Quarterly.
Analysis of the mechanics and findings of survey research; regular thematic presentation of poll results.

Interest Groups

Cigler, Allan J., and Burdett A. Loomis. *Interest Group Politics.*
Examines interest groups in the policy-making process—a rapidly changing field.

Close, Arthur C., and John P. Gregg. *Washington Representatives.*
Lists Washington representatives of major corporations, unions, and national associations as well as registered foreign agents and the organizations represented by an individual or an office in Washington.

Congressional Quarterly. *The Washington Lobby.*
Lobbying developments in strategies and techniques, highlighting political action committees (PACs); explores federal laws, regulations, and court cases that govern lobbyists as well as interest group ratings of members of Congress.

Gruber, Katerine, Susan M. Boyles, Kathleen Dombrowski, Michael A. Pare, and Karin E. Koek, eds. *Encyclopedia of Associations.*
Guide to over 23,000 organizations, both national and international, spanning various sectors of society.

Interstate Bureau of Regulations. *State Political Action Legislation and Regulations: Index and Directory of Organizations.*
Information on regulation of political action committees in the states.

Malbin, Michael J. *Parties, Interest Groups, and Campaign Finance Laws.*
Early (1980) collection pulling together analyses in an increasingly investigated area.

Weinberger, Marvin I., and David U. Greevy. *The PAC Directory: A Complete Guide to Political Action Committees.*
Useful assemblage of information on political action committees in the political process.

Congress

Barone, Michael, and Grant Ujifusa. *The Almanac of American Politics.*
Data-rich political analyses of each state, congressional district, representative, senator, and governor; current composition of committees; state maps with congressional district and county boundaries.

Congressional Quarterly. *American Leaders 1789-1987.*
Material on more than 11,000 members of Congress: age, religion, occupations, women, blacks, turnover, and shifts between chambers; data on congressional sessions, party composition, and leadership. Also includes biographical summaries of presidents, vice presidents, Supreme Court justices, and governors.

Congressional Quarterly. *Congress and the Nation.*
Akin to *Congressional Quarterly Almanac* (see below), but each volume covers a presidential term.

Congressional Quarterly. *Congressional Districts in the 1980s.*
Profiles of each congressional district containing statistics on election returns, economic makeup, and demographics.

Congressional Quarterly. *Congressional Quarterly Almanac.*
Each volume now covers legislation for a single session of Congress, appendices contain particularly useful data on Congress and politics.

Congressional Quarterly. *Congressional Roll Call.*
Annual compilation of every roll-call vote by every member of Congress and summary voting measures (ideology, party unity, presidential support, and voting participation).

Congressional Quarterly. *Guide to Congress.*
Massive, rich accounting of how Congress works and how it developed. Check here first for data covering all but the most recent years.

Congressional Quarterly. *Politics in America.*
Data-rich political analyses of each state, congressional district, representative, and senator; current composition of committees; state maps with congressional district and county boundaries.

Ornstein, Norman J., Thomas E. Mann, and Michael J. Malbin, eds. *Vital Statistics on Congress, 1987-1988.*
Data on characteristics of members, elections, campaign finance, committees, staff, expenses, workload, budgeting, and voting alignments; most data series stretch back to World War II, some longer.

Parsons, Stanley B., William W. Beach, Dan Hermann, and Michael J. Dubin. *United States Congressional Districts and Data.*
Demographic and geographic data about American congressional districts. Currently two volumes available, covering 1789-1883.

U.S. Bureau of the Census. *Congressional District Data Book.*
Census data by congressional district with maps.

U.S. Congress. Joint Committee on Printing. *Official Congressional Directory.*
Biographical data on current members, statistics on the sessions of Congress, useful reference source on committees and subcommittees, foreign representatives and consular offices in the United States, press representatives, and state delegations.

The Presidency and the Executive Branch

Congressional Quarterly. *Federal Regulatory Directory.*
Descriptions and data provide extensive profiles of the major and minor regulatory agencies—over 100 in all.

Congressional Quarterly. *Presidential Elections Since 1789.*
Facts and figures on presidential elections; electoral college vote since 1789; primary returns since 1912; major-party candidate vote shares state-by-state; minor candidate vote totals; recent turnout and party support trends.

DeGregorio, William A. *The Complete Book of U.S. Presidents.*
Biographies of presidents and cabinet members.

Kane, Joseph Nathan. *Facts about the Presidents: A Compilation of Biographical and Historical Information.*
Chapter on each president and comparative statistics on all presidents.

King, Gary, and Lyn Ragsdale. *The Elusive Executive: Discovering Statistical Patterns in the Presidency.*
A statistical evaluation of the presidency in its various aspects, focusing on post-war presidencies with some longer time series.

U.S. Government Organization Manual.
Official federal government handbook detailing the organization, activities, and current officials in legislative, judicial, and executive governmental units.

Weekly Compilation of Presidential Documents.
Highly useful collection of presidential activities; includes texts of proclamations, executive orders, speeches, and other presidential communications; supplements include acts gaining presidential approval, nominations submitted for Senate confirmation, and a list of White House press releases; indexed.

The Judiciary

The Conference of State Court Administrators and the Court Statistics and Information Management Project of the National Center for State Courts. *1984 State Appellate Court Jurisdiction Guide for Statistical Reporting.*
Data on judicial workload in the state appellate courts.

Congressional Quarterly. *Guide to the U.S. Supreme Court.*
Solid, broad coverage of the Supreme Court and the development of the law; an excellent source that also refers readers to additional references.

Curran, Barbara A., et al. *The Lawyer Statistical Report: A Statistical Profile of the U.S. Legal Profession in the 1980s.*
A statistical profile of a changing profession, by age, gender, and place of employment; also profiles 1980 lawyer populations within states, metropolitan, and nonmetropolitan areas.

Dornette, W. Stuart, and Robert R. Cross. *Federal Judiciary Almanac.*
Data on various aspects of the federal judiciary.

Director of the Administrative Office of the United States Courts. *Annual Report of the Director of the Administrative Office of the United States Courts.*
Data on workload in the federal courts.

Friedman, Leon, and Fred L. Israel, eds. *The Justices of the United States Supreme Court.*
Biography on each justice including several typical opinions; useful tables and charts.

Judges of the United States.
Information about individuals serving in the nation's courts.

Federalism: State and Local Government

Beyle, Thad L., ed. *State Government.*
Congressional Quarterly's guide to current issues and activities in the states.

Council of State Governments. *The Book of the States.*
Definitive reference to the current data on state government activities across the board.

Council of State Governments. *State Administrative Officials Classified by Functions.*
Lists state administrative officials by function; before 1977 issued as a supplement to *The Book of the States.*

Council of State Governments. *State Elective Officials and the Legislatures.*
Lists state elected officials and legislators; before 1977 issued as a supplement to *The Book of the States.*

FYI Information Services. *The New Book of American Rankings.*
Compares 50 states and principal cities on 300 items.

Garwood, Alfred N., ed. *Almanac of the 50 States: Basic Data Profiles with Comparative Tables.*
State-level summaries of data on government and elections, policy, federal aid, population characteristics, crime, and so forth.

Holli, Melvin G., and Peter Jones, eds. *Biographical Dictionary of American Mayors, 1820-1980.*
Covers 679 mayors in big cities (Baltimore, Boston, Buffalo, Chicago, Cincinnati, Cleveland, Detroit, Los Angeles, Milwaukee, New Orleans, New York, Philadelphia, Pittsburgh, San Francisco, and St. Louis); appendices contain lists categorizing mayors by characteristics such as party, religion, and ethnicity.

International City Management Association. *The Municipal Year Book.*
Reliable source for urban data and developments.

Marlin, John Tepper, and James S. Avery. *The Book of American City Rankings.*
Nearly 300 thematic tables with data on the 100 largest U.S. cities.

National Association of Counties and International City Management Association. *The County Year Book.*
Surveys issues and trends in county government and administration; a reliable source of data on county government.

State statistical abstracts.
A list of state statistical abstracts (or near equivalents) can be found in the *Statistical Abstract of the United States, 1987,* 884-887. They are of widely varying quality.

Tax Foundation. *Facts and Figures on Government Finance.*
Data on government revenues, spending and debt at the federal, state, and local levels.

U.S. Advisory Commission on Intergovernmental Relations. *Significant Features of Fiscal Federalism.*
Convenient compilation of comparative state data on revenues, expenditures, and related matters; tables and figures present comparisons across states as well as state-by-state in-depth treatment.

U.S. Advisory Commission on Intergovernmental Relations. *The Transformation in American Politics: Implications for Federalism.*
Wide-ranging treatment (much broader than the subtitle implies) of major recent trends in American politics with emphasis on relevant data.

U.S. Bureau of the Census. *City Government Finances; Government Finances; State Government Finances.*
These three series summarize government finances at city and state levels; supply great detail for states and the larger cities.

Foreign and Military Policy

Cochran, Thomas B., William A. Arkin, and Milton M. Hoenig. *Nuclear Weapons Databook.*
Descriptions, specifications, and deployments of American and Soviet nuclear weapons systems.

International Institute of Strategic Studies. *The Military Balance.*
Statistical analysis of military forces and defense spending; figures given for countries and regional organizations such as NATO (North Atlantic Treaty Organization).

U.S. Arms Control and Disarmament Agency. *World Military Expenditures and Arms Transfers.*
Annual statistical accounts of military spending and the arms race.

World Armaments and Disarmament: SIPRI Yearbook.
Overview of the arms race and efforts to promote disarmament; detailed data on world military spending.

Social Policy

Bogue, Donald J. *The Population of the United States: Historical Trends and Future Projections.*
Extensive description of nation's population characteristics, focusing on the years since 1960; topics include poverty, income, housing, educational attainment, ethnicity, migration, and so forth.

Joint Center for Political Studies. *Black Elected Officials: A National Roster.*
Lists black elected officials by office and address with summary tabulations on the historical trends and comparative state figures.

National Center for Health Statistics. *Health, United States.*
Statistical sourcebook covering determinants and measures of health, health care resources and their utilization, health care expenditures, health care coverage, major federal programs, and so forth.

National Urban League. *The State of Black America.*
Yearly review assessing the conditions of blacks in the nation.

U.S. Department of Education. Center for Statistics. *Digest of Education Statistics.*
Current data on school enrollments, teachers, retention rates, educational attainment, finances, achievement, schools and school districts, federal education programs, and so forth.

U.S. Department of Education. Office of Educational Research and Improvement. *The Condition of Education: A Statistical Report.*
Data survey reviewing trends in elementary, secondary, and higher education; data portray student characteristics and performance as well as fiscal, material, and human resources deployed in education.

U.S. Department of Energy. Energy Information Administration. *Annual Energy Review.*
Data on energy supply and disposition, exploration, and reserves.

U.S. Department of Justice. Bureau of Criminal Justice Statistics. *Sourcebook of Criminal Justice Statistics.*
Brings together nationwide statistical data on the criminal justice system, public opinion, illegal activities, persons arrested, judicial proceedings, and persons under correctional supervision.

U.S. Department of Justice. Federal Bureau of Investigation. *Uniform Crime Reports for the United States.*
Variety of charts and tables on types and frequencies of crimes, persons arrested, and law enforcement personnel; several forty-year trends.

Economic Policy

Hoel, Arline Alchian, Kenneth W. Clarkson, and Roger LeRoy Miller. *Economics Sourcebook of Government Statistics.*
Ranges across inflation, general business conditions, interest rates, employment and earnings, international finance and trade, and the budget; critical discussions of over fifty major statistical series produced by the federal government in these areas; also refers to primary and secondary sources containing the series.

Office of Management and Budget. *Budget of the United States Government.*
Multi-volume annual presentation of data on federal revenues and expenditures; while the details of the federal budget documents may be numbing to the uninitiated, even the novice can find two volumes particularly useful: *Historical Tables* and *The Budget in Brief,* both of which are designed for the general public.

O'Hara, Frederick M., and Robert Sicignano. *Handbook of United States Economic and Financial Indicators.*
Defines a couple of hundred economic indicators culled from over fifty sources; provides information on publication schedules and historical trends.

Survey of Current Business.
Monthly publication with data on U.S. income and trade developments.

U.S. Bureau of Labor Statistics. *Employment and Earnings.*
Various statistics on the nation's nonfarm work force, including lengthy time series with data beginning in 1909.

U.S. Bureau of Labor Statistics. *Handbook of Labor Statistics.*
Collection of data concerning employment, unemployment, earnings, school enrollment and educational attainment, productivity, prices, strikes, and so forth.

U.S. Bureau of Labor Statistics. *Monthly Labor Review.*
Covers most Bureau of Labor Statistics series, giving data concerning employment, hours, pay, strikes, prices and inflation, and so forth.

U.S. Council of Economic Advisers. *Economic Indicators.*
Data on total output, income, and spending; employment, unemployment, and wages; production and business activity; prices, currency, credit, and security markets; and federal finance.

U.S. Department of Agriculture. *Agricultural Statistics.*
Vast array of agricultural data, including politically relevant displays, such as farm economic trends, price-support programs, and agricultural imports and exports.

U.S. President. *The Economic Report of the President.*
Reviews the national economic situation; presents a substantial appendix with long time series of critical economic data.

Reference List

Abraham, Henry J. *Justices and Presidents: Appointments to the Supreme Court*. 2d ed. New York: Oxford University Press, 1985.

Abraham, Henry J. *The Judiciary: The Supreme Court in the Governmental Process*. 6th ed. Boston: Allyn and Bacon, 1983.

Alexander, Herbert E., and Brian A. Haggerty. *Financing the 1984 Election*. Lexington, Mass.: Lexington Books, 1987.

Alexander, Herbert E., and Jennifer W. Frutig. *Public Financing of State Elections: A Data Book and Election Guide to Public Funding of Political Parties and Candidates in Seventeen States*. Los Angeles: Citizens' Research Foundation, 1982.

Alexander, Herbert E., and Mike Eberts. *Public Financing of State Elections: A Data Book on Tax-Assisted Funding of Political Parties and Candidates in Twenty States*. Los Angeles. Citizens' Research Foundation, 1986.

America Votes. See Scammon, Richard M., and Alice V. McGillivray. *America Votes*.

Arterton, F. Christopher. "Campaign Organizations Confront the Media-Political Environment." In *Race for the Presidency: The Media and the Nomination Process*, James David Barber, ed. Englewood Cliffs, N.J.: Prentice-Hall, 1978.

Austin, Erik W., and Jerome M. Clubb. *Political Facts of the United States Since 1789*. New York: Columbia University Press, 1986.

Bain, Richard C., and Judith H. Parris. *Convention Decisions and Voting Records*. 2d ed. Washington, D.C.: Brookings, 1973.

Balinski, Michel, and H. P. Young. *Fair Representation*. New Haven, Conn.: Yale University Press, 1982.

Ball, Howard. *Courts and Politics: The Federal Judicial System*. 2d ed. Englewood Cliffs, N.J.: Prentice-Hall, 1987.

Barone, Michael, and Grant Ujifusa. *The Almanac of American Politics: The President, the Senators, the Representatives, the Governors: Their Records and Election Results, Their States and Districts.* Washington, D.C.: National Journal, 1972-. Biennial.

Bartley, Numan V., and Hugh D. Graham. *Southern Elections: County and Precinct Data, 1950-1972.* Baton Rouge: Louisiana State University Press, 1978.

Baum, Lawrence. *The Supreme Court.* 2d ed. Washington, D.C.: CQ Press, 1985.

Beyle, Thad L., ed. *State Government.* Washington, D.C.: CQ Press, 1985.

Blaustein, Albert P., and Roy M. Mersky. *The First One Hundred Justices: Statistical Studies on the Supreme Court of the United States.* Hamden, Conn.: Shoe String Press, Archon Books, 1978.

Bogue, Donald J. *The Population of the United States: Historical Trends and Future Projections.* New York: The Free Press, 1985.

Book of the States. See Council of State Governments. *The Book of the States.*

Broadcasting Publications. *Broadcasting Cablecasting Yearbook.* Washington, D.C.: Broadcasting Publications, 1982-. Annual. Continues *Broadcasting Cable Yearbook,* which combined *Broadcasting Yearbook* (1968-1979) and *Broadcasting, Cable Sourcebook* (1973-1979).

Brown, Roger G. "Party and Bureaucracy: From Kennedy to Reagan." *Political Science Quarterly* 97 (1982): 279-294.

Burnham, Walter Dean. "The Turnout Problem." In *Elections American Style,* A. James Reichley, ed. Washington, D.C.: Brookings, 1987.

Cantor, Joseph E. "Political Action Committees: Their Evolution and Growth and Their Implications for the Political System." Washington, D.C.: Congressional Research Service, Report no. 82-92, November 6, 1981. Updated May 7, 1982.

Center for the American Woman and Politics. *Women in Public Office: A Biographical Directory and Statistical Analysis.* New York: R. R. Bowker, 1976.

Cigler, Allan J., and Burdett A. Loomis. *Interest Group Politics.* 2d ed. Washington, D.C.: CQ Press, 1986.

Clements, John. *Taylor's Encyclopedia of Government Officials: Federal and State.* Dallas: Political Research, 1967-. Biennial.

Close, Arthur C., and John P. Gregg. *Washington Representatives.* New York: Columbia Books, 1977-. Annual.

Cochran, Thomas B., William A. Arkin, and Milton M. Hoenig. *Nuclear Weapons Databook.* Cambridge, Mass.: Ballinger, 1987.

The Conference of State Court Administrators and the Court Statistics and Information Management Project of the National Center for

State Courts. *1984 State Appellate Court Jurisdiction Guide for Statistical Reporting.* Robert T. Roper, Mary E. Elsner, and Victor E. Flango, eds. Williamsburg, Va.: Conference of State Court Administrators and the National Center for State Courts, 1985.

Congressional Information Service. *American Statistics Index: A Comprehensive Guide and Index to the Statistical Publications of the U.S. Government.* Washington, D.C.: Congressional Information Service, 1973-. Annual, with monthly supplements.

Congressional Information Service. *Statistical Reference Index: A Selective Guide to American Statistical Publications from Sources Other than the U.S. Government.* Washington, D.C.: Congressional Information Service. 1980-. Annual, with bimonthly supplements.

Congressional Quarterly. *American Leaders 1789-1987.* Washington, D.C.: Congressional Quarterly, 1987.

Congressional Quarterly. *Congress and the Nation.* Washington, D.C.: Congressional Quarterly, 1965-. Quadrennial.

Congressional Quarterly. *Congressional Districts in the 1980s.* Washington, D.C.: Congressional Quarterly, 1983.

Congressional Quarterly. *Congressional Quarterly Almanac.* Washington, D.C.: Congressional Quarterly, 1945-. Annual.

Congressional Quarterly. *Congressional Quarterly's Guide to Congress.* 3d ed. Washington, D.C.: Congressional Quarterly, 1982.

Congressional Quarterly. *Congressional Quarterly's Guide to U.S. Elections.* 2d ed. Washington, D.C.: Congressional Quarterly, 1985.

Congressional Quarterly. *Congressional Roll Call: A Chronology and Analysis of Votes in the House and Senate.* Washington, D.C.: Congressional Quarterly, 1974-. Annual.

Congressional Quarterly. *Elections '80.* Washington, D.C.: Congressional Quarterly, 1980.

Congressional Quarterly. *Elections '84.* Washington, D.C.: Congressional Quarterly, 1984.

Congressional Quarterly. *Federal Regulatory Directory.* Washington, D.C.: Congressional Quarterly, 1979-. Annual.

Congressional Quarterly. *Guide to the U.S. Supreme Court.* Washington, D.C.: Congressional Quarterly, 1979.

Congressional Quarterly. *National Party Conventions, 1831-1984.* 4th ed. Washington, D.C.: Congressional Quarterly, 1987.

Congressional Quarterly. *Politics in America.* Washington, D.C.: Congressional Quarterly. 1981-. Biennial.

Congressional Quarterly. *Presidential Elections Since 1789.* 4th ed. Washington, D.C.: Congressional Quarterly, 1987.

Congressional Quarterly. *The Washington Lobby*. 5th ed. Washington, D.C.: CQ Press, 1987.

Congressional Quarterly. *Washington Information Directory, 1987-88*. Washington, D.C.: Congressional Quarterly, 1987.

Congressional Quarterly Weekly Report. Washington, D.C.: Congressional Quarterly, 1946-. Weekly.

Congressional Record. Washington, D.C.: U.S. Government Printing Office, 1873-.

Congressional Research Service. *The Constitution of the United States: Analysis and Interpretation*. Washington, D.C.: U.S. Government Printing Office, 1973. 92d Cong., 2d sess., S. Doc. 92-82.

Converse, Philip E., Jean D. Dotson, Wendy J. Hoag, and William H. McGee III. *American Social Attitudes Data Sourcebook 1947-1978*. Cambridge, Mass.: Harvard University Press, 1980.

Cooper, Joseph, David William Brady, and Patricia A. Hurley. "The Electoral Basis of Party Voting: Patterns and Trends in the U.S. House of Representatives, 1887-1969." In *The Impact of the Electoral Process*, Louis Maisel and Joseph Cooper, eds. Beverly Hills, Calif.: Sage, 1977.

Corsi, Jerome R. *Judicial Politics: An Introduction*. Englewood Cliffs, N.J.: Prentice-Hall, 1984.

Council of State Governments. *The Book of the States*. Lexington, Ky.: Council of State Governments, 1935-. Biennial.

Council of State Governments. *State Administrative Officials Classified by Functions*. Lexington, Ky.: Council of State Governments, 1977-. Biennial.

Council of State Governments. *State Elective Officials and the Legislatures*. Lexington, Ky.: Council of State Governments, 1977-. Biennial.

Council on Governmental Ethics, The Council of State Governments. *Campaign Finance, Ethics, and Lobby Law: Blue-Book, 1984-85*. Lexington, Ky.: Council of State Governments, 1984.

Criminal Justice Institute. *The Corrections Yearbook*. New York: Criminal Justice Institute, 1981-. Annual.

Crotty, William, and John S. Jackson III. *Presidential Primaries and Nominations*. Washington: CQ Press, 1985.

Curran, Barbara A., et al. *The Lawyer Statistical Report: A Statistical Profile of the U.S. Legal Profession in the 1980s*. Chicago: American Bar Foundation, 1985.

David, Paul T. *Party Strength in the United States 1872-1970*. Charlottesville: University Press of Virginia, 1972. Updated for 1972 in *Journal of Politics* 36 (1972): 785-796; for 1974 in *Journal of Politics* 38 (1974): 416-425; for 1976 in *Journal of Politics* 40 (1976): 770-780.

DeGregorio, William A. *The Complete Book of U.S. Presidents.* New York: December, 1984.

Director of the Administrative Office of the United States Courts. *Annual Report of the Director of the Administrative Office of the United States Courts.* Washington, D.C.: U.S. Government Printing Office, 1940-.

Director of the Administrative Office of the United States Courts. *Federal Court Management Statistics.* Washington, D.C.: U.S. Government Printing Office, 1985.

Dixon, Robert B., Jr. *Democratic Representation: Reapportionment in Law and Politics.* New York: Oxford University Press, 1968.

Dornette, W. Stuart, and Robert R. Cross. *Federal Judiciary Almanac 1986.* New York: Wiley, 1986.

D. T. Skelton Service Associates, Inc. *Campaign Finance Law 84.* Washington, D.C.: Federal Election Commission's National Clearinghouse on Election Administration, 1984.

Editor & Publisher—The Fourth Estate. New York: Editor & Publisher Company, 1884-. Weekly.

Editorial Research Reports. *The Women's Movement: Achievements and Effects.* Washington, D.C.: Congressional Quarterly, 1977.

Edwards, George C. III. *Presidential Performance and Public Approval.* Baltimore: Johns Hopkins University Press, forthcoming.

Elliot, Stephen P., ed. *A Reference Guide to the U.S. Supreme Court.* New York: Facts on File, 1986.

Farah, Barbara. "Delegate Polls: 1944-1984." *Public Opinion* 7, no. 4 (1984): 43-47.

Federal Election Commission. *Annual Report.* Washington, D.C.: U.S. Government Printing Office, 1976-.

Federal Election Commission. *Reports on Financial Activity.* Washington, D.C.: U.S. Government Printing Office, 1980-.

Fisher, Louis. *The Politics of Shared Power: Congress and the Executive.* 2d ed. Washington, D.C.: CQ Press, 1987.

Frankfurter, Felix, and I. M. Landis. *The Business of the Supreme Court.* New York: MacMillan, 1927.

Friedman, Leon, and Fred L. Israel, eds. *The Justices of the United States Supreme Court, 1789-1978: Their Lives and Major Opinions.* New York: Chelsea House in association with Bowker. Volume 5 covers 1969-1978.

FYI Information Services. *The New Book of American Rankings.* New York: Facts on File, 1984.

The Gallup Poll: Public Opinion 1935-71. 3 vols. New York: Random House, 1972.

The Gallup Poll: Public Opinion. Wilmington Del.: Scholarly Resources Inc., 1972-. Annual. Years 1972-1977 contained in 2 vols.

The Gallup Report: Political, Social and Economic Trends. Princeton, N.J.: American Institute of Public Opinion, 1965-. Monthly. Previously titled *Gallup Opinion Index* and the *Gallup Political Report.*

Garwood, Alfred N., ed. *Almanac of the 50 States: Basic Data Profiles with Comparative Tables.* Newburyport, Mass.: Information Publications, 1986.

General Social Survey. Chicago: National Opinion Research Center, University of Chicago, 1972-. Annual.

Glashan, Roy R. *American Governors and Gubernatorial Elections, 1775-1978.* Westport, Conn.: Meckler, 1979.

Goldman, Sheldon. *Constitutional Law: Cases and Essays.* New York: Harper and Row, 1987.

Goldman, Sheldon. "Reagan's Second Term Judicial Appointments: The Battle at Midway." *Judicature* 70 (1987): 324-339.

Graber, Doris. "Hoopla and Horse-Race in 1980 Campaign Coverage: A Closer Look." In *Mass Media and Elections: International Research Perspectives.* Winfried Schulz and Klaus Schönbach, eds. Munich: Verlag Olschlager, 1983.

Graber, Doris. *Mass Media and American Politics.* 2d ed. Washington, D.C.: CQ Press, 1984.

Grimes, Alan P. *Democracy and the Amendments to the Constitution.* Lexington, Mass.: Lexington Books, 1978.

Grofman, Bernard F. "Criteria for Districting." *UCLA Law Review* 33 (1985): 77-184.

Gruber, Katerine, Susan M. Boyles, Kathleen Dombrowski, Michael A. Pare, and Karin E. Koek, eds. *Encyclopedia of Associations.* Detroit: Gale Research Company, 1960-. Annual.

Halpern, S. C., and C. M. Lamb. *Supreme Court, Activism and Restraint.* Lexington, Mass.: Lexington Books, 1982.

Haynes, George H. *The Senate of the United States.* New York: Russell and Russell, 1960.

Heard, Alexander E. *The Costs of Democracy.* Chapel Hill, N.C.: University of North Carolina Press, 1960.

Henshaw, Stanley K. "Characteristics of U.S. Women Having Abortions, 1982-1983." *Family Planning Perspectives* 19, no. 1 (1987): 5-9.

Henshaw, Stanley K., and Ellen Blaine. *Abortion Services in the United States, Each State, and Metropolitan Area, 1981-1982.* New York: Alan Guttmacher Institute, 1985.

Henshaw, Stanley K., Jacqueline Darroch Forrest, and Jennifer Van Vort. "Abortion Services in the United States, 1984 and 1985." *Family Planning Perspectives* 19, no. 2 (1987): 63-70.

Historical Statistics of the U.S. See U.S. Bureau of the Census. *Historical Statistics of the U.S.*

Hoel, Arline Alchian, Kenneth W. Clarkson, and Roger LeRoy Miller. *Economics Sourcebook of Government Statistics.* Lexington, Mass.: Lexington Books, 1983.

Holli, Melvin G., and Peter Jones, eds. *Biographical Dictionary of American Mayors, 1820-1980.* Westport, Conn.: Greenwood Press, 1981.

Information Please Almanac: Atlas and Yearbook. Boston: Houghton Mifflin. 1947-. Annual.

International City Management Association. *The Municipal Year Book.* New York: International City Management Association, 1934-. Annual.

International Institute of Strategic Studies. *The Military Balance.* London: International Institute of Strategic Studies, 1959-. Annual.

Interstate Bureau of Regulations. *State Political Action Legislation and Regulations: Index and Directory of Organizations.* Westport, Conn.: Quorum Books, 1984.

Inter-University Consortium for Political and Social Research. "Candidate and Constituency Statistics of Elections in the United States, 1788-1984," (machine-readable data file). Ann Arbor, Mich.: Inter-University Consortium for Political and Social Research, 1986.

Jacobson, Gary C. *Money in Congressional Elections.* New Haven, Conn.: Yale University Press, 1980.

Jacobson, Gary C. *The Politics of Congressional Elections.* 2d ed. Boston: Little, Brown, 1987.

Joint Center for Political Studies. *Black Elected Officials: A National Roster.* Washington, D.C.: Joint Center for Political Studies, 1971-.

Joint Chiefs of Staff. *Military Posture for Fiscal Year 1988.* Washington, D.C.: U.S. Government Printing Office, 1987.

Joslyn, Richard. *Mass Media and Elections.* Reading, Mass.: Addison-Wesley, 1984.

Judges of the United States. 2d ed. Washington, D.C.: U.S. Government Printing Office, 1983.

Kallenbach, Joseph E., and Jessamine S. Kallenbach. *American State Governors, 1776-1976.* Dobbs Ferry, N.Y.: Oceana Publications, 1977-1982.

Kane, Joseph Nathan. *Facts about the Presidents: A Compilation of Biographical and Historical Information.* 5th ed. New York: H. H. Wilson, 1985.

Keech, William R., and Donald R. Matthews. *The Party's Choice: With an Epilogue on the 1976 Nominations.* Washington, D.C.: Brookings, 1976.

Kernell, Samuel. *Going Public: New Strategies of Presidential Leadership.* Washington, D.C.: CQ Press, 1986.

King, Gary, and Lyn Ragsdale. *The Elusive Executive: Discovering Statistical Patterns in the Presidency.* Washington, D.C.: CQ Press, 1988.

Kirkpatrick, Jeane. *The New Presidential Elite.* New York: Russell Sage, 1976.

Kurland, Philip B., and Ralph Lerner. *The Founder's Constitution.* Chicago: University of Chicago Press, 1987.

League of Women Voters Education Fund. *Easy Does It.* Washington, D.C.: League of Women Voters, 1984.

Magazine Index. Belmont, Calif.: Information Access Co., 1977-.

Malbin, Michael J. *Parties, Interest Groups, and Campaign Finance Laws.* Washington, D.C.: American Enterprise Institute for Public Policy Research, 1980.

Marlin, John Tepper, and James S. Avery. *The Book of American City Rankings.* New York: Facts on File, 1983.

Mediamark Research Inc. *Multimedia Audiences.* New York: Mediamark, 1986.

Miller, Arthur H. "Is Confidence Rebounding?" *Public Opinion* 6, no. 3 (1983): 16-20.

Miller, Warren E., and M. Kent Jennings. *Parties in Transition: A Longitudinal Study of Party Elites and Party Supporters.* New York: Russell Sage, 1986.

Miller, Warren E., Arthur H. Miller, and Edward J. Schneider. *American National Election Studies Data Sourcebook, 1952-1978.* Cambridge, Mass.: Harvard University Press, 1980.

Mitofsky, Warren J., and Martin Plissner. "The Making of the Delegates, 1968-1980." *Public Opinion* 3, no. 5 (1980): 37-43.

Moe, Ronald C. "The Federal Executive Establishment: Evolution and Trends." Prepared for the U.S. Senate Committee on Government Affairs by the Congressional Research Service. Washington, D.C.: Congressional Research Service, 1980.

Mueller, John E. *War, Presidents and Public Opinion.* New York: Wiley, 1973. Reprinted in 1983 by University Press of America.

Mullaney, Marie. *American Governors and Gubernatorial Elections, 1978-1987: A Statistical Compilation.* Westport, Conn.: Meckler, 1988.

Murphy, Arthur. "Evaluating the Presidents of the United States." *Presidential Studies Quarterly* 14 (1984): 117-126.

National Association of Counties and International City Management Association. *The County Year Book.* Washington, D.C.: National Association of Counties and International City Management Association, 1975-. Annual.

National Center for Health Statistics. *Health, United States, 1985.* Washington, D.C.: U.S. Government Printing Office, 1985.

National Elections Studies. Ann Arbor, Mich.: Center for Political Studies Institute for Social Research, University of Michigan, 1952-. Biennial.

National Journal. Washington, D.C.: Center for Political Research, 1969-. Weekly.

National Newspaper Index. Belmont, Calif.: Information Access Co., 1977-.

National Opinion Research Center (NORC). *See* General Social Survey.

National Standards Association. *National Directory of State Agencies.* Bethesda, Md.: National Standards Association, 1976-. Annual since 1986.

National Urban League. *The State of Black America.* New York: The National Urban League, 1976-. Annual.

Nielson Television Index. Northbrook, Ill.: A. C. Nielson. Annual.

Nimmo, Dan. *The Political Persuaders: The Techniques of Modern Election Campaigns.* Englewood Cliffs, N.J.: Prentice-Hall, 1970.

Nunn, Clyde Z., Harry J. Crockett, Jr., and J. Allen Williams, Jr. *Tolerance for Nonconformity.* San Francisco: Jossey-Bass, 1978.

Office of Management and Budget. *Budget of the United States Government, Budget in Brief.* Washington, D.C.: U.S. Government Printing Office, 1951-. Annual.

Office of Management and Budget. *Budget of the United States Government, Fiscal Year 1988: Historical Tables.* Washington, D.C.: U.S. Government Printing Office, 1987.

Office of Management and Budget. *Budget of the United States Government, Fiscal Year 1988: Special Analyses.* Washington, D.C.: U.S. Government Printing Office, 1987.

Office of Personnel Management. *Affirmative Employment Statistics.* Washington, D.C.: U.S. Government Printing Office, 1978-. Annual.

Office of Personnel Management. *Federal Civilian Workforce Statistics, Employment and Trends.* Washington, D.C.: U.S. Government Printing Office. Bimonthly.

Office of Personnel Management. *Pay Structure of the Federal Civil Service.* Washington, D.C.: U.S. Government Printing Office, 1946-. Annual.

O'Hara, Frederick M., and Robert Sicignano. *Handbook of United States Economic and Financial Indicators.* Westport, Conn.: Greenwood, 1985.

Opinion Research Service. *American Public Opinion Index.* Louisville, Ky.: Opinion Research Service, 1981-. Annual.

Orfield, Gary, and Franklin Monfort. "Are American Schools Resegregating in the Reagan Era? A Statistical Analysis of Segregation Levels from 1980-1984." Paper no. 14, National School Desegregation Project Working Papers. Chicago: no date.

Ornstein, Norman J., Thomas E. Mann, and Michael J. Malbin, eds. *Vital Statistics on Congress, 1987-88.* Washington, D.C.: Congressional Quarterly, 1987.

Parsons, Stanley B., William W. Beach, and Dan Hermann. *United States Congressional Districts and Data, 1788-1841.* Westport, Conn.: Greenwood, 1978.

Parsons, Stanley B., William W. Beach, and Michael J. Dubin. *United States Congressional Districts and Data, 1843-1883.* Westport, Conn.: Greenwood, 1986.

Pious, Richard M. *The American Presidency.* New York: Basic Books, 1979.

Posner, R. A. *The Federal Courts.* Cambridge, Mass.: Harvard University Press, 1985.

Public Opinion. Washington, D.C.: American Enterprise Institute for Public Policy Research , 1978-. Bimonthly.

Public Opinion Quarterly. Chicago: University of Chicago Press, 1937-.

Radio Advertising Bureau. *Radio Facts.* New York: Radio Advertising Bureau. Annual.

Reader's Digest. *Reader's Digest Almanac.* Pleasantville, N.Y.: Reader's Digest, 1966-. Annual.

Republican National Committee. *The 1985 Republican Almanac: State Political Profiles.* Washington, D.C.: Republican National Committee, 1985.

Republican National Committee. *1984-1985 Election Summary: National Tables, Maps and Charts.* Washington, D.C.: Republican National Committee, 1986.

Robinson, Michael J., and Margaret A. Sheehan. *Over the Wire and On TV: CBS and UPI in Campaign 1980.* New York: Russell Sage, 1983.

Runyon, John H. *Source Book of American Presidential Campaign and Election Statistics, 1948-1968.* New York: Frederick Ungar, 1971.

Scammon, Richard M., comp. and ed. *America at the Polls: A Handbook of American Presidential Election Statistics 1920-1964.* Pittsburgh: University of Pittsburgh Press, 1965.

Scammon, Richard M., and Alice V. McGillivray, comps. and eds. *America at the Polls: A Handbook of American Presidential Election Statistics 1968-1984.* Washington, D.C.: Congressional Quarterly, Elections Research Center, 1988.

Scammon, Richard M., and Alice V. McGillivray, comps. and eds. *American Votes: A Handbook of Contemporary American Election Statistics.* Washington, D.C.: Congressional Quarterly, Elections Research Center, 1956-. Biennial.

Schapsmeier, Edward L., and Frederick H. Schapsmeier. *Political Parties and Civic Action Groups.* Westport, Conn.: Greenwood, 1987.

Schlozman, Kay Lehman, and John T. Tierney. *Organized Interests and American Democracy.* New York: Harper and Row, 1986.

Schuman, Howard, and Stanley Presser. *Questions and Answers in Attitude Surveys.* New York: Academic Press, 1981.

Senate Library. *Presidential Vetoes, 1789-1976.* Washington, D.C.: U.S. Government Printing Office, 1978.

Smith, Tom W. "The Polls: America's Most Important Problems." *Public Opinion Quarterly* 49 (1985): 268-274.

Southwick, Leslie H. *Presidential Also-Rans and Running Mates, 1788-1980.* Jefferson, N.C.: McFarland, 1984.

Stanwood, Edward. Revised by Charles Knowles Bolton. *A History of the Presidency, 1788-1916.* Boston: Houghton Mifflin, 1916.

State Information Book. Rockville, Md.: Infax, 1985-. Biennial.

Statistical Abstract of the U.S. See U.S. Bureau of the Census. *Statistical Abstract of the U.S.*

Sterling, Christopher H. *Electronic Media: A Guide to Trends in Broadcasting and Newer Technologies: 1920-1983.* New York: Praeger, 1984.

Stouffer, Samuel A. *Communism, Conformity, and Civil Liberties.* Garden City, N.Y.: Doubleday, 1955.

Tax Foundation. *Facts and Figures on Government Finance.* Englewood Cliffs, N.J.: Prentice-Hall, 1941-. Biennial.

Television Digest. *Cable and Station Coverage Atlas, 1986.* Washington, D.C.: Television Digest, 1986.

Television Digest. *Television and Cable Factbook.* Washington, D.C.: Television Digest, 1946-. Annual.

Television Information Office. "America's Watching: Public Attitudes Toward Television." New York: Television Information Office, 1987.

Television Information Office. "Public Attitudes Toward Television and Other Media in a Time of Change." New York: Television Information Office, 1985.

Tolchin, Susan J. *Women in Congress: 1917-1976*. Report no. 94-1732. Washington, D.C.: U.S. Government Printing Office, 1976.

U.S. Advisory Commission on Intergovernmental Relations. *Significant Features of Fiscal Federalism 1985-86 edition*. Report M-146. Washington, D.C.: U.S. Advisory Commission on Intergovernmental Relations, 1986.

U.S. Advisory Commission on Intergovernmental Relations. *The Transformation in American Politics: Implications for Federalism*. Washington, D.C.: U.S. Advisory Commission on Intergovernmental Relations, 1986.

U.S. Arms Control and Disarmament Agency. *World Military Expenditures and Arms Transfers*. Washington, D.C.: U.S. Government Printing Office, 1965-. Annual (title varies).

U.S. Bureau of Labor Statistics. *Employment and Earnings*. Washington, D.C.: U.S. Government Printing Office, 1961-. Annual.

U.S. Bureau of Labor Statistics. *Handbook of Labor Statistics*. Washington, D.C.: U.S. Government Printing Office, 1927-. Frequency varies.

U.S. Bureau of Labor Statistics. *Monthly Labor Review*. Washington, D.C.: Bureau of Labor Statistics, 1915-.

U.S. Bureau of the Census. *Census of Governments*, vol. 6, no. 4 (1982), Historical Statistics on Governmental Finance and Employment. Washington, D.C.: Government Printing Office, 1985.

U.S. Bureau of the Census. *City Government Finances*. Washington, D.C.: U.S. Government Printing Office, 1909-. Annual.

U.S. Bureau of the Census. *Congressional District Atlas*. Washington, D.C.: U.S. Government Printing Office, 1960-. Frequency varies.

U.S. Bureau of the Census. *Congressional District Data Book*. Washington, D.C.: U.S. Government Printing Office, 1961-. Frequency varies.

U.S. Bureau of the Census. *County and City Data Book*. Washington, D.C.: U.S. Government Printing Office, 1952-. Frequency varies.

U.S. Bureau of the Census. Current Population Reports. Population Characteristics, series P-20. *Voter Participation*. Washington, D.C.: U.S. Government Printing Office, 1964-. Biennial.

U.S. Bureau of the Census. Current Population Reports, series P-60, no. 150. "Characteristics of Households and Persons Receiving Selected Noncash Benefits: 1984." Washington, D.C.: U.S. Government Printing Office, 1985.

U.S. Bureau of the Census. Current Population Reports, series P-60, no. 152. "Characteristics of the Population Below the Poverty Level: 1984." Washington, D.C.: U.S. Government Printing Office, 1984.

U.S. Bureau of the Census. Current Population Reports, series P-60, no. 157. "Money Income and Poverty Status of Families and Persons in the United States: 1986." Washington, D.C.: U.S. Government Printing Office, 1987.

U.S. Bureau of the Census. *Federal Expenditures by State for Fiscal Year [year].* Washington, D.C.: U.S. Government Printing Office, 1983-. Annual.

U.S. Bureau of the Census. *Governmental Finances.* Washington, D.C.: U.S. Government Printing Office, 1965-. Annual.

U.S. Bureau of the Census. *Historical Statistics of the United States, Colonial Times to 1970.* Bicentennial edition. Washington, D.C.: U.S. Government Printing Office, 1975.

U.S. Bureau of the Census. *Historical Statistics on Governmental Finances and Employment.* Washington, D.C.: U.S. Government Printing Office, 1985.

U.S. Bureau of the Census. *Public Employment in [year].* Washington, D.C.: U.S. Government Printing Office, 1966-. Annual.

U.S. Bureau of the Census. *State and Metropolitan Area Data Book.* Washington, D.C.: U.S. Government Printing Office. Biennial.

U.S. Bureau of the Census. *State Government Finances.* Washington, D.C.: U.S. Government Printing Office, 1916-. Annual.

U.S. Bureau of the Census. *Statistical Abstract of the U.S.* Washington, D.C.: U.S. Government Printing Office, 1879-. Annual.

U.S. Commission on Civil Rights. *The Voting Rights Act: Unfulfilled Goals.* Washington, D.C.: U.S. Government Printing Office, 1981.

U.S. Congress. *Calendars of the U.S. House of Representatives and History of Legislation.* Washington, D.C.: U.S. Government Printing Office. Annual.

U.S. Congress. House. *Constitution, Jefferson's Manual, and Rules of the House of Representatives of the United States.* Washington, D.C.: U.S. Government Printing Office. Biennial.

U.S. Congress. Joint Committee on Printing. *Official Congressional Directory.* Washington, D.C.: U.S. Government Printing Office, 1865-.

U.S. Congress. Joint Economic Committee. *The Military Budget and National Economic Priorities.* 91st Cong., 1st sess. Washington, D.C.: U.S. Government Printing Office, 1969.

U.S. Congress. Secretary of the U.S. Senate. *Nomination and Election of the President and Vice President of the United States Including the Manner of Selecting Delegates to National Political Conventions.* Washington, D.C.: U.S. Government Printing Office, 1984.

U.S. Congress. Senate. *Biographical Directory of the American Congress, 1774-1971.* 92d Cong., 1st sess., S. Doc. 92-8. Washington, D.C.: U.S. Government Printing Office, 1971.

U.S. Council of Economic Advisers. *Economic Indicators.* Washington, D.C.: U.S. Government Printing Office, 1948-. Monthly.

U.S. Department of Agriculture. *Agricultural Statistics.* Washington, D.C.: U.S. Government Printing Office, 1937-. Annual.

U.S. Department of Commerce. *Survey of Current Business.* Washington, D.C.: U.S. Government Printing Office, 1921-. Monthly.

U.S. Department of Education. Center for Statistics. *Digest of Education Statistics.* Washington, D.C.: U.S. Government Printing Office, 1962-. Annual.

U.S. Department of Education. Office of Educational Research and Improvement. *The Condition of Education: A Statistical Report.* Washington, D.C.: U.S. Government Printing Office, 1975-.

U.S. Department of Energy. Energy Information Administration. *Annual Energy Review.* Washington, D.C.: U.S. Government Printing Office, 1977-.

U.S. Department of Health and Human Services. Social Security Administration. *Social Security Bulletin, Annual Statistical Supplement 1986.* Washington, D.C.: U.S. Government Printing Office, 1987.

U.S. Department of Justice. Bureau of Criminal Justice Statistics. *Sourcebook of Criminal Justice Statistics.* Washington, D.C.: U.S. Government Printing Office, 1974-. Annual.

U.S. Department of Justice. Federal Bureau of Investigation. *Uniform Crime Reports for the United States.* Washington, D.C.: U.S. Government Printing Office, 1930-. Annual.

U.S. Department of State. Office of Public Communication. *A Short History of the U.S. Department of State 1781-1981.* Washington, D.C.: U.S. Government Printing Office, 1981.

U.S. Department of State. *Key Officers of Foreign Service Posts.* Washington, D.C.: U.S. Government Printing Office, September 1987.

U.S. Government Organization Manual. Washington, D.C.: U.S. Government Printing Office, 1935-. Annual.

U.S. President. *The Economic Report of the President.* Washington, D.C.: U.S. Government Printing Office, 1947-. Annual.

Watson, Richard A., and Norman C. Thomas. *The Politics of the Presidency.* 2d ed. Washington, D.C.: CQ Press, 1988.

Wattenberg, Martin. *The Decline of American Political Parties, 1952-1984.* Cambridge, Mass.: Harvard University Press, 1986.

Wattenberg, Martin. "The Hollow Realignment." *Public Opinion Quarterly* 51 (1987): 58-74.

Weekly Compilation of Presidential Documents. Washington, D.C.: U.S. Government Printing Office.

Weinberger, Marvin I., and David U. Greevy. *The PAC Directory: A Complete Guide to Political Action Committees.* Cambridge, Mass.: Ballinger, 1982.

Wolfinger, Raymond, and Steven Rosenstone. *Who Votes?* New Haven, Conn.: Yale University Press, 1980.

The World Almanac and Book of Facts. New York: Pharos Books, 1868-. Annual since 1886.

World Armaments and Disarmament: SIPRI Yearbook. Stockholm: Almqvist & Wiksell; New York: Oxford University Press, 1970-. Annual.

Index

JK 274 .S74 1988
Stanley, Harold W.
Vital statistics on American
politics (89-099)